Idolatry Of The Campus:

Idolatry Of The Campus:

—⁓—

How it entered our Universities and may ultimately lead to complete moral decay, bankruptcy, and destruction of our nation

Charles L. Carter PhD

ISBN-13: 9781974263233
ISBN-10: 1974263231

Forward

They perish for a lack of knowledge! We are often unknowingly worshipping idols and even teaching them. If we say we have no sin, we deceive ourselves, and the truth is not in us. Man has been and still is an idol factory. Idolatry is anything that removes or distracts from the glory and honor of the one true God---Creator of everything. More specifically, paying obeisance to or worshipping in any way or attributing to something else that which is due Creator-God. This book addresses the history of idolatry, how these ancient gods are still with us on the campus, and identifies and traces the gods of Humanism, pseudo-science, naturalism, materialism and the false religion of the campus. Are the faculty and students involved in "respectable" idolatry? The consequences for a people and nation into this idolatry is as judge Bork describes us as "Slouching to Gomorrah". When you listen to professors and teachers please identify the hidden agenda of idolatry. Though the campus is and should be a place where the "enterprise of ideas" presides, we try to uncover the deception of idolatry on campus for the purpose of inoculating the student from this enormous, in fact "infinite" error. This is written in textbook fashion for the parent and student preparing them for what will come from the university system. Charles L. Carter PhD, Emeritus Professor

This book does not seek condemnation of anyone. We are all condemned by our own thoughts and actions and are in need of the Messiah, the loving Savior of all mankind; who teaches us about himself: "I am the Way, the Truth, and the Light, no one comes to the Father except through me."[1]

He would that none would be lost![2]

Remember, the teacher is held to a higher standard.[3] You must learn what happens to a person and a nation that teaches or follows after a false god or gods.[4] You must know who those false gods are, which is the theme of this book.

He tells us that for anyone that harms His children, it is better for them that they drown with a millstone tied around their neck.[5] Teacher. These are the children that sit in front of you from first grade to graduate school! Put this on your desk where you can see it.

Creator-God's "demo" nation is Israel. To review what happened to a nation that turns to Idolatry observe the ancient destruction of Israel in 1Kings 9:6 as well as the wrath required by a Just Creator-God in 1Kings 14:9,1-, 1Kings 16:13 & 26, and in Revelation 9:20-21. Note that our nation has committed the same errors as Israel in ancient times. We can stave off our destruction only by repentance before and acceptance of our Creator-God.

You will notice as you read the following chapters and subsequent pages that many quotes from many people have been cited. These quotes and

---

1 John 14:6

2 2Peter 3:9

3 2Peter 2:1-2

4 Acts 14:15. When the people of Iconium tried to make Paul and Barnabus gods, they turned to them and said, "Men, why are you doing these things? We also are men with the same nature as you, and preach to you that you should turn from these vain things to the living God, who made the heaven, and earth, the sea, and all things that are in them."

5 Matt 18:6

citations are tools for you to help ponder what is actually happening in real time making you part of the history that will, perhaps, be read by future generations. There is one book that is cited herein that is typically ignored and, worse, maligned without proof by scientists and academia as a whole: The Word of God called the Bible. It is only fair to use passages and quotes from it as well as quotes and passages from others who disagrees or agrees with it. It is very important to be fair and balanced in your research. It will be up to you to make the decision that makes sense which requires logical thought. What is so difficult is there is little teaching given regarding how to use clear, logical thought to come to a conclusion – of any kind. Seek coherent answers.

The 4 most important questions we all must answer, and our children must learn are:

1. Is there a God?
2. Is the bible the word of God?
3. Is there only one way of salvation?
4. Is this life all there is? I pray the answers are in your input information stream.

IDOLATRY of the campus:
How it entered our Universities and may ultimately lead to complete moral decay, bankruptcy, and destruction of our nation
By
Charles L. Carter Ph.D.

Book Summary

They perish for a lack of knowledge! We are often unknowingly worshipping idols and even teaching them. If we say we have no sin, we deceive ourselves, and the truth is not in us. Man has been and still is an idol factory. Idolatry is anything that removes or distracts from the glory and honor of the one true God---Creator of everything. More specifically, paying obeisance to or worshipping in anyway or attributing to something else that which is due Creator-God. This book addresses the history of idolatry, how these ancient gods are still with us on the campus, and identifies and traces the gods of Humanism, pseudo-science, naturalism, materialism and the false religion of the campus. Are the faculty and students involved in "respectable" idolatry? The consequences for a people and nation into this idolatry is as judge Bork describes us as "Slouching to Gomorrah". When you listen to professors and teachers please identify the hidden agenda of idolatry. Though the campus is and should be a place where the "enterprise of ideas" presides, we try to uncover the deception of idolatry on campus for the purpose of inoculating the student from this enormous, in fact "infinite" error. Ultimately what counts is your "faith", and where it is anchored.

FAITH in THE WISDOM OF MAN vs. FAITH in POWER of CREATOR-GOD

Paul had the equivalent of 2 PhD's when he went to the Corinthians to teach them and he said, "For I determined not to know anything among you except Jesus Christ and Him Crucified....That your faith

should not be in the wisdom of men but in the power of God." [NKJV 1Corin:2:2-5]

If the University builds your faith, your world, it has to maintain it. It cannot do that! Since eternity is beyond its capacity as are many things of the future.

This book is to help you identify when Idols are being taught, false concepts that negate the word of Creator-God (ie. the bible), and to at least suggest if you begin with the plain word of Creator-God your science will help you understand the world better. This is a text opposed to the religion of Idolatrous Humanism....where the false wisdom is narrow and incomplete and will lead you nowhere a 1000 years from now.

This book is written in textbook fashion for the parent and student preparing them for what will come from the university system. Charles L. Carter PhD, Emeritus Professor

7 chapters 442 pages, 133,957 words
60 definitions, 475 notes 9 Figures 2 Tables
Bibliography of 207 Authors or speakers cited
Index
Copyright © CL Carter 2017

Dedication

To Mighty Creator-God. Maker of Heaven and Earth

To my sweet wife Sandy. Without her this work of 8 years would have never happened and I would have missed the mark.

Prologue

This book does not seek condemnation of anyone. We are all condemned by our own thoughts and actions and are in need of the Messiah, the loving Savior of all mankind; who teaches us about himself: "I am the Way, the Truth, and the Light, no one comes to the Father except through me."[6]

He would that none would be lost![7]

We are to follow Paul's teaching in 1 Corinthians 4:1-5 "Let a man so consider us, as servants of Christ and stewards of the mysteries of God. Moreover it is required in stewards that one be found <u>faithful</u>........Therefore judge nothing before the time, until the LORD comes, who will both bring to light the hidden things of darkness and reveal the counsels of the heart; and then each one's praise will come from God." We are required to remain "faithful" as servants of Christ and stewards of the mysteries of God. When Christ returns He and He alone has knowledge of each person's heart and can judge. Until then we are not to judge, but to be Lovers of Creator-God and our fellow man. If we can show them the way, let's do it. By Lovers I am referring to Agape Love (see glossary-definitions and the end of the book).

---

6 John 14:6
7 2Peter 3:9

Remember, the teacher is held to a higher standard.[8] You must learn what happens to a person and a nation that teaches or follows after a false god or gods.[9] You must know who those false gods are, which is the theme of this book. He tells us that for anyone that harms His children, it is better for them that they drown with a millstone tied around their neck.[10] Teacher. These are the children that sit in front of you from first grade to graduate school! Put this on your desk where you can see it.

Creator-God's "demo" nation is Israel. To review what happened to a nation that turns to Idolatry observe the ancient destruction of Israel in 1Kings 9:6 as well as the wrath required by a Just Creator-God in 1Kings 14:9,1-, 1Kings 16:13 & 26, and in Revelation 9:20-21. Note that our nation has committed the same errors as Israel in ancient times. We can stave off our destruction only by repentance before and acceptance of our Creator-God.

This nation needs a mighty educational system….and a mighty academy of its universities and colleges that can train our children to think logically, to seek the truth, and learn in environments where the "enterprise of ideas campus " includes the words and ideas given to us by Creator-God…one that respects and does not denigrate the Bible. Respects true science and identifies what is not known by man. After all, who founded the universities in the first place?

---

8 2Peter 2:1-2

9 Acts 14:15. When the people of Iconium tried to make Paul and Barnabus gods, they turned to them and said, "Men, why are you doing these things? We also are men with the same nature as you, and preach to you that you should turn from these vain things to the living God, who made the heaven, and earth, the sea, and all things that are in them."

10 Matt 18:6

Table of Contents

Headings index

Introduction

"Their sorrows shall be multiplied who hasten after another god."[Ps 16:4]

This book is an attempt to identify those gods. Their identity is enormously deceptive but they have plagued mankind since day one. You may be surprised where they may be found; we even hide them in our heart and fail to recognize them. Who of you, dear reader wants his sorrows to be multiplied?

"May our spirits bow only to the One who made us"

"You shall not bow down to their gods, nor serve them, nor do according to their working; but you shall utterly overthrow them and completely breakdown their sacred pillars."[Ex 20:5,23:13, Deut. 12:30-34, Num 33:52]

"As in the days of Noah so will the signs of the coming of the son of man be." {Jesus Christ}

This last statement is a prophecy that has not been understood by most people and certainly not by me. I woke up one morning and understood that this refers both to before and to the time after the flood, the 400 years Noah lived after the flood.....when he would be surrounded by those who would hear his story of Creator-God who was "just" and destroyed the 6 billion people who only had evil in their hearts continually from their youth. Noah's Creator-God would be a great contrast to the descriptions that others would invent....idols of the mind and idols of matter. That time had certain key characteristics. The first characteristic was the formation of the first kingdom under a man named Nimrod. It wasn't just a simple kingdom; it was the first "**one world government**". Nimrod's government had inserted many forms of idolatry, seeds that were sown throughout civilization and exist to this day. The idols of Nimrod's kingdom needed teacher-priests and authority. The academy was formed to spread their religion…the word "academy" can be traced to the very district of " Accad" where much of the social structure of this seminal culture began. Let's trace these idols from Babylon to the Baals of the Canaanites, the Assyrians, the people of Mesopotamia and the Greek Pantheon, Tarsus and Pergamos where those priests of Nimrod moved north of Rome to Etrusca, there are their college of priests called "the August body" would teach idolatry to Rome. So today we find the earth filled with the idolatry that was sewed during the days of Noah after the flood, sewed initially by those Noah had cursed …they lived up to their infamy. Modern "humanism" found all over our teaching institutions is the ultimate degenerate antromorphization of these pagan gods. This idolatry can be found in the Academy, in our schools, throughout our airways, and in our streets and homes in large part due to the spiritual work of the enemy of man and his minions. What would parents do if they found out that their child was being taught to worship at the feet of the god Moloch, and they were paying for it? We battle not against flesh and blood, but against principalities and powers in high places. Our enemy is not the faculty but the powerful forces controlling their thoughts, driving a false reality, and a false science. If you want a window into this spiritual battle, read Daniel 10. Note that Daniel is writing words that expose this battle to our understanding like no other writing. He came under an attack such that the Messenger (likely the angel Gabriel) was hindered by the demonic head of the Principality of Persia (Iran) called the "Prince of Persia" who fought with him for 30 days with such power that Gabriel requested the Mighty Angel Michael to free him so he could deliver the message from heaven to Daniel. To this day the book of Daniel is called a book of poetry by the Jews, blinded to the truth of it as a pure prophecy of the Messiah to come, an amazing fact in itself.

Dr D. James Kennedy tells of the unusual experience of a missionary to Russia one year before the disunion of the Soviet Union. He was the first to gain the approval of the department of education to distribute bibles to one Soviet high school in Moscow. The principle received him and thanked him for a book that he was giving him to teach with. The man said "thank you for this book on religion. I have been thinking about possibly teaching a course on religion next year, and I'm sure this would prove to be helpful." The missionary said, "Excuse me sir. There seems to be some misunderstanding. This is not a book on religion. This is a Bible." The man's eyes open wide in amazement and he said, "A Bible, a Bible!" He clasped it to his breast and said, "A Bible! We were once a great Christian nation, but we turned our backs on God, and we have destroyed ourselves."

Who Are We?

"We are made in God's image. The sheer fact that we could spend the rest of our lives Contemplating what it means to be made in God's image, without beginning to scratch the surface, reminds us that we are God's image, not gods. We are, in some ways, to God as our mirror image is to us. There is a resemblance, a connection, but the difference is one of ontology, dimension. Thus, God creates, we create. But when we look at creation more closely we find that He speaks things into reality, while we rearrange what He has already created. I'm stringing words together; He spoke language into being. Adam named the animals, but God formed them........ Renaming isn't the same as remaking. And <u>one thing man will never be is secular</u>. When someone claims,' I'm not a very religious person' translate that to be more accurate, ' I'm not a very truthful person. 'We are religious people. That we name our worship something else doesn't change its true nature. We are still worshiping. The trouble is that the things we don't call gods, but treat as gods, are merely his image bearers." [1]

The tremendous stature of man is not understood by modern man because he relates himself to a machine and an animal so murder is not inherently different from any other crime! But it is inherently different because we are made in the image of God….it is profoundly different.

And "We've been called to have dominion over the earth to the glory of Creator-God, but we want dominion for the glory of man"[2] What went on at Babel was an evil twisting of the legitimate task Creator- God had given mankind. It's perfectly OK with Him for us to create wonderful things and explore and describe His Creation, but they are to be done under the authority of Creator-God, not mere man. When we create for our own glory, whether it is a nation or a city or a structure, it is to be before the face of God *coram Deo,* under the authority of God, and unto the glory of God. Even Shakespeare knew this and wrote in the song at the end of King Henry IV noted "unto you o God is the glory" in Latin. "Babel is representative of the Whole human enterprise that we are so busily engaged in. 'Let's build a city. Let's make a name for ourselves….The greatest building project man kind ever attempted was resisted by God. and it ended in chaos and confusion"[3] The teaching of the university almost completely omits this understanding to our children. The Humanism religion excludes out Creator, a fatal flaw. Would you say that we have chaos, division, and confusion, and raw anger amongst our members today?

We worship creation rather than Creator-God, and none more frequently that that two dimensional copy of God, man. The fact that the recent President of the United States calls America a "secular" nation is not a good sign for this nation. It follows then that, if President Obama's label for us was accurate, then we are not a very truthful nation. How did we become an idolatrous nation?

There is a story of Caesar, when chased by his enemies across a river, easily threw off his royal robes, but held high his books as he kicked across the river. He became admired as "Caesar who loved learning more than his royal robes".

"For the time is coming when people will no longer listen to sound wholesome teaching. They will follow their own desire and will look for teachers who will tell them whatever their itching ears* want to hear. They will reject the truth and chase after myths." [2 Tim 4:3]$_{NLT}$ [1]

*(note: to have one's ears tickled by what it hears is a Greek idiom…. what seems compelling to them.)

Knowledge tends to puff up all of us. I certainly know what happened to me. Soon after teaching a subject I know well, I often opened the lecture hall doors just in case someone walking by might chance to hear my wonderful thoughts. Was I deluded? Or was it worse than that.

Failure to recognize a reality higher than our own is a common error of faculty, indeed of all people who study a lot of information and pass exams and feel themselves proven in that area of knowledge. Is it possible that recognizing only your own personal "truth" is a big-time error?

As David Kupelian puts it quoting a Psychiatrist M. Scott Peck M.D. from his classic best-seller, *People of the Lie:*[4]

"Malignant narcissism is characterized by an unsubmitted will. All adults who are mentally healthy submit themselves one way or another to something higher than themselves, be it God or truth or love or some other ideal. They do what God wants them to do rather than what they would desire. "Thy will, not mine, be done," the God-submitted person says. They believe in what is true rather than what they would like to be true.

> *… In summary, to a greater or lesser degree, all mentally healthy individuals submit themselves to the demands of their own conscience. Not so the evil, however. In the conflict between their guilt and their will, it is the guilt that must go and the will that must win."*[5]

The mechanism of teaching "me, me, I, I" to students when that is the orientation of the particular faculty is a hard problem for the individual. Hard to identify in oneself, and hard to address in an honest manner. We must recognize that there are forces smarter than any faculty operating here and the moral destruction of a culture is a major outcome of this malignant narcissism. This thinking extends to all who: Knowing there is no real false god, wrongly believe they can teach an open form of idolatry (as I define it) with little consequence by subconsciously pointing to their own reality, choosing to laugh at the search for real truth, and walk with their society into the abyss, declaring as it did, that the abyss, and the demons of the abyss do not exist. So they merrily refer to the gods of Babylon, the demigods of Babylonian-Greek and Roman culture and the morality of that period in their teaching.

I repeat, how would mom and dad respond if they knew their child was asked to bow before the pagan Idol Moloch and Isis for example? That Idolatry was imbedded in the lecture notes, the exams, and the whole ambience of the University. They pay the bill, or their child goes in great debt for this overlay that is not in the literature of that institution's offer to educate their child. Are they aware that Humanism is idolatry of the highest level… the theology of the imagined!

What would you think if you sent your child to college to get a better job but find out that the function of many of the faculty is to steal your child's eternal life! We know that between 61 and 70% of children that believe before they leave for college have a loss in their faith. 81% of all teens have attended church of at least 2 months or more of those but after college 61% of those are disengaged.[6]

"They became futile in their thoughts and their foolish hearts were darkened. Professing to be wise, they became fools, and changed the glory of the incorruptible (Creator) God into an image made like corruptible man….." [7] God describes himself carefully in scripture so man would not rightly describe Him by his (man's) imaginations saying, "my god is different", in the way of human discourse.

If you want an answer to what is happening to America, ask and find an answer to the question, What is the Final Reality? If the answer you find is: There is an infinite Creator God, then your answer is at odds with what is taught to most students on our campus, our future and past teachers in the departments of education, and our future professionals in this nation. The campus teaches the final reality is: there is a material or energy which has always existed, shaped into its present form only by pure chance leading logically to the conclusion that man is the measure of all things. This Humanist conclusion is a grave contradiction that I will explain in this book, giving no meaning for life, no basis for a value system and no basis for law. Knowing that man has only knowledge of himself and is (except for Christ) not a witness of creation; tending to be faulty in his observations of many things with only his 5 senses, his invented value system must be arbitrary as well as the basis of his law. Christ was not just the only one witnessing creation, He is the Creator man-God. If a child is taught he is a grownup worm, why should he consider life so valuable, even his own? Do you know our supreme court operates only on arbitrary law. Have they been removed as a solid anchor for our nation?

Wise parents know that their children should be raised up in a manner that develops the three part nature of the child with equal emphasis on their spiritual their intellectual and the physical. For they know there's a world of feeling, a world of thought, and a world of things... to fill three kinds of needs, spiritual intellectual and physical. That our child was given three capacities that match those needs: the capacity to worship, to reason, and to create. A good parent wants balance so the tripart spiritual, mental, and physical capacities are developed. Today's university over emphasizes the physical and the philosophical and, while it knows that the spiritual must be taught, it fails to teach an honest spiritual development by substituting an idolatry that we call "humanism" that has become the religion of the university. We want our children to be sane, complete, and know what reality is but without this balance we're driving our children, our nation and our civilization away from sanity and reality! History is replete with the destruction of nations.[8]

"The Glory of God is the hardest truth of all for people to accept" [9]

Logic of Idolatry: (The most basic act we do against Creator-God)
If we <u>don't</u> acknowledge the sovereignty of Creator-God, the justice of Creator-God, the omniscience of Creator-God, and the immutability of Creator-God, then whatever god we are acknowledging is **NOT**

Creator-God. Idolatry can be done in a crass manner with a statue of a icon or, "In a more sophisticated, intellectual sort of idolatry----the reconstruction of our doctrine of God in such a way as to strip Him of those attributes with which we are uncomfortable. All of us have a propensity to reconstruct a god who is not holy, who is not wrathful, who is not just, who is not sovereign. We find it easy to take attributes of God we like and reject the ones we don't. When we do that we are as guilty of idolatry as a person who is worshipping a graven image. [10]

If this book exposes the principle of Idolatry taught openly in America's Colleges and Universities I have achieved my goal. Idolatry is giving credit or honor or authority to anyone or anything other then the One truly responsible for the Universe and the forces operating here. It's a misdirection, a deception, and a lie to give this credit or honor to anything other then Creator-God. And the seriousness of this error is the ultimate destruction of the culture in which it occurs. Honest history supports this understanding, from ancient Babylon to Nazi Germany; from all the empires of the past to the collapse of modern nations.[11] The desire I have is to present this book in gentleness and respect. That is not an easy task by any measure.

Why would a society, knowing this truth, engage in such an absurdity? This is an enormous question that must be raised? What are we doing? I realize this concept of Idolatry is somewhat foreign in that it is not a piece of wood or stone but even more dangerous, a mental image. The ancients were somewhat more honest in their idolatry with little carved images that they worshiped while modern man has these things in his head with, most often, a key word or phrase that invokes them…..one that is quite the deception! Man, the first Adam, was created in the image of God. God is not created by the imagination of man. When we create an idol our hearts become darkened (blind) to the truth.

Probably the greatest condemnation of the university comes from Ravi Zacharias in his observation that, "Universities deliver meaninglessness in large doses. On campus after campus, in culture after culture, I have listened for hours to intellectuals, young and old, who testify to a deep seated emptiness." [12] We all fall into the dichotomy of Cain or Abel....into the "two humanities" One declares no Creator-God or one of their own imagination and tries to come to him in their own way while the other humanity comes to Creator-God in God's way. There is no neutral ground.[10] Who among the faculty are not guilty of this charge? When we step back from the podium and realize we spent our time integrating the lesson material utilizing evolution or social evolution or some such imagined theory, we must remember in no way are we filling the hole in our students heart; that deep understanding is just not there because the theory is empty and unsatisfying to something deep inside of us. I hope to present an alternative way of thinking in this book. The theoretical physicists often talk of additional dimensions. They write them in their equations and lose most of us in the process. However there is an unseen dimension to this universe that has historically been a part of history for thousands of years. The spiritual realm is recognized by almost everyone, but it is not in those equations. Can't faculty bypass their intellect and speak from their heart? Or are we afraid? Are we afraid that would not appear authoritative? Or is it we have no words for that dimension? I might suggest that we reconsider; such words exist.

What profit is idolatry? We are told around 600 BC by a prophet of Creator-God by the name of Habakkuk who wrote to us while his nation Judah was in its death throws; in the process of being conquered by the Babylonians because of their idolatry. "These images "are a **teacher of lies**, that the maker of its mold should trust in it, ...Arise it shall teach!... But the LORD is in His holy temple. Let all the earth keep silence before Him."[13]

The Idolatry itself teaches the lies as well. Does it gain even more power if the Professor invokes it? Indeed, "pride" can be idolatry.

Who am I to criticize the great universities and their faculty? This book however is a disputation of the religion of the humanist fundamentalists, secular fundamentalists, the "religion of the campus", and evolution fundamentalism that have crept in to wage war on truth. Having taught at 4 great universities and studied under excellent professors of whom I have a great respect, I found myself, after 30 years of teaching, joining a small

Christian Faculty breakfast discussion group. I soon became aware how offensive the mere existence of this group was on campus and how great were the efforts to block and decimate the group. I became aware as well of the unfriendly atmosphere where I found myself. Open believers are not welcome today on campus and the truth is how held in disdain or at least "tongue in cheek" if Creator-God is contained in written or spoken statements! (see:"Candlelight on the Campus" Appendix 1)

To prove that Creator-God is offended by our giving His Glory or His praise to others. we must listen to one of the greatest of prophets, Isaiah 42: 5-9:

> Thus says the God the LORD,
> Who created the heavens and stretched them out,
> Who spread forth the earth and that which comes from it,
> Who gives breath to the people on it,
> And spirit to those who walk on it:
> "I, the LORD, have called You in righteousness,
> And will hold your hand;
> I will keep You and give You as a covenant to the people,
> As a light to the Gentiles,
> To open blind eyes,
> To bring out prisoners from the prison,
> Those who sit in darkness from the prison house,
> *I am* the LORD, and that is My name;
> And My Glory I will not give to another,
> Nor My praise to graven images.
> Behold, the former things have come to pass,
> And the new things I declare;
> Before they spring forth I tell you of them."

My attitude in this book is one of warning to everyone me included. Everyone has a part to play. We can all be used for a valuable purpose by our Creator-God.

Why is the "New Covenant" He gave us in Jeremiah 31:31-34 important? It's because man couldn't keep the Old Covenant Law He gave to Moses. Why doesn't the LORD speak to us audibly: Why doesn't He do something spectacular and unmistakable? <u>Because not only is Jesus preparing a place for us (John 14:2), but He's also preparing us for the place.</u> That is, He's stripping us of our dependence on the physical and material world. He wants us to hear with our ears of the spirit (that still small voice), and to see with the eyes of the spirit. Jon Courson makes this point:

"I believe the Church would expand exponentially if Christians would simply obey when the Holy Spirit says, 'Talk to Him. Give to her. Love them.' "He'll show us things about out kids so we can minister effectively to them. He'll show us things about ourselves that we need to correct. He'll give insight how to witness to those who seem so closed to the gospel. God has given us the written Word to correct us when we're not hearing Him clearly and confirm what He speaks to us. Thus it's not a matter of dos an don'ts, but confirmation and correction—of the Word written on paper working in tandem with His will written on our hearts.[14]

His nature is that of a Jealous Creator-God and He must be who He is. This book is designed to point out the offense of inventing our own god or gods. That blocks us from His preparing us for the wonderful eternity He has planned for us. We are in training! Creator-God's outrage for idolatry will be a function of His very nature, He must respond once our nation crosses the line! Help us to break away and back away from the line we must be approaching!

I repeat, what would a society think once it discovers we're teaching their children to worship Moloch and the Baals, the gods of ancient Babylon among many other such gods? The wonderful things that we do in preparing students for a job in that culture might allow us to survive the outrage (perhaps) but it's not going to be pleasant.

i

The Creator-God of the Bible vs. Ancient gods

Part 1. Creator-God

Who is The Creator-God of the Bible?

"In the beginning God created the heaven and the earth."[Genesis 1:1]

The first words of the bible are entirely unique. No other ancient paganism or modern cosmogony including naturalism mentions or even alludes to the absolute origin of the Universe.[1] If you study these others carefully you will see they all begin with space and time and matter already created…. so they all have little more to say than even Carl Sagan who told us that physics doesn't address where the Cosmic egg came from in the "Big Bang" cosmology. (was there a cosmic chicken then?) Michio Kaku who seems to have replaced him as the salesman for the "Big Bang" announced that with the discovery of the Higgs Boson, there was a type of Higgs Boson that was the trigger for the "Big Bang", as he theorized, but no statement for who made the cosmic egg so their theory would work. Is Mekio attesting to a science of the observable, in that there are no doubt, many physicists who would attest to observing explosions that created order? And a theory that requires at least a temperature of 1×10^{100} degrees K. required to give the Microwave background we find today, seen as so profound without an explanation where the energy comes from for that enormous heat. Although that is not quite fair for their theory of beginnings. The word "singularity" means "miracle" to the physicist implying no reproduction or observation is possible; meaning it can't be tested. Clearly establishing a "faith based physics"….a lot of faith! Creator-God made things in a way to allow the creation of the profession of physics so man would have employment and gain great skills in math and imagination, but only one observer was present at the creation and He is kind enough to declare to us not only what he did, but how he did it. Since we have no idea what is the true nature of an electron or a photon, or graviton, or why we weigh anything or why inertia, we cannot claim anything more than a very primitive science compared to the straightforward presentation of the One observer whose creation obeys His spoken word.

A reasonable question to ask of the Physicists is: Why should the "Physics of maintenance of the universe" be the same as the "physics of creation of the universe"? What do we study for we only have a created universe to observe. Since science is of the observable, what basis is there for Humanists theories? No scientists has honestly seen a star born. Such expressions are common but without convincing support. We read such expressions bantered about as "Star-forming region" in Messier 33 (Galaxy). Any where they see stellar gas they are quick to label it "star birth" regions or ie. "stellar nursery in the Eagle Nebula". Yet they admit "Researchers still do not know the details of how clouds of dust and gas collapse to form stars."[2] They are just "best guessing" are they not. A infra red signature of a forming star is not known. That is not science facts but hypothesis formation.

5 reasons why Creator-God exists.

William Lane Craig of the Talbot school of Theology tells us 5 key reasons why Creator-God exists and describes the characteristics of what Craig refers to as "that Transcendent cause":

1. Creator-God is the best explanation of the origin of the universe.
2. Creator-God is the best explanation of the fine-tuning of the universe for intelligent life.
3. Creator-God is the best explanation for the existence of objective moral values and duties.
4. Creator-God is the best explanation for the historical facts concerning Jesus of Nazareth.
5. Creator-God can be personally known and experienced.

Big Bang arguments that quantum mechanics allows for particles to pop in and out of existence apparently from nothing does not explain the quantum vacuum where they come in and out of existence. This seething Quantum vacuum before these events occur is certainly not nothing. It is a <u>SEA</u> of energy in the seething vacuum and is full of what is needed and obeys physical laws for everything to exist that we see now. The quantum vacuum state couldn't have existed in infinity past it had to have a beginning. so what brought the universe into existence. This points to a Transcendent cause of the universe and that Transcendent cause had these characteristics:

1. an uncaused being
2. a non-physical and immaterial being because it created all the matter in the universe
3. a Timeless non-temporal being because it created time
4. the changeless being
5. an enormously powerful being
6. a personal being which is required to link a temporal effect with a beginning from a permanent time with a cause that has existed from eternity. because once the sufficient conditions exist as a cause then the effect would have to follow. For example: for water to freeze the conditions required are the temperature must be below freezing. How can water not exist and not be frozen when the conditions for freezing exist for it? An agent must act or will to act to bring this into being. and that agent has a will just as a person "wills" to stand up after he's been sitting."

"We know from simple logic that once the conditions are given the effect must follow if there's sufficient conditions." So the effect would have to be there permanently without any will. Therefore God is a person in fact he is three persons in one ....,far more complex than anything we can grasp with our little water brains.

" Again, if the conditions are given from eternity then the effect would have to be present from eternity.....the cause of water freezing is because the temperature is below 0 degrees Celsius. If the temperature were below 0 degrees Celsius from eternity past it would be impossible for the water to just begin to freeze a finite time ago. so how do you get a temporal effect from the beginning from a permanent cause?

A Transcendent cause must be a PERSONAL AGENT who freely chooses to create a new effect without any prior determining conditions.....so we are brought not just to a Transcendent cause of the universe but to its personal creator.....Creator-God."[3]

The characteristics of Creator-God vs. Idols

Most of us have a very small Creator – God. When we say Creator or "God almighty", what does that mean. Many of the words used to describe Creator- God exist only to describe him. Many terms set him as the standard for the word..... the ultimate.

Creator -God is impeccably honest, he cannot lie showing that he only is Veracity or truth completely. He alone is God. He tells us He has searched the heavens and found no other God. That means all others claiming or claimed by man to be god are fake. We are told they have a demon spirit behind each of them. If there is an atom, particle, or energy anywhere in the universe that He does not control, then He is not Creator- God. So his sovereignty is perfect. This also means that nothing happens by chance in that he always knows the final outcome. So He can "allow things" or he can "change things" and that all is within his will. We all question untoward and bad events and sometimes our prayers are not answered. There is however a war in heaven and on earth that is unseen by us. In the book of Daniel we see a window on the war that is happening. We are told that Daniel had asked Creator-God what would happen to his people but the answer from heaven was delayed. The Heavenly Messenger was delayed 21 days because the prince of the kingdom of Persia withstood him until Michael (the Archangel) came to help him in the battle. After the Angel relayed the message from Creator-God, the Angel explained that he must return to the battle with the "Prince of Persia" and later the "Prince of Greece" will come (to battle)" [Daniel 10:10-21.] We are given a unique window into the heavenly battle between Creator-God and the Principalities and powers of Creator-God's enemy. There are indeed powerful dark forces at war with Creator-God and we are often in the middle. I realize many readers do not believe there are in existence enemies of God and man who can drive the universe that was made "good" off the charts into such big trouble as we see all around us. I see a creation were "work" is to be done which, whether gravity, lifting a weight, or energy expenditure, or a movement causing heat from friction, or spiritual work, all involve RESISTANCE of some kind. Without tungsten resistance wire in the light bulb, the current would not produce light. Even free space has a resistance (Impendence) of $120x\pi$ (ohms), which has much to do with light properties and antenna operation. What is comforting is that what may be intended for bad, Creator- God tells us He will turn to good ultimately. I take him for his word. Note that the Herods, Hamans, and Hitlers's and Hamas and Hezbollah of the world have attempted to destroy His Messiah's coming, but notice how it worked out for them, all of them.

> Creator-God is love. He wants to interact with us in everything we do. He is full of care and compassion dressing the flowers and trees with beauty as well as the man and woman he created. He exists outside of time because time is part of the workings of his creation, required for it to work. For work to be done, it must be done in "time". God is holy and righteousness completely. God is separated from sin and corruption (or degradation). R.C. Sproul notes that the writing of the Prophet Isaiah 6:3 describes Creator - God as "Holy, Holy, Holy" and that only once in sacred scripture is an attribute of God elevated to the third degree. ie. The bible never says love, love, love. [4]

He is described by the terms "omnipotent" (supremely all powerful) and "omnipresent" (exists everywhere and all times as the all – perceiving all –concealing foundation of reality). Creator-God is "omniscient" or is all-knowing, he has all knowledge of all things knowing the end from the beginning. His wisdom is perfect and that he knows human nature and all natures and we'll see his will accomplished in heaven and earth (Romans 16:27). So He alone is wise. God is one, a single infinite being of Father, Son, and Holy Spirit called Triune and all personal relating to himself and personal relating to us. He lets us see this relating to himself in holy scripture in communications and shares this with us. The characteristic of one bestowing grace or un-merited favor on us is most amazing in that a Creator-God with such attributes would extend this grace freely to those who bow to Him and Him alone. This graciousness is extended unconditionally as well as conditionally. Finally His immutability or unchanging character must be known. He tells us he doesn't change and is the same "from everlasting to everlasting". [Psalm 90:2, Psalm 103:17, Psalm 106:48]

I lay out this description of the Creator-God for the purpose of contrast with pagan and mythology gods that we will see that are manmade. In truth our Creator-God is impossible to describe fully because our water brains, all of them together, can't grasp all that He is and can do ....we are left with terms He has given us from which He describes himself. Demigods, pagan gods, and idols, please note, are so removed from all of these characteristics that they are easily filtered out of reality, once you know the nature of Creator-God. As the ancient and modern idols are described please observe the enormous contrast to the one true God.

Man's feeble attempt to exclude Creator-God in his "science" requires a total escape from commonsense. Lee Smolin, a physicist I respect, identifies the strings of "string theory" as "made of nothing" . Smolin is finally getting at truth in theoretical physics. We are told that Creator-God made the universe "*Ex nihilo*" (out of nothing). If it is maintained by his face shining photons from every possible direction (the zitterbewegung vacuum or background energy)then we have an explanation for the enormous amount of what is fallaciously called 'dark energy and dark matter". A signal on all sides of a sensor cannot be detected. So we haven't measured this sustaining power yet. Faith seems to be part of the design of things! This energy and its precision was shown by Beyer and Putoff [5] while assuming the ground state electron of hydrogen, emits Larmor radiation which causes it to spiral inward, but does not lead to collapse of the electron orbit because the electron absorbs a zero–point–energy." By treating the electron as undergoing harmonic oscillation the Lamor emission and the harmonic –oscillator – type absorption prove to be in balance <u>EXACTLY</u> at the Bohr radius (average minimal radius of the electron from the proton). This model has been modified in 1995 by Ibison and Haish. (see: www.calphysics.org/zpe.html)

So all matter operates with his will and his word and perhaps His super energetic face. Any attempt to describe reality by smashing some pieces of matter and looking in the trash to reassemble reality are studies in frustration by the poor physicist who follows his university training in theology leaving out that which allows the universe to be created from nothing. They can't possibly assemble reality from smashed atoms or particles by excluding <u>everything</u> especially what holds it all together, Creator-God. Too much like the anthropologist, having been trained in evolution, who looks at painted pictures on cave walls and publishes a paper describing what he calls a 100,000 year old description of what he interprets as the "stone age" with no idea of the absolute age of the paint ....the hard questions of science; choosing, as usual, the shallow answer... Which is likely a lie.

A Brief Declaration and Vindication of The Doctrine of the Trinity by John Owen in 1669: [6]
"*God is one*; — that this one God is *Father, Son, and Holy Ghost*; — that *the Father is the Father of the Son*; and *the Son, the Son of the Father*; and *the Holy Ghost, the Spirit of the Father and the Son*; and that, in respect of this their mutual relation, they are distinct from each other. This is the *substance* of the doctrine of the Trinity, as to the first direct concernment of faith therein. The first intention of the Scripture, in the revelation of God towards us, is, as was said, that we might fear him, believe, worship, obey him, and live unto him, as God. That we may do this in a due manner, and worship *the only true God*, <u>and not adore the false imaginations of our own</u>

<u>minds</u> it declares, as was said, that this *God is one*, the Father, Son, and Holy Ghost; — that the *Father is this one God*; and therefore is to be believed in, worshipped, obeyed, lived unto, and in all things considered by us as the first cause, sovereign Lord, and last end of all; — that *the Son is the one true God*; and therefore is to be believed in, worshipped, obeyed, lived unto, and in all things considered by us as the first cause, sovereign Lord, and last end of all; — and so, also, of the Holy Ghost....... Wherefore, to deny that the Lord Christ, in his death and suffering for us, underwent the punishment due to our sins, what we had deserved, that we might be delivered, as it everts (overturns) the great foundation of the gospel, so, by an open perverting of the plain words of the Scripture, because not suited in their sense and importance to the vain imaginations of men, it gives no small countenance to infidelity and atheism."

So man's effort to exclude Jesus Christ the Messiah as God is a clear denial of the only path made available for man to be saved for eternity. This leaves only the many paths that sadly lead to destruction of all that go there. We are told that these words are meaningless to those who are perishing.

Rejection of Christ as God: the Arian-Unitarian Heresy
The Unitarian heresy was decided with the arguments presented for the "Arian heresy" at the Council of Nicea in 325 AD and rejected completely only to be resurrected again and again as the Arian-Unitarian heresy. [7] We will see the transformation of Harvard into a Humanist University as a result of the ascendency of this Arian-Unitarian heresy in Boston 1545 years later.

A Strange Characteristic of Idolaters with many Idols: Why some characteristics are so hard to decipher in the ancient writings
One of the characteristics of idolaters is they attribute to whichever idol they select an attribute they <u>feel</u> they need at the moment. Somehow miraculously, the idol will grant them their desires like a Genie. Sort of like a waiter or bell-hop totally under the control of the requestor. If the event happens as requested, then the little god came through, if not, they must

have not selected the correct god, performed the right ritual or sacrifice, or perhaps their god wasn't listening. The Canaanites used the location of family-god idols to denote real property locations. Whenever a battle was fought, the idol invoked was a key communication within the pagan culture. The people must have used a weak form of inductive logic...Bayesian thinking in an attempt to gain a reasonable likelihood of success. This was a system so full of holes that anyone could be fooled by the causal reality or weak correlations that, "seemed good to a man". Barnhouse notes that the author of the Encyclopedia Britannica confesses a confession among scholars concerning the attributes of the Egyptian deities, and seemed disturbed about it, " but when we consider that there were local deities who took on various characteristics at home and were overlapped by national deities, the difficulty disappears. The polytheistic mind is liable to consider that any god has any attribute in time of need. We can study the same phenomenon today where various powers are ascribed to a certain statue of the Virgin Mary not possessed by other statues of the same person, and where, for example, the Virgin of Lourdes and the Virgin of La Salette and the Virgin of Fatima vie for the faithfulness of different devotees in the same church building."[8]

One of the characteristics of the pagan world was its insistence that its god was tied to a specific region of some area, state, city or principality. We know that is true of certain Demons such as the "Prince of Persia" (Iran), but in no way describes the True God. This is best described about 800BC by the words of Naaman, the king of Syria's top general who was cured of leprosy by dipping in the Jordan river (Jordan means judgment). Once he realized the only true God was Creator-God of Israel, he requested, "two mules burden of earth " or dirt of Israel so he could go back to Syria and build a place to sacrifice on top of that dirt of Israel.[2 Kings 5:1-28] [NKJV] [Nelson] It is not to difficult to see this bizarre local land attribute of Idols/gods led to many murderous wars. We also know in ancient times people used their idols to stake out their property boundaries as well.

Because of what we see in Creator-God's character we can contrast this to others man has set up as god(s).

Table 1. frequent characteristics of the representative pagan gods we will trace through time to the campus

god supposed characteristic	frequent Characteristics
Epicurus's Pantheon of Greek gods that are supposedly blessed and immortal.	Do not interest or concern themselves with man. Ethics defined simply as good=absence of pain and pleasure=absence of suffering
Molech (king) Nimrod/Marduk	Requires child sacrifice
Tiamat	Torn to become the stuff of the universe
<u>Apis(bull-god) & (cow headed) Hathor</u>	Sacred cow of Egypt
Giant scarub Dung God, Amon-Ra, the Beetle headed king of Egyptian gods, the sun god Brought light from the darkness Along with Aten, the sun's disc And ankh, symbol of life from the sun	Since they rolled perfect balls across their fields, they must bring the sun back from the netherworld.. the seed of life
Thoth, ibis-headed god of intelligence, medicine and learning Apis, Serapis, Imhotep	gods with powers of healing
Horus, hawk-headed sky god of upper Egypt Shu, the wind-god, god of light Nut, the sky goddess	Control Storms and outbreaks of nature
Osiris, head of the Hamatic Trinity (with Isis and Horus)	Agricultural god
Ermutet, Egyptian	Goddess of childbirth and crops
Ishtar	(Nimrod & Tammuz's (her son) wife)
Cybel, Diana, Rhea, Semiramis	Mother of the gods
Sin	Deified Heth's brother Sumerian and Assyrian god
Ammon of the Egyptians	Deified Ham (2nd son of Noah)
Astarte, Aphrodite, Venus, Semiramus, Easter, Beltus queen of heaven, Ishtar, Idaia Mater or "Mother of Knowledge"(Eve), Rhea or Cyble Queen of Babylon, Minervia goddess of wisdom inventor of Arts and Sciences, The Moon]	Mother of Heaven and Earth, Goddess of love and beauty, Goddess of Towers (war), Pagan hope of the world

Why is a physical image of the Creator-God a grave error?

Albert Einstein said "I see a pattern, but my imagination cannot picture the maker of that pattern. I see a clock, but I cannot envision the clockmaker. The human mind is unable to conceive of the four dimensions, so how can it conceive of a God, before whom a thousand years and a thousand dimensions are as one?" [9] While Einstein has arrived at his conclusion of the problem, we see the wisdom in his statement. We see why any image of Creator God is absurd and totally unrepresentative. We learn that idolatry is man building himself a mental image of something man can't picture and then giving this false mental image characteristics and descriptors the man desires. Absurd!

"You shall worship the LORD thy God and Him only shall you serve." (Matthew 4:10, Luke 4:8)

The idea that we can create images or imagine other gods is actually quite foolish, and instructing students to follow these false gods in any manner is not wise, and I will make the case, can harm the nation. But the creator god has a name above all names and we are to trust in that very name. That name is a sound in our minds that He does allow. The Jews usually write it "G_d" while the King James Version of the Bible represents the name as LORD with all caps, the writers are representing the Hebrew ( ) YHVH or sometimes as 'JA'. Not as an image but a very important word for our minds to solve the problem Einstein addresses….. A word that can then be associated with the attributes he attributes to himself in the collection of 66 books of the bible. If he is all powerful he can certainly inform us of what is true, and light, and give us direction as we pour, blind, and naked stumble through life.

If the future "Revived Roman Empire" can be called the "Daughter of Babylon" then what names can we attach to the educational system that is underlying the development of this "Revived Roman Empire"? Babylon is far deeper into these modern times then most will admit. I would like to make the case that the thinking by the leaders of ancient Babylon continues today.

Part 2. Truth of Genesis and Creator-God's Word

Veracity of the Book of Genesis

To be consistent with the doctrine of Biblical inspiration and authority as well as the accurate historicity of its records I take the position that the book of genesis is accurate and precise and in fact all that man has on the subject of beginnings. Jesus Christ himself, accepted the genesis record as history. "it is arrogant and presumptuous for modern day scholars to undertake to correct Christ and the apostles on this vital matter. Scholars that claim the entire book is allegory are incorrect. There are no allegory in the book of Genesis except where the dreams interpreted by Joseph are so described. It is evident from at least 11 *toledolth or* divisions that represent the original documents from which genesis was collection. The collection includes 11 "These are the generations" two of them are about the Edomites and one of them about Ishmael while the rest begin with "the generations of heaven and earth" to "the generations of Jacob" at the end [10] it seems that the writer of genesis (no doubt Moses) is an editor or compiler of these at least eleven documents contained in the book of genesis. He compiled this work all by a work of the Holy Spirit who infallibly guided him in the process. A clear understanding of Genesis requires an understanding of the New Testament and the Index of it all, the book of "The Revelation of Jesus Christ".

There are many who reject "Noah's flood", but we find the evidence is quite overwhelming. For example: the most ancient Chinese ideograph for boat is a picture of "an ark and 8 souls". How is it that the inventor of the Chinese language knew about Genesis 7. The four couples that survived the flood traded the occupation of master shipbuilders for farming. The patriarch Noah, who was "contemporary" with Adam or his son Seth (Genealogies of the Masoretic text) and Noah and his son Shem were contemporary with Abraham. So "Shem's story" (Genesis 10:1b-11:10) and the other 10 segments of Genesis are as close as we can get to those that witnessed or were told by Creator-God. What is even better is that the Man-Creator-God Jesus confirmed what was written. We cannot ignore that both Noah and his son Shem outlived the one that started the rebellion of Idolatry, Nimrod by many years apparently…although there may have been another individual by that name many years later.

Man is to trust in Creator-God for He can be trusted

'And in His name shall the gentiles trust' (Matt 12:21). Trust, what an amazing story since the beginning of time. Is trust the key? Is trust in God the key to it all? It is possible that when two people are allowed to start an increase in population and multiply at the rate of two percent, within sixteen hundred years in ideal conditions there would be over a trillion people on this earth. There was an enormous number of people when the flood occurred but only one man and his family trusted in God. He could convince no one else it seams. That man, Noah started and seeded everyone else on earth today. God taught man not to murder other men because of the incredible value of each person. " For in the image of God made he man" (Gen 9:5-6). Man is to hold man in high respect because each of us is an image-bearer of God. At least Adam was when he was made; we are at least similar to Adam with at least 5000 years of many heritable errors in us (approximately 200 per generation). "Modern man who relates himself to the machine and to the animal does not really understand the tremendous stature of man and therefore he sees no reason why murder is inherently different from any other crime." [11] The first men gave rise to each of the cultures we learn about. And in Genesis 1-11 we find two distinct cultures, the culture of the godly line and the culture of the un-godly line.

A man of the godly line was not to be unequally yoked….was not to marry a woman of the un-godly line, a culture without the true God, the line of Cain who killed his brother; one in which the concept of love of his brother has been lost. This attitude is a Humanism-pride like attitude and we will see it raise its ugly head again after the flood. "Since Cain, everyone in the world stands in the place of Cain or the place of Abel. From this time on in the flow of history there are two humanities. The one says there is no God or makes gods after his own imagination, or tries to come to the true God in his own way. The other humanity comes to the true God in God's way. There is no neutral ground."[12]

Part 3. Deception-Idolatry

The History of the Deception

While the history of idolatry is extremely difficult to document and scholars are not in agreement, there are important considerations that seem logical. Most highly regarded writing is in Genesis where Moses notes in the Garden of Eden that the Savior for mankind will, "....be the seed of the woman (note: women don't have seed, implying the virgin birth) and will crush the serpents head but the serpent will bruise his heel". (Genesis 3:15)

This Savior who will save mankind is first described to us through the records of only eight people (and perhaps any writings Noah brought with him). Also noting that Noah talked with the ancients that knew Adam for Adam lived 950 years. My point is that as man multiplied and dispersed over the earth it should not be surprising that parts of the story of a "savior of mankind" would be retained by many of the societies. A piece of truth can often be found in the epics and pagan narratives from that time on. Also it is commonly known that the enemy of man often deceives man by trying to imitate using similar concepts such as "gods dying as some weep for Tammuz". Even the name of the local gods often referred to the "savior". And the blood of the pagan god referenced in the sacrifices that developed.

The enemy of man has always sought to turn man from the love and worship of the Creator – God and his provision of Himself as the "God–man" Jesus as the entrance for man into eternal life. Recall the attempt of Satan during the 40 days of the temptation of Christ in the desert in which Satan offered all the kingdoms of the world (which he owned) and their glory if Christ would worship him(Satan); which Christ declared "Be gone, Satan! For it is written, You shall worship the LORD your God and him only shall you serve." (Matthew 4:9-10) Instructing us who follow in the correct path. Also recall the first of the 10 commandments, "you shall have no other gods before me" (Exodus 20), ruling mental imagery as well as the second law ruling all material idolatry. Homer's most ancient writing of the *Iliad* at least 2600 years ago use the Greek term "Ichor", known as the blood of god.

"From the clear vain the immortal Ichor flowed,

such stream as issues from a wounded god,

Pure emanation, uncorrupted flood, unlike our gross, diseased terrestrial blood"[13].

So we see incorporated into "hero –worship–gods" a little truth from the two people that lived a long time after the flood who knew the truth, Noah and his son Shem. Rebellion against Creator–God begin with Noah's son Cush and followed with his descendants in what seems became the Roman and Greek pantheon of gods and goddesses and their accompanying myths and poems. Any attempt to trace this path is difficult at best and fraught with controversy, but what would you expect from the enemy of the true Creator–God and his collection of fallen angels or/and demons who, we are told, are behind every false god and idol.

About the same time Charles Darwin was inventing his theory to supply humanism with its theology, several careful writers where describing the development of modern idolatry, false gods, and goddesses. William Burckhardt in "Lares and Penates" in Cilicia on the "Magi and Monks", followed by H.J. Jones in 1852 on "Is Rome Babylon", which was not received well followed by a work of incredible thoroughness by Rev. Alexander Hislop called "The Two Babylons" with reference to 270 works quoted or referred to with an average of seven sites in footnotes on each of his 323 pages of his third edition (which can't be read without his amazing footnotes which are not in the e-books.[14] F. F. Bruce in 1941 carefully corrected Hislop's work which Bruce called a "radical revision" because "the science of philology no longer depends on fortuitous similarities ----referring to the laws of development and change in language that were unknown and capped Hislop's time. Hislop's Mysteries of Babylon made a very convincing case for the pagan rituals found in modern religions throughout the world. This new knowledge convincingly placed all modern ideology flowing on a continuum from Nimrod and his wife to the religions of the world, infecting all except the bible. Once you carefully read Bruce's radical revision of Hislop you will find yourself on a stronger footing. [15]

The History of Idolatry

While there is academic debate about the person of Nimrod or Nimroud as well as just who is this Babylonian "mother and child" figure that is found so often in Babylonism. Most recent archeological findings of these most ancient individuals have not clarified the matter. I will start with the authority of the Bible which identifies the historicity of Nimrod and notes he was the first king noted whose kingdom was Babel, Ereeh, Accad, and Calneh in the land of Shinar. He was also described as a "mighty hunter before the LORD"and a mighty one on the earth, who later built Nineveh, Rehoboth Ir, Calah and Resen between Nineveth and Calneh. I am also following the evidence and support of Flavius Josephus, Henry A. Ironside, George Rawlinson, Henry Morris and others. And for SemiRamus I as the Babylonian Madonna there is some support, but her name is not found in the Bible. However there seems to be indirect reference to her when the term "Mystery Babylon" is mentioned. It is also remarkable that statues of mother and child certainly abound and are worshiped and prayed to even today. "She is reputed to have been the founder of the Babylonian Mysteries and the first high-priestess of idolatry."[16] Ironsides describes this Babylonian Madonna as the founder of the "Babylonian Mysteries" and considers her the "first high-priestess of idolatry".[14] As noted by Justin Martyr, "everywhere the cult of mother and child became the popular system....(in which) worship was celebrated with the most disgusting and immoral practices."

Other writings of support are those of Justin Dionysis, Diodorus Siculus, Ovid, Layard, Athenagorus, Lucian, Herodot, Augustine, Heisod, and Mary Whitby's Chronicon Paschale as well as Alexander Hislop and many others.

Most civilizations began with one god or creator and then follow pseudonyms or descriptors of characteristics of that deity with a progression of hero worship etc.(See :Custance Ref. 23-25) The progression of the religion of "Mystery Babylon" began with Nimrod-king (Moleck)-Marduk symbolized by the snake/serpent/dragon with pseudonyms as follows:

ENKI/Apsu/god of wisdom, ASTALLULDI (Greek Asesculopius)/ Chiron/Centarus/Titan/Atlas

Bel/BAAL or Herculeus/MelKarth(Greek) ie.Baal-Peor, Baal-Hermon, Baal-Zebub/Triton, Meri-Baal Nabul/NEBO /Apollo-Hermes(Greek) Mars, Orion/Ninus.

While Semiramis-Astarte as Madonna and child (Tammuz) who was worshipped as fire itself[17] and she appears paired with her reincarnated husband-son as Ashtoreth/Tammuz, Isis and Horus in Egypt, Aphrodite and Eros in Greece, Venus and Cupid in Italy, and many other names in distant lands. Within 1000 years, Babylonianism had become the RELIGION of the world, which had rejected divine revelation and replaced it with man's vain imaginations. [18]

"Men had proved unwilling to obey god's simple instruction to fill the earth, dividing into many separate, but parallel, governmental units. They preferred to remain together under one great centralized and highly regimented government, and this union had quickly lead to a vast unified anti-God religious philosophy as well. The key was their ability to cooperate and organize together, and this depended on their ability to formulate and implement complex plans. Basic to everything was their ability to communicate with each other. They were all of one lip and one vocabulary, speaking with the same sounds in formulating plots the same way." [19] Creator-God instructed the people to multiply and fill the earth. But by the time that Nimrod had attained leadership of the people he recognized two choices (1) systematic colonization and development of all parts of the earth each with its own local government, in accordance with god's commands (found in Genesis 1:28; 9:1), or (2) establishment of a strongly centralize society with controls over resources and occupations, which would soon be able to produce a self sufficient civilization capable of controlling the entire world. Nimrod made choice number (2) which would better serve the purposes of Nimrod and his fellow rebels and of course the invisible satanic conspiracy as well. A self sufficient society integrated under powerful and brilliant leaders would be a society no longer dependent upon a Creator-God, which was Nimrod's aim."[20] Nimrod's big work was the building of a tower UNTO heaven that was dedicated to heaven and its angelic host in the deceptive guise of spirituality, glorifying human achievement in both the technical, spiritual, and demonstration of power. The first real demonstration of Humanism. Nimrod no doubt:

> "provided a center and an altar where men could offer sacrifices and worship God. The signs of the zodiac ....signifying the great story of creation and redemption, as told by the antediluvian patriarchs.......soon however the worship of the Creator was corrupted into the worship of the 'creature' (Romans 1:21-23,25) meaning statues and pictures of men and birds and four footed beasts an creping things..... The Virgin, whose sign among the stars once reminded men of the promised Seed of the woman (Messiah), began to assume the proportions of an actual 'Queen of Heaven'; and Leo, the great sidereal lion at the other end of the zodiac, became a great spiritual 'King of Heaven'. Soon the stars, the physical "host of heaven," were invested with the personalities of the angels, the invisible spiritual heavenly host..... Acknowledging and worshipping these angelic spirits, the people no doubt felt very pious and religious. There were specific angels and stars concerned with every aspect of human life and terrestrial processes.... The system soon became so complicated that it required a specially devoted class of

men and women to dedicate their lives to study and interpretation for guidance (thus forming the priest class, the famous 'Nimrod's Priests' college). As the consciousness of Gods personal nearness receded, so did their concern to obey him. But also this absence of true spiritual communion left a spiritual vacuum in their souls which can only be satisfied by some other kind of personal spiritual communion. The vacuum was filled by rebellious angels ----the evil spirits and demons that had no inhibitions. They reveled in and encouraged this idolatrous worship; for all this was in accord with the desire of Lucifer their master, to become god himself.,,,,, as they have done before the flood these evil spirits begin to control the minds and bodies of those human beings who were open to such possession and guidance, especially those of the priests and priest-ess who have become devoted to the system of worship." From such beginnings soon emerged the entire complex of human religion - - and evolutionary pantheism, promulgated via a system of astrology and idolatrous polytheism, empowered by occultic spiritism and demonism." [21]

The entire basis of idolatry established by Nimrod and his wife Semiramis, who perpetuated this system that permits us to trace its evil hand into today's university,

Part 4. Babylon

Babylon and hero - god - worship

The humanist religion began with Nimrod at a most ancient time soon after the flood and while that time is somewhat uncertain, it can be traced back to the time of the building of the tower of Babel under the direction of "the founder of the world's first kingdom, Nimrod–bar–Cush, the son of the Cush. Nimrod is referred to as our Orion, or Kronos, "the horned one" who married the infamous Semiramus I, reputed to be the foundress of the Babylonian "Mysteries" and the first high priestess of idolatry.[22] Scholars have studied her extensively in trying to understand the selection of December 25 for the celebration of Christ's birth which coincided with the roman festival of Saturnalia which is held annually in honor of the birth of the son of Semiramus, the Babylonian "Queen of heaven" (see: Jer 7:18, 44:15-30). Dr. Jones tells us that she was known as "Isis" who gave birth about the time of the winter solstice.[23] This mystery religion spread from Babylon to all the surrounding nations with the same symbols. The "queen of heaven" with the babe in arms found everywhere on carvings as well as discussed in ancient writings. It is amazing that this Babylonian Madonna was carried all over by the seafaring Phoenicians known as Nimrod, the sun-god) worshipped with the mother as Astoreth and the child as Tammuz Adonis.

"The deification of kings and the worship of them during their reigns were characteristic of Sumerian religions in the time of the last dynasty of Ur and the succeeding dynasties of Sin and Ellasar when the "god–kings" died. They, like Tammuz, perished; for in life they were husband's of Ishtar"

[24](as was Tammuz). However the persistence to this day of Ishtar (Nimrods and Tammuz wife+) is quite amazing. (See: table 1. p 12)

I am in agreement with Arthur C. Custance PhD an amazing archaeologist, anthropologist, scientist, and inventor, trained in cuneiform, Hebrew and Greek, and the former head of Canada's Human Engineering Laboratories of the Defense Research Board of Ottawa. His logic followed Prebendary Roe who observed, "…it is more sensible to start with the known and reason upon it towards the unknown than start with the unknown in the hope of being able to explain the known"[25]. Scholars of cuneiform and hieroglyphics found tremendous numbers of gods and goddesses, demons, and lesser spiritual powers. "…As they studied earlier and earlier tablets the extreme Polytheism began to be replaced by something more nearly approaching a hierarchy of spiritual beings arranged into a kind of a court with one Supreme Being overall.[26] Langdon of Oxford was perhaps the first to see this trend in 1931.[27]

Custance arrived at the position that in the older civilizations, Sumerian (as Langdon also took note) "there was a rapid decline from monotheism to extreme Polytheism and widespread belief and evil spirits. It is in a very true sense the history of the fall of man. While T. J. Meek[28] opposed Langdon's argument, which according to Langdon, the Sumerian religion was "swallowed up" by the Babylonianism about 3000 BC with 5000 gods while only 750 appear 4000 BC and only three gods are found on the 300 or so tablets Langdon found in Jamdet Nasr; the sky god "Enil", the earth god in "Enki", and the sky god "Babbar". Langdon translated 575 tablets from Uruk which dated between 3500 and 4000 BC which contained only two deities the sky god "An" and the mother goddess "Innina". Frankfort completely supported Langdon's conclusion in subsequent excavations at Tell Asmar houses and Temples that show on cylinder seals where a "single god" was the central figure of the community.

Therefore Custance concluded that, contrary to previous theory, "Polytheism never did arrive by evolution of polydemonism, but because the attributes of a single god were differently emphasized by different people until those people in later years came to forget they were speaking of the same person. Thus attributes of a single deity became a plurality of deities. Custance's theory is that this special emphasis on characteristics of greatest significance help explain what is seen in history. ie, "...a warlike people are not too likely to emphasize the gentleness of God nor the legalistic people the forgiveness of God. They would rather emphasize His power in the one case and His justice and the other." He makes his case in what he called his Doorway Papers[29] where he exposes the possibility that Noah's son Shem emphasized the spiritual quality of life - - - a God of pure spirit, Hamites on the practical concerns of life, with gods of power and Japhethites or Indo-Europeans emphasized gods of light in the sense of being gods of understanding."[30] Constants even felt that Matthew, Mark, and Luke, was fit to each of these respectively.

"When the Babylonians took over from the ancient Samaritans the Babylonian pantheon are designated as one with and one in the god Marduk, set forth under the name "Ninib" the "Possessor of Power", under the name "Nergal" or "Zamama", as "Lord of Battle" under the name "Bel", as "Possessor of Lordship" under the name "Nebo", as "the Lord of the Prophet"; under the name "Sin" as "Illuminator of the Night"(moon) under the name "Shamash" as "Lord of all that is Just"; under the name "Addu" as God of rain." Marduk therefore was "Nimib" as well as "Nergal", Moon-god as well as sun-god, the names being simply different ways of describing his attributes, powers, or duties.[31]

Max Miller tells us in his "Science of Language" that mythology was the "bane of the ancient world, in truth a disease of language"[32]. So when we hear of the epic of Gilgamish or any ancient epic we see invented poetic names that were gradually allowed to become new heathen gods with certain traits. Custance makes the case that China and India also fit this mold citing Edward McCrady's note that even the Reg veda (book one, page 164) shows us that in the early days the gods were regarded simply as diverse manifestations of a single divine being.... "They call him Indra, Mythra, where Varunna, Agni - -that which is One, the Wise name by different terms",[33]

So we have Shem and the following Hebrews with a pure spirit God YHVH of ancient days pure throughout the old and new testament. Yet a totally different story for the Hamites who, emphasizing the practical concerns of life, immediately went for power claiming that power initially in Nimrod and holding onto that power through his wife Semiramus. Japheth's descendents, are viewed as emphasizing the philosophical aspects of life seemingly inventing gods of light, in the sense of being gods of understanding. Of the four sons of Ham, Cush is associated with the peoples of southern Arabia and Ethiopia. Mizraim, an ancient Hebrew name for Egypt became the father of the Egyptian empire totally devoted to material interests. Phut is associated with Lydia west of Egypt while the fourth son, Canaan was initially in and around Palestine, and later much more widespread. [34]

The linkage of these Hamite gods of power with modern Humanist idolatry is amazing and their practical or power and control characteristic seems to have come to the fore as the spirit of the modern university. This is to also recognize that there are many wonderful faculty preparing our children for the future, under control of a system that calls itself proudly "secular" thereby isolating these excellent faculty and muting their influence. But there is admittedly almost a complete falling away from teaching Creator-God as Creator-God and replacing Him with false idols that will lead to devastating results.

Is Trust in God, as in the very emblem of America, the key element lacking in Nimrod's idolatry?

But Cush begat Nimrod. and Cush and Nimrod seemed to be contrary to trusting in God. After Noah recovered from a drunkenness situation, Noah cursed his son Ham's future grandson Canaan, in that Ham's descendents would serve his other two brothers descendents. Noah's words show great disappointment in Ham but more important Ham shows us his rejection of Noah's Creator-God and His instructions. This could and probably did create a deep family jealously that would grow. Cush then named his first son "he rebelled" or Nimrod and raised him to rebel against God. Nimrod excelled in wickedness, "mighty in wickedness" is one translation. It is possible that his heroes reputation was from slaying and hunting giant animals that proliferated after the flood.[35] We then see the first public declaration of Humanism, "let us make bricks". God sees man as individuals each with unique characteristics like we see in untouched stones. Nimrod sought to make everyone alike or equal (into bricks) both for administrative convenience and spiritual control...consider him the John Dewey of his day. To paraphrase what Nimrod and his followers say next, "Go to, let us build a tower that reaches unto heaven. Let's make a name for ourselves so that we can maintain a human unity and we can achieve social stability." By building the walls and tower for the genuine protection of the "fear" of the wild animals that must have proliferated after the flood he would certainly have a following. Are they proud Humanists? It is not unreasonable to think that if Nimrod was "great" before God, he was proud and that he refused to trust in the God of Noah (remember pride is "not fearing Creator-God"). And in so doing he started all the paganism and all the untruth and all the humanism that we have today. Let's explore that idea, that so many have promulgated before. For you will see that Nimrod and his consort becomes the basis of Idol worship to this day.

Not satisfied from protecting his people from the fear of wild animals that had proliferated, he proceeded to protect them from the fear of Noah and Shem's Creator-God. Answering the question "why are we here?" with his own answer, not the answer given by Creator-God who knows the answer. It is also not unreasonable to think that there were people on the earth early on who knew and could see that there had been a world-wide flood and that millions and perhaps many billions had died. People had at least two choices, to fear a God that had the power to do what was done, or to rebel against that authority and subsequently decide not to trust the God that had destroyed all those that were corrupt and filled the earth with violence. And in not trusting that God, introduced Humanism.... man's invented answer for everything. In the process he introduced idols. False gods pointing away from the Creator-God to himself(or later His wife pointing to the dead Nimrod she claimed was now an astral god in the form of Orion the hunter, the "sky god". Behind every false god we know is a demon. So how many false gods has Nimrod and his people put together?

Babylon

The word Babel has two different meanings. One it is called Babel; because the LORD did there confound the language of all the earth." In Hebrew the word Babel means confusion. The Babylonians themselves used the word to mean "We are the gate of God," and the Jews said, "No, you are confusion. The word we use, Babylon is simply Babel with a Greek ending."[36] We need to follow the line of those who did not follow the true God but made up gods after their imaginations to reach the false gods of the campus today.

Throughout the book of Genesis a literary form is in place that lays out the facts central to the main theme first quickly and then the record returns to the main theme and treats it at length.[37] Has modern man still following those false gods? When we look at Nimrod and Simiramus his wife or consort or whatever she was, we see the two of them in a direct linkage to all the gods that were moved from Babylon to Pergamos by Nimrod's priests. We are taught that Pergamos became the "seat of Satan" (Revelation 2:12-13). Then we see that Nimrod's priests moved to a city north of Rome, Etrusca where they presented themselves as the teachers of Rome. We say the "Greeks" taught the Roman children. They were the college or university for Rome. And Rome for the first 200 years before Nimrod's Priests set up their college and described a city with no record of divorce recorded as noted in Plutrarc's Lives. And yet, once the educational systems were setup with Nimrod's false gods, Rome became incredibly pagan and defiled, filled with the same things we saw in Babylon, in the land of Shinar and Nineveh. Each city had its own favorite god but each man could choose from the pantheon of gods that suited his character. A Rome where women bragged of as many marriages and divorces as their age in years. This History of the Roman and Greek Pantheon is inextricably linked to the Egyptian pantheon. A history of the Dynasties of Egypt follow the lists of 1500 or so deities of Egypt. The best archeology we have to explain this can be found in the most ancient Egyptian papyri and monuments.

Egyptian Deities linked to Babylon and Rome

Ancient man may well have known that these idols were not the Creator-God but they knew there was a god with a demon behind them. Nevertheless they identified with them, they had characteristics that they decided "that's the god I want for me". They chose that god because they thought that god would look after them when they died, Because they had not trusted in the Creator-God. Did we see in Mohammad's father a cabal with 360 gods with the head god the moon-god Sin. Is it just a continuation of this into modern times. And do we see those who reject Jesus Christ as God even though he called himself God, He said "I Am" using the "Ego Eimi" expression, the very unusual Greek words God used to identify himself to Moses 1500 years earlier which means "Yahwah". The identity of the true God and the understanding that He is 3 persons in Unity. That Trinity, each time rejected leads to the worship of false gods. Lets move to modern times. Where do we see men's downfall and subsequent damaged by worshipping a false god and choosing a false god because in all cases he did not trust the Creator? He didn't trust Jesus Christ as fulfilling everything that is needed for salvation. He had to add this or that. In Emperor Constantine we see a situation where as he had conquered he merely turned to Nimrod's priests and the pagan priests all around him to declare "you are now Christian priests". In so doing he imbedded distrust in the Church and kept it there.

We often don't see a challenge particularly from a scientists or a thinkers point of view until we come in history to a man like Isaac Newton at Oxford and Rene Descartes in the Sorbonne in Paris both about the same time, both using reason better than most had used reason until that time as a scientists. We see Descartes standing in front of the priests, the Jesuits, in front of this wonderful Paris University explaining why we should trust God. Science can observe and trust its observational skills to identify reality, that we do exist and can do these things. We have a God we can trust. And we find Newton spending the last 40 years of his life dedicated to the study of the Word of God and developing a timeline as to when the end would come with the return of the Hebrew Messiah. A man who moved on from the simple observations of what light and lights performances are and how gravity operates as well as the mathematical relationships that describes that performance. He moved on to something far more important to him and to all human beings. Is there anyone that doesn't want to go to heaven..... doesn't truly want to live forever? How does that person get there if he has had a false god shoved down his throat? Or If he is worshipping a demon and doesn't know it. The purpose of this book is to document these two pathways. The pathway of trusting in the Creator of the universe to be who he says He is..... trusting in His word verses the path of distrust, the path of Nimrod. The path to nowhere, to Chaos. The path that would introduce a massive contradiction in a persons head if he arrived at the time of Darwin. And Darwin would merely say what many others who thought as he did; like his grandfather Erasmus, who weren't trusting in God either, that random processes or **Random = Information**, an enormous contradiction that no man can understand and would therefore worship. That information could be created by random. Or that matter by itself could create information. Later on a physicists might argue that although no one has ever seen an explosion that created order, yet an explosion created order in the big bang, with no explanation what came before. Is that a failure to trust. I think so!

Those who trust in God would be driven to read his Word and to understand the clarity of what it being taught to us. The clarity in who He is when He sends himself as a man to save us and to cover us from our sins. So that we can be part of Him since no error can be part of a Holy God. A holy God could not allow the sinful things we are doing down here without something very special to cover those errors...those things we think and do that are "missing the mark". So who are we to distrust our creator? Who are we to distrust? Do we have that kind of authority? A secular university must try its best to dull our conscious of the guilt that resides there because of the sins against Creator-God. Guilt suppression by convincing our children that they are "victims" is a misdirection and enormous lie, that really doesn't work if the child understands truth before arriving at such instruction. I want to remind you that in Job 41 at the very end of that chapter the point is made that the head of all those that are proud is the Leviathan or the Dragon. And that is none other than Satan. What kind of pride does it take to distrust the creator who created everything and knit us together in the womb? It takes pride, it takes enormous pride. Is that what we battle against, the same pride that caused the fall of Lucifer?

Ps 2:12 "Kiss the Son, lest he be angry, and ye perish from the way, when his wrath is kindled but a little. Blessed are all they that put their trust in Him.

Lets revisit Genesis 10:8 "and Cush begat Nimrod; he began to be Mighty on the earth". Nimrod was the youngest and most illustrious son of Cush. He was given a name that means "let us rebel!". He was apparently trained by his father for this purpose. He is called "a mighty one" as the first great Emperor. Nimrods name is preserved in numerous legends and geographical sites in Babylon. It is written throughout the cuneiform tablets, thousands of them. After his death he was evidently deified, evidently worshipped as Merodach or Marduck (from *Mered* to rebel, and *Dakh* the great)or Mars among the Romans [38]. He was a "mighty hunter before the Lord" we are told in Genesis 10:9. Wherefore it is said "even as Nimrod the mighty hunter before the Lord. The beginning of his kingdom was Babel and Erech, and Accad, and Calneh, in the land of Shiner. Out of the land went forth Asher and buildeth Nivieth and the city of Rohobath, and Calah and Resen between Niveth and Calah the same is a great city." Twelve centuries after Nimrod build Nineveh, Assyria's greatest city it was still recognized as "the land of Nimrod" (Micah 5:6).

"Now a mighty hunter." Henry Morris, a student of the bible and a PhD in Hydraulics and a hydraulics engineer as well who wrote the textbook in Hydraulics that many great universities used for many years said. "A mighty hunter", this phrase connotes a man mighty in wickedness. It is possible his hero's reputation was gained in hunting and slaying the giant animals that proliferated after the flood and were considered dangerous to the small human population of the first century. He built a great kingdom with the capital at Babel in the plain of Shinar no doubt equivalent to Sumer in the Tigris-Euphrates valley. Nineveh is the capital city of Assyria was named for Ninus, evidently another name for Nimrod although both Babylonia and Assyria were later conquered by Semites. The Hamite Nimrod was their founder and first king. Nineveh was 200 miles north of Babylon on the Tigris River.

Jeremiah 51:7 notes that all Idolatry is one. How is that so? And again lets document that Nimrod is the first of the Mighty one after the flood. One would assume he was not trusting. Baal abreven is called the "winged one". Nin or Ninus, Centaur, and Saturn are all the" son" the mighty horse hunter. We have Cronus in Egypt, equivalent of Nimrod. Osiris is the god whose mother is the god of the Egyptian Madonna. The insignia is the young calf or the bull which is Saturn. We see Absus, we see Nebrod, we see Kisus in Greek, Baucus the Babylonian Messiah which used the symbol of the cross. And Nimrod the apostate as the first to defile. Phaeton, Asclepius, Moloch (Nimrod's title). Tammuz was the son of Ishtar Ezekiel 8:14 tells us. Atlas, we understand, made heaven afar off for the unbelievers, he held up heaven away from the earth, therefore they built many artifacts that exist today thinking that Atlas had lifted the heavens away from man therefore emancipating him from God. We see Sybil or Diana also as Rea also as Venus the mother of the gods, the consort of god. Now lets move to the fact that when we see the word "father" we disturb the Muslims who have been taught that for anyone to be called father he must have a consort and that is attributing to their Allah that he has a wife or a consort and to have sex. The Muslims have difficulty with our expression "Aba Father" because of course the pagan gods all had consorts. We also see from the writings of Alexander Hislop (p32) that Ala Mahocin was Nimrod, the head god. We are also to understand the head god was named Zoroaster, the first Zoroaster (note p59). And of course modern man at least often calls him Zarthustra, as in "Thus Spake Zarathustra" by Friedrich Nietzsche, a book that identified the "ubermensch" the superman to Hitler along with a great deal more.

The god Janus, the two face Janus is the Babylonian Messiah. The incarnation of Noah supposedly, with Dagon the fish god of the Philistines, Babylonian, and Nineveh. Isis the mother of corn Ceres which is worshipped by the Druids. And the sun is Moloch "round water" and that is Baal. We know that Orion is the same as Nimrod in Persia. We see that as documented in "Two Babylons" [39]. The sacred heart is the Bel of Moloch.[40] We see in the worship of Rome that Isis is the mother, Horus is the Child and Seb (the Egyptian trinity) Seb is the father of these gods. That is the Egyptian trinity .[41] So to summarize: we see the long list of pagan gods, ancient gods. Zeus means nothing more than Nimrod. Zarathustra…. repeat all of these gods mean nothing more then false gods with demons behind them that all seem to stream out of the first one to defile god by not trusting Him. Recall that Nimrod, who declared himself an emperor and was the first one able to hunt and shoot a bow and arrow from his horse and trained his troops as archers on horses. He must have been competing with someone that lived in that area, his great grandfather or great grand uncle Noah and Shem. Remember that Noah and Shem outlived Nimrod by 200 years. Imagine Noah and Shem living in the area where Nimrod lived, and everyone knew about Noah, he had the truth of the past..he had the truth of a God that could be trusted and that Noah trusted. When Nimrod was either eaten by a wild boar or killed by Shem and cut up and sent to all the known provinces. Subsequently his wife Semiramus wanted to remain in power as an Empress. We are told she declared her husband the god Orion and apparently had relations with whoever was in the temple, became pregnant and called the child Tammuz the reincarnation of her husband Nimrod. Tammuz as we all know is worshipped on December 25th. Tammuz was called by almost all the names of the promised Messiah: Adonai, the Lord, Adon or Adonis and under the name of Mithras was worshipped as Mediator and 'Lord of the covenant'. Please be aware that the Mithras religion took over the Roman Army. There are estimates of many thousands of Mithraic monuments throughout the Roman Empire by the 3rd Century A.D. One of the most well-documented phenomena of antiquity. While Arnold Toynbee called the Cult the "Crucible of Christanity", the Cult was organized as a series of "grades" or levels of initiation through which the male only members gradually rose. A truly secret society, with something to do with the killing of a Bull and the discovery of the procession of the equinoxes.[42] Tammuz and Nimrod worship can be shown to influence not only ancient Babylon but continues in history to the present.

How is it that Nimrod is the first Humanist? What is a Humanist? A humanist is one that if you turn to him and ask how you got here and why you are here will answer with a position without knowledge of the truth because the truth is only known by the one that was there at Creation, the One that observed it all, documented it and gave us that knowledge and understanding from His word. The humanist is one that attributes creation and man's existence to a series of things he calls evolution in which once there was nothing, it exploded, it created order and the order of matter then created or assembled man with natural processes and that man is made by nature and that nature (which is a product of Creator-God) is what is to be worshipped. So we see environmentalism loving nature, worshipping living things and treating them as if they were the creator, which is not true. Nor is it true that all things start simple and become better and better with time, a very silly notion that speaks of willful ignorance of the 2nd law of thermodynamics. Which tells us that increasing disorder is what is observed in the universe.

So we have now identified a great many of the instructors and teachers throughout the world who teach everyone that they were created by a product…the product that Creator-God created; and in so doing they eliminate or at least hide the trust that one might have in the One that created us. How can you trust in a nature that is uncontrolled in which billions and trillions of things have had to die they say to assemble man. There had to be tremendous struggles, fights, and wars and everything else among everything from the insects and all the way up through the funny tree they have assembled until finally man, a collection of genetic errors and mutations arrives. Unfortunately there is no evidence that errors can create order and that genetic mutation creates information. As we move from an ape to a man we see more informational content in the man and all of the processes that are described in evolution particularly speciation or phylum generation do not provide for a system to increase informational content. We don't see the genome having more informational content. And yet both the monkey and the man have 50% of the same genome as a carrot. All living things are very similar because they all come out of the same laboratory, the same genius, the same mind of our Creator-God and his active right arm Jesus Christ, who knows the end from the beginning and therefore made no errors at the start. We add the errors by ourselves. Infinite errors, that only He can nullify.

Is it possible that understanding and logic would open our eyes to the truth once we see how we got here and the path we took as well as how deceptive it was and continues to be...would open our eyes to the truth. It was so easy, it was so simple for that deception to creep in. All because of the failure to really think through the presuppositions. They presuppose that God could not be trusted and therefore they had to add to who He was and in so doing establish the enormity of their pride. Their pride was enormous to be able to stand before a holy God and basically say He is incompetent. He couldn't write his Bible. He couldn't get the ink right on the page. He can move the stars around with his fingers, but he can't get the ink correct on the page. We find the Unitarian who rejects Jesus as Creator-God, thereby walking away from who God is and not trusting in Him. Clamoring for humanism at every juncture in history. We find them as leaders of the society as editors of Journals, and there is no limit to the harm that has been done by walking away from the fact of who Jesus is.

Part 5. Pathology

The continued existence of complex life revolves around smart control systems that allow or maintain what physiologists call "homeostasis", that fixity of the internal environment that keeps us all alive. These control systems are smart and have a "policy" that is "purpose and direction". Negative feedback control is the role throughout so that with more of something the intelligent control system brings that parameter back to normal. It turns out that all living systems are constructed during the development of the embryo, maintained in a finely tuned state by this negative feedback control in which if something exceeds a certain healthy limit it is driven back to within the design limits. All pathology is positive feedback ….with an increase we get more of an increase. In this case there is a loss of control to bring it back into design limits causing dysfunction or disease. The only "normal" exception is birth and death which are unique! And if the baby is not borne the results is death of the mother. Likewise, the pathology of religion, is man adding more and more "imagined" characteristics to Creator-God who we, as children, are unable to understand. Failing to grasp the only true descriptors, those He Himself has given us. We are silly thinking that we can think like Creator-God let alone imagine him. What he tells us is to hold him in a relationship with us. This is our correct position with respect to Him while most religions are something entirely different. That is, a society can be seen as operating in a similar manner. The genius in all there control systems has a focus, the One who designed them in the first place. I see positive feedback control causing pathology in the society as the teaching and practice of idolatry. Something that with "more of it" you get "more of it" until it destroys the society. It is interesting to note that this is a spiritual matter. Dealing with a part of man that is not visible yet a part that gives him "purpose and direction", the very definition of a control system.

It is reasonable to observe this physical universe as designed in a manner similar to the process that man's body maintains homeostasis. Far to many physical and chemical constants exists to say otherwise. It is also not outside of reason to assume the spiritual universe is designed to maintain a "constancy" or "fixity" as well. How might that be?

Life is "blood based" and spirit is "Creator-God" based. That is all things are in reference to Creator-God and kept within design parameters by and through Him. Positive feedback disease would then be Idolatry out of control. This "misdirection" of the spirit to anything other than Creator-God is what is defined as Idolatry. We would only know this if He told us it was so. Which He has! All cultures that have imbedded themselves into idolatry have been destroyed or taken into captivity (ie. the Babylonian Captivity of the Hebrews) or as in Nazi Germany we find Hitler's abuse of theology dismantled the moral fiber of a nation...creating passive onlookers of what was moral activists. By unifying all denominations under the National Reich Church in 1933 naming his man Ludwig Muller as head and all church property as now owned by the state with only "National Reich Church Orators" allowed to meet only on Saturday night, and the removal of all bibles, alters, and all crucifixes, with *Mein Kampf* Germany's new sacred book, replacing all bibles. Hitler's church directive "does not allow communion and does not recognize the forgiveness of sin but that "a sin once committed will be ruthlessly punished by the honorable and indestructible laws of nature and punishment will follow during the sinners lifetime." [43] Hitler's idolatry was the worship of him, his book, and his government. If you open your mind to the fact that this pattern is continuing, as if man's enemy is not so creative, seeming to do the same thing because it has worked in the past. (until America and the free world fought back)

The pagan gods of Nimrod and Cush (Some of the ones that are hidden on Campus NOW)

1. Timat, Bel, Janus (Chaos "stuffing material of the Universe", confounder, god of beginnings)
2. Gaia, Ceres (earth mother) Ma-Ka, Asherah, Allat, Queen of Heaven
   Heaven, Inanna/Ishtar, Aristotle used the word "Physis" for Nature
3. "Man is the measure of all things" Protagoras
4. Minerva, Sheng Ti (goddess of civilization, wisdom, the arts, war)
5. Eros, Cupid
6. Pan (Nature)
7. Justice (Roman law of nature)
8. Lucifer (light bearer) illuminator of deceptive understanding and thought
9. Marduk, Nimrod (rebellion against the authority of Creator-God)
10. Molech, the god of the Ammonites requiring child sacrifice in a giant bonfire[44] months after community orgies.

Movement of Idols
Movement of Nimrod's Priests from Babylon to Pergamos, the "seat of Satan"

The pantheon of poly-demonism set up by Nimrod and his consort was so complex that a priesthood had to be established to do the work. Professional priests were needed to oversee the temples, perform the rites, and teach and maintain the libraries and archives. This system would persist for centuries until a major event would force them to migrate elsewhere. See: William Burckhardt Barker "Lares and Penates", ch 8, "Magi and Monks" where the author describes certain relics of Anatolian religion from which the author deduced that after the Persian conquest of Babylon, the headquarters of the Babylonian hierarchy were transferred to Pergamum, whence they passed to Rome in 133BC.[45] When Attalus III, the last Pergamene king, bequeathed his kingdom to the Roman state.[also Hislop as noted by F.F. Bruce refers to the oracle of Apollo quoted by Pausanias x. 15, which addresses Attalus I as "bull-horned:, an epithet belonging to Bacchus.] As Hislop elsewhere identifies Bacchus with Nimrod (ch ii), he concludes that the Attalids sat in the seat of the priest-kings of Babylon, and "were hailed as the representatives of the old Babylonian god."

Professor Anthon of Columbia University (in 1851) cites Heroditus and many others identify the Magi with the priest class founded by Zoroaster. "...the Magi formed one of the six tribes into which the Medes (today's Kurds) were originally divided"[46] but, on the downfall of the Median empire were retained at the court of their conquerors with a great deal of power and authority, even attempting to take over the throne by a man called "Smerdis the Magi". The Magi were divided into three classes: the first class of inferior priests, who conducted the ordinary religious ceremonies; the second presided over the sacred fire; the third was called Archimagus or high-priest who had supreme authority over the whole order. That this whole order was linked to fire worship idolatry is evident in the order of their Temples.

1. Common oratories where people performed devotions and sacred fire was kept only in lamps.
2. Public Temples with altars on which the fire was kept continually burning where the higher order Magi directed public devotions and the people assembled.
3. The grand seat of the Archimagus visited by the people only at certain seasons with solemnity. Each person must visit the seat and maintain or repair it once in his life.

We are told that there were Babylonian magi far more ancient than the Persian magi. The reading of their history is fraught with warnings that whole libraries were written as deceptions to hide their secrets and their true power. So much of their written history is spurious because writings and libraries were a display of power even if the writings were false. On the one hand we have the statement of Diogenes Laertius [1,6, seqq]. "...they are employed in worshipping the gods by prayers and sacrifices as if their worship alone would be accepted; they teach their doctrine concerning the nature and origin of the gods, whom they think to be fire, earth, and water; they reject the use of pictures and images, and reprobate the origin that the gods are male and female; they discourse to the people concerning justice; they think impious to consume dead bodies with fire; they allow of marriage between mother and son; they practice divination and prophecy; pretending the gods appear to them; they do not wear ornaments in dress; they clothe themselves in a white robe; they make use of the ground as their bed; use herbs, cheese, and bread, for food; and use a reed for their staff." [47]

Tammuz was called Adon or Adonis and under the name of Mithros was worshipped as the Mediator [Plutarch, De Iside et Osivide vol ii, p369 and 478] the inscription found in Rome which identifies 2 dieties Mithros and Phanes, represents Mithras at the moment when he broke the cosmic egg and cause the light to shine which was to illuminate the world. Pliny sites the view of Eudoxus that Zoroaster lived 6000 years before the death of Pluto.[48] Aristotle's statement as found in Theopompus lays out that the magi are more ancient than the Egyptians.[49] Plato's Republic[50] says that Eros Armenius (also called the 4th Zoroaster[51] in [Clericus, De Chaldaeis vol 2, p195] died and rose again after 10 days and communicated what he pretended to have learned in Hades. Wilson speaks of the fire worshipping magi in the days of Hoshang, the father of Tahmurs, who founded Babylon.[52] Muller (p86) puts Ninus the head of the fire worshippers suggesting that Ninus, Nimrod, and the first Zoroaster were the same.[53]

We see in Ezekiel 8:14 Jewish women were "weeping for Tammuz". This rite is identical to the ancient rite for Adonis and Osiris. Even Maimonides notes that when Tammuz was put to death, the weeping for that death was in the temple at Babylon.

A very interesting puzzle comes from seemingly senseless words of Plutarch's 4th book where he says "the Egyptians were of the opinion that darkness was prior to light, and that the light was produced from mice (Aakbar, a Chaldee word) and Gheber (Arabic) in the fifth generation at the time of the new Moon.[54] If, as many experts agree, Noah is placed as the sun of the world as pagan representations and therefore the greater light, than his son Shem would be the Mona (moon) or lesser light. So with Plutarch's statement, this dissatisfaction in the fifth generation from Noah, the Moon enlightenment was somehow replaced by Nimrod. Picture the community gathering of tree trunks for a great unity fire (community organizing) and the observance of the mice running in all directions from the great fire - -where the people or the Ghebur worshippers would think the Akbar were producing the fire during the new Moon causing a crescent to arise, as Nimrod was set up in a position to Shem, as the representative of Noah, and "the great enlightener of the world.[55] This, no doubt may represent the greatest Rebellion against Creator-God since the Great Flood, and continues to have repercussions today! Today's enlighteners are to be found at our institutes of learning, standing on their words in the libraries, and directing us to what they say are truths that do not follow from the truth Noah has given us or that Noah even existed; even denying the flood.

So Nimrods priests, that group of magi as purveyors of magic and divination and supposedly purify with fire, also prove a pagan idolatry to the world in secret colleges of "Augurs", so named when they reach Etruska and then Rome. The spread of the history of idolatry is very difficult to follow but if you study magi and the augury, even though the secrets are kept secret, the work of those who walked away from the god of Noah into idolatry can be followed or inferred. Since, I repeat, entire libraries exist written as a deception, and since we are talking about the father of lies and deception, what would one expect to encounter! It's almost as if the writings are chaotic to prevent clarity in describing what happened.

The Persian magi were called Pyrethi or worshippers of fire (Strabo) who renewed the sacred fire in the Temples with accompanying ceremony and music. While the magi of the Medes and Persians were said to be founded by one named Zoroaster although the first Zoroaster is in question, this order in 521 BC usurped the throne of Persia and one year later Smerdus the magi or his pretender Cambyses is murdered by Darius Hystaspis and and six conspirators.[56] The following "great slaughter of the Magi" it is thought is the cause of the flight of the order to Pergamos, although it is hard to document, this event continued as a famous celebration. The occultic learning and practice of the Persian magi is considered the definition of the Greek Mageia as well as the Latin Magi.

Nebuchadnezzar captured Jerusalem and brought Daniel to Babylon. Daniel and his three friends brought the world of Creator-God to Nebuchadnezzar which once he bows to Creator-God (after 7 years of insanity) would be an enormous affront to Nimrods priest class.

The evidence they escaped to Pergamos to continue the pantheon certainly fits the understanding that the most religious city was Pergamos many centuries later where a new age term "universal life regeneration force" which was nothing more than the "eight wheel path of enlightenment", that of strange sex with the sacred goddess or god-king through a supposed temple virgin (or perhaps 72 virgins) as a temple rite of the "black arts". Also the magic of the supposedly healing at the temple of Aesculapius at Pergamos, the serpent god, the Caduceas is also found to be a symbol of Cybele, equated with Diana, Rhea, Ala Mahozoine, or Semiramus--- mother of the gods, and in ancient Persia as Mithras, father of the gods (Saturna in Rome) exposed as a form of the hidden Babylonian mysteries. The fact that their idols were worshiped under these many names helps us to understand why the actual name of the one true God (YHVH) is so extremely important.

Movement of Nimrod's Priests from Pergamos to the Po valley of Etruska (Hetruria) Tuscany

One of the most difficult areas of ancient study is the Etruscan or Hesychius. There is great mystery here because authors have declared these people "the most religious people that ever lived". There is obviously been an enormous effort to destroy their libraries, and there are thefts systematically. The likely culprit is Rome. It is as if everything from the Roman pantheon, teaching, engineering, and philosophy has its pre existence in Eturia and Rome tried to hide the truth. So logically linking the most religious people of Pergamos with the Etruscans seems logical, that is no doubt difficult to demonstrate without the opening of ancient cultural records in Rome. The motive for such a withholding of information require that you spend two or more years studying a book by Hislop called "Two Babylons". It is also true that Roman historians had a patriotic ax to grind or the ancient Greek historians in writing about the Etruscans who actually lay the foundations of the city of Rome. So what we know comes indirectly from others. While the Etruscan alphabet is known and is unique, their language is not completely understood. However the very name Rome is Etruscan.[57] Etruscan religion had enormous influence on roman religion in the identity of the mother-goddess "Thufltha" who was also the goddess of the night and of the dead.

The Trojans and the Phrygrans of Asia minor practiced the Babylonian animal sacrifice – prophecy of Haruspice (exam of the liver). The Etruscans inherited this ritual, and the same ritual continues in Rome until Gratian (375AD). Attalusi of Pergamom performed the Haruspice before an important battle to secure Pergamon's independence and found "NIKE" on the liver to boost the army's morale. After the battle built a shrine to Nike and to the Athenaeum of Pergamon on the Pergamon Acropolis. The Etruskan had an entire priesthood – college teaching the knowledge of the Haruspice and practice of divination. FA Bruce ties the settling of Etruska with the Aeneas legand (Virgil's Aenid) the Ageans who escape from Troy and Naeoius (235BC)with their family and national gods (Lares and Penates) and the black meteorite "Palladium" (kept in the temple of Vesta [58]while Herodotus says they came from Lydia (p i,94) called (Tuppnvoi)Gr. Which relates to Tursa, part of the sea peoples that attacked Egypt in 1221 BC. Their language has a resemblance to the inscriptions in Lemnos.[59] In Ezekiel 21:21 the king of Babylon stands at the fork in the road at the head of two routes. He looks for all signs: he shakes arrows, he consults idols, he examines animal livers. Into his right hand comes the portent (divination) for Jerusalem. (or the omen mark on the right of the liver).

Sir Robert Anderson in his book "The Bible or the Church" p. 42 maintains that mystery cults which were so popular throughout the Roman empire and the early centuries of our era given appeal to the fathers that cannot take the place of an appeal to the apostles. "the most honored of the fathers were men whose minds were impregnated by the superstitions of pagan religion, or the subtleties of pagan philosophy.... They were' near the fountain' of Christianity, forsooth; yes, but they were near still to the cesspool of paganism. And the inquiry will show that it is to the cesspool that we should attribute every perversion of the truth which today defaces what is called the Christian religion."[60]

One way or another the Polydemonism and the college of Agury made it to Rome in a big way. The Etruscan Menrva (Minerva) stemming from the moon goddess "Meneswa" or She who measures who came from the head of her father Zeus whose throne was called the "Seat of Satan" in Pergamos was a syncretism between Greek and Etruscan which was the pagan goddess of wisdom, war, art, schools, and commerce. She is found today on more than 40 Universities as the goddess of wisdom or whatever and on seals of California as well as the title to the Demonist Aleister Crowley's rituals, the medal of Honor, and the seal of the American Academy of Arts and Sciences in Cambridge to name a few. Statues of the Goddess abound in teaching institutions throughout the world, perhaps for want of anything else to copy. Roman school had statues of Minerva and school masters received a gift called "Minerv". Thus was formed the Augures college.

Babylonian gods found in the cult of Mithros college at Tarsus
Two key events brought the many tribes and city-states together through the conquering of Alexander the Great and again the conquering of Constantine 7 centuries later. In 67 BC Tarsus was absorbed into the new Roman province of Cilicia. A university was established that became known for its flourishing school of Greek philosophy. The famous first meeting between Mark Antony and Cleopatra took place there in 41 BC. Strabo praises the cultural level of Tarsus in this period with its philosophers, poets and linguists. The schools of Tarsus rivaled Athens and Alexandria. 2 Maccabees records its revolt in about 171 BC against Antiochus IV Epiphanes, who had renamed the town Antiochia on the Cydnus. In his time the library of Tarsus held 200,000 books, including a huge collection of scientific works.

David Ulansey's scientific American article on Mithraic mysteries noted that, "Tarsus, the capital of Cilecia was the home of one of the most important intellectual communities in the Mediterranean. The community was dominated by stoic philosophers who were famous not only for their fatalism (which led them to be firm believers in astrology) but also for their traditions of personifying natural forces in the forms of gods and heroes. Most likely Mithraism arose as intellectuals in Tarsus, speculating about the force responsible for the newly discovered precession of the equinoxes, personified that power in the local Cilician god Perseus. (identified with the constellation Perseus)".[61] What better way to keep a secret religion secret is to hide even the actual name of the god they worshipped. They chose the name Mithra, because the Iranian god of light and truth was Mithras; Perseus was thought in antiquity to be the founder of Persia; the king of Pontus, king Mithridates, came from the dynasty named after Mithra supposedly descended from Perseus leading to the "star map" hypothesis of Ulansky, visiting Prof. of Religious Studies at U C Berkley, Roger Beck of the Univ. of Toronto, Stanley Insler of Yale, Michael Speidel of U. of Hawaii, and Alessandro Bassani of U. of Rome.

The importance of this strange cult-religion is that when the Roman army ruled or occupied much of the world from Britain, Rome, Ostea, Numidia, Dalmatia, Greece, Egypt, and Syria or anywhere the Roman Army had major outposts we find hundreds of underground Temples to Mithras all with painting and carvings of a young man killing a bull and an open area to view the stars.[62] While Ulansky claims it's all about the discovery of the previously unknown god who intellectuals at Tarsus decided could move the heavens in the precession from Taurus the bull 2000 years earlier to the constellation that they found the equinox located when they founded the religion at Tarsus. Tarsus is a very special city. We get a description of life in Tarsus from the book "Lares and Penates" by William Barker describing the household deities that were found in Tarsus for the protection of home and the state.....both local family deities and many others. What was always found in each home was a Statue of Apollo. (at Mount Nemrut, Mithras is shown beardless, wearing a Phrygian cap seated on the throne with other deities beside King Antiochus I who erected the colossal statuary. The inscription on the back of the throne included the name Apollo Mithras Helios, (Ἀπόλλωνος Μίθρου Ἡλίου)[63]

Ulansey's case for the star or astral link for Mithraism, the favorite religion of the roman army (along with the usual roman pantheon of pagan gods) is greatly strengthened by the fact that the astronomer Hipparchus had just discovered that the equinoxes, the points on the Celestial sphere where the sun appears to be on the first day of spring and the first day of autumn. The astrologers describe the Celestial sphere as follows: the ecliptic is an imaginary plane that would pass for the earth's orbit around the sun why the Celestial equinoxes tilted 23.4°from the ecliptic. As you look out from the earth, the constellation that the vernal (spring) equinox points to was Tarus the bull he called the "age of Tarus" about 2000 BC. The worship part was of a god who, his worshipers claim could move the heavens from Tarus to the next constellation.

As an aside, the consequence of the procession is a changing north pole star. The wobble of the earth's axis of rotation meant the pole star was the star Thuban in the constellation Draco the dragon 2000 BC and it is today the star Polaris, the entrance to what the ancients called the sheep gate (little dipper), though this is controversial.

"So a power they called sol Invictus Mithras the priest-astrologers-college claimed this special "sun" had the power to move the entire heavens or the 'entire universe' and they apparently endowed Mithras with the ability to overcome the 'forces of fate' they thought resided in the stars and could guarantee the soul a safe passage through the planetary spheres after death. They kept this secret knowledge for selected initiates to understand this new god."[64]

"Cicero pointed that the Stoics were looking for the "great year" when the planets and the sun and moon returned to their "original" position followed by the *ekpyrosis* which was a conflagration where the cosmos returned to the form from which it began. [65] Ulansky notes that this conflagration was accepted dogma in the Roman Period referencing Arnold, *Roman Stoicism*.[66] It appears that once the discovery of the procession of the equinoxes allowed a date for this "great year" by the mathematicians, the Mithraic followers felt they had their answer or their special knowledge, even though followers of

Plato and Aristotle would not allow such talk. We see the figure of Mithras emerging from an egg, surrounded by the zodiac." [67]

This fits perfectly with Nimrod's wife Istar or Easter emerging from an egg in the pagan tradition of the Easter egg roll of the 20th century. We also have a suggestion that the city of Tarsus was built by Sennacherib in Cilicia "in the image of Babylon" [68] suggesting that Tarsus was a copy of Babylon, a conceptual home of the gods…where the great temples symbolized the cosmos and had to have at least 3 certain features: 1. Holy Mound, 2. Dais Of Destinies', and 3. "Assembly Hall of the Gods". The temple would presumably have Mesopotamian texts in a library, scholars, priests and astronomers attached to it. Also the special god of that city was Sandon-Marduk [69] where Sandon is the logogram for Marduk in the Hittite texts.[70] The gods of Tarsus resembles great Assyrian gods of the seventh century shown standing on their characteristic animals with a disk above the god's head from Sennacherib's rock sculpture at Maltai and from the cylinder seals of 700 BC were all figures had a hoened animal like Marduk's red Dragon. These were continued for almost 1000 years on coins of Tarsus.[71] This hero-god shown as "the victorious one" comparable to Ba'al and Bel, a title bestowing on the hero-god in recognition of his victory over chaos was portrayed so in which the god or Tarsus was modeled after Zeus by Alexander the Great on Macedonian coinage. Dalley notes the special relationship between Babylon and Tarsus goes back to 240BC when the Stoic philosopher Diogenes of Babylon had a famous student from Tarsus, one Archidemus, who according to Plutarch, went on to found a new school for Stoics in Babylonia. Also Another Tarsian pupil of Diogenes was Antipater who succeeded his teacher as head of the stoic school at Athers.[72] The neo-Assyrian cuneiform tablets found at Tarsus contain an incantation for warding off evil omens identical to those taken from Sennacherib's palace at Assur. These incantations were accompanied by rituals in which certain stones were used for their magical powers, especially the chalcedony stones[73]. The stones were placed near a sleeping woman to ensure safe pregnancy and child-bearing; used by men to avert hair loss, or trembling hands or evil caused by snakes.[74] Copies of these stones were the characteristic holy beads found at that time.

Mithric initiates entered a class or grade as they climbed up the ladder of this secret society-religion. Clauss argues that the grades represented a distinct class of priests, *sacerdotes.*

The highest grade, *pater,* is far the most common found on dedications and inscriptions - and it would appear not to have been unusual for a Mithraeum to have several persons with this grade.

Characteristics associated with the Pater Grade;Mitre, shepherd's staff, garnet or ruby ring, chasuble or cape, elaborate robes jewel encrusted with metallic threads, and the planet deity was Saturn. The form *pater patrum* (father of fathers) is often found, which appears to indicate the *pater* with primary status. There are several examples of persons, commonly those of higher social status, joining a Mithraeum with the status *pater* - especially in Rome during the 'pagan revival' of the 4th century. [75] It can't be emphasized the level of secrecy is almost complete. So much so that controversy of it's rites continue today.

It cannot be shown that any Mithraeum continued in use in the 5th century. The coin series in all Mithraea end at the end of the 4th century at the latest. The cult disappeared earlier than that of Isis. Isis was still remembered in the middle ages as a pagan deity, but Mithras was already forgotten in late antiquity.[76]

But again, Meyer holds that the Mithras Liturgy reflects the world of Mithraism and may be a confirmation for Ulansey's theory of Mithras being held responsible for the precession of equinoxes.[77] David Ulansey finds astronomical evidence from the mithraeum itself.[78] He reminds us that the Platonic writer Porphyry wrote in the 3rd century AD that the cave-like temple Mithraea depicted "an image of the world"[79] and that Zoroaster consecrated a cave resembling the world fabricated by Mithras.[80] The ceiling of the Caesarea Maritima Mithraeum retains traces of blue paint, which may mean the ceiling was painted to depict the sky and the stars.[81]

The creation of a "new" pagan religion of idolatry at Tarsus based on a syncretism of a new finding in the science of the day "Procession of the equinoxes" with "special knowledge" or gnosis actually has a parallel on today's campus. "Throughout history the ancient mystery religions have taken many forms from paganism and witchcraft to humanism and secular psychology. Today they may be classified under the general name of "Theosophy," the blending of science and religion to create a universal brotherhood of man under a one-world state wherein an ethical society will flourish. The term, 'theosophy' (lit., 'Divine Wisdom', or 'Wisdom of the gods') has several synonyms, some of the more common being 'the Esoteric Philosophy,' 'the Wisdom-Religion,' 'the Secret Doctrine,' 'the Ancient Wisdom,' and 'the Esoteric Tradition.'"[82] The esoteric teachings are the foundation for the New Age movement-today's expression for the "higher" mysteries permitted for the masses while only the academic initiates are given the deep secrets or "truths". This is all so remarkable to the heresy of Gnosticism of an earlier age with a new cover and a little archeo-biology and archeo-astronomy and all the rest "archeos-" of the evolutionary pantheon. Together with the "Unity in Diversity" and "Tolerance" creeds and doctrine of today's campus to make up the hidden theology of the campus often cited as "secular" hidden behind the claim of "non-religious and non-spiritual". All in the spirit of non-judgmentalism by the encouragement of the student to form his own moral and ethical system.....effectively telling the student he is god. If that isn't within the definition of idolatry as we began, I don't know what is.

College of Nimrod's Priests began instruction of Roman children
We are told in "Pleutrarch's Lives" that there is no record of divorce in Rome during the first years of it's existence. While later in it's history there are women boasting they have more marriages and divorces than their age. Plutarch, in like manner, tells of the early religion of the Romans, that it was imageless and spiritual. He says Numa "forbade the Romans to represent the deity in the form either of man or of beast. Nor was there among them formerly any image or statue of the Divine Being; during the first one hundred and seventy years they built temples, indeed, and other sacred domes, but placed in them no figure of any kind; persuaded that it is impious to represent things Divine by what is perishable, and that we can have no conception of God but by the understanding".[83] The Etruscin Augury colleges

and schools were the location that Rome's elite sent their children for training. Very little originality is found in Rome, but it did incorporate what it found from each culture it encountered. The Roman Idolatry is legion and the ethical structure of Rome is legion as well. Follow it to Nero's famous and greatest toga party where he castrated a 12 year old boy and married him. And the incredible battle between two Roman army generals (and their troops) for that boy after Nero committed suicide. Moral decadence must be defined by what Rome became.

The education of Rome and it's intellectual climate was established by the Etruscan Auguary. What was found in what we would call a counterpart dining rooms, or *triclinia* were to be found above ground in the precincts of almost any temple or religious sanctuary in the Roman empire, and such rooms were commonly used for their regular feasts by Roman 'clubs', or *collegia*. They could function as guilds, social clubs, or burial societies; in practice, in ancient Rome, they sometimes became organized bodies of local businessmen and even criminals, who ran the mercantile/criminal activities in a given urban region, or rione. The organization of a <u>collegium</u> was often modeled on that of civic governing bodies, the Senate of Rome being the epitome. The meeting hall was often known as the *curia*, the same term as that applied to that of the Roman Senate.

In ancient Chaldia there was a god called in Babylon Nebo, and in Egypt Nub or Num.[84]And among the Romans, Numa, for Numa Pompfelius, the great priest-king of the Romans, occupied precisely the position of the Babylonian Nebo [85] he was called" Tages" among the Etruscans were the Romans got most of their rites. Tages came up out of the earth or a hole on the ground or well. In Egypt this god was represented with the head of horns and ram just as in Etrusca where he was presented with the head of horns of a ram.[86] The name Nebo signifies "The Prophet," and as such this god "gave oracles, practiced augury, pretended to miraculous powers and was adept in magic. He was the great wonder worker, and claimed to cause fire to come down from heaven in the sight of men." This Tages is the one who was said to have taught the Romans augury, and all the superstition and wonder-working ".[87] Some of the magic that these gods did was to float in the air. This was the case with Zoroaster while luminous rays came out of his body while a fire was resting on his head.[88] The idea of the birth of a god from a hole in the earth or a cave is very common in the pagan mysteries. Mithra was fabled to have been produced from a cave in the earth according to Justin Martyr[89] and please remember there are other religions with these divine ones come up out of the well or speak to you in caves and of course the apocalyptic beast also "comes up out of the earth" as described in Revelation 19: 20. The Imperial standard of Rome was a "Red Dragon" the universal symbol of fire-worship suggested, in a pagan culture, the safety of the empire rested on that system of worship. This was true in Egypt where kings ie. Moloch were identified with fire and blood which was true you will recall of Nimrod as well .[90] Which cave did he reside in?[91]

The Early Collegium
Early history of the Collegium or College

By law, only three persons were required to create a legal collegium; the only exception was the college of consuls, which included only the two <u>consuls</u>. There were four great religious corporations (*quattuor amplissima collegia*) of Roman priests. They were, in descending order of importance:The highest was the *Pontifices* (also known as College of Pontifices, headed by the *Pontifex Maximus*, a title taken first by the 2nd Roman king Numa Marcius and then the Caesars from Augustus, Julius Caesar, to Gratian. The main duty of the Pontifices was to maintain the *pax deorum* or "peace of the gods.[92] His real power lay in the administration of *jus divinum* or divine law. His responsibilities seemed to include:

1. The regulation of all expiatory ceremonials needed as a result of pestilence, lightning, etc.
2. The consecration of all temples and other sacred places and objects dedicated to the gods.
3. The regulation of the calendar; both astronomically and in detailed application to the public life of the state.

4. The administration of the law relating to burials and burying-places, and the worship of the *Manes* or dead ancestors.

5. The superintendence of all marriages by *conferratio,* i.e. originally of all legal patrician marriages.

6. The administration of the law of adoption and of testamentary succession.

7. The regulation of the public morals, and fining and punishing offending parties.

   In the Pagan tradition the secret keys of the Chaldean Mystries, the "book of the grand interpreter Hermes Trismegistus" the Interperter of the gods was for the Pontifiex Maximus.

The next level of religious academics were the *Augures.* The augur, usually depicted with a crooked or curved staff was a priest and official in the classical world, especially ancient Rome and Etruska. His main role was to interpret the will of the gods by studying the flight of birds: whether they are flying in groups or alone, what noises they make as they fly, direction of flight and what kind of birds they are. This was known as "taking the auspices." The ceremony and function of the augur was central to any major undertaking in Roman society—public or private—including matters of war, commerce, and religion.

The Roman historian Livy stresses the importance of the augurs: "Who does not know that this city was founded only after taking the auspices, that everything in war and in peace, at home and abroad, was done only after taking the auspices.[93]

The next college was called the *Quindecimviri.* In ancient Rome, the **quindecimviri sacris faciundis** were the fifteen (*quindecim*) members of a college (*collegium*) with priestly duties. Most notably they guarded the Sibylline Books, scriptures which they consulted and interpreted at the request of the Senate. This *collegium* also oversaw the worship of any foreign gods which were introduced to Rome.

Originally these duties had been performed by *duumviri* (or *duo-viri*), two men of patrician status. Their number was increased to ten by a Licinio-Sextian law in 367 BC, which also stipulated that half of these priests were to be plebeian. During the Middle Republic, members of the college were admitted through cooption. At some point in the 3rd century BC, several priesthoods, probably including the *quindecimviri*, began to be elected through the voting tribes.[94] The fourth collegia of priests was called the *Epulones. quindecimviri sacris faciundis.* The *epulones* arranged feasts and public banquets at festivals and games *(ludi)*, duties that had originally belonged to the pontiffs. Initially there were three *epulones*, but later their number was increased to seven; hence they were also known as the *septemviri epulonum*, "seven men of the *epulones.*" Julius Caesar temporarily expanded the college to ten, but after his death it was reduced again to seven. Their college was founded in 196 BC, long after reforms had opened the magistracies and most priesthoods to plebeians, who were thus eligible from the beginning. [95]

Finally there were many many colleges of gods and societies for example the College of Aesculapius and Hygia. The College of Aesculapius and Hygia was an assoassociation founded in the mid-2nd century AD by a wealthy Roman woman named Salvia Marcellina, in honor of her dead husband. The college served as a burial society and dining club for its members. Usually of the plebian (poorer) class of Roman Citizens.

The conclusions of pagan worship or the development of religion
"Most of us have been brought up in the tenants of orthodox ethnology, and this is largely an enthusiastic and quite uncritical attempt to apply the Darwinian Theory of Evolution to the facts of social experience. Many ethnologists, sociologists, psychologists still persist in this endeavor and will persist as long as they have the curious notion that everything possesses and evolutionary history - - -(toward "better and better" whether it is religion, genes, society, or the psych of man and animal so cleverly suggested by Herbert Spencer and Taylor during the dark heyday of Evolutionism. An *a priori* assumption of an upward development of mankind along a single line with the absence of any proof that single stages of the process have any historical connection with one another." [96] (ie. The simple always precedes the complex). The principle of the pagan idolatry went directly to exalt fall and humanity, to consecrate its lusts, to give men licensed to live after the

flesh, and yet, after such a life, to make them sure of eternity. Janus the divinity commonly worshipped in Phrygia (west central part of Anatolia, now part of Turkey) along with Rhea or Cybele who was once called the father of the gods and the Mediatorial divinity was worshipped under the name *Idaia Mater*, "The mother of knowledge," and she bore in her hand as a symbol the pomegranate which to pagans is the fruit of the forbidden tree. So we can expect to encounter this pagan concept later in the institutes of learning, the Universities.

So we see the "Evolutionary Presumptive" rejecting the great evidence laid down by Wilhelm Schmidt, Edward H. Schaeffer, Axel W. Pearson, Andrew Lying, Samuel Zwemer, Cannon Titcombe, and finally Paul Radin (American Indians) and claiming their "gods" developed from primitive simple crude, or naïve and leading to the complex, refined, or sophisticated to the present.[97] Quite the opposite of this "presumptive".

However, to the contrary, devolution – degenerate was the case. If primitive cultures are placed in ascending order, the lower groups have the purest concept of God who has neither wife nor family. Under Him and created by Him are the primal pair from whom the tribe descended. As you moved up from cultural complexity introduced in the degeneracy, worship of dead ancestors supplant the worship of the Supreme Being (who can't be seen) and then the anthropomorphization of the gods results in making images or at least mental images of the pure spirit of the Supreme Being which is now reduced to a caricature of a dead man or thing of nature - - - be more easily conceived in the mind's eye he soon displaces Creator – God altogether.[98],[99]

If we think the "gods of the campus" are a more sophisticated religion taught by a more sophisticated priestly class of faculty we are mistaken. They think their hidden gods are "evolved" when in fact they are devolved and degenerate idols, stealing glory and honor from the one true Creator-God and tearing at the spiritual fabric of the nation.

Religions do need development and progressive addition. Christianity is instead a relationship with the Creator not a bundle of rituals and tasks to "win" favor of some sort of image of some sort of power. The relationship should be a personal one as described by Creator-God Himself. We are to worship Him "in spirit and in Truth", and to have the training and insight to discern false gods and false Messiahs. He has the power to have printed 6 billion copies of his history of interaction with us. The educational establishment does have a task, but they have abandon it completely for the glory of political correctness, diversity, religious "tolerance", and the presumed power of worshipping the Hammite gods. I will elaborate on the unusual characteristics of the idols assembled by the descendents of Ham, noting how worshipping the stars, the earth, the moon, yourself, "just do what thou wilt", and pantheism fit that mold. The claim that institutions are "not religious" or instead functioning as so-called "secularism" is the rejection of the instruction given by Creator-God in the Bible, so is within the descriptors of idolatry.

Today's Idolatry
Modern Idolatry

Idolaters are known to attribute to their particular Idol any attributes or special benefit that is needed at the moment. For example there can be many different groups worshipping before different statues of the same image in the same building, claiming quite different benefits from the same image. Just like the ancient blacksmith or the ancient woodworker, "...extract, infer, invent, craft, shape, whittle, or design a god, modern man thinks up a god of their own making, amenable to their own desires, and completely false and unprofitable. The carpenter has been replaced by the scholar, but the method and result are the same." Blinded by their own creativity and ingenuity, fooled by their own cleverness, misled by the beauty of their work, persuaded by the plausibility of their own arguments—so they do not and can not see that the god whom they have "proved"or rendered "probable" is not the God of the Bible, but merely an attenuated and tenuous part of creation, a god of their own making.[100] They are doing just what has been done throughout history, pseudonyms of idolatry that worship and serve the creature and not the Creator-God.

ii

How are these ancient gods still with us on the campus?

Part 1. Humanism

Herd of Independent minds

The editors of an excellent monthly review, The New Criterion[1] noted: "Look almost anywhere in academia: What Hardol Rosenberg called "the herd of independent minds" has huddled together in bovine complacency, mooing ankle-deep in its own effluvia, safe within its gated enclosure."

Let's look at idolatry documented in the bible. Who initiates idolatry and why does man fall for this terrible error?

We're told the "carnal mind" is enmity against Creator–God. That is the "worldly – minded", those that have envying, and strive, and divisions. "For the mind that is set on flesh is "hostile to God, for it does not submit to God's law; indeed it cannot." [Romans 8:7] $_{ESV}$. "Self – centeredness" as opposed to "God centeredness"; a life ruled by the flesh is a life dependent on finite human effort and resources, a selfish life as opposed to one directed by God's spirit.[2] Where God's spirit is not a special part of the person but the "power" of gods presence.[3] People error when they think of a person as a bifurcation of an upright spiritual part and a "immortal bodily" part. That is Neo-Platonism introduced by the Gnostics and not Christianity.[4] As mere mortals we cannot stand against sin for we don't have the weapons of war to deal with evil things. For the weapons of the spirit are for the pulling down of the strongholds of Satan (and his fallen angels), such weapons as "Shields of faith, helmet of salvation, and sword of the spirit, which is the Word of Creator–God."[Eph 6:16] So man in the flesh leans away from Creator–God, His Word, and the tools and weapons He has provided to battle the invisible war between good and evil. The flesh predisposes us all to idolatry.

Balak's plan to destroy the nation of Israel in 1400 BC was to pay a hireling prophet to tell him to send the women of Moab to seduce the men of the camp of Israel and the men fell for these women and soon attended the sacrifices of the gods of the Moabites, partook of their feasts, and worship their Idols ....called Baal-peor who then infected Israel.

So the enemy of man was repeating his simple battle plan and taking down a nation by seduction of those who worshipped idols, false gods with a demon behind them. While it would seem Satan had won and Israel would be permanently destroyed by God's wrath, Satan seemed to know nothing of the loving kindness of the divine heart ..... he had no knowledge of the doctrine of grace or of permanent error correction Creator-God would bring by sending himself in the form of a man for us all to follow out of this "carnal" world into a wondrous eternity!

If Satan had no knowledge of the things of God as loving kindness, tender mercy, and longsuffering, then man certainly is not born with this incredible knowledge and can be taught in a manner and way of thinking that is just like the Moabite women, the sensuality of the flesh following after the false gods of the Epicureans that we will find firmly established on today's campuses.

Lets take a look at today's campus and the attitude toward a Loving Creator-God that appears to be pervasive. It's as if everything that can be done to the entering student to defile him/her is occurring. The motive in most cases is claiming that "secular", interpreted as directing the student in a manner that would "cleans" them of their beliefs, directing them toward a self-centered decision-making ethics in which they are their own little god deciding what is good, there is no "evil" supposedly "no shame" and that if there is any law it is not related to the law of Creator-God. I've never recently found a class of graduate students that can name the 10 commandments collectively or individually let alone know what the commandments mean. The idea that all men "miss the mark" and must repent before a pure and Holy God and claim the righteousness of the Hebrew messiah who died and rose again for them personally is not permitted in the classroom. It can be discussed one on one in the Faculty's office but albeit carefully. Why are these not allowed on today's campus? Obviously the aforementioned would be offensive to those who want nothing to do with it, or have belief in other god or gods. Fine, but that is not the same as what is occurring. The student is being directed openly at false IDOLS by the teaching, giving credit and glory that is due Creator-God to something else by misdirection or illogical arguments that have the appearance of Science but are at their core deceptive. The University couldn't openly do this when the tuition they receive that is not from the Government is from those parents that would likely scream "foul"! The secular intelligentsia filled with what is called in the bible "philosophies and vain deceit" ["Beware lest any man spoil you through philosophy and vain deceit, after the tradition of men, after the rudiments of the world, and not after Christ." Colossians 2:8]

"The philosophy of the school room in one generation will be the philosophy of government in the next" (Abraham Lincoln).

"It is reported that the director of religion and culture for a major University exposed her theology on a flight from Chicago to Boise while sitting beside a quiet Christian. She quickly began her three hour verbal dissertation of her religious beliefs and philosophy. Three hours of going in circles, trying, I think, to convince herself of her beliefs. She talked of Quantum Physics, a parallel universe, the great religious leaders of the past and present (listing them), frequently noting. "God is in everything and all of us are going to heaven!" she said with much conviction. Three hours of one continuous sentence. Her talking without breathing. Him listening and wondering how much longer this flight could go on. Waiting. Patiently, or not so patiently waiting. Sooner or later, she has to wear out. Then, silence. He looked up, Smiling. Oh, how peaceful the silence! 'You are smiling! You must be thinking? I have got you thinking, haven't I?' She looked like the woman at the fair who just won the Grand Prize for her giant pumpkin. Now, finally, it was his chance to ask some questions. I had about fifteen minutes before we were landing."

"For three hours now, you have been giving me your opinion and religious beliefs. You may or may not want to hear what I have to say, but I will give you the only absolute truth that there is and that is the Word of God, the Holy Bible. You mentioned the great religious leaders of the past and present. One of those you mentioned was Jesus. Who was this Jesus to you?"

"Jesus was a great man and prophet!"

"Do you see that emergency door? If this plane were on fire, you would want to escape the danger through that emergency door, wouldn't you?

"Yes!"

"And if this plane were on fire, you would want to help me get off this plane and out of danger as well wouldn't you?"

"Yes! Of course I would!"

"Jesus is the Way, the Truth, and the Life. No man comes to the Father, but by Him. Jesus is the only door by which you or anyone else can get to heaven. You have said we are all going to heaven. I agree. Why? Because the Bible tells us in Ecclesiastes that the spirit of man will return to God who gave it. Yours and my spirits will return to God in either a saved or an unsaved condition. We will all stand before God in heaven.

We will just not all stay there. Only those who have repented of their sins, been born-again, and received Christ as their Savior will remain in heaven. Go to all of the great religious leaders tombs and what will you find? A tomb with a body in it. Only Jesus the Christ rose from the dead and had the power to do such a thing. You have said that God is in everything. The seats of this plane. In you and I. In everything. (he then smashed the coffee cup in his hand) Was God in this coffee cup? No! The Bible says that God is in us and through us and He is alive, not in the inanimate objects. The believer is in fact the Temple of God's Holy Spirit, the third personage of the Trinity. But, you must be born-again for the Holy Spirit of God to live within you."

It was at this time that she said, "Who are you and what do you do?"

"His name was Pastor Daniel Lane, Corporate Chaplain for an international company which has divisions out here that he was going to visit."

And, with this said, she needed to suddenly take a nap. With only minutes left in the flight.

What was her position in life? The "Director of Religion and Culture" for a major University. (Pastor Daniel Lane)[5]

Lets take a look at the idols she is worshipping. Her gods are not that remote from the gods of Babylon we have been discussing. When she describes god as in everything and we are all going to heaven. Is it Tiamat that god of Chaos that was torn to make up all the stuff of the universe. The poly-demonism of the Mystery religions all allow you to choose one of the gods you want special favors from based on some supposed characteristic but for most, salvation was a gift due to certain rites or sacrifice.....always your works to reach up to that god to get what you want at the time. Her collective salvation sounds a lot like comments by President Barack Obama.

The northern Kingdom of Israel was beset by the Idolatry of Baal of the Zidonians or Sidon, where in Sidon, the people dwelt "quiet and secure with no magistrate to judge them or put them to shame on anything. They worshipped the moon goddess Ashtoreth and Baal, the male god of the Phoenicians often identified with Molech [Jer 19:5;Judg 2:11;10:10 1Kings 18:18;Jer2:23;Hos 2:17] and was afterwards the religion of the ten tribes in the time of Ahab [1Kings 16:31-33;18:19,22] and for a time in the kingdom of Judah [2Kings8:27;2Chron28:2] unto the time of captivity [Zeph 1:4-6]. The sun-god under the title of Baal; was the chief object of worship of the Canaanites. Each locality had its special Baal, the various local Baals were summed up under the name of Baalim, or "lords" each Baal had a wife, a colorless reflection of himself.[6]

King Ahab was converted from worshipping JHVH the God of the Hebrews to his wife Jezebel's Phoenician gods which lead to the social and moral deterioration of the northern kingdom then leading to the downfall of

Samaria completely. Jezebel's demise was not good in that she was shoved out a 2nd story window and her body was eaten by dogs. Apparently her husband also met a similar fate and his blood was licked by dogs or pigs or both.

Donald Gray Barnhouse describes a truly carnal and worldly woman:

"Many years ago and elderly woman came to a minister at the beginning of his ministry in a certain church and began to warn him against a woman in the congregation. He should not entrust her with any spiritual task because, according to the gossip, she was "worldly." The pastor had been apprised of the true situation in the church and came to the accused's defense. His informant persisted, saying that the woman in question danced, drank cocktails, smoked and used too much makeup. The pastor knew his scripture and said, "On the contrary, you have not told me one item that would make me think she is worldly. She is what the scripture calls "carnal" it is you who were the worldly one." The woman was aghast and protested that she did not do this, she did not do that; that she abstained from this and avoided that. The minister replied, "Nevertheless, you are the worldly one. All the things you mentioned against her are in the realm of the flesh. You are worldly because you are the one who wishes power and who loves display. You want to be the head of organizations. You delight in show and position. When the various circles were meeting in different homes, the other women finally return to the church for the meetings because none of them could keep up with you. When the woman had gone to your house, you had made an ostentatious show of your linen, your china, your crystal. As you have had no children, you have had more income to spend on other things. Your conversations concerned the cloth and napkins you had bought in the Azores, the ornament from Dresden, and the antique from a little shop in England. Your suppose coat-of-arms was framed in a prominent place on your wall, and every time anyone remarked on any of your heirlooms you explain from which ancestors it had come and described without understatement his particular honors in life[7] Note: the truly worldly woman who claimed how she "did not do this or that", abstain from this, and avoided that because she wishes power and loves display, delighting in the show and position with an ostentatious show of linen, China, and crystals and told how great were her ancestors and heirlooms. Not the woman she accused who danced, drank cocktails, smoked, and used too much makeup. That woman was not who she claimed she was.

They also seem to respond with the attitude of Shakespeare's Prospero in Winter's Tale, i.e. "they protest too much". Why, if people are committed to scientific pursuit of truth do they refuse to answer honest questions of logic and evidence?

Ryan Rotela, a student at Florida Atlantic University at Davie Florida reported that his instructor in intercultural Communications class, Dr. Deandre Poole (also Vice Chair of the Palm Beach County Democratic Party) told his class to write the name "Jesus" on a piece of paper and then stomp on it on the floor, When he refused and spoke up about it, he was suspended from the class. The Prof. was doing a textbook exercise entitled, "Intercultural Communications: A Contextual Approach, 5th ed. The exercise is part of the new secular disciplines of 'diversity' and 'tolerance ' words that seem to relieve certain peoples guilt and make them feel good…demonstrating the contempt the instructor has for people of Christian faith.[8]

What can we expect from Idolatry? An example from history:

After Assyria's Antiochus gave his daughter Cleopatra to the king of Egypt to put a spy in the palace but she fell for the king and rejected her father….her father Antiochus got upset and went on a war rampage but was stopped by Rome and was eventually murdered. His descendent a "raiser of taxes" was also killed and is replaced by a "vile person" Antiochus Epiphanies who obtained the kingdom by flatteries (and deception). He began to devastate the Egyptians, he robs all the riches he finds and buys the allegiance of all the renegades he needs to perpetrate his crimes. He infiltrated the kingdom and got his enemy poisoned by those seated at his own table. Both these kings (Antiochus and the king of Egypt)hearts shall be to do mischief. They couldn't settle their differences on the battlefield so they sat down to make a treaty. Antiochus was again stopped by the Romans in his exploits so in his "grief" he decided to attack the Jews using the rebellious Jews among them. He came into Jerusalem so angry because he couldn't do what he wanted to do with Egypt and slaughtered every child he could find right on the street, every woman he could find he had raped and then killed. He took the idol Zeus into the Jewish temple of YHVH and put it on the temple worship center. He stopped all the Jewish sacrifices and tried to make all the Jews bow down to Zeus then he slew a pig, took chalices and filled them up with blood of that slain pig and went with his men through all the temple and threw that pig's blood all over the temple desecrating everything they could find...there was pigs blood all over the walls and over the holy vessels. They took some of the pork from the slain pig and lined the priests up and forced them to eat it by jamming it down their throats. Then offered the pig as a sacrifice on the Jewish alter...an abomination of desolation so great that the temple itself was desolate, nobody could go there. It was emptied out because of what Antiochus did to the Jews.[9] Daniel wrote this more then 500 years before it happened for he was told this detail by a messenger Angel. (Historians have not yet completed all the details given by Daniel because what Daniel was told are by the only observer (of what happened before it happened).

Humanism is pervasive!

A false presupposition of Evolution, is that everything has a evolutionary history. There is no evidence for this at all. "The corollary of this, though not usually thought through, was that in reverse everything must have been worse and worse as one passed back into history and prehistory......that progress was automatic. This pervasive philosophy of evolution seemed to have been contagious and one by one each branch of historical research succumbed to the temptation to reconstitute its data in ascending scales starting with the simple, crude, or naïve and leading to the complex refined, or sophisticated at the present. The history of art, technology, social organization, everything in fact....including religious beliefs...was assumed to fall into this pattern. There was a logical compulsion about it all.... indeed it appeared self evident that it must be so."[10] I plan to show that modern "humanism" is a belief system that is the ultimate degenerate anthromorphization of the pagan gods of ancient time; which can be shown to be a devolution from a powerful monotheism. It is a enormous error in the argument that polytheism arose by the evolution of polydemonism and not by the emphasis of differently expressed attributes of a single God by a people that in later years came to forget that they were speaking of the same Person so that the attributes became a plurality of deities. The writing just before Darwin set the stage for his theory by cleverly defining "how it all began" without any data that was convincing. Spencer and Lewis Browne decided, without anything but an empty theory, that religion began with the worship of the dead, sometimes ancestors, by poor crude half-ape man, nursing his wound in some draughty cave, in fear throughout most of his life...which, because of his superstitious and unscientific nature "naturally gave rise to feelings of awe and dread which slowly evolved into structured religious beliefs." (And this over "millions and millions of years" where I will show the absolute dating of the paint on cave-man art does not support these thoughts at all.)This was a perfect introduction to religion by a Humanist professor who had been taught the same theory. Lets examine this theory through the eyes of anthropologist Wilhelm Schmidt the founder of the famous journal <u>Anthropos. A more reasonable observation of man's behavior is a strong tendency towards spiritual degeneration theoughout history.</u> In fact the idea that man is "getting better and better in every way" is bizarre and certainly, despite the fact that we have technology and can develop things does not speak to our spiritual side at all.

Experts that have spent their life studying the following civilizations gave the following statements.

1. Stephen Langdon of Oxford on the Sumerian (oldest) civilization
    "I mainly fail to carry conviction in concluding that both in Sumerian and Semitic religions, monotheism preceded polytheism".

"The Sumerian religion, which is the most powerful cultural influence in the ancient world, could be traced by means of pictographic inscriptions almost to the earliest religious concepts of man...indicate a primitive monotheism, and the totemistic origin of Hebrew and other Semitic religions is now entirely discredited".[11]

2. Henry Frankfort from subsequent excavations at Tell Asmar from the third Millennium B.C.

    "We discover that the representations on cylinder seals, which are usually connected with various gods, can all be fitted into a consistent picture in which a single god worshiped in this temple forms the central figure. It seems, therefore that at this early period his various aspects were not considered separate deities in the Sumero-Accadian pantheon." [12]

3. Friedrich Delitzsch from a report by T.G. Pinches on a tablet:

    "This tells us that the highest of the deities in the Babylonian pahtheon are designated as one with the god Marduk. Marduk is set forth under the name "Ninib", as Possessor of Power"; under the name of "Nergal" or "Zamama," as "Lord of Battle"; under the name "Bel," as "Possessor of Lordship"; under the name "Nebo," as "The Lord the Prophet"; under the name "Sin," as "Illuminator of the Night"; under the name "Shamash," as "Lord of all that is Just"; under the name "Addu," as "God of Rain." Marduk therefore was Ninib as well as Nergal, Moon-god as well as Sun-god, the names being simply different ways of describing his attributes, powers, or duties."[13]

4. George Rawlinson noted:

    "The deity, once divided, there was no limit to the number of His attributes of various kinds and of different grades; and in Egypt everything that partook of the divine essence became a god. Emblems were added to the catalogue; and though not really deities, they called forth feelings of respect which the ignorant could not distinguish from actual worship."[14]

5. Paul of Tarsus, Rabban Gamaliel the Elder's student who had the equivalent of 2 PhD's by the time he was 23. One of the most educated men of the times. Wrote in Romans 1:18-23:

    "...men, who suppress the truth in unrighteousness, because what may be known of God is manifest in them, for God has shown it to them. For since the creation of the world His invisible attributes are clearly seen, being understood by the things that are made, even His eternal power and the Godhead, so that they are without excuse, because, although they knew God, they did not glorify Him as God, nor were thankful, but "became futile in their thoughts, and their foolish hearts were darkened. Professing to be wise, they became fools, and changed the glory of the incorruptible God into an image made like corruptible man—and birds and four-footed animals and creeping things...and served the creature rather than the Creator"[NKJV]

Apparent benefits to Faculty who teach Humanism

1. Claimed Authority "Nature and me will tell you how it is. By removing the true mover and authority—puffs them up. They can easily answer all hard questions from the inquiring High School student by arguing from evolutionism that "... all evolves from the simple to the complex of today".
2. Fallacious arguments succeed on the campus because of self-authority. Puffed up by knowledge is not proof of reality.
3. Heideggers influence [Camus, Existentialism, Jean Paul Sarte, Nietzsche Hitler & Zoroaster]
4. Faculty supermen and semantics. The terminology employed rendered all formal logical assessment hopeless....Deeply fallacious.

The Idolatry of Faculty Marxists.
Words that remove us from reality
　Government directed Protection….all men are victims

- Protecting the German gene
- Protecting the citizen from failure
- Protecting the citizen from poverty
- Protecting the citizen from risks
- Protecting the mother from the baby

Government directed Compassion

- Gov. compassion replacing the Family
- Compassion on those with bad judgment mistakes
- Compassion on the life of the pregnant woman
- Compassion on the lawbreaker
- Compassion on the murderer
- Compassion on the citizen with a poor quality of life
- Compassion on the person to decry the family
- Compassion on the elderly

Part of the church went along. [15]

Is Pseudo science asking the student theology questions that science hasn't the capacity to answer?

We can summarize humanism as now containing the re-direction of what is due God into man and man's philosophy-religion and gods ie. false Messiahs **Because He is God and there is none else!**

"Ye are My witnesses saith the LORD, and MY servant whom I have chosen: that ye may know and believe ME, and understand that I am HE: before ME there was no God formed, neither shall there be after ME. I, even I, am the LORD, and beside ME there is no Savior." [Isaiah 43:10-11] NKJV

The Idolatry of Faculty Marxists.

If a faculty worships at the feet of Karl Marx, I would argue that they have accepted Marx's god in the form of rank idolatry. In joining in with Marx they have accepted the reasoning and philosophy of an individual that is no doubt brilliant, and one deeply imbedded in Greek history and philosophy, but he developed a communist doctrine that, the case can be made was that of a man following the dictates of the father of idolatry Satan according to work by Richard Wurmbrant (1818-1883) titled "Was Marx a Satanist?"

If you read Marx's writing and poems as a young man, you are impressed with him as a brilliant "word smith". He seemed able to write poetry on most any topic that no doubt, leads the world to openly debate where his heart really rested. He is so like young Darwin struggling with the bible and God and Romance. I'm not really sure I can totally categorize the man as an Idolater all his life. He seems to have had an early period where he understood who the Christ was ("religion itself teaches us that the ideal being whom all strive to copy sacrificed himself for the sake of mankind, and who would dare to set at naught such judgments" .[16] While I may be giving Marx a gift here he certainly wrote a great deal that identifies him as thoroughly anti-Creator-God, as if choosing the very incorrect path he concerned himself with in his youth.

Marx may give the appearance of an angel of light ....a compassionate visionary who truly cared for the poor but lets look at his poetry, his plays and the underlying structure of his philosophy to find something altogether different, in fact quite phony. Today one third of the world is Marxist. Many are convinced that Marx gave the answer about how to help the hungry, destitute, and oppressed on earth, the ground work for "modern liberalism". He claimed that: "The abolition of religion as the illusory happiness of man is a requisite for their real happiness." Marx came up with the answer to the world's problem as the abandonment of religion, replaced with the state, because religion obstructs the fulfillment of the communist ideal. We don't know what created "the new Marx" when he was 18 he begin to write anti-God, pro-Satin-like verses as: "I wish to avenge myself against the One who rules above." And:

"So a god has snatched from me my all
In the curse and rack of destiny.
All his worlds are gone beyond recall!!
Nothing but revenge is left to me!
I shall build my throne high overhead,
Cold, tremendous shall its summit be.
For its bulwark—superstitious dread.
For its Marshall—blackest agony."

Perhaps the motivation for this desire for a throne high overhead like Lucifer's proud boast in Isaiah 14:13 can be found in a drama Marx wrote in which he uses a satanic inversion of "Emmanuel" for the title "Oulanem" in which Wurmbrand points is a Marx confession:

The hellish vapors rise and fill the brain,
Till I go mad and my heart is utterly changed.
See this sword? The prince of darkness sold it to me...
For me beats the time and gives the signs.
Ever more boldly I play the dance of death
And they are also Oulanem, Oulanem.
The name rings forth like death, rings forth
Until it dies away in a wretched crawl.
Stop, I've got it now! It rises from my soul...

Yes I have power within my youthful arms
To clench and crush you [i.e. Personified humanity] with tempestuous
    force,
While for us both the abyss yawns in darkness.
You will sink down and I shall follow laughing.
Whispering in your ears, "Descend, come with me, friend.[17]

Marx, a student of Shakespeare "loved the words of Mephistophenles in Faust" 'Everything in existence is worth being destroyed: Note that Marx ends Oulanem with:

If there is a Something which devours,
I'll leap within it, through <u>I bring the world to ruins</u> (my emphasis)…
The world which bulks between me and the abyss
I will smash to pieces with my enduring curses.

Wurmbrand points out that Oulanem is probably the only drama in the world in which all the characters are aware of their own corruption, which they flaunt and celebrate with conviction…..all are satanic, corrupt, and doomed. [p15]. Marx is writing what the devil does: he consigns the entire human race to damnation. Marx is seen as wishing to bring the world to ruin, building himself a throne. Marx and his partners in the First International Mikhail Bakunin who wrote "..here steps in Satan, the eternal rebel, the first free-thinker and the emancipator of words..urging him to disobey and eat of the fruit of knowledge"…He writes:"In this revolution we will have to awaken the devil in people, to stir up the basest passions." [Wurmbrand p 22]

In Marx's poem "Human Pride":
With disdain I will throw my gauntlet full in the face of the world
And see the collapse of this pygmy giant whose fall will not stifle my ardor
Then will **I wander godlike and victorious through the ruins of the world**
And giving my words an active force, I will <u>feel equal to the Creator</u> (my emphasis)

If this is Marx, he could care less about anybody but Marx! Idolatry at it's simplest. Claiming god-hood for himself. The Best example is his poem "Human Pride":

"With disdain I will throw my gauntlet full in the face of the world,
And see the collapse of this pygmy giant whose fall will not stifle my ardor.
Then will I wander godlike and victorious through the ruins of the world

73

And giving my words an active force, I will feel equal to the Creator." [18]

I can argue that his "word smith" genius which I would argue is as the problem of Human Pride.

<u>Human Pride</u> by 19 year old Karl Marx (sent to his Rabbi Father)

When these stately Halls I scan
And the giant burden of these Houses,
And the stormy pilgrimage of Man
And the frenzied race that never ceases,
Pulse's throbbing do I sense
And the giant flame of Soul so proud?
Shall the Waves then bear you hence
Into Life, into the Ocean's flood?
Shall I then revere these forms
Heavenward soaring, proud, inviolate?
Should I yield before the Life that storms
Towards the Indeterminate?
No! You pigmy-giants so wretched,
And you ice-cold stone Monstrosity,
See how in these eyes averted
Burns the Soul's impetuosity.
Swift eye scans the circles round,
Hastens through them all exploringly,
Yearning, as on fire, resounds,
Mocking through the vast Halls and away.
When you all go down and sink,
Fragment-world shall lie around,
Even though cold Splendor blink,
Even though grim Ruin stand its ground.
There is drawn no boundary,
No hard, wretched earth-clod bars our way,

And we sail across the sea,
And we wander countries far away.
Nothing bids to stay our going,
Nothing locks our hopes inside;
Swift away go fancies fleeing,
And the bosom's joy and pain abide.
All those monstrous shapes so vast
Tower aloft in fearfulness,
Feeling not love's fiery blast
That creates them out of nothingness.
No giant column soars to Heaven
In a single block, victorious;
One stone on the other meanly woven
Emulates the timid snail laborious.
But the Soul embraces all,
Is a lofty giant flame that glows,
Even in its very Fall
Dragging Suns in its destructive throes.
And out of itself it swells
Up to Heaven's realms on high;
Gods within its depths it lulls,
Thunderous lightning flashes in its eye.
And it wavers not a whit
Where the very God-Thought fares,
On its breast will cherish it;
Soul's own greatness is its lofty Prayer.
Soul its greatness must devour,
In its greatness must go down;
Then volcanoes seethe and roar,
And lamenting Demons gather round.
Soul, succumbing haughtily,
Raises up a throne to giant derision;
Downfall turns to Victory,

Hero's prize is proud renunciation.
But when two are bound together,
When two souls together flow,
Each one softly tells the other
No more need alone through space to go.
Then all Worlds hear melodies
Like the Aeolian harp full sighing,
In eternal Beauty's rays
Wish and Soul's desire together flowing.
Jenny! Do I dare avow
That in love we have exchanged our Souls,
That as one they throb and glow,
And that through their waves one current rolls?
Then the gauntlet do I fling
Scornful in the World's wide open face.
Down the giant She-Dwarf, whimpering,
Plunges, cannot crush my happiness.
Like unto a God I dare
Through that ruined realm in triumph roam.
Every word is Deed and Fire,
And my bosom like the Maker's own.

Marx has pity on himself as one "mourned by demons"! How else can this be taken then as one following the enemy of Creator-God....(Lucifer-Satan)

Moses Hess, called Marx and Engles's chief theoretician as well as the Communist Rabi is to be respected for his work on the return of the Jews to Zion, however Hess, like Marx had a "..common derivation from Hegel and Feuerbach on the one hand, and their common struggles against other oppositional tendencies on the other."[19] The strange Idolatry Hess seemed to push is that the gift to the world by the Jews would be communism rather than the promise of the Hebrew Messiah. This, according to Hook, was "born of a desire to find the fundamental principles of social organization which would make possible the elimination of all conflict between man and man, and class and class". Hess was a student of Torah but walked away from it and believed that these valid principles of social order could be derived <u>only</u> from a knowledge of the metaphysical structure of existence...virtue arises from the knowledge of our status and function in the all-embracing totality—called by both Spinoza and Hegel, God. Hess only slightly modified this Spinoza's god. It seemed that their theology was that everything was blessed with necessity, and that evil was non existent.

The Idolatry of Hess and Feuerbach is seen in the following:

The essence of God, says Feuerbach, is the transcendent essence of man, and the real theory of divine nature is the theory of human nature. Theology is anthropology. Hess wrote in his "Holy History of Mankind"[20] that the original harmony that the Jews had with God was lost, but that now the Jews had the opportunity to reestablish this harmony through socialism. Hess claims the Jews had a unconscious union with God before Christ, that Christ "disjoints the harmony", but the disjuncture does not reach its climax until the Middle Ages which laid the foundation for private property in modern society. We see the theology of the communists developed not from the Holy Bible at all but:

Where God says it's sin   (missing the mark) as Creator-God has laid down the law.
Communists say its Property. (The great misdirection)
[see:Moses Hess exposed][21]

Thinking he knew Jesus was really a Essen, he claimed Jesus did what he did according to the class of society as Hess, a foundation communist, would think. For Hess incorrectly describes the prophets of the bible as primarily interested in "Social Justice" . A poor read of both the books of the Kings and the 2 books of the Chronicles in which the prophets were concerned with Jewish king after Jewish king going after Idolatry and sinning against Creator-God. Causing destruction of the Jewish cities and ultimately their removal from the land God gave them...to Assyria for the

Northern Kingdom and Babylon for Judah. How can Hess mistake the plain reading of the scriptures ie. all is about class and property not sin against Creator-God. I am beginning to wonder if there is an idolatry of "social justice" designed by the far left to be something to worship as if it were much more than the 2 words plainly infer. Busily doing the work of "social justice" rather than describing the sin against Creator-God's 10 commandments that will lead us to the need for the Hebrew Messiah who took all such sins upon himself on the cross which requires us to accept His Gift of redemption which leads us down the narrow path to eternal life. Thinking like Hess that we can cure the world's injustice and defeat man's enemy with communist theory rather than look at ourselves and the log in our eye is the height of hypocrisy! How humble the socialist faculty!

The Progressive Liberal says He is the only one smart enough to be the "taskmaster", so that all will be equal. Something as equality of outcome was rejected by America's founding Fathers as they studied the French Revolution. The problem is derived from defining the nature of man as social, involving the cooperative activity of all individuals for the same ends and interests. The true theory of man, the true humanism is the theory of human society. In other words:

THEOLOGY = ANTHROPOLOGY = SOCIALISM [22]

How many faculty believe this lie? So trite! They walk into the realm where man makes up theology or writes the word of their god as Feuerbach's "essence" and Feuerbach's truth. Since Jesus the messiah, the Son of God said he was the "way and the truth" we have a clear choice between Feuerbach's truth that has no power to save us from our violations of Gods 10 commandments since we have all lied, stolen, and looked on others with lust (committed adultery in our heart), and desired our neighbor's property for ourselves. And that is only 4 of the 10 commandments. If you have never "hated" someone in your heart then have you not murdered someone in your heart; most of us have! And if we break His law in one part we break them all. Feuerbach's god will not save you, and the professor had you on the "wrong path" or way. "Enter in by the Narrow gate; for wide is the gate and broad is the way that leads to destruction, and many are those who enter by it. How narrow is the gate and restricted is the way that leads to life! Few are those who find it." [webb Matthew 7:13-14] "Beware of those who come to you in sheep's clothing, (and with sheepskins) but inwardly they are ravening wolves." [Matt 7:15 KJCS] A ravening one is a predatory one that lives by preying on others… Like the Raven that can be found (like the crow) in the nest (the family) of another, voraciously devouring their young. Buyer beware!!

Part 2. Naturalism

Naturalists worldview and Idols

"…the fundamental difference between a naturalist worldview and a religious world view is the moral framework. While the naturalist may choose to be a moral person, no compelling rational reason exists why one should not be amoral. Reason simply does not dictate their pragmatism. Reason alone does not allow one to defend one way or another….. Pure practical reason, even with a good knowledge of the facts, will not take you to morality."[23] "in every religion except Christianity, morality is a means of attainment…. So different from the naturalist who has an extreme problem and must go to great lengths to deduce even that there is no such thing as good or evil; all of us merely dance to our DNA." Ravi Zacharias points out that every rebirth in Hinduism is a means to pay for the previous lives shortcomings. Karma is systemic to the Hindu belief while in Buddhism every birth is a rebirth, the payback is impersonal because Buddhism has no essential self that exists or survives so every birth as a rebirth of an impersonal karma. Only the best of Buddhist scholars are even qualified to discuss these very intricate ideas. In Islam only Allah makes the decision about whether an individual gets rewarded with heaven. In the later days of Israel, Hebrews and in turn, the Christians, two realities make a crucial systemic and distinguish indifference. "First and foremost Creator-God is the author of moral boundaries not man and not culture….. Eating the fruit from the tree of the knowledge of good and evil basically gave humanity the power to error, to redefine everything. Creator-God had given language, identification, in reality to humankind. He imparted to humans the power to name the animals while essential to created order was a moral framework that the creation was not to name or define. This was the prerogative of the creator, not of the creation. This is the key to understanding the naturalists worldview and his idols." "And the Christian faith, simply stated, reminds us that our fundamental problem is not moral; rather, our fundamental problem is spiritual. It is not just that we are immoral, but that a moral life alone cannot bridge what separates us from Creator-God. Herein lies the cardinal difference between the moralizing religions and Jesus' offer to us. Jesus does not offer to make bad people good but to make dead people alive."[24] Creator-God wants us to understand our own hearts, and nothing shows this more than the stringent demands of a law that discloses we are not Creator-God .... and neither had we better play God.... The moral threads of life were intended to reflect and honor the God we served; they are not a means of entering heaven. Why does a man honor his vows? Why does a woman honor her vows? Is it to earn the love of their spouse or is it to demonstrate the sacredness of their love? True love engenders a life that honors its commitment. That is the role of obedience to Creator-God's moral precepts ....putting hands and feet to belief, embodying the nature of one's ultimate commitment reflects ....the very character of Creator-God. Jesus said to let our lives so shine before people that they would glorify God as a result (Matt 5:16)."[25]

So we see the naturalist must set himself up as the final arbiter of good and evil...making himself god and an idol.....so often the instruction in today's classroom, working so hard to liberate the student from the laws of Creator-God, and condemning him to eternal death and separation from his Maker.

Leaving Hess's theology of communism and confronting Lenin's Dilemma allows us a peak at Lenin's agreement with Freud (whose picture is on the cover of this book) that man was a stimulus-response mechanism without spirit or soul, just a lump of protein molecules wired with nerves.

Radical Feminism and Idolatry
This difficult and personal topic invades our culture and our worldview of the family and basically all of our institutions. That it has a large component

of idolatry is undeniable. Lets look at the cover of the National Organization for Women (NOW).

"NOW is the time to take back control of our lives. NOW is the time to make reproductive freedom for wimmin of all classes,"

Cultures, ages and sexual orientations are reality. NOW is not the time to assimilate too bureaucratic puppeteers who want to control, degrade, torture, kill and rape our bodies. NOW is the time to drop the boot hill in the growing of patriarchy. NOW IS THE TIME TO FIGHT BACK. NO GOD, NO MASTER, NO LAWS.[26]

Judge Bork points out that this short paragraph expresses the rage, the nihilism, and the incoherence of Feminism today "Wimmin" (a word ending in "men" must be avoided) have lost control of their lives, though it is not stated when they had control and how they lost it.[27]

Radical Feminism and its twisted theology
Feminism begins with "Liberation Theology".

Presuppositions of Feminist Theology:

1. Ruether and Russell accept Mary Daly's dynamic nature of revelation.
2. Therefore the bible is a tool as to how God worked to free the oppressed.
3. Discard parts of the bible that did not agree with "their vision of sexual equality" and therefore decided that part of the bible was outdated.
4. ie. relative only to a <u>particular time</u>
   <u>And a particular culture</u> (therefore morally relative truths)
5. Biblical interpretation must change according to their will
6. Method to be applied is Cultural Reflection (CR)
   Which allows the formulation of applicable doctrine.

Therefore Women's' personal interpretation is greater than God's revelation.

7. CR is inductive not deductive and therefore experimental. ie. Seeking a question to try out a hypothesis.

8. Russel claims the purpose of doing theology is to apply "discoveries" to the action of "Social Justice".[28]

Russel was one of the 1st women graduates of Harvard Divinity School. And a pastor for 10 years who lived in Guilford with her partner Shannon Clarkson.

The key to Russel thinking is her "New Creation" concept in which she describes new creation after Feminist theory. She describes, "Shaping Reality which leads to creating alternatives for social reality". Russel names God as other than Father! [29]

When we apply the dialectic as Marx does to Russel's thinking of oppression we must name the key oppressed and ask just who was the oppressor?

EGYPT   → symbol of the WORLD
(oppressed the people of God)
Satan   → the accuser of the Brethren
Lawlessness and Sin   → Destruction of the Body and Nation

Problem of Feminism in Christianity

Feminism claimed using female as well as male pronouns to address God would de-sexualize Him. But the opposite occurred. "The switch from masculine to feminine reduced God to sexuality."[30] "They presented an image of a deity that is bisexual or androgynous rather than one who transcends the polarity of the sexes." [31]

Renaming God in a way that was other than He had named himself logically leads to an erosion of God's independent personality in their eyes. God became a much less personal "force". ie. Virginia Mollenkott extended God's name from He/She to He/She/it! [32]

Impersonalizing God is bad bad theology. "It would have been easy for a Creator to sacrifice a Redeemer, but it was not so easy for a Father to sacrifices His Son. …. Understanding God - - -Father/Son/Holy Spirit - - - as being in relationship within Himself is essential to understanding God. In denying this relationship, radical feminists deny who God is.[33] Further reading will help you identify the link between secular Feminism and spirituality----between the women's movement and the immemorial Craft of Wicca (witchcraft) [34]

Changing of the Gods

"The new wave of Feminism needs to be not only many faceted but cosmic and ultimately religious in its vision. This means reaching outward and inward toward the God beneath the gods who have stolen our identity."[35] Radical feminism rejected the Judeo – Christian God which left a vacuum to be filled. Feminist reached into themselves and used themselves to fill the hole and used the goddess as a symbol of their inherent right and power to do so".[36]

There are now many more than 600 undergraduate and several dozen graduate programs in women's studies in American colleges and universities. The student taking Feminism courses is libel to be exposed to rank idolatry of the ancient Welch pantheon of gods or the druidic idolatry, all imbedded in goddess worship or rituals or chants and magic. Hardly different than Kundalini Yoga's gods or the peeps and chants of the Etruscan augurs from Babylon.

The Hebrews that engaged in such idolatry were destroyed and their nation sent into captivity. Their descendants became slaves. Why would anyone seek after false gods playing into the hands of man's enemy who is the "father of lies" whose will and *modus operandi* is to "rob, kill, and destroy". Many women in a group of any kind, even just two, seem OK until a man enters the situation then strife seems to enter, whether its feminine bullying or any kind of strife. A strategy that unites women is to "put down" man or man's supposed control to "get off" on it. Radical feminism is taking all this to extremes - - - even to the form of "womanist theology". The ultimate in pettiness. There are no male/females differences in heaven. The strife will end, thank goodness!

The late judge Robert H. Bork in his chapter on the politics of sex noted "..radical feminism's assault on American culture warns us to not dismiss today's feminism as a "mildly amusing but an utterly inconsequential fit of hysterics. That would be a mistake." [37] He describes radical feminism as the most destructive and fanatical movement to come down to us from the Sixties. Instead of the Marxist oppression of the proletariat, Feminists believe that the oppressors, the source of all evil, are men. Replacing the "establishment "of the 60's with the "patriarchy". He notes that "Feminism rode into our cultural life on the coattails of the New Left but now it certainly deserves its only place in the halls of intellectual barbarisms." It's not a woman's reform movement but entirely something else. There are more women than men in the universities today as well as large numbers in business and professions … Yet this seems only to fuel the rage of feminists"[38] If a radical feminist has any dissatisfaction in any experience it is the fault of others, namely men allowing her to function in the movement in "solidarity and common purpose" just like the identity politics of racial and ethnic programs on campus.

"Today's radical feminism aspires to be much more than this. It bids to be a totalizing scheme resting on a grand theory, one that is as all inclusive as Marxism, as assured of its ability to unmask hidden meanings as Freudian psychology, and as fervent in its condemnation of apostates as evangelical fundamentalism. Feminist theory provides a doctrine of original sin: The world's evils originate in male supremacy."[39]

My mother was the first secretary to female congresswoman in the House of Representatives which is where I was introduced to Bella Abzug who, at the time, represented the 20th district of New York. She was someone you didn't forget. All by herself she pushed radical feminism into mainstream America and the world. One of her pet peeves was to attack the language used in everyday discussions in a way that left the plain and simple biological definitions of what men and women are to a term that misdirected the simple God-given understanding into the realm of "relative truth" - - -that of the socially constructed word "gender" which would allow an expansion into five "sex is": men, women, lesbians, gays, and bisexuals.[40]

"The gender perspective of radical feminism is easy to ridicule but must be taken seriously. It attacks not only man but the institution of the family, it is hostile to traditional religion, it demands quotas in every field for women, and it engages in serious misrepresentations of fact. Worst of all, it inflicts great damage on persons and essential institutions in a reckless attempt to remake human beings and create a world that can never exist. As we will see, among the institutions that have been seriously damaged by radical feminism are the American educational system and the American military."[41]

Judge Bork outlines the intellectual collapse of radical feminism. Those who make attempts to equate men and women physiologically are bizarre, demanding equality on all matters. Truth simply describes "... Males as almost always larger, stronger, and faster with greater upper body strength without the sweat gland fatigue of the female that leads to overheating in hot environments that require endurance. Today there is a stopwatch on every female on the flight deck of an aircraft carrier for a reason (see Dr. Carl Gisolfi's work with the U.S. Navy). Where the early kibbutz movement attempted to "raise boys and girls in a way that would destroy sex roles... We found the program collapsed within a few years. Boys and girls returned to different sex roles. Milford Spiro and American sociologist who studied this phenomenon found, "(against his own intentions), that I was observing the influence of human nature on culture." [42]

If you want to read an idolatry based anti-Biblical Feminism, read Shere Hite's "The Hite report on the family: growing up under patriarchy"[43] where the "Basic feminist fallacy continues, there is no such thing as' fixed human nature'. Rather, it is a psychological structure that is carefully implanted in our minds as we learn the love and power equations of the family - - - for life. Fortunately the family is a human institution: humans made it and can change it."[44] These are key word changes the radical feminist requires:

Sex → "gender"
Family → "household"

Bork notes that feminist ideology is a fantasy of persecution - - -such best-selling books as "Backlash: the undeclared war against American women"[45] "in the 600 or more undergraduate and dozens of graduate programs and women studies in American colleges and universities… Intellectual integrity comes in a distant second to political correctness." Bork notes that the university, dedicated to reason and knowledge, should be feminism's sworn enemy but are instead the center of power. He points to the proof of the politization of higher education as the so-called disciplines such as African-American studies, Hispanic studies, gay and lesbian studies.[46] Were feminists are altering what are found in textbooks of high school and elementary school and with their "sensitivity" training designed to limit what can be spoken and written on campus. Bork notes, "…the campuses are now extremely unpleasant for white Males, were they are subject to harassment and demands that they tow the feminist cultural and political line. Where "evidence and logic are running heavily against the no-difference position so " must be identified with the enemy to exalt intuitive and emotional "women's way of knowing"[47] claiming to perceive all of reality through a sex/gender lens.

Pati and Koertge identify "total rejection" feminists (TOTAL RE) who claimed everything must go - - - even logic, mathematics, and science, and the intellectual discipline of objectivity, clarity, and precision as well.[48] Bork jokes that "nobody knows what a radical feminist physics would look like…. Allowing feminist rocket scientists to place satellites in orbit and without any of Newton's laws of motion." It is noted that, "no axiom or proposition of feminist science that explains or predicts anything or as capable of being tested empirically exists".[49] All the previous work by men labeled WMS or white male system, with a bizarre thought that, "knowledge and modes of reasoning are socially constructed: that is that there are no objective truths and no single valid method of reasoning. That is a very convenient position for someone making irrational assertions. It would be rather difficult to

uphold intelligent, or even and intelligible discussion with someone holding that position, and it would be impossible to win an argument with her.
That, of course, is the point of the exercise.... Women's studies programs
and courses are abysmal swamps of irrational dogma and hatred..... Were
classroom agreement with the ideology is mandatory."[50]

So while radical feminists dismantle college curricula they describe a
false reality. Since their truth and reality are clearly a monstrous idolatry
where Creator-God's creation must be rewritten after their false dogma that
is as much theology as the imperialism of Marxism and fascism.

Judge Bork quotes professor Christian Hoff Sommers who would like to
see the label on the women's studies programs of the more extreme institutions with the following.

> "We will help your daughter discover the extent to which she has
> been in complicity with the patriarchy. We will encourage her to
> reconstruct herself through dialogue with us. She may become
> enraged and chronically offended. She will very likely reject the
> religion and moral codes you raised her with. She may change her
> appearance, and even her sexual orientation. She may end up hating
> you (her father) and pitting you (her mother). After she has com-
> pleted your reeducation with us, you will certainly be out of thou-
> sands of dollars and very possibly be out of one daughter as well". [51]

And we might add, this re-education has embedded within it incredible irra-
tionalism with a hatred of the logic, science, and sensibilities of the known
world along with and infused hatred. "They should be spared what they
obtain there (women's studies); total immersion in a false worldview coupled
to a forth-rate education.... Working to acquire belligerent attitudes and
misinformation... Instead of preparing students for the world. Programs
that impose handicaps upon them."[52]

You ask what could be so wrong with educational programs that
demean women who choose to work primarily as mothers and home-
makers.....Telling them that if they become one of these, their lives are

essentially worthless... Which is a grand lie! Some women have commented, "America today is a nation full of ironies... Including a feminist elite more fiercely committed to the good name of Feminism then to the welfare of women."[53]

Judge Bork makes the point to young women, "It should be a source of great pride to bear the next generation and to train that generation's mind and morals. That is certainly a greater accomplishment then churning out tracts attacking men and families" [54]

We know that the once greatest angel in heaven who was kicked out, Lucifer, became man's greatest adversary and accuser after "iniquity was found in him"[Eze 28: 12-19]. That "Iniquity" was "Pride and a haughty spirit" which he now by choice deceives the whole world. Open your eyes at these deceptions and lies to see the idol at whose feet you find yourself. Worshipping the Idol of radical feminism and its advocacy of the destruction of the family, engendering hatred between the sexes, degrading our military, our universities, and our daughters as well. If you read genesis three you'll see we have been warned for thousands of years of this fallen angel. Only now it's up close and personal

Donald Barnhouse has an interesting theory that Satan may be the king of deceit but he himself can be deceived leading to the "chaos of history". Barnhouse supports his theory when he noted Satan's struggle during WWII when the far superior Japanese fleet lay just over the horizon and started attacking but the US Naval fliers destroyed the bridge of the ship of the Japanese commanding admiral, destroying the command communication for the entire Japanese fleet forcing each captain to operate on his own. The Japanese fleet began to fire on their own ships and the naval battle was a rout.. Satan was unable to unify his own forces here suggesting the chaos of history is a confusing record of the mess of deception, confused and lost communication/control of his forces. So we note that the histories of Spengler and Toynbee have created great philosophies of history that see the disintegration without seeing the cause.[55] We are firing on each other here today because we can't hear or see our Commander-God's instructions in the Bible. Perhaps you can see and hear the chaos now....listen!!!

Part 3. Secularism

Secularism and Idolatry: They chose to believe a lie

There is great treachery in the word "secular". The word is used in laws made to control and even to declare correct speech and correct thought. It is a word for the institutions of our society to hide behind claiming to "beg the question" and dismiss all questions of "Religion". But we have defined religion as those theologies in which man seeks to enter heaven by works, rituals, or similar means to please what he thinks is his god and thereby earn eternal life. While Christianity is a "<u>relationship</u>" with a Creator-God who is reaching down to man (and dying for him) to cleanse him and clothe him in the righteousness of the Son of God, Jesus the Christ. So if secular means excluding "religion" but including seeking a "relationship" with Creator-God then the word and its institutions have value with respect to the things of heaven. But if it attempts to also remove the relationship with man's Creator-God it has no value and benefits man little!! If on the other hand the term "secular university or college" is intended to exclude Creator-God completely from the campus.....if that is the intention, then there is evil afoot. That intention, while claiming fairness and political correctness opens up a space for "Humanism" as the Idol (hidden as a stealth Idol behind a word}.

Do we naturally all have some "good or divine spark" in us that "by our own boot straps" we can be made better, and better (evolve) into a perfection that will save us? This carries with it a strong "suggestion" that man is perfectible by man. Any nation that thinks they are secular carries this heavy burden. If this nation subsequently teaches its children that it is a secular nation and its institutions are also secular then this lie will become pervasive and but few will discover or even be exposed to the truth. Especially if history is modified and "Religion" is substituted for theology in all of the teaching institutions so that few come to understand that Creator–God has given mankind His Ten commandments as the moral basis for man, far above the cultural ethics.

Who among us has never lied? This makes the person (and all of us) a liar. Who among us has used Creator–God's name as a cuss word and thereby blasphemed the One who "knit us together in the womb"? Who among us has not looked at someone with "lust"? That makes us an adulterer at heart. Have we envied something or someone that another person has, and wanted them for ourselves? The thoughts and intents of our heart is who we are. That rotten heart, that secular soul is doomed! The secular nation and its secular institutions are dedicated to keeping us in this defiled state. The state may then pay for our burial but we are then little more than food for worms because Creator–God Himself has paid the price of our misdeeds and miss-thoughts by His own blood. Do we accept the free gift or reject it? How can you if you remain secular? If you were to die tonight and came before a perfect holy Creator–God would He find you innocent or guilty as a lying, thieving, adulterer at heart…. "Missing the mark". Or will you be covered by the One He sent to cleans you of this guilt and escaped the secularist's religion and it's idols or false hidden gods. The bible tells us that Creator-God's law is a "schoolmaster" to bring us to the truth because "God would that ALL would be saved. [1 Timothy 2:4]. While that is His desire, we have to repent of our sins and accept The payment of Jesus Christ's Death on the cross for those sins. This defeats the "pride" Creator-God's enemy thrust upon humanity. Remember a "humble" person is not a weak person but one who "fears" Creator-God!

All nations and societies in history that have secular idolatry have ended up on the dunghill of history. They have "slouched toward Gomorrah" like the U.S. is today and did not recover.

Who are the secular idols?

The false "spark of divinity" claim is in every one of those deadly idols. Refusing to replace that completely deprived heart with the Hebrew Messiah Jesus the Christ who has paid our price before Creator–God is what the secular idol demands. It blocks our true knowledge of our self and speaks to us the same that it spoke to the first humans. "God has not said you will surely die". There is nothing really new under the sun. Man's enemy has had such destructive success with his hidden lie and our universities and schools take his lie "hook, line, and sinker"!

The claim that a secular institution is "not taking sides" is also a lie. Just look at the curriculum dedicated to the inference that there is no Creator–God and His Word the Bible as well as religions are some sort of phenomenological thing that happens with people so we can learn tolerance of the society, encouraging a path that leads to complete destruction. Remember our real enemy seeks to "rob, kill, and destroy" each and every one of us. The secular idol guarantees the success of man's enemy.

Claiming a false "spark of the divine" in all people as in the idolatry of secularism has incredible implications. At a time when Egypt is struggling to become "secular" to save itself from the destruction of fundamentalist religion in which at least 100 clear or implied war verses direct the murder or enslavement of those that don't accept it by compulsion does confuse the student. Here "religion" has nothing to do with a relationship with the One who gave His life for you so you're depraved heart would be replaced with His pure and completely "good" heart. Here the desire for a "secular" Egypt is for a "neutral" state and institutions that have "freedom to choose" whose god you have faith in. Not compulsion but freedom from compulsion.

Table 2. Babylonian gods. Is Babylon still with us?

[Isaiah 46:1 Nebo in Moab, worshipped also by the Moabites]

NAME	Other NAMES	Where Worshipped	What They Stand For	What the Worship includes
Bel Marduk	Enil	Babylon	Weather, War, Sun god	Prostitution, child sacrifice
Son of Marduk	Nebo, Nabu	Babylon	Learning, Astronomy, god of Science	Prostitution

The hidden self-righteousness of the secular idolatry

This faults "divine spark" of supposed goodness the secularist claims is also the idol of self-righteousness and vain or empty deceit. This is a base form of pride that condemns us. The Pharisees and the Sadducees in Jesus time were told, "it will be storming today, for this sky is red and threatening, you know how to interpret the appearance of the sky, but you cannot interpret the sign of the times. And evil and adulterous generation seeks for a sign but no sign will be given except for the sign of Jonah".[Matthew 9: 11].

This idolatry is no different than the pagan who chopped a stick of wood, burned part of it for warmth in the fireplace then carved part of it into some image and dropped to his knees before his carving to worship the divinity he thought he had imparted to it. Rank self–deception-------but at least he is open and honest about what he had done compared to the self-righteous professor dedicated to the destruction of the faith of his students. That deceit and pride is damnable before Creator–God. Judge Robert Bork notes in his "Slouching toward Gomorrah" that the fortress of "modern liberalism" (Hollywood, network news, universities, church bureaucracies, the New York Times, or the Washington Post) have control of the culture and, "The tyrannies of political correctness and multiculturalism will not be ejected from the universities by any number of conservative victories at the poles" until the culture is recaptured".[56] Since the schools and the universities have captured the culture with their "modern liberalism" that excludes Creator–God at every doorway with this tyranny of political correctness and multiculturalism designed as a cultural self-righteousness to hide the guilt of the sub-pagan culture they have created. Professor Bork doesn't even rank this culture as plain pagan but, because of this rank deceit, calls it "sub–pagan". Or even less than or below pagan. By demanding that the children of this sub–pagan society created by the fortress of modern liberalism bow to whatever resentments and sensitivities prevail today they must uphold this stranglehold on this empty culture with "women's rights to choose" or "gay marriage", manufactured to resonate with the imbedded tyrannical words they have planted within their students' minds of "political correctness" and "multiculturalism", mindless anti–intellectual terms that destroyed and defile, maintaining control of a once free nation. This monster is a component of these "divine sparks" of so called goodness or self righteousness whereby the intellectual class of our nation confronts the true righteousness of Creator-God, His Word, the bible and all truth. Thereby attempting to destroy any chance for the young to end the burden each carry before God. Preventing this understanding of the need for repentance and openness to the One who made us as well as His provision for our "path of true righteousness", His righteousness in us.

The source of the secularists "divine spark"

Let's ask an important question. Where did Nimrod get his authority to declare himself the king and spiritual leader of Babylon, from his wife? From whom? It was certainly not from Creator–God for he decided a path far different, one of authority that was not of Creator-God. Where does the modern secularist claim as the source of his "divine spark" of goodness that he will parley for the "better and better" evolution ploy? Indeed the secularist will claim the authority to control the spiritual content of the nation. President Obama's recent pronouncement that we are a "secular" nation contains within it the guise of tolerance and multiculturalism and includes the power of poly-demonism. This time by attempting to negate Creator–God by simply not recognizing Him or making Him something other than what He tells us who He is. A free country cannot exist without recognizing and accepting the direction of Creator–God.

A leading secular-atheist proves God

Richard Dawkins was with the former Dean of Saint Paul's Cathedral on the BBC live when Dawkins was asked to give the full title of his favorite book. Dawkins said it was "Darwin's origin of... Species" a? My God"!!! (Dawkins' exclamation). The ultimate evidence of God is that someone who doesn't believe in Him calls upon Him to remember the full title of his favorite book. Yet Dawkins claims he believes that God doesn't exist. [Ravi Zacharias]

The faculty that invented the concept that man is weak at this point in history and therefore invented Creator-God because of fear but later, when man has arrived due to "progress" which they never quite define, will allow him to drop the invented god because god is man's invention. This professor is described in 2nd Thessalonians 2:10, "..... And with all wicked deception for those who are perishing, because they <u>refused</u> to love the truth and so be saved. Therefore God sends them a <u>strong delusion</u> so that they may believe what his false, in order that all may be condemned who did not believe the truth but had pleasure in unrighteousness."[2Th 2:10-12] ESV

If you follow this fellow, you're following the pied piper who has pleasure in teaching you that which will defile you before almighty Creator-God. This professor has "refused to love the truth" which he rejects or redefines as always culturally "relative" and believes himself divine...... deciding Creator-God doesn't exist........and thus setting himself up as an idol. This introduces us to the humanist religion.

Jesus told us in Luke 11:23, "Whoever is not with me is against me, and whoever does not gather with me scatters" [Matt 12:30] ESV

Robert Fitch's work "The Obsolescence of Ethics: Christianity and Crisis" noted:

"Ours is an age where ethics has become obsolete. It is superseded by science, deleted by philosophy and dismissed as emotive by psychology. It is drowned in compassion, evaporates into aesthetics and retreats before relativism. The usual moral distinctions between good and bad are simply drowned in a maudlin emotion in which we feel more sympathy for the murderer than for the murdered, for the adulterer then for the betrayed, and in which we have actually begun to believe that the real guilty party, the one who somehow caused it all, is the victim, and not the perpetrator of the crime."[57]

iii

How the Humanist have developed: the ones who teach us, the answers are only from man

They are instructing us to "read the library" for the truth, choosing to ignore any of the more than five billion copies of the Words of Creator-God breathed into man's heart and onto the pages of the Bible.

Part 1. Early Foundations of Humanism

One of the great mathematicians and Scientists Blaise Pascal wrote the following:

"...for after all what is man in nature? A nothing in relation to infinity, all in relation to nothing, a central point between nothing and all and infinitely far from understanding either. The ends of things and their beginnings are impregnably concealed from him in an impenetrable secret. He is equally incapable of seeing the nothingness out of which he was drawn and the infinite in which he is engulfed." [1]

"Shem, who saw Lamech, who saw Adam, saw also Jacob, who saw those who saw Moses; therefore the deluge and the creation are true. This is conclusive among certain people who clearly understand it" [2]

"The prophecies are the strongest proofs of Jesus Christ. For these therefore God has made the most provision; since the event which has fulfilled them is a miracle existing from the birth of the Church to the end. Therefore God raised up prophets during sixteen hundred years, and during four hundred years afterwards he dispersed all these prophecies with all the Jews, who bore them into all regions of the world. Such was the preparation for the birth of Jesus Christ, whose Gospel exacting belief from every man made it necessary not only that there should be prophecies to inspire this belief, but that these prophecies should be spread throughout the whole world, so that the whole world should embrace it. Prophecies.—If one man alone had made a book of predictions concerning Jesus Christ, both as to the time and the manner of his coming, and if Jesus Christ had come in agreement with these prophecies, the fact would have had infinite force. But in this case there is much more. Here is a succession of men for the space of four thousand years, who without interruption or variation, follow one another in foretelling the same event. Here is a whole people announcing it, existing for four thousand years, to testify in a body their certainty, from which they cannot be diverted by all the threatenings and persecutions brought to bear against them; This is in a far greater degree important. But it was not enough that the prophecies existed, they needed also distribution through all places, and preservation through all time. And in order that this agreement might not be taken as an effect of chance, it was necessary it should be foretold. It is much more glorious for the Messiah that they should be spectators and even instruments of his glory, beyond the fact that God had preserved him. Proof.—Prophecy with accomplishment. That which preceded, and that which followed Jesus Christ" The Bible (Old Testament) is the most ancient book in the world, and the most authentic. Mohomet forbade (us) reading (the Bible) the Apostles and Moses order us to read it.......the Old Testament is a Cipher." [3]

But when Muslims don't know how to answer a question (ie. Why was Jesus miraculously born of a Virgin?) they are instructed in the Qur'an in Surah 10:94 that they are to ask Christians-people of the Book (the Bible):"If you are in doubt concerning that which We have revealed unto you, then ask those who are reading the Book [the Taurat (Torah) and the Injil (Gospel)] before you.". Muslims are amazed at the fact that Jesus (Isa) is mentioned 93 times in the Qur'an : Muhammad is referred to by name only four times. They are instructed to read what Jesus said. They can't do this without reading the Injil (Gospel)! I mention this because Muslims are sometimes told that Christians make Jesus an Idol, which is totally incorrect because Jesus and God are" One" in Christianity.

Human Beings as gods

[Gen 3] "...you will be like God". The lie Satan spoke to the first humans.

[Psalm 16:4] "Their sorrows shall be multiplied who hasten after another god;"

[Psalm 118:8,14] " It is better to trust in the LORD than to put confidence in man......And

He (Creator-God) has become my salvation"

I remember in a lecture on "Truth in Science" saying to my students, "You know you didn't create yourself". I looked up from my notes to see many graduate students quizzically surprised at the statement, one commented, "I hadn't thought of that", to my amazement. I had no intention of profound thought, but to some of these students, which were some of the best on campus, this was profound! How did their minds and hearts arrive at this position?

Arnold Toynbee in his 12 volume "Study of history" concluded after surveying civilizations across history that, "self worship was the paramount religion of mankind," even though it had many numerous and diverse guises.[4] From earliest history man has exulted man to deity, and practiced open idolatry without any attempt at concealment or subtlety. From ancient Assyrian to the Greek philosopher Protagoras (481-420 BC) who declared, "Man the measure of all things". Schlossberg tells us that Italian Renaissance Humanism gave a secular face to high Renaissance culture (15th and 16th century) but did not break with their Christian past. It wasn't until the 17th century that English Deism broke openly with the Christian faith. The 19th century theorist August Conte's introduction of idolatry on the campus it turns out would become the theoretical deification of the human race. Humanism most solid footing as a religion began with August Comte. The major assumptions of sociology and social science were given by him .....one who advocated the worship of the "Great Being", defined as humanity past, present, and future. His four volume set "Instituting the Religion of Humanity" (1851-4) gives us a clue. In 1848 he founded the "Positivist Society" and modeled it after the "Club of the Jacobins", the infamous group of the French revolution. Early on he was a student and secretary of Saint-Simon where he wrote, "Science transformed into philosophy and 'The System' was transformed into religion". In 1852 he wrote the "Catechism of Positive Religion" and in 1855 functioning as the "high priest of humanity" sent an emissary to the Jesuits and Rome proposing an alliance with Ignatius. In his work "The System" he wrote that his goal was to destroy the people and monarchy authority of divine right and reorganize life irrespective of God and king.[5]

He elevated human history to the divine in which his (Comte's) religious calendar suggested the worship of intellectual people he named. He claimed that as religion weakened, he would replace it with the theology of "social physics", his name for Sociology. He died in 1857 before he could write and publish the text he had announced 35 years earlier on "Treatise on Universal Education". In all cases he gave the "learned" the authority and power he called "Spirit". By equating "Complete Positivism" with the continuing dominance of the heart (his definition of love) he claimed to "act from affection" and by elevating human feelings to the divine.....making humanity a deity by describing to man the attributes of God. ie. sovereignty, autonomy, complete rationality, and moral perfection. Strangely, almost like one who soon follows him (Charles Darwin), he claimed man is improving more and more onto a future "Unity". Which is the opposite of the "devolution" seen in mankind's "slouching toward Gomorrah" today. So we see the father of humanist sociology instituting the religion of humanity with sacraments, sacred calendar, priesthood, prayers, and a social system of "Positivist Societies". The religion of humanities "positivist" calendar of 1848 replaced the titles of saints with those he thought had advanced civilization (i.e. Guttenberg and Shakespeare). His catechism was positivism. At his death there was a ceremonial gathering of English and French to commemorate the one who had established their religion.[6] Few social studies or sociology teachers will reveal the idolatry rampant in their discipline. A discipline that Comte claimed was a "Science above all of the sciences". No doubt because he sought to make it a god or the study of humanity as god.

Hess and Comte on history and Europe

The similarity of the thought of the theologians of Marxism and the father of sociology are quite remarkable. The biography in the 1911 Encyclopedia Britannica describes him as one with, "Exaggerated egoism, and the absence of all feeling for reality, which marked is latter days". They both worshipped the idol they called "Spinoza's god". Hess in his "Holy History of Mankind" considered the first work of socialism in Europe, laid the groundwork for the NAZI party (the National Socialist Party) and the Marxists attack on private property by the "Re-established unity of spirit and matter" enunciated by Spinoza. If this is a pantheist idol than it is understood? What was Spinoza's god is somewhat debatable and surrounded with controversy. Some say Spinoza as a rationalist was committed to a form of a universal idealism by placing consciousness as identical with objectivity which is so abstract as to be biting. I read and suspect Spinoza's god was only in his mind and remains buried with the other zillion idols in the dustbins of history. Erasmus Darwin wrote a poem on "The origin of Society", a Poem with philosophical Notes in 1803. Darwin and Wallace read Malthus "Essay on Population" and were inspired by it. The interaction of these thought processes seem highly likely.

Those that glorify or make divine man's history, worshipping in Comte's "Religion of Humanity" have divined from somewhere that all that happens was imbedded in what has happened without an effort or control from Creator–God outside of both time and history. Of course Creator–God interacts with his creation and has well documented both who He is and what He has done, is doing, and will do. He tells us we will know He wrote the existing 5 billion documents called "The Bible" by the fact that He, "tells us what will happen before it happens". [Isaiah 48:5, John 13:19] For more is written of the prophecies of the bible than any futurist work. You will find the accuracy and truth of these ancient writings is very well documented. I will mention some of these in chapter seven.

While I dearly love Hess's writing on the future of Zion, his projection for the future of Europe is much like Comte's. He interpreted the French Revolution as the road to "social unity" and saw the communist commonwealth somehow springing out of the disappearance of private property at the same time as he proposed that the Jewish princes like the Rothschild's and Montefiore, Albert Cohen, Fould, and others organize a "Society for the Colonization of Palestine" in 1862.[7] Hess is not easy to describe in a few sentences. He is a brilliant writer that succumbed to the utopia of socialism just as Comte and his close friend Ernst Ranan. Calling the beginning of what he called the "Messianic era" starting with Spinoza's god (who seem to capture many minds) and culminating with the French revolution. Somehow the great divide was cemented between two of Gemaliel's students, Judah Ben Zachai and Saul of Tarsus when the former joined with Gemaliel's son setting up synagogue worship after the destruction of the temple and 70 AD and the latter writing a large part of the New Testament as the apostle Paul. This divide is in part because the Jew is blinded in part. And that he will be made whole again with the second coming of Messiah and will indeed rule and reign with Him during the Millennium at the end of the coming seven years of tribulation and the battle of Armageddon.[Revelation 16,20 and Romans 11:25]

Lets trace the history of early self-worship to today's "modernity – humanism" and long development of today's fundamentalist humanist. Nimrod and his tower of Babel declared his independence from Creator-God. I repeat Herbert Schlossberg in his seminal work "Idols for Destruction" follows the noted historian Arnold Toynbee's conclusion that "self worship" was a paramount religion of mankind. Not long after Nimrod we're read a Stella of the king of a Syria who was declaring himself and his powers as manifesting:

"I am regal, I am a lordly, I am exalted, I am mighty, I am honored, I am glorified, I am preeminent, I am powerful, I am valiant, I am lion brave, I am heroic. I, Assur –Nasir – Pal... Chosen of Sin, favorite of Anu, beloved of Adad, mighty one among the gods. I am the merciless weapon that strikes down the land of his enemies."[8]

Isn't t this king so full of himself that he considers himself like a god? His people were famously brutal. Do you think he considers himself the law-giver? Or do you see him as inclined to bow to a righteous judge. How much of this self-worship bled into the classical literature of renaissance human-ism which produced students that couldn't help but contain the "pagan assumptions" imbedded in the classical humanist literature.

Historicism

Recall that Hegel was what I see as the philosophical generator for many of the academic historians. He taught that history was seamless and that all that happened is contained in what happened before. This makes "the his-tory" an idol. It excludes interventions from Creator–God, failing to recog-nize Him. In fact history is an artifact of His Creation and not something to be divinized after the fashion of Hegel and most humanistic writers. History is important but "not all important".[9]

> Schlossberg gives an excellent description of the,"... Biblical view
> of history that had a beginning and will have an end, and that
> both beginning and end are in Creator-God's hands. Therefore,
> what comes between them is invested with meaning and purpose;
> the Creator is not the prime mover of ancient philosophy, and the
> Terminator is not the bleak exhaustion of resources or the running
> down of the sun. Will and personality dominate everything and
> make history a moral arena. This conception takes lordship out of
> history, recognizes God as Creator, Sustainer, and LORD of the
> Universe.... (history) is no longer to be idolized".[10]

The poor student that feels he must read the humanist historian to find some sense of what will be his place in history is given nothing to trust or have faith that his future has any personal meaning. What have these bankrupt writers and professors have for them.....nihilism, solace in suicide or what?

"Ressentiment" and Nietzsche

Schlossberg describes a special term from Nietzsche's celebrated attack on Christianity, "res sentiment" was and continues to be used by sociologists to describe in much stronger terms than simple resentment. It describes both the "perceived injury that may have a basis in fact, but more often is it occasioned by plane envy of another person or their property" (the 10th commandment). "...it's that perception is not either to sublimate and or assuaged by doing some injury to the object of the feeling, the result is a persistent mental condition, stemming from the repression of emotions that are not acceptable when openly expressed. The result is **hatred** and the impulse to spite and to say things that detract from the others worth."[11] Schlossberg continues, "One of the most common elements to be repressed is "Schadenfreude", the rejoicing in another person's misfortune", vengeance.... This res sentiment has much to do with so called 'senseless action'."[12] Res-sentiment values its own welfare less than it does the debasement or harm of its object. Many crimes of vandalism, brutality, bullying, and murder might be explained this way... "A" is affirmed, valued, and praised not for its own intrinsic quality, but with the on verbalized intention of denying, devaluing, and denigrating "B". "A" is played off against "B". Therefore what appears to be a positive affirmation of the worth of others are really disguised attacks on still others.... Altruism glories in the praise of the weak and base, even at their expense, if that will also debase the strong and the good! [13]

Scheler sees the "altruistic" urge as a form of hatred, of self-hatred, posing as its opposite (love) in the faults perspective of consciousness. In this same way, in res sentiment morality, love for the 'small', the 'poor', 'the weak' and the 'oppressed' is really disguised hatred, repressed envy; an impulse to detract.... Directed against the opposite phenomenon: wealth, 'strength', ' power', 'largess'."

When hatred does not dare to come out into the open it can be easily expressed in the form of ostensible love-love... Love for something which has features that are opposite of those of the hated object. This can happen in such a way that the hatred remains secret.[14] Remember Jesus Christ taught us that anger without a cause or hatred of a man or untruthfully denigrating his reputation is in danger of judgment.[See: scripture Matthew 5:22, Exodus 28:13].

As I mentioned before, altruism is clearly seen as a, "counterfeit of Christian love, informed by the ideology of humanism and powered by res sentiment. It permeates demeaning the successful, or those who display in the form of superiority, by pulling over the act the mask of concern for the poor and weak."[15] Schlossberg noted that in Nietzsche's time the church was so infused with humanism that Nietzsche confused Christian love for its imitator. He continues quoting Scheler that Christian love does not help the week, sick, and helpless because it values those attributes but because of concern for the person who lies behind them. And because the bible clearly instructs us to show concern and caring for them, the general welfare of humanity is not a point of Christian love. The individual is the point of Christian love, each and every person. The Christian would expand his resources to help support the needy as opposed to seek to utilize other's resources to accomplish that goal. It is certainly not feeling and empathy but " action and movement". Remember it was Judas who criticized Mary when she anointed Jesus with precious ointments out of the false concern for the poor because it was worth "300 denari" and could've been sold and given to the poor. But we learn that Judas kept the money box and stole what was put in it. [John 12: 5-6] Note the close similarity between Judas and the person filled with Nietzsche's ressentiment-altruistic urge.

Attack of the Anti-Christs

The young student faces a devastating attack from three directions. I call these the attack of the antichrists. They all three represent a form of idolatry an assault on: 1. "The Way", 2."The Truth", and 3."The Life ".

1. Assault on "The Way"---the path

The way to eternal life is not of the flash or of the altar of a person but of the heart. Religion, religiosity, worship of self or any other idol, philosophy, or vain deceit to not lead us on a path of righteousness before our Creator-God. Jesus Christ tells us "He is the way, the truth, and the life... And no one comes to the father except by Him." [John 14:6] A child needs to gain understanding in things of the spirit.

2. *Attack on "The Truth"*

Students taught that there is no absolute truth will believe it if they haven't learned how to recognize the great "lie".... Relativism. The false teaching that nothing can be known, i.e. No "True Truth" as Dr. Francis Schaeffer called it, making all statements a matter of opinion or "true for me" and nothing more. Students are so vulnerable because as noted in Monroe's book "Finding God at Harvard", students feel safer as doubters than believers, and as perpetual seekers rather than eventual Finders". [16]

3. *Attack on "The Life"....dead in our sins against Creator-God.*

The 10 commandments are a schoolmaster for us to see the need for redemption. Adam and eve became dead to "eternal life" when they sought and got the "knowledge of good and evil" - - - -they could make up their own "values" citing for themselves what was good and walking away from what Creator–God taught as against Him. Without God's word, the idea that man has no common set of rules or laws that apply to all of us equally is a path to destruction and a life of meaninglessness and purpose....a list-lessness leading to nihilism and the thoughts of depression and suicide accompanied by enormous loneliness. Remember, we know we didn't create ourselves. Not good! That path to redemption....too life, is the only way out of the Morass.

Listen carefully to certain "redistribution" politicians or, as Schoeck points out, "...that 'equalitarians' are striving with greater urgency to whip up among poor people a keener sense of resentment against their neighbors."[17] It is evident to many that they are political tools and this act is despicable!

Equalitarianism - Egalitarianism

Schlossberg is right on the mark when he puts the problem and historical perspective with Nietzsche's "res sentiment" as the motive.

Class struggle or "leveling" (equalitarianism-egalitarianism) has a motive, that of lowering the upper class and raising the lower class tacitly referring to "birth and position"...so nobility and heredity of office were removed in the new America. Making a person's "qualities and efforts" responsible for their achievements.[18]

The Equalitarian doesn't like the result of the equality given us by our nation's founders. They, the organizers of humanity, believe they are made of finer clay then the rest of mankind. If these organizers have received from heaven and intelligence and virtue that place them beyond the nub of mankind; if so, let them show their titles to the superiority.[19] Interesting that president Obama's first executive order was to block inquiry into his personal records. These executive orders have the full force of law.[20]

The humanist delusion, that of believing he is some sort of god---a final moral arbiter by his sentiment of what is good and bad or, as Creator–God put it, "Knowledge of good and evil." The disobedient Eve acted out bringing death and ended a previously perfect world that had been "good". [Gen 2:9]. Schlossberg says it best:

"...if I succumbed to the humanist delusion, the ultimate egoism of believing that my own sentiments have the force of supreme law ..... that is if I succumbed to the serpents temptation by declaring myself a god who determines good and evil .....I can do anything at all with confidence in its legitimacy. The supreme

law giver ..... I myself has ruled. With all the confidence of being
on the side of supreme god, I can go on a blood rampage as
Assur-Nasir-Pal did, and exalt in my divine attributes." [21]

Man's Perfectibility? Perfect before Creator - God?
One of the hallmarks of the Humanist University is driven by a vision
of "man's perfectibility". We saw it with a driving but insane term
Evolution - - -"things are getting better and better" - - -man is evolving.
Once you fall for man's "perfectibility" you tend to fall away from the
real truth of history, that man is a sinner. That means you have chosen a
lie and walked away from the Bible, see no need for a saving messiah and
therefore no need for Christ. For if you decide there is no hell then what
did Creator–God do when he became a man and died on the cross for
you... You walk away from it all. Humanism is Satan's perfect ploy, buy
it and your future will end in the most horrible surprise known to man!

Another path from Hagel that alters American Thinking
Adrian Rogers describes 5 key men that have shaped and modified humanism in America. Starting with (1) Hegel in 1820's, while he claims a belief,
declares there are "no moral absolutes. His reasoned argument or dialectic
is that all history is made up of thesis, antithesis, and synthesis. So with an
idea as a thesis verses it's opposing idea comes a synthesis that becomes the
new thesis. This new thesis is the new accepted model for "truth". So for
philosophical and social evolution there is no fixed standard of right and
wrong. Today, if you ask most High School or college students you would
get this reply, "What is right for you might not be right for me!" The classical answer for a believer in "relative truth. Hegel believed the strongest
idea wins, following a position that history is evolutionary. Next comes (2)
Feuerbach (1830's) who built on Hegel's thought of 'no absolutes' that there
can be no God...who would be the source of absolute truths. Feuerbach
decided that man is not in the image of God but God is in the image of man.

Since moral flux causes a deep insecurity in the mind of man, "Christianity has in fact long vanished, not only from reason but from the life of mankind, it is nothing more than a fixed idea" (fixed ideas don't survive the Hegelian system). This is a clear definition of **Humanism**. Fuerbach is the transition to his great admirer, (3) Karl Marx, who subsequently build on Hagel and Fuerbach by asking, "If there are no absolutes and no God, then what is the future and purpose of mankind? Where are we going? Marx's answer was his "Communist Manifesto" where the new term Dialectical Materialism is invented to make it appear more of a philosophical treatise rather than the religious leaning work it was. Marx laid out the dialectic as:

Thesis: Capitalism, the right to own property and the right to be productive for yourself was wrong. VS.

Antithesis: The desire for equality and fairness in the hearts and minds of the working people.

Synthesis: Socialism and Communism. A Godless, unspeakable, immoral system because it does not recognize the worth of the individual. Marx decided that we must have revolution, no matter the suffering. There must be violent change. "We must be like a foreign body within the existing system that will accelerate its death". (know of anything that is accelerating America's death today?)

Millions and millions were put to death under godless communism...40-50 million executed so far, so that a Humanist-godless utopia can be brought in. Observe the Venezuela of 2016, the destruction and misery brought by socialism/communism. "The suffering and sacrifice of violent changes constitutes the price that man has to pay to have any essential progress at all. (we will get 'better and better' as Darwin demands). Rogers points out that Communism is dying in Cuba and other countries like Red China but has the most life in the Universities of America today! The next of the 5 men was (4) Charles Darwin (1859 Origin of Species,1871 Descent of Man) who tries to tell us, If no god, then how did we get here? Evolution can be considered a philosophy, "The Philosophy of Evolution".......the next best guess for a mind that cannot accept Devine Creation. Darwin declares, "We ourselves are the product of mere chance"...we cannot escape the evolving web. One of Darwin's philosophers later noted, "The mystery of the universe is explained, the Deity is annulled and a new era of infinite knowledge is ushered in."[22] The final ghost from the past responsible for humanism is Sigmund Freud (1856-1939) who moved humanism into the 20th century. Since Feuerbach said we create the idea of god, Freud said our idea of God comes from our childhood father when we were children. (you must remember most of Freud's theories come out of his own most unusual life). He decided that mankind's is motivated chiefly by pleasure (sexual pleasure) and eroticism..everything begins and ends with sex. If people are not allowed to fulfill their sexual and erotic desires then they get a neuroses. (creates a society of extreme permissiveness with sex outside of marriage...if you hold the children back, they will be frustrated!

Then in 1929, a man arrived on the scene of Europe that was a student of Hegel, Fuerbach, and Marx....Adolph Hitler; who decided he had a better idea than Marx. "No more that nature desires the mating of the weaker with the stronger, even less does she desire the blending of higher with a lower race. Since, if she did, her whole work of higher breading or perhaps hundreds of thousands of years might be ruined with one blow". "All great cultures of the past perished all because the original creative races died from blood poisoning (intermarriage)..... The man who created the culture must be preserved. Preservation is bound up with the rigid law of necessity, the right to victory of the best and the strongest in the world. Those who want to live, let them fight and those who do not want to fight in this eternal struggle do not <u>deserve</u> to live. This is how it is!²³ Hitler's argument for the extermination of the Jews was.....he reclassified them as "non-persons". Today, thanks to the thinking of humanism in America we have reclassified the fetus as a non-person. Instead of 6 million gassed we have 55 million non-persons eliminated. The modern word for liberals is "Choice". "Choice" is what one does in his own personal gas chamber and that is his own business. We should remember that the applicable logic in a era of 'survival of the fittest' is Old People Die. Today we have, "sewn the wind and we are reaping the whirlwind"(Adrian Rogers).

The greatest problem for the 5 creators of "Humanism", is they do not have the truth. Dr Rogers would have the pulpits of America filled with those that would teach "Thus saith the LORD".

Ontological victimhood: destructive misdirection

Have you noticed your professors and teachers describing populations of victims? "Victimhood" is a characteristic of all members of a humanitarian society worshipping humanitarian idols of the exalted week, sick, helpless, and anguished as well as the strong and prosperous. They make all into victims.

"Denying the possibility of strength for the week keeps them week. Being freed from dependence would bring the victim back into the human family, responsible for himself and others.

How much better to remain a victim, shielded from trouble and responsibility by altruism."[24]

Note the people paying the tab for all this due to a "false guilt" cannot be happy.

Ressentiment elicits a counter ressentiment and so accentuates the self-righteous hypocrisies of both rich and poor and drags the whole of society into the strife that can drive it down in a cycle of destruction, the opposite of any uplifting stratagem that would make us more innovative and productive - - -"The ubiquitous fear of envy destroys economic incentive, for anyone who receives what his neighbors do not have makes himself vulnerable".[25] What a way to destroy the economy of a nation!

Listen to the hatred of George Bernard Shaw for the poor to identify with the humanist idolatry. He said anyone who cannot justify their existence should be killed. Shaw, the idol–god statesmen pouring out hatred and scorn on humans after seeming to elevate humans as gods. What chaos! The intellectual, the professor, the teacher, that has no fear of Creator–God realizes that people are like machines and need to be programmed and they with their government help can be the programmers. If, as they have accomplished a cultural morality based on "individual sentiment" must guard against the logical outcome... Anarchy and the disintegration of society.[26] Humanists argument for powerful central government may seem convincing. But the chaos of a society with no Creator–God's 'handed-down – law' but only 'sentiment values' of each individual is what we're getting. They have worked so hard to convince us that "man is a grownup worm", Darwinian Materialism of the biologist...... Leading to its enslavement of us all. Moral principles hang in midair today allowing half of America to agree to the murder of our children and the destruction of the family under the guise of silly terms "reproductive freedom" and "sexual freedom". Terms so freely used in 1939 Germany's cabarets. The elite will then dominate, especially if a crisis reigns. As Schlossberg says, "...the theology that divinizes man, it turns out, only divinizes some men. The objects of humanitarian concern (poor, needy, etc.) Become less than men, so that the humanitarian can't execute the prerogatives of a god, the god that will fail." [27]

The Orginal Source is" non-reason"

Ravi Zacharias quotes C.S. Lewis in <u>Miracles</u> "Reason might conceivably be found to depend on [another reason] and so on; it would not matter how far this process was carried provided you found reason coming from reason at each stage. It is only when you are asked to believe in reason coming from non-reason that you must cry halt!"[28] The worshippers of man identify their law with man an attribute power in goodness with man and from man. As Frederic Bastiat has noted, "If we are free, does it not follow that we shall no longer recognize the power and goodness of god? Does it follow that we shall than cease to associate with each other, to help each other, to love and succor our unfortunate brothers, to study the secrets of nature, and to strive to improve ourselves to the best of our abilities?" [29] Or will you adopt the idols of your humanist teacher and become so self-absorbed with a false sense of the false power he infuses along with the nihilism and emptiness of final purpose as he teaches you to turn from Creator-God.

Part 2. You are Being Indoctrinated

Secular Humanism is a Religion, the one promoted by government schools. Is it the religion of the state?

This is the religion taught in certain churches, and promoted by many faculty and teachers at all levels of education, and by certain government administrations." It is a non-neutral perspective, complete with a philosophical view of ultimate reality (metaphysical naturalism) and a set of normative ethical ideals. In short, it is a distinct and particular worldview. It is not derived in some generic way from microscopes and telescopes. Rather, it is firmly grounded in philosophical naturalism, non-theism, evolutionary theory, ethical relativism, and political globalism. In addition, it has clergy members, social ceremonies, and a developing symbolism."(see: in definition, "Religion").[30]

"Education is the most powerful ally of Humanism, and every American public school is a school of Humanism. What can the theistic Sunday Schools, meeting for an hour once a week, and teaching only a fraction of the children, do to stem the tide of a five-day program of humanistic teaching?" [31] This was a vision of a Humanist Unitarian Minister for America's schools. It's a stealthy way to do the work of Creator-God's enemies.....and attempt the takeover of the United States by imbedding itself in government schools while hiding from the courts and the constitution. A high level of deception only Satan himself could contrive.

It's as if the founders of the Fundamentalist Secular Humanism we see in today's classrooms and on the ubiquitous teaching screens of Secular Media looked at the Bible, and especially Jesus Christ, and failed to see that

He called himself God many times (the "I AM, or *ego Eimi*) and decided he was a product of his local culture and that was it. Failing to grasp the truth of the Word of Creator-God, they cleverly sought to amalgamate the weak so-called science of evolution and sociology/ anthropology/ social science and appear to elevate man as the law-giver over Creator-God. A false sense of freedom from a Creator-God who will ultimately hold us accountable for what we have done with our lives. Not far removed from the worship of the pagan god Atlas, who lifted Heaven away from man "a far off" so as to rest man's conscious sense of guilt. Allowing its religious followers a footing firmly seated in mid-air.....quite close to the lie Satan told Eve, as he misquoted Creator-God in Genesis 3. It's a masterful invention, dwelling on all that is difficult to grasp in Christianity, creating a music like the pied piper and leading our children in "Slouching toward Gomorrah". Fundamentalism for the ones that consider themselves wise in their own conceit....something viewed by Creator-God 2500 years ago, so it is not new. If you follow what I have written about Nimrod thousands of years ago you will also see the same kind of sales pitch for power and control with the same sort of Idolatry. You have to see yourself as the final moral standard to follow them....creating yourself as an idol. It might feel good until you come before your Creator-God, then not so much.

Moral Relativism

Why doesn't it work for mankind to decide what is good and what is evil. Ravi Zacharias noted:

> "...eating the fruit from the tree of the knowledge of good and evil basically gave humanity the power to redefine everything. God had given language, identification, and reality to humankind. He imparted to humans the power to name the animals. But essential to the created order was a moral framework that the creation was not to name or define. This was the prerogative of the Creator-God, not of the creation. I believe that this is what is at stake here."
> "Does mankind have a right to defined what is good and what is

evil? Have you ever heard this refrain in culture after culture: 'what right does any culture have to dictate to another culture what is good?' Imbedded in that charge is always an another charge:' The evil things that have happened in your culture deny you the providence to dictate to anyone else.

'.......I recall that Malcom Muggeridge once said that human depravity is at once the most empirically verifiable fact yet the most staunchly resisted datum by our intellectuals. For them, H2O as the formula for water is indisputable; but in ethics, man is still the measure—without stating which man. This is the fundamental difference between a transcendent worldview and a humanistic one. But the question arises as to what makes the Christian framework unique. Here we see the second cardinal difference between the Judeo-Christian framework and the others. It is simple this: no amount of moral capacity can get us back into a right relationship with God....our fundamental problem is not moral; rather, our fundamental problem is spiritual.

...Jesus does not offer to make bad people good but to make dead people alive.

....In the Hebrew-Christian tradition, the law unifies people. No one is made righteous before God by keeping the law (the Ten Commandments). It is only following redemption that we can truly understand the moral law for what it is--- a mirror that indicts and calls the heart to seek God's help. (this also helps removes the proud haughty spirit we once had). This makes moral reasoning the fruit of spiritual understanding and not the cause of it. ....Any life that does not see its need for redemption will not understand the truth about morality."[32]

The Empty Cry "Nobody knows the answer"

Why would humanist—atheist faculty who live a life of utter hopelessness and purposelessness and despair seek to put this bankruptcy upon their students? Is it they think they are the new breed of spiritual icons, a glass full of altruism and enlightenment. Are they the ones who will make men good with their new ideas .....control man's evolution with the power of their mouth? On to a better world and a better man? What does science and history really point to that can be trusted? Has humanist religion made any one a better person in anything other than their own delusional eyes?... Those that see themselves as a god.

Wake up students, follow their nihilism into oblivion at your peril!

"..In the pride of his face the wicked does not see Him; all his thoughts are' there is no god' [Psalm 10:4 ESV]

"The fool says in his heart there is no God." [Psalm 14:1]

False Presuppositions

((**Speciationists (evolutionists)** unsubstantiated conjecture about the past.)

The Reprobate mind generates self-defining instruments defining good and evil.[Ravi Zacheriah]

A good example of cognitive idolatry being taught today: Physicists and Professor Emeritus Victor J. Stenger in his book "Has Science Found God: the latest results in the search for purpose in the universe", describes his idol as follows (p188):

> "We have seen that zero external energy was required to produce the mass and energy of our universe. We have seen that order can spontaneously arise from disorder. We have seen the complexity can evolve from simplicity. We have seen that time has no fundamental arrow, and so the very concepts of cosmic beginnings and causal creation are problematical. No known scientific principles are necessarily violated in a model of our universe that is causally self contained, in which everything that happens, happens within."[33]

He appears quite proud before a Creator-God, Stenger has the argument that answers the Word of God, teaching that these trite series of "we have seen" describes reality. Notice the cleaver use of the word "problematical".

He rests with the statement that cosmic beginnings are difficult to solve. That means he provides no answer whatsoever to the student searching for purpose in the Universe (within the title of his book). Claiming there is no purpose or direction to the universe. He discusses Chaos theory without describing that it as one of the control system designs where the outcome is very sensitive to initial conditions…meaning that the outcome from a chaotic event would only be understood by the One outside of time…. Creator-God. So it is not at all without direction….just not under Stenger and other Humanist understanding. Once you believe "the Lie" that there is no Creator-God, you can indeed arrive at Stenger's Idol.

Stenger has built his world view on presuppositions from a humanist worldview probably taught to him as he ran away from Creator-God….His morality is invented and driven by himself, his philosophy, and his narrow view of reality. That the physics of materialism is all there is and a possible physics of non-materialism is irrelevant to him. He is probably a faculty who would have supported the renaming of the Theology Department to the "Religion" department for the purpose of demoting it to some kind of social science-like status.

Part 3. Evolution and Society

Evolution: A deceptive word that contains a big lie combined with truth The word Evolution is a Humanist Construct
What does the word evolution mean, and how deceptive is it? It's even self-deceptive if you make false premises or assumptions.

> "Men Occasionally stumble over the truth, but most of them pick themselves up and hurry off as if nothing had happened" [Winston Churchill]

THE <u>ONLY</u> <u>Absolute</u> BARRIER TO THE TRUTH IS THE PRESUMPTION THAT YOU ALLREADY HAVE IT!![34]
If you start out with A <u>false</u> presupposition, there are an INFINITE (∞) number of FALSE conjectures that can explain the spaces in the datum. These probably only describe our ignorance to describe reality! In contrast there is only one conjecture that describes TRUTH. I repeat. There is only one conjecture that describes TRUTH![35]

8. **Evolution**- an unstable theory or better an unsubstantiated conjecture about the past treated incorrectly as a theory of everything best characterized as containing 2 hidden terms; 1) Genetic Adaptation- which best fits the data as slow changes over time within species. and 2) Speciation (or phylum generation)...the creation of all species from one species after the spontaneous generation of life from dead

matter, requiring the contradiction that: The organizing power that created the amazing life around us was "random forces" doing the selecting. Hiding all in the term "natural" as if that clarified it all.

9. **Natural Selection**- Implying a "selector" as a deception designed to replace the creationists "Divine Watchmaker" with what is supposed to be an impersonal force like a ghost that is an external agency of some type that disintegrates under scrutiny...unless Darwin gave "selection" omnipotent power embarrassing evolutionists in the process.

Many evolutionists claim a false correlation between the act of selection by breeding and Darwin's phantom selector-----Darwin's hocus-pocus. Who is this mysterious mover making new life:

RANDOM = INFORMATION

Look carefully at his equation......note that it is a contradiction
...... that cannot be understood by anybody; and is found as the basis of many belief systems or religions invented by humans since the time of Nimrod in Babylon. (Random by definition does not contain any information)

Evidence for Speciation
Surprisingly, there is no agreed upon evidence for speciation! In spite of the fact that we have a extensive **fossil database**. Millions of fossils have been collected and fill our museums. There is agreement that all life forms appeared suddenly fully formed. Many call it the Cambrian explosion. There are NO, NO agreed upon transitional species. You would think the embarrassment of this and the finding of soft vascular tissue in dinosaur bones; impossible if the "millions of years" claim were true![36] [March 25 Science, 2005 report: "Tyrannosaurus Rex fossil yields flexible tissue" Mary H. Schweitzer et al] Next we look at the all important

"Rate of Beneficial Mutations" or the frequency of beneficial mutations without which there could never be a created "new" species.....the soft underbelly of evolution. If that database is empty, your professors face should be very red as he lies to you, although I must say the physiology of blushing according to Born Folkow, is not understood either. There is high quality free software written by an eminent Astrophysicist and a Geneticist to test as many generations as you want to test (depending on the number of computer processors you have) called "Mendel's Accountant: a numerical analysis program". It allows most all parameters involved in the analysis of "speciation" but it does ask for the frequency of mutations among other key input data.[37] If you read the beneficial mutation rate literature, you will be shocked to find most all the literature where actual data are gathered (over the past 20 years) does not speak of "speciation" nor do they demonstrate anything of the kind. In fact if you look at even very recent papers such as Silander et al. 2007 Plos Biol 5:922-931 available free on line you will find mostly the language of genetic adaptation not speciation, because once a constant environment is achieved, genetic changes "plateau", certainly not favoring the movement to new species.[38] How many "new" species of "adapted animals are found today? Is the rate of deleterious mutations/beneficial mutations a positive number. You can imagine all kinds of extreme environments, and they do, but the supposed data under stress is non-existent except in bacteria and virus which, find poor agreement in species classification in the first place. Silander et al 2007 using a DNA bacteriophage (ThetaX174) were unable to find any beneficial mutations in the "high-fitness" phages but only in "low fitness" phages could beneficial mutations be "inferred". In fact the "Beneficial Mutation Rate" papers should jump out at you from Google Scholar but we find such work indicating "reverse evolution in fly's" where much evolution lab work proceeds.[39] Fly's do well in evolution labs it seems. A more productive term for analysis is "Mutation Extinction". Which is very much supported in the literature. Is the weeding out of the "un fit" all that Darwin has added to science. If mutation rates increase significantly, many populations cease to exist quickly. The fact that a random error in the genome would be permanent and would lead to a beneficial "fitness" and also be inheritable by the following generation...by the making of previously non-existing proteins, that would be acceptable to the nuclear pore, that controls all that goes in and out of the nucleus in cellular animals leading to a new trait is certainly a wonder because it is not probable except in the case of genetic adaptation where such potential resides in the genome in the first place. If these data clearly show "speciation"...the creation of entirely new species by this process then Darwinian Evolution is proven, but I am afraid evolutionists are unsuccessful at showing us such data. They know that this data is highly unlikely. If they assume the circular argument that man descended from the monkey, or is it "ascended". Looking at observed/expected values to determine the beneficial direction of movement for the creation of a new species is just not correct. As usual the "beneficial" judge is the evolutionist with the preconceived idea of what is "beneficial" . Almost like the "sentiment" basis for moral decisions just don't cut it either. Nevertheless, for all these "beneficial" random mutations to add up to new proteins and then a new species will take an enormous period of time. Lets look at this idea of enormous periods of time.

Darwin's geologist, Charles Lyell (Darwin considered himself a geologist too) knew his work needed a "lot of time". Could he explain the sea shells on the top of Mt. Everest and all he found in the rocks? Lyell travelled to Niagara Falls to study the rate of recession of the falls in 1867. He was told by the local inhabitants that the falls ate into the rock formations at the rate of about 3 feet/year. Lyell thought that a conservative number for his book would be 1 foot/year which would be his best guess and just happened to fit the 35,000 feet of the 7 mile gorge as lake Erie drops into lake Ontario-----which he extrapolated to 35,000 years apparently to fit his belief in the doctrine of Uniformitarianism which Darwin considered a mainstay of his theory as well, slow steady changes in the earth. Travel in 1979 published 4 to 5 feet/year as the more accurate measure. From 1842-1905 published Horseshoe Falls erosion rates actually made, gave from 1.05 SD .47 Meters/year to 1.24 SD .53 Meters/year as our best measurements. Today much water is diverted by hydroelectric power so erosion is back to < 1 ft/year or less. Anyway Lyell was considerably off with his estimate of 1 foot. Assuming the large glacier melt much earlier would produce even faster erosion 35,000 years is absurd. Considering man's written history is about 5,000 years and the definitive answer for man existence on this earth, the radio dating of cave paint by "cave man", still without convincing data of eons. We find no definitive data that the questionable processes needed for Darwinian speciation have the time they would need for random production of all the species we find. What the observations show so far is that all the major life forms appear suddenly and that many species are disappearing fairly rapidly.

I don't know the date the earth was created....the Bible doesn't tell us at all. We are told it was setup for our habitation about 6 to 10,000 years ago, with all the things man needs for life, all the foods and environmental needs. It appears a lot of catastrophic events have occurred here, and they are in the geologic record. I'm not sure how long it has been since the earth was formed, that is a number Creator-God is keeping from us for some reason, He knows why. Devolution or negative evolution seems to be occurring in which many species are losing in their fitness. There is no evidence that mankind is not losing some of his smarts either. Notice how few Newton's and Einstein's are appearing. It now seems it takes a group not an individual to see new things that others have not seen. If as some speculate, we have 200 errors/generation in the Human genome one can wonder how long the devolution will continue. It is obvious to a Christian that our Creator-God would not allow things to continue that long...the point where we could no longer comprehend Him with our water-based brain. If you want to read about beginnings start with John 1:1 "In the beginning was the Word..". The book of Genesis is a wonderful book but is burdened by a million attacks and distortions as well as total misunderstandings requiring great study all the way to the index of the entire work in the book of Revelation to get the big picture. Consider He is speaking or "breathing" His words through people of his creation from outside of time, it makes sense that the time and dates would be hard for us to deal with. We see everything as with a Beginning, middle and end. That is the way all things appear to us. It seems as if Creator-God wanted us to have his detailed Word that is so multidimensional and complete as to require a lifetime of study to grasp what

He has written. But many questions remain unanswered….so many that the answers could take an eternity to learn. Something to look forward to.

The Evolutionists present the Chimpanzee as our closest living relative. Just what does that do for us?

Warning: America is Composed of Religious Political groups and hundreds of hate groups

"Cultural fault lines are being drawn, and rather than being a melting pot nation, the United States is composed of religious and political groups, plus hundreds of hate groups,"[40] The study was based on a three-day workshop by its Center for Strategic Leadership which deals with issues using the project team concept. The study, entitled "In the Dark: Military Planning for a Catastrophic Critical Infrastructure Event," concluded that there in fact is "very little" in the way of back-up capability to the electric grid upon which the communications infrastructure is vitally dependent.

Our Nation is in trouble. How has the Humanist contributed to the dissolution of the bonds among American Citizens?

Endless variations of this theme can be cited. Basic to all these "funny money" concepts were two essentially religious premises.[following is after Rousas, John Rushdoony, in *"Gold is Money"* by Hans F. Steinholdz, p177]

First, man was seen as a creator, replacing Creator-God. Man's declaration of independence from Creator-God means the supplanting of Creator-God by man. This is how the bible presents original sin, the desire of every man to be his own god, "knowing or determining good and evil in terms of himself (Genesis 3:5). Just as God created heaven and earth out of nothing, so man creates values out of nothing. In Christian theology, values are what God declares them to be. In humanism, values are what man declares them to be. If man or the state declares that *fiat* money has value it therefore has value. The application of the word *fiat* to money is theologically significant. It is Latin for "Let it be done."

The *fiat* power of god has been transferred to man and applied to money. Man is now the creative force of the world, and it is man's word and will that governs reality in fact makes reality and establishes value. The position of Hagel, "the rational is the real," means that what man's autonomous reason establishes is thus the new reality, or the reality in process of becoming. For Marx, this meant that man now recreates the world in terms of his rationality, because no other reality has any meaning. In his *Thesis on Feuerbach*, Marx declared "The philosophers have only interpreted the world, in various ways; the point, however, is to **change** it." (emphasis mine) As Jerry Rubin made the point in 1960's declaring, "We create reality wherever we go by living our fantasies."[41] If the rationale is real, then the intellectual elite of statism can create *fiat* money in the assurance that their ideas must work if implemented with full force of rational planning. It is the natural consequences of modern religious humanism that men should, as his own ultimate god, issue fiat money, values, and laws. The logic of humanism requires it.

Second, the logical corollary of this is that man, as his own lawmaker now, is freed from past laws. As the new god of being, modern statist man is no longer bound by the word of the old God of scripture. Perhaps it is unfair or unkind to remind anyone that, a decade ago, when the hoarding of silver coins began, there were those who insisted that Gresham's law was no longer operative. That it did operate, some hold, was because too many men were still governed by reactionary concepts. Given sufficient re-education away from the ostensible myths of hard money, man, it is held, will no longer operate as though classical economics were true, or as though God ordained hard money in his law. Re-educated men, it is maintained, will be free from past laws and will be able to prosper under fiat money. The presupposition of this position is that there is no reality beyond the mind of man. It presupposes the economic Christian Science: the only reality is Mind, and what the elite planning mind decrees is ipso facto reality. However, no more than a universal belief in Christian Science would eliminate toothaches and broken bones will a belief in Christian Science Economics eliminate the consequences of fiat money...... "Fiat money is political money of the state."[42]

Why would someone believe that the Universe is not Created?

The big question is why would someone believe that the universe was not created? Who first laid out that proposition? The Bible does answer this if you read it carefully. Isaiah 14:12-15 and Ezekiel 28:11-19 are addressing it seems to the kings of Babylon and Tyre. But the wording indicates the words are addressed to the evil spirits that possessed the human kings. And this possession was by Lucifer himself. Henry Morris in his book "The Long War Against God" asks the correct question:

> How could Lucifer "...possibly think that he, as one of God's created beings, could ever manage to vanquish his Creator? He was 'full of wisdom,' so surely he was intelligent enough to realize he could not possibly defeat his Creator." But we are told that once God created him, Lucifer found himself on the face of the waters, so he could choose to accept God's explanation for his existence or pridefully choose the eternal watery chaos as his creator in error.
>
> *"Unless, that is, he did not believe that God really was his Creator!* After all, the only evidence he had was God's word, and he evidently chose not to believe what God had told him. There seems no other possible way to rationalize what seems otherwise to have been an incredible foolish decision on Satan's part.
>
> But if God had not created him, then who did? And who made God? What could Lucifer have been thinking?
>
> It would seem that the only possible alternate solution that Lucifer could imagine would be evolution[1]. Perhaps---just perhaps---both he and God had somehow evolved out of primeval chaos, with God just happening to precede him chronologically. If so, they were both really the same kind of being, as were the other angels. Therefore, a well-planned rebellion, just might be successful!
>
> This seems like an absurd proposition, but Lucifer was both proud and desperate and there was evidently no other possible way to account for their mutual existence. Anyway, how can it be so "absurd", when this is essentially what all anti-creationists have

always believed? The ancient pantheists believed that the gods created themselves out of the primeval chaos, and modern scientific
evolutionists believe that human beings have evolved out of the
chaos of the primeval big bang. So far as Lucifer new, all the angels
could have evolved along with himself and god, either slowly over
long ages or very rapidly. Since they were not able to observe the
process who could know?

Lucifer's first moment of awareness (and the same would apply
to all the angels) after God created him was one of waters all around
him. The angels were probably created on the first day of creation
week immediately after the creation of space\matter\time cosmos
itself. This is the implication of the remarkable statement in introduction to Psalm 104." [43]

Bless the lord, O' my soul. O Lord my God, thou are very great;
thou art clothed with honor and majesty. Who covered thyself with
light as with the garment; who stretches out the heavens like a curtain: Who layeth of the beams of his chambers in the waters: who
maketh the clouds his chariot: who walketh upon the waters of
the wind: Who maketh his angels spirits; his ministers a flaming
fire: Who laid the foundations of the earth, that it should not be
removed forever. [Psalm 104:1-5]

"There is an important twofold question remaining. Assuming
this analysis to be correct, as all evidence seems to suggest, Satan
and his principalities and powers of darkness have been actively
promoting anti-creationism behind the scenes all through the
ages. Depending on times and places and circumstances, this can
sometimes take the form of overt Satanism, for the ultimate goal of
Satan is to usurp the throne of God himself (e.g. Isa 14:12-14) and
win the obedient worship of all God's creatures. More commonly,
his anti-creationism takes the form of pantheism or humanism or
atheism, all of which dethrone God as Creator but do not immediately enthrone Satan as the high god he aspires to be. Certain
forms of applied pantheism eg. polytheism, animism, Idolatry, and

demonism) involve obedience to invisible spirits other than the true God and thus comes close to Satanism." [44]

Morris continues: "This explains the fact that not only the Sumerian cosmogony (the *Enuma Elish*), but also that of the Egyptians and most of the others that have been handed down by various tribes and nations, all began with an eternal watery chaos from which the gods eventually evolved by some unknown process. This was Lucifer's best guess as to his own origin, and so this is what he would have to use to persuade men to join with him in opposing the God of creation….if there is some better and more realistic way of accounting for Satan's long war with his Creator, we should be open to it, but something like the above is surely strongly implied.

This means, finally that the very first evolutionist was not Charles Darwin or Lucretius or Thales or Nimrod, but Satan himself! He has not only deceived the whole world with the monstrous lie of evolution but has deceived himself most of all. He still thinks (to this day) he can defeat God because, like modern "scientific" evolutionists, he refuses to believe that God is really God" [45] He chose to believe a lie, as do all those who reject the Creator.

Albert Einstein looked to the Universities:

"Being a lover of freedom, when the (Nazi) revolution came I looked to the universities to defend it, knowing that they had always boasted of their devotion to the cause of truth; but no, the universities took refuge in silence. Then I looked to the great editors of the newspapers whose flaming editorials in days gone by had proclaimed their love of freedom; but they, like the universities, were silenced in a few short weeks. I then addressed myself to the authors, to those who had passed themselves off as the intellectual guides of Germany and among whom was frequently discussed the question of freedom and its place in modern life. They are, in tern, very dumb. Only the Church stood squarely across the path of Hitler's campaign for suppressing the truth. I never had any special interest in the Church before, but now I feel a great affection and admiration for it because the Church alone has had the courage and persistence to stand for intellectual truth and moral freedom. I am forced to confess that what I once despised I now praise unreservedly" [46]

It turns out that the Universities were not silent but it seems embraced the German National Socialist Workers' Party (German: Deutsche Nationalsozialistische Arbeiterpartei, DNSAP) agenda and in many cases wrote the intellectual underpinnings Hitler needed to carry out his agenda. I do not believe Hitler would have been successful without great assistance from a great many Professors. This is very strange and was unexpected by the outside world. Those Scientists and Faculty who had met with these people at international conferences and interacted with them intellectually must have been amazed. What had taken place in the minds of Faculty to permit the adoption of the Unfit Jew mentality? Could it be the acceptance as fact of Darwin's theory of Evolution first published with an amazing title and subtitle *Origin of Species by Means of Natural Selection, or the Preservation of Favoured Races in the Struggle for Life;* with respect to certain "Favored" races. This appeared as planned by one desiring the destruction of the Jews long before the appearance of Hitler no doubt, an enemy of man from the start.

The word "Evolution" is a Humanist Construct
The eminent evolutionist Leigh Van Valen summed up a conundrum akin to that of natural selection:

Yes, fitness is the central concept of evolutionary biology, but it is an elusive concept. Almost everyone who looks at it seriously comes out in a different place. There are literally dozens of genuinely different definitions, which I won't review here. At least two people have called fitness indefinable, a biological primitive....Or is it that we can't define it because we do not fully understand it. [47]

"Darwin's application of mystical powers to natural selection was immediately spotted and severely ·criticized. Darwin and his followers have all been forced to concede that selection is a false term when applied to interactions at the organism-environment interface—but they always justify metaphorical usages. Selection was resisted for decades precisely because there was no empirical evidence for a selector—evidence that still remains non-existent."[48]

The illusion that natural selection operates on unconscious environmental features, like any other idol, but it induces people *not* to give the Lord credit for the Selection is idolatrous in the basest of ways. Not only does it ascribe intelligence-like powers; incredible intelligence and machinery He has built into His creatures that enable them to adapt to environmental features. The innate mystical problem of selection was addressed yet again by two distinguished atheists in 2010 in a book urging fellow evolutionists to end appeals to selection's omnipotent power and to consider new mechanisms:

Familiar claims to the contrary notwithstanding, Darwin didn't manage to get mental causes out of his account of how evolution works. He just hid them in the unexamined analogy between selection by breeding and natural selection...we can claim something Darwinists cannot. There is no ghost in our machine; neither God, nor Mother Nature...and there are no phantom breeders either. What breeds the ghosts in Darwinism is its covert appeal to intentional biological explanations....Darwin pointed the direction to a thoroughly naturalistic—indeed a thoroughly atheistic—theory of phenotype [trait] formation; but he didn't see how to get the whole way there. He killed off God, if you like, but Mother Nature and other pseudo-agents got away scot-free. We think it's now time to get rid of them too.[49]

Survival of the Fittest: Darwin's great legacy

In an interesting work by Weinrich, *Hitler's Professors* we see the following instructions to faculty, all teachers and the Universities:

"The law of Nature concerning 'the survival of the fittest' should be presented so as to admit no exceptions. The unfit is doomed to Ausmerze (extinction) and if he does not go voluntarily, he must be helped out of existence. This law of Nature would be, then made to apply to groups or, in more mystical terms, to races; and in the order of fitness the Jews would appear the lowest group predestined for Ausmerze, while the top folk of the Germans would emerge as the Crown of Creation." [50]

Consider the work of Emeritus Professor Phillip E. Johnson, Professor of law at Boalt School of Law at the University of California, Berkeley, where he served on the active faculty from 1967 to 2000. Johnson has served as deputy district attorney and has held visiting professorships at Emory University and at University College, London is a graduate of both Harvard University and the University of Chicago School of Law and served as clerk for U.S. Supreme Court Justice Earl Warren. With this incredible background in the law and reasoning in the law we find his writing on Evolution remarkable, logical, and devastating to the evolutionary scientist who claims he is teaching you science. Professor Johnson provides clarity in the bible when he teaches creation from the Gospel of John. "In the beginning was the Word, the word was with God, and that Word was God. He was with God in the beginning." [John 1:1]. He is a person, it is a Being with intelligence and purpose, a being who was with God and who was God. In this book he's called Creator–God to distinguish Him from all the false gods. Continuing in the book of John, "..all things were made through him, and without him was not anything made that was made. In him was life, and the life was the light of men the light shines in the darkness, and the darkness has not overcome it..... And the Word became flesh and dwelt among us". I wonder who that could be? Isn't this the right way to begin a discussion of creation rather than Genesis 1, so encumbered in word traps by the haters of the word of God.

The religious evolutionary faculty of the university have a creation doctrine as Phillip Johnson weeds them out in the open with the real creation myth;

"...in the beginning were the particles and the impersonal laws of physics. The particles somehow became complex living stuff, and the stuff imagined God."

"That is man created god; the stuff imagined god. You cannot be out of the right relationship with particles because the laws do not care what you do. Your behavior is not their concern. They are not thinking about you because they are not thinking about anything. And if man created God, than what we need to know is that god is an illusion, and then we turn to a different priesthood to tell us how to live - - -the scientific priesthood."[51] The particle story is what you would call a "creation myth". How much of America is linked to this idolatrous "creation myth" today. It seems to be separating the sheep from the goats as it were.

Remember John spoke of light and dark, "The light shines in the darkness, but the darkness has not understood it." Speakers of this creation myth are in the dark and do not understand. The Light came into the world, but it was rejected. Now why is there this pattern of rejection? Why is it that people, often the most intelligent ones, often the professors, often the ones to the highest IQs and with the most learning, are rejecting the creator?

"For since the creation of the world, His invisible qualities – His eternal power, and divine nature – have been clearly seen, because they are understood from what has been made, so people are without excuse." [Romans 1:20][NET]

Dear student, remember you cannot see the light itself, but you can see everything else because of the light. The light illuminates everything else. If you get started in the right way in your thinking and you can see everything else, then you can understand everything; but not if you are started in the wrong way, and you are shrouded in darkness."[52] Just like the poor faculty selling you this myth. What Johnson points out that the light shines in the darkness, and so that is the starting point for all our knowledge. But that is not what they teach at the University of California, the California State University, or even many ostensibly Christian colleges. No, they are teaching that the particle story is the light. The World story is the darkness of superstition, which is dispelled by the light of scientific knowledge and tells us our true creator is a mindless, purposeless evolutionary process that does not control us; **we can control it**. Are those not thoughts of idolatry? And if this is the great promise of genetic engineering and that is the great dream which comes out of the human genome – sequencing project. We, not you and me, but we, the people who control science, can take under our control the very creative power of the universe. The process of evolution. Before this evolution was an unindicted purposeless process. The particles are unthinking; they just become complex living stuff. But now the stuff that imagined God in the first place can become god because it can take under its control the very creative power of the universe, the process of evolution, and make people better, a new kind of people. Now that is a powerful dream of life, a powerful dream of scientific conquest. [53] Is that a power trip? If you're mind has been run afoul with relative truth you will follow their logic when they say the "World story" is religious truth, but not scientific truth.

"The true truth is the scientific truth. The religious truth is the thing you pretend to believe on Sunday mornings, because it somehow makes you feel good baby, it makes you better people, it works for you in some way so what is true for you that we would not teach it to young people as if it really happened. It is imaginary, and it follows from this that everything else in the doctrine is just imaginary.

Jesus rose from the dead - - -oh, that is a pretty story. But, no, people do not get up from the grave after they are dead. So they've closed the casket on the gospel of Jesus Christ; so they think!"

Remember creation stories are the foundation of everything else. Your worldview depends on it. So does your eternal life! Our American culture is being trashed and terrible things are happening right in front of you. Why is it thought to be unconstitutional to put up a copy of the 10 commandments in a public school? Law Professor Johnson says it doesn't have anything to do with documents that you can see in the National Archives building called the Constitution and the Declaration of Independence of the United States. It does not have anything to do with the thinkers and framers of that document; that is not what they had in mind at all. The rule that it is unconstitutional to put up the 10 commandments, as if they were authoritative, comes from modernist thinking; it comes from the particle story of evolution. If the particles somehow became complex living stuff, what becomes of God's Commandments? Well, they are illusory, just as God himself is, so they have no authority. The 10 Commandments become obsolete, and we have to make up a morality for ourselves.[54] We have an established religion of the country, established by the government with its priests paid out of your tax money. In complete violation of the Constitution of the United States..... why our forefathers walked away from the "Church of England". Please remember the cultural pathology that has followed that thinking. What happened to the 10 Commandments —"thou shalt not commit adultery". What happens to marriage? Previously marriage had been thought to be a divinely instituted sacrament, a holy thing which is established by God and which human beings were not free to alter as they like. Once Gods authority becomes illusory, then marriage becomes just an agreement between two people. I'm sure you are aware the Ideologies of sex, the politics of sex, hating masculinity, and the sexual militant's destructive work on the family is having its result. "These social pathologies in turn rationalize most all domestic public spending, **which is now bankrupting the Western democracies.**

Virtually the entire domestic budget of every government from Italy to Missouri is justified by problems proceeding from single-parent homes and connected forms of family dissolution."[55]

Continuing Johnson's thinking, "…to imagine a biologist questioning the theory of evolution is to imagine something that just about never happens, because they are taught that it would be bad thinking. If you are going to be a good biologist, you just assume the Theory of Evolution and work out the details, but you never question the basic truth of the doctrine. Johnson reasoned that we have two definitions of science in our culture, not just one. The educational authorities will tell you that they are the same and there is no need to distinguish between them but they are not the same; they are really very different, the key to the error of the theory right out of the legal mind of Professor Johnson:

What is Science?

1. Science is the business of making <u>observations</u> of nature with microscopes, telescopes, and mathematical calculations, doing experiments, and interpreting the results without prejudice. That is why science has to be independent of any governmental authority or religious authority. You cannot have a bishop saying you cannot make that observation; you cannot come to that conclusion because it violates our doctrine. Science has to be independent so it can be unprejudiced.

2. Science is the business of giving <u>explanations</u> for everything that exists in terms of natural causes and natural causes only. Science assumes by definition that there is an explanation for every phenomenon in terms of natural causes. That is just a starting point, a definitional point.

If you want to ask, "can the particles become complex living stuff" or, to put it another way, "Can non–living chemicals swirling around in a chemical soup spontaneously combine to make a living organism?" it has never been seen to happen. There is no experimental evidence that it occurs. Strangely and illogically they claim the proof is the fact that life exists. That is not proof of their theory. It is called circular reasoning. It is as well true that there is no evidence for "speciation" either! "if the student asks what natural selection can do... What it has been seen doing in nature, you find that it has never been seen creating anything, let alone writing volumes of information that exceed the entire sets of the Encyclopedia Britannica, as the information contained in one copy of the human genome found in each of your trillion or so cells of your body.

All that matches selection has ever been seen to do in nature is to effect certain changes in population shifts. If you spray a mosquito population with DDT the DDT resistant mosquitoes are the ones that are going to survive. And eventually the whole mosquito population is DDT resistant, and DDT does not work well anymore. The Darwinists have decided that the only thing they know that can make any change at all and must be responsible for doing all the creating. If it were not, the alternative would be well, we do not even think about that. The purpose of the whole thing is keeping God out of reality. [56]Remember that your worldview is how you see a reality! These people are messing with your sanity if this is a false reality. What kind of mental pathology that can destroy you can come from cramming this in your head? Reality is serious business. This has everything to do with the process of idolatry, and idolatry is worshiping the created thing rather than the Creator–God. You turn the created thing into the creator; the particles somehow became complex living stuff. So you are worshiping the forces of nature represented by idols, and the naturalistic theory of evolution. The theory that nature did its own creating is just our century's fashion in idolatry. They exchanged the truth of God for a lie and worshiped and served created things rather than Creator–God.[57]

Why would the teachers do this?
The Bible tells us this truth is denied because of the power of sin (missing the mark), because of the desire to evade the true Creator–God. Once we wake up and see that we have violated (all of us) all 10 of Creator-God's commandments and are in a wrong relationship with Creator–God we realize that we must do something about it! Jesus asked his followers, "….. who do you say that I am?" and as the good Professor Johnson points out that is the key question we must take too a dying culture and explain to people why it is so important. "Why is the Light that illuminates the darkness in that cave and then enables people to see everything else and find their way out" so important. Please answer that yourself. [58]

"…if generally one's personal convictions are a matter of loyalty to a particular heritage or tradition. It is amazing how much belief is based not on fact but on blind allegiance to an institution or a political party or a church priest or pastor or religious system….. The same holds true in the secular world. Beliefs are held for social reasons …..to remain acceptable in one circle of friends or among one's colleagues. For example not to believe in evolution would cause one to be ridiculed by his peers and even to lose one standing in the academic community. Robert Jastrow, one of the world's leading astronomers, was the founder (and for years the director) of the Goddard space institute that send Pioneer and Voyager into space. An agnostic, Jastrow shocked his colleagues by admitting at the national conference of the Association for the Advancement of Science (AAAS) that the evidence seems to demand an intelligent Creator of the universe. He also found the courage to write:"

'Astronomers are curiously upset by…..Proof that the universe had a beginning.

The reactions provide an interesting demonstration of the response of the scientific mind …..supposedly a very objective

mind - - when evidence uncovered by science itself leads to a conflict with articles of faith in their profession.... There is a kind of
religion and science".[59]

The senior paleontologist at the British museum of natural history, the center of modern evolution has confessed in a production
by Douglas Deewar and EL Davies".[60]

"Evolution itself is accepted by zoologists not because it has
been observed to occur or...

Can be proved by logically coherent evidence to be true, but
because the only alternative, special creation, is clearly incredible."
(i.e. Something many scientist don't want to admit)

The eminent British astronomer Sir Frederick Hoyle reminds us of the
mathematics that:

"...even if the whole universe consisted of organic soup the chance
of producing the basic signs of life by random process without intelligent direction would be approximately one in 10 with 40,000
zeroes after it. In other words it couldn't happen - -ever! Says Hoyle,
"Darwinian evolution is most unlikely to get even one polypeptide
sequence right let alone the thousands on which living cells depend
for survival."

"The situation (mathematically impossible) is well known to
geneticists and yet nobody seems to blow the whistle decisively on
the theory...

"Most scientists still cling to Darwinism because of its grip on
the educational system... You either have to believe the concepts, or
you will be branded a heretic."[61]

Your instructors are just like everyone else they don't like to be wrong. It
would be especially humiliating to admit that the religious faith of a lifetime
of Darwinian evolution has been misplaced and that the religion inherited

from one's ancestor to or the flawed scientific point of view picked up and taught at universities was in fact false science properly called religious faith.[62]

"The greatest shortcoming of most attempts at liberal education today, with their individualized, unfocused, and scattered curricula, is their failure to enhance the students' understanding of their role as free citizens of a free society and the responsibilities it entails. Every successful civilization must possess a means for passing on its basic values to each generation. When it no longer does so, its days are numbered". [63]

Is the Fear of man responsible?

We all seek to avoid persecution because of the "idols of approval"," comfort", or "pleasure". The idol of approval, of losing man's favor.

Man often compromises to win favor and approval. ("The fear of man is the default setting". Faculty warm themselves at the fire of acceptance.)[64]:

> Few professors follow the great instruction of Americas Greatest Physicists Richard Feynman in his famous 1974 commencement address at Caltech by warning against self-deception, the original sin of science, "...the first principle is that you must not fool yourself, and you are the easiest person to fool. To avoid self- deception scientists must bend over backward to report data that cause doubt on their theories." Specifically to scientists who talk to the public (like students).
>
> "I would like to add something that's not essential to the science, but something I kind of believe, which is that you should not fool layman when you're talking as a scientist....I'm talking about specific, extra type of integrity that is not lying, but <u>bending over backwards to show how you're maybe wrong,</u> and (integrity) that you are to have when acting as a scientist. And this is our

responsibility as scientists, certainly to other scientist, and I think to laymen."

Students, look for this level of humility from your teachers. If it's not there, beware!

> One of the characteristics of material humanists is self-deception. How many would admit the religious zeal about something they must incorporate in their person to succeed as a teacher or professor. How many editors of "good" publications will permit anything other than materialist terms in the papers they submit? "...when materialism is fully understood, objective truth goes into the trashcan along with objective morality. The postmodernist irrationalism that is sweeping our universities is thus the logical outcome of the scientific rationalism that prepared the ground by undermining the metaphysical basis for confidence in objective truth. A wrong view of mind has come out of science because science has become confused with materialist philosophy. And that wrong view has become a compulsory dogma for every discipline and for the intellectual culture in general"[65]

How common is the materialist picture of reality?

Paul Feyerabend put it this way, "Scientists are not content with running their own playpens in accordance with what they regard as the rules of the scientific method; they want to universalize those rules, they want them to become part of society at large, and they use every means at their disposal.....argument, propaganda, pressure tactics, intimidation, lobbying ..... to achieve their aims." With these tactics that have been successful in imposing a naturalistic religious philosophy on the entire culture.[66]

Have your professors fallen into the trap they teach, but fail to recognize their impossible logic that, "in the beginning were the particles (not Creator-God) and that mind itself is a product of matter", so how is it possible to have knowledge of an objective reality like objective science? Just like a Marxism, Darwinism is a liberation myth that has become a new justification for ordering people not to think for themselves. Freeing them from the responsibilities of recognizing who they are and how they relate to their Creator–God...The most important question of their life. This religion is an infection imbedded in our literature, our lectures, our media and is required for success in academia. What a trap! This religion teaches that Biblical religion is an oppressor to be overthrown. And just like the movie "Inherit the Wind", Stanley Kramer's great contribution to the destruction of Christianity, portrays the moral side of Darwinian triumph over Christianity, materialist faculty teach that the theological content of Christianity amounts to threatening people with damnation if they dare to think for themselves. This is an enormous lie! By hiding you from our violations of the 10 Commandments of Creator–God and thereby blocking our acceptance of the free Gift to all men/women, covering those violations with Jesus Himself, the gift of salvation and eternal life which is why He sent his Son for us all in the first place. If blocking that understanding isn't evil, then I don't know what evil is! Creator–God is truly gentle, kind, and loving that he would lay his life down for us. And he did.

> John Bunyan points out that there is an ungodly fear of God demonstrated by Adam when he ran from Creator-God and clothed himself in sticky painful fig leafs to hide himself from Creator-God's presence. As long as we're alive this forgiving God is so gracious he offers us complete forgiveness...His great gift.....Himself. That is real love![67]

A picture of The Modern Humanist

Sociology, social psychology, and social anthropology are modern disciplines that are quite guilty of leading us in this strange path to "relative truth". Somehow through trials in twisted logic, following Joseph Fletcher's "Situation Ethics" into Davel Noebel's "The homosexual revolution", all outcomes from the false assumption that nature is relative move us to "Slouching to Gimmorah".

> "Nature is not relative. It is unaffected by remorse, tears, love, or forgiveness, and it very seldom gives us space to repent. That is why we have human laws! The law of man may be just a bit more flexible, but this is to warn us of the exactions of inflexible nature.......
> the 'relativistic float' in the minds of individuals by millions and nations by the score is one of the most clear and present danger in our society."[68]

Part 4. Relative Truth

Plutarch's translator of "Cicero" tells us the word Doxa, the Greek word for "the desire for glory" is employed by the philosophers to express 'opinion' which may be false as opposed to 'knowledge' **which must be true.**

Relative Truth = Doxa is not knowledge which must be true.

And, if the Greeks are correct, a great many faculty fed us "doxa" from a "desire for glory" with far less search for the real truth or recognition it even exists. That permits a false reality for the young mind in which the sanity of truth really required thinking with words and expressions that represent reality. Is Alfred Korzybski's "Science and Sanity" applicable here?[69] Our brains are being wired in a manner unrelated to reality which is quite harmful to mankind. We must ask our teachers if they are speaking "Doxa" to us!! These teachings interfere with the three silent levels of mental functioning as they are made into linguistic reactions. The early teaching "words-meanings" are so removed from reality that the student's language system becomes removed from reality....we think with these words for heaven sake! (please see figure2. below).

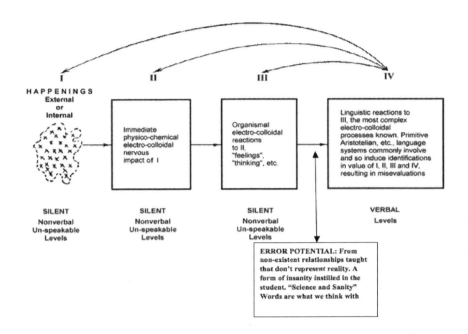

Fig 2. Korzybski's institute of General Semantics diagram
(circa 1946 by permission .modified)

[Kendig, M., Alfred Korzybski's An extensional analysis of the process of
abstracting from an Electro-Colloidal Non-Aristotelian point of view""
General Semantics Bulletin, Autumn-Winter 1950-51, Numbers four
and five. Institute of General Semantics, Lakeville, CT. pp9-10]

The bizarre terms introduced that somehow claim to represent reality of
the "socio-cultural" field which cause the student to speak unembarrassed
about "Value Phenomena", Value Situations", "Value Fields" and "Value
Framework" all terms mauled by departments of social relations and, as
Prof. David Aiken of Harvard University (1952) tells us "…has lost all ves-
tiges of bony structure. In such a predicament it is the part of sanity to
refuse flatly to acknowledge…" Ethics historically had effective terms like
"good" and "ought" that were both vague enough and flexible enough but
those seeking the insanity of relative truth have chosen to play with the
terms "Value" to either make it everything to everybody or make it into an
excuse for the so-called science of the social, an excuse for the disciplines

that spring from the "loosely defined" (where correlations of .2 and .3 that do not explain 70 to 80% of the data are acceptable). As Aiken noted, "Free stipulation, like free association, however is of little interest, save to the clinical psychologist. It's philosophical significance is precisely nil-or if it isn't, then let someone spell out the reason why. Still, there comes a time, at last when one must protect against anyone taking about values at all until he has first made quite plain what on earth it would be like to confront one of the slippery creatures in the flesh." [70]

If science is a moving train, then the relativity of social science has its feet firmly planted in mid air.

The sociology of Humanism and it's gods

19th century French sociologist Emile Durkheim borrowed the word "ANOMIE" from French philosopher Jean-Marie Gayan and used it in his influential book "Suicide" (1897) outlining the social causes of suicide, characterized by a rapid change of the standards or values of society and an associated feeling of alienation and purposelessness. (much more akin to nihilism) Durkheim also formally posited anomie as a mismatch, not simply the absence of norms. Thus a society with too much rigidity and little individual discretion could also produce a kind of anomie, a mismatch between individual circumstances and larger social mores. Thus, fatalistic suicide arises when a person is too rule-governed, when there is ...no free horizon of expectation.[71] Robert Merton, writing on Anomie Theory, describes "..anomie becomes the explanation for high rates of deviant behavior in the U.S. compared with other societies, and also an explanation for the distribution of deviant behavior across groups defined by class, race, ethnicity, and the like".[72]

Our students are told to constantly focus on their "feelings" to their destruction.

Even Star Wars teaches them this error. If the correct path is determined by "feelings" alone, we are looking at the end of morality and the end of our society as we know it! That path can be called "Slouching to Gomorrah".

"Anomie" found in many existential authors and advocates who, for the most part consider the question of, "does Creator-God exist" a moot point....and in most cases are blind to the "Salvation" offered by the Creator-God. It would seem that anyone declaring themselves an expert on society (ie. sociologist) who rejected the teaching of the Bible because they do not understand those teachings or in most cases have failed to study them in a reasonable manner, fall into the trap Aiken describes. Grasping at anything in society he "felt" was stable....grasping a science he did not understand as a moving train, unstable and dependent upon discovery, imagination, unable to fathom infinity, random, nothingness, "outside of time"; in short a bleak contrast of a reality generated by vastly limited man verses a reality as Creator- God designed for man. He simply rejected the truth of the bible. Kurtz's father did not teach him the God of the Torah and his website was http://kurtz.pragmatism.org, clearly links him to the father of American Pragmatism old Harvard's William James.

Kurtz called himself a "skeptic" in the form of atheist Voltaire (God is dead) :

In the "Skeptics magazine" written just after his Death we find:

Martin Gardner, magician James Randi, psychologist Ray Hyman, and philosopher Paul Kurtz played primary roles in the foundation and planning of the organization and the subsequent movement (of Humanists-Skeptics) .... experimental psychologists had tested the Israeli psychic and determined that he was genuine.

Kurtz glorifies eugenicist Margaret Sanger as wonderful as Einstein, Beethoven and Mark Twain in his writing. No doubt her founding of Planned Parenthood would meet with his approval.

The Creator-God who is responsible for the publication of his "Word", the Bible, tells us He cares for all of us and He knows the result of all of human history. With that knowledge He has written a love letter to us to direct our paths-----dealing with every possible aspect of the 'best path' for man to take as in such writing as Proverbs and the ten commandments defining what is "deviant" from that path. We must learn the whole counsel of Creator-God then we will understand! Not as Jack Kerouac tried to teach us in "On the Road" (Starting The Beat Generation) that we must experience all paths first and then decide.....strange because he considered himself a Catholic, anti-Marxist, Buddhist, and then again a Catholic in his lifetime. Our youth, in its ignorance of outcomes, hidden from the "good" and "ought" paths find rebellion comfortable, deviance comfortable because they have this fuzzy logic monster switch imbedded in their brain called "relative truth". Mocking virginity, family, normality, and embracing nihilism, for they have no idea why they were put on this earth..... How does a society and its culture survive?

A students role as a free citizen of a free society is to possess the wisdom to stabilize a successful civilization. A basic value example is one based on the <u>anatomy and histology</u> design of man and woman. Teaching ignorance of this and a high-risk life style in which longevity may end before 43---a lifestyle of a generation who's days are definitely numbered. Lets look at an example of "Natural" in the hands of progressives ....so obliterated a term today that it barely allows any discernment. The "natural" anatomy and "histology" (tissues) of a man's rectum and a woman's vagina. A physician at the U.C. Berkley's student health has accurately compared the two structures in her book "Unprotected" .[73] The vagina has a 25 to 45 cellular thick lining with a low pH all protective of infection, in which is found under the lining layer of target cells and no "M" cells laying out convincing evidence that vaginal transmission of Aids is quite rare. The vagina also is rich in elastic fibers followed by a layer of muscle and then more elastic fibers. You could say the vagina is naturally designed to protect from infection from both bacteria and viruses like HIV/AIDS. The rectum on the other hand has a very different structure. "As part of the gastrointestinal system, it has a lining who's primary function is absorption, bringing in molecules and food and water. The pH is higher, also a vulnerability. Most importantly, the rectal lining---the barrier to be breached to reach the blood stream is only one (1) cell thick. Below that delicate lining are blood vessels and target cells, elastic fibers are absent. The rectum also has abundant specialized "M" cells on the rectal surface that actively latch onto the HIV virus, take it in, and deliver it to the target cells[74] [Owen, Robert L.,"Uptake and transport of Intestinal macromolecules and microorganisms by "M" cells in Peyer's

Patches". Seminars in Immunology 11:154-163, 1999] They deliver the virus directly to the lymphocyte in 10 minutes meaning the HIV infection is then in the blood. Remember the vagina has no"M" cells so vaginal sex is natural with respect to tissue design while rectal sex is not. The progressive advocate of rectal sex is not supporting anything natural so extremely high risk enters the human race and spreads by this behavior. Can't say we were not warned thousands of years ago:

"And likewise also the men, leaving the natural function of the women, burned in their lust toward one another, men doing what is inappropriate with men, <u>and receiving in themselves the due penalty of their error.</u>" [Romans 1:27]

"Be not deceived. God is not mocked, for whatever a man sows, that will he also reap. For he who sows to his own flesh will from the flesh reap corruption. But he who sows to the Spirit will from the Spirit reap eternal life.[Galatians 6:7-8]

The New Progressive as an enemy of man or The Progressive Humanist Exposed
John C. Greene in his book "The Death of Adam" [Iowa State University Press, 1959] accurately describes Darwinism and the work of Darwin's inner circle as a "synthesis"..inferring a clever Hegelian dialectical operation of opposites, with the assumption always of the progressive "progression of formless to the formed, inorganic to the organic, blind force to conscious intellect and will".[75] Green doesn't like what he calls "static creationism" of the bible and cries out "I can see no excuse for doubting that all are coordinated terms of Natures great progression.." My answer to Green is if you follow the application of "Progression" in the theories of the so called "Natural" creation of the universe without Creator-God who created knowing the end from the beginning, from Aristoltle's..for the sun and stars are born not, neither do they decay, but are eternal and devine (384-322 BC), through the publications of William Whiston's new theory of the earth, modified by a "true son of the French Enlightenment" Buffon who decided to remove the Bible from natural history, progressing to Thomas Wright's (1711-1786) publication followed by Immanuel Kant's description of reality as a necessary

outcome of the application of Newton's laws of motion, then to Sir William Herschel's brilliant observations that all the stars are in motion, degrading to the crude deduction by Pierre- Simon Laplace (1749-1827) of how the galaxies and planets formed by "accretion" excludes Newton's God. None of these early thinkers were wise in their understanding of Plasma physics which applies to 90 percent or more of the known universe. Plasma Physics, today is little more than in its early elementary understanding by man. My point of the speculations of Nature and Random causing the order of things without Creator-God, differently than He has taught us in His 5 billion copies of his publication the Bible, are ideas devoid of the full knowledge of things. Somehow theology is embedded in each and every one of these false ideas and Voltaire, who declared "God is Dead" and the bible would be forgotten would find the bible published today in the very house he occupied.

Many of these "Progressives" follow Lyell in their paganism:

...in fine, he (Lamarck) renounces his belief in the high genealogy of his species, and looks forward, as if in compensation, to the future perfectibility of man in his physical, intellectual, and moral attributes. [76]

Pointing to human self-perfectibility, that everything is getting better and better...the frequency of beneficial mutation (which is a negative number) all a crude and empty dream of Humanism, giving something other than Creator-God the glory and honor due Him. Lyell and Lamarck had great influence on Darwin and Darwin had great influence on Voltaire, Hegel, and all Humanists, Unitarians, and Religions of man. The failure of astronomers to find that Aristotle's belief the sun and stars are eternal and divine. Something nowhere found in the bible. In fact Creator-God will not always strive with his creation but will turn his face away from it so to speak and all matter will turn into a "fervent" heat (or energy)[2Peter 3:10] and he will speak His Creation words and all things will be new. That level of technology is not something man can aspire to, especially since we have at least 200 errors in the genome with every generation. So the key ideal of the progressive, to dream the impossible dream, is a farce most likely placed in our heads by the same declaring that "God hath not said you will die if you eat of the forbidden fruit of the knowledge of good and evil". The universe is indeed following the second law of thermodynamics and falling into disorder "more and more". Just who do we think we are? Are we able to alter Plank's constant by .0001 % or any really fundamental underpinning of the things that make up the universe? Man may be made in the image of Creator-God but there's nothing about man to be worshipped nor given honor or Glory that is instead to be given to our Creator-God.

The University Liberal has become "Illiberal liberalism"
"The old liberalism of Burke or John Stewart Mill didn't worry much about offending people.

It sought political freedom, freedom of conscience, and freedom to seek the truth.....not interdiction but more speech.....the new illiberal liberalism, on the contrary, prattles on about tolerance and diversity, but it practices intolerance and demands conformity whenever it is challenged. 'Racism' 'Homophobic' 'Islamophobia'. These are the weapons in its armory of intimidation (as instructed by Saul Alinsky in Rules for Radicals) : not so much torts as silencers in a war of Ideological grievance-mongering..... What we are witnessing is the establishment of a network of intolerance that employs the rhetoric of liberalism in order to pursue an illiberal agenda of conformity. Participants in an orgy of intolerance by those intoxicated by the spectacle of their own virtue." [77]

Kimball raises up the spectacle of 1930's rise of fascist Germany "Build a bonfire and you to can be torched at the stake...as Brian equivalently put it to Max in "Cabaret" : ".Do you think you can control them?" The once great center of freedom Brandeis University (whose motto "Truth even unto its innermost parts") Removes the brave and freedom fighting Ayaan Hirsi Ali, and Condi Rice from their free speech list. Distinguished Scholar Daniel Piper's middle east forum is banned from the British Library and Brendan Eich is removed as CEO of Mozilla, making a strong parallel between the PC liberals and the National Socialist Party of 1936 Germany.[78]

Possible Collapse of our Culture and Nation

Results in Degradation of Humanity

The collapse of popular culture is inevitable if we don't wake up and smell the coffee. "Our culture is rapidly sinking to barbarism. The leaders of our culture, the University Faculty are leading us into the abyss. If you know the words to Snoopy Dog's song "horny", perhaps you've listened to the Nine inch Nails "big man with a gun". The obscenity is staggering without artistic distinction and or even mediocrity,..... little more than noise of the beat with lyrics that range from perverse to mercifully unintelligible. It is difficult to convey just how debased rap it is.... The songs can be heard as paeans of revenge. As the young have always chafed under authority; the difference now is that obscene assaults on authority have become culturally acceptable."[79] Where is virtue? Where is beauty? Where is shame? Were is conscience? Is this slide the outcome of the attitude and teachings that man is merely a grownup worm, evolved from the mire, and destined for oblivion? To be selected out of the animal kingdom by the brutal idol "Selection". That there is no real truth, only the bar-room saying "who says"! I don't believe the materialist philosophy's relative truth has any greater future then those ancient books of the dark ages on how to mutate lead into gold, just as worthless as reading last years social column. I think that's the future of large segments of lecture notes before students in the universities, and those teaching the teachers as well. Truth is what will lift us up and is the dawn of our salvation.

We have described the development of "Human beings as gods" from the earliest recorded rulers, man's history for worshipping man. Nietzsche's

"Ressentiment" describing the mental illness of hate that drove the Nazi mind and much evil today as well. We have also described the deception and disinformation of Marxism and materialism and how it is aligned with ontological victimhood----all products of non-reason as is moral relativism. We have pointed out the lie component of evolution as a false-science and how it perpetuates through a sociology of its own...leading to the question, how could this infection inter into a bible-believing nation of 1800s and captured the minds and hearts of the American Universities?

iv

From Nimrod to Harvard: how these foreign gods entered America's Universities

Part 1. Formation of the University: It's Christian beginnings

We described in the early pagan mystery religion colleges of Nimrod priest's, the Etruscan Auguary, and the Roman Colleges of Mythras at Tarsus. Just what is the origin of modern scholarship?

80-110 Ad

The charge by Jesus was to teach others seriously. The early Christians were mostly Jews who came from a long standing Jewish tradition that valued formal education. There was a strong emphasis on teaching in the great commission that Christ gave to us. So Creator–God in Matthew 28: 19-20 motivated Christians to "teach the world" (all nations) all that He has commanded them. Indeed Christ spent his entire three year ministry teaching. His words were the writings responsible for the great literacy in America's beginnings. Indeed, Paul who wrote much of the new testament was a special student of Gamaliel, the most famous teacher of the Middle East. Some consider he had the equivalent of two Ph.D.s by the time he was 23. Thomas Jefferson's commission to survey the state of literacy in the first states and found that fathers had read the bible to their children and the children were thereby taught to read. Almost no illiteracy was found in that survey. While today almost ¼ of Americans (one of four) were functionally illiterate or "could not make low level inferences using printed materials".[1]. Quite a decline in literacy! Are books even in the residences of that population today? Or are their fathers present? Man is "free to choose good or evil …..that is freedom!!" but don't rewrite the "laws of the land" so the evil is lawful."He who despises the Word will be destroyed but he who fears the commandment will be rewarded." [Proverbs 13:13b] and numbers 15:3 (will be cut off). "but…..God is no respecter of persons" (but rewards the righteous). Which is the only true statement of equality, check it out!

To Christians, reading "the Word" of Creator–God was a requirement of life, it was reasonable to early Americans as well as today's modern Christians that literacy is fundamental for all!

110-900 Ad

Just after 110 AD the "Didache" instruction Manual appeared and records indicate the Bishop of Antioch urge that children be taught the holy scriptures and a skilled trade continuing the tradition of the Jewish fathers.[2] Justin Martyr (AD 150) the "great scholar of the Christian Church", established institutions first in Ephesus and Rome and later Alexandria Egypt. All of which became famous. The school's primarily taught doctrine however the school in Alexandria included mathematics, medicine, and grammar in the curriculum.[3] It is to be noted that the stated object of instruction was to include both sexes and all social classes for Creator–God is not a respect of person's …..or does not discriminate who a child is or where he is from. It is to be noted that "before the birth of Christ, Roman gymnasia did not formally educate girls in literary skills… and most boys were only from the privileged class.[4] Saint Augustine is quoted as claiming that Christian women were often better informed in divine matters than the pagan male philosophers. D.D. McGarry in his work on "Mediaeval Education" notes the cathedral epispical schools also taught the seven liberal arts (the Trivium) grammar, rhetoric, logic, and the "quadrivivum" arithmetic, music, geometry, and astronomy.[5] The teachers were scholasticii appointed by the bishop and while the students were often the children of royalty and higher social ranks the monasteries and nunneries were not of that class. The middle ages had many famous Christian educated women:

930-1400 Ad

"Hrotsvitha of Granderscheim (930 to -1002) wrote plays, poems, legends, and epics. Hildegard of Bingen (1098-1179) founded her own monastery, wrote a mass, and corresponded with Popes, Emperors, and Bishops. Brigitta of Sweden (1303 – 73) opposed higher taxes and founded a religious order. Catherine of Siena (1347?-89) labored for peace and wrote letters of council to men of authority. Christina de Pizan (14th century) authored a number of books as well as Queen Isabella(1451-1504) who underwrote Columbus' trip to America." [6]

The Mediaeval Universities

James B. Mollinger of Saint John's College, Cambridge, suggest today's university started as a scholastic guild. Since the Latin *universitas* was a very general term describing any community or corporation the additional words *magustorium scholarium* was needed to denote what we think of as a teaching university. These were "those noted as *studium* or *studium generale*" in the 13th and 14 centuries found in most European cities.

The license to teach was most often granted by the Chancellor Scholasticus or official of the cathedral church, especially in the north of Europe. A few famous schools were developed in Paris (1210AD) Bologna (1000AD), and the first stadium at Salerno's school of medicine (9th century) but according to H. Rasdall in his massive work on the "University of Europe in the Middle Ages" [7] nothing approaching a regular university ever existed in Naples, only a medical school.

Remember the Greco–Roman tradition has always excluded girls and women. It was Christ who taught women and men together at the Sermon on the Mount or Mary and Martha at home. The western culture of educating females is not of Greco Roman tradition but a result of the practice of Creator–God in the form of the man Jesus Christ.

Historians such as Will Durant notes the teaching of Christianity was "without reservation to all individuals, classes, and nations; it was not limited to one people, like Judaism, nor to the freedmen of one state, like the official cult's of Greece and Rome.[8]

Luther and the Protestant Reformation: 16th century

Martin Luther visited the church at Saxony (Germany) and found widespread ignorance among both the common people and many pastors whom he considered incompetent to teach. Students of Luther note his emphasis on "cultivating the human mind was absolutely essential because people needed to understand both the Word of scripture and the nature of the world in which the Word would take root".[9] "...and although he never denied that one of his purposes of education was to train pastors for the church, he also wanted children to serve Creator-God and society in all stations of life".[10]

Luther was the first it is believed, to advocate tax-supported public schools because he had "lost faith" in the church in the cathedral/Episcopal schools and monasteries. Since parents were not able to teach their children, Luther saw the future doom of both church and society unless public funds would be used to educate the youth. Indeed the first public school system in Germany was implemented by Philipp Melanchthon (1497-1560) Luther's principle coworker together with Johannes Burgenhagen (pastor of the church Luther attended). Compulsory education was also the doctrine of Luther:

"I hold that it is the duty of the temporal authority to compel its subjects to keep their children in school, especially the promising ones we mentioned above."[11]

Graded education was introduced by a Lutheran layman named Johann Sturm (1507-89) rewarding the student by advancing in grade. He also was credited with the formation of the "gymnasium" secondary level in Strasbourg, France that later could be found throughout Europe.[12]

Another devout Christian originated the Kindergarten, Frederick Froebel (1782-1852) who discerned that children needed to be introduced early in life to the fact that the world of man and nature were connected by Creator-God. [13]

The contribution to education by Christians inspired by the bible is immense. Just as the collection and organization of the written Word into libraries for study was driven by the Christian community.

While secularism dominates most colleges today in America, "… Every collegiate institution founded in the Colonies before the Revolutionary War (except U. Pennsylvania) was established by some branch of the Christian church".[14] A survey in 1932 by Donald Tewksbury, "The Founding of American Colleges and Universities Before the Cival War", also found 167 of 182 colleges and universities were founded by Christian denominations.[15]

Part 2. Religion without the Bible

Nimrod to European Institutes of Learning
Breakdown of the German view of Creator-God and his word: Whence came Jeulis Wellhousen?

Hume, Kant. Madame de Stael, or Anne-Louise-Germaine Necker claim superiority and power of the human mind..over God's Word.....

Germany had to fill its bookshelves with Wellhousen's theology, destroying the word of God or making the bible a mockery so the Idol of "The love of one's own people" was made an absolute.[16]

Robespierre, the leader of the French revolution described to his national convention what his goal was. The peaceful enjoyment of liberty and equality... The Terror is nothing other than prompt severe inflexible justice".[17] However his reign of terror was completely unjust and as a result Robespierre was detained without a trial. So what went horribly wrong? ..."unknowable principle became possessed, went insane, and ultimately accomplish the very opposite of the justice the revolutionaries sought."[18] Timothy Keller asks, "... what happened? Idolatry. When love of one's people becomes an absolute, it turns into racism. When love of equality turns into a supreme thing it can result in hatred and violence toward anyone who has led a privilege life or can turn this into a political cause and then into counterfeit gods. People can look to romantic love to

give fulfillment they found in religious experience. Nietzsche, however believed it would be money that would replace Creator-God.
We can even look on our political leaders as "messiah's," and turn
political activities into a kind of religion.[19]

The point to all these failures of society is that once you have
lost the reality of Creator-God or not respected His Word, you are
open for the destruction of idolatry. That is the lesson of history.
Not the bumbling vain philosophies we hear from the blind, professing themselves to be wise as they interpret history to us, the so
called experts that fill our university libraries and textbooks.

Dietrich Bonhoeffer had a critical view of the phenomenon of religion and
asserted that revelation abolished religion (which he called the "garment"
of faith). Having witnessed the complete failure of the German Protestant
church as an institution in the face of Nazism, he saw this challenge as an
opportunity of renewal for Christianity. While Hitler hanged this wonderful pastor just before our troops arrived, his legacy lives on in a theology and
teaching that I hold in high regard. [20]

The concept of Bonhoffer's that revelation abolished religion opens up
the problem with the pre-Nazi German church. The revelation of truth in
the Bible faced a group of "intellectuals" who felt they had the power to
reject that truth for something they came up with, as if they were witness to
history as well as creation rather than who they really were. The Church was
so very weakened by the vain "Philosophy of Rational Materialism" that
placed the "water-brain" of man over Creator-God. Open blatant Ideology!
But first the "Word of Creator-God" had to be attacked with this vain
materialist philosophy. The development of German Rationalism as sum-
marized by Hagenbach is a serial development:

"...But Kant surrendered his work to Fichte, Fichte to Schilling,
Schelling to Hegel, and there it reached the end. In concentration,
abstraction, grasp and force, those men were singly of the mightiest.
But they were linked : they make a chain : each took up the task

dropped by the one before him and forwarded the work. The conditions for solving the problems of religion without the Bible could not conceivably be finer. Whatever men could do, they could do. But what was the end of their work… Nothing but miserable doubt, uncertainty, blank, unmitigated hopelessness. A 'born Hegelian ' is the most compact term to define a man who, in relation to religion, is always seeking but never finding. At the end of this long search Germany had gained not a single step : it was 'Blinded with doubt, in wildering mazes lost,' But not even Newton's one pearl on the shores of the ocean of infinite truth had it attained. The nation had been cut loose from its moorings. As were the leaders so were the followers. F. A. Bahrdt, the extreme product of the infidel reaction in the last century, ended his days in an ale-house, the clergy were the most unbelieving of all classes ; the gospel idea of regeneration was utterly lost sight of, and the process of raising the world by self-culture, by educating the inner life to a perfection attainable of itself, was the only moral specific. The failure was utter, final, irremediable. At the end of this long career of " protesting," the simple way was to leave the generation to die in its infidelity" .[21]

Was the action of Julius Welhausen and De Witte to Degrade Creator-God's Word in preparation for successful attack on the German Church (a church so degraded it could not stand up to Hitler)?

Where is the source of the Progressive-Liberal German Church just before Hitler crushed it?

When Dr. Tholuck (1826) was appointed Professor in the great University of Halle, where there were hundreds of students preparing to enter the ministry, he could find but one who ever read the Bible for devotional purposes, and his own house was attacked, his windows broken, and he himself rudely treated in the streets, because he believed in the Scriptures as the word of God. In the beginning of this century the work of infidelity had been so thorough going, that the Bible and evangelical religion, represented by a handful of true souls, had arrayed against them the three great worlds, of literature, education and art. Most unnatural divorce! Those divine gifts which ought to illumine and illustrate each other, were rudely sundered; the "faith once delivered to the saints " was compacted in a little isolated body, while poetry, philosophy, scholarship, educational science, music, and all art either ignored it or ridiculed it, or assailed it. The Bible had been protested out of all knowledge of men, out of all the domain of culture or breeding, or forceful thought. Great minds then tried to deal single-handed with religion. Without the Bible as their chart, they ventured out into the dim void, and felt their own way. With their own unaided eyes, they tried to " find out the Almighty to perfection."[22]

Julius Wellhausen degraded the very special history of the Jews by his writings in the German language by describing them as:

"Pre-mosaic religion and Israel had been polydemonism in the form of totemism, animism, ancestor worship, fetishism. Recent investigations in the countries of the ancient Orient, however, have demonstrated that the religions of the Near East as far as can now be ascertained, did not sink to such levels; they were polytheistic in character (star worship, personification of natural forces), and tapered off to the monarchial system. Rather than evolution, there was retrogression, because the number of gods gradually increased. Furthermore, prehistory testifies that primitive man was in no way intellectually inferior to his descendants, and that at least in the realm of art he was quite superior. Ethnology also refute the theory of religious evolution, for the concepts of the so-called primitive peoples are purer than those of their neighbors already engaged in agriculture and cattle raising. Therefore, we need to give scant attention to those passages which have been cited as containing traces of the above mentioned "isms."[23] Wellhausen's documentary hypothesis of the Pentateuch, enhances his view that the bible is nothing but a collection of interesting documents rather than the word of Creator–God and is infected with Wellhausen's account of pre-history that is quite bizarre in light of our understanding today. This was before the archeological discovery of many modern findings totally supporting biblical veracity and dating of the bible like the dead sea scrolls, the discovery of the Hittite empire, let alone the work of Sir Robert Anderson showing the very day of "Palm Sunday" predicted by the plain text in the old testament, the establishment of Israel in 1948 and the prediction of events in the Daily News today by the bible. Today we have overwhelming evidence supporting the present text so that a belief accepting the "original text" as the Word of Creator–God is not unreasonable. Modern translations such as the online free "Net Bible"(net bible.org) assembled by 25 of the world's great scholars has 56,000 translation and textual notes explaining why this or that word was used to translate the text. For the New Testament alone 121 papyri fragments and more than 20,000-30,000 manuscripts and it least a million textual references in the writings of the early church fathers allow no doubt of the accuracy or veracity of today's New Testament. There's amazing agreement on the Greek words that likely made up the original autographs.[24]

The Practice of Textual Criticism

The goal of textual criticism should be to establish the original reading of the text that is in the autograph or original writing. The method is to sift through the manuscripts carefully comparing them with one another to determine how the variations occurred, leading to a fair rendering of the text. Usually the effort is limited by the scarcity of manuscripts and their closeness to their original and time. ie. There are only 693 copies of Homers work. The oldest is at least 500 years after Homer wrote.

The first list of Old Testament manuscripts was made by Benjamin Kennecott (1776 to 1780) and published at Oxford, which listed 615 manuscripts from libraries in England and on the continent. Giodonni De Rosi (1784-1788) published a list of 731 manuscripts. Since that time the dead sea scrolls (1947, manuscripts date from 250 BC), in the Cairo –Geniza (1890) and the Old Synagogue in Cairo were found 10,000 Biblical manuscripts.[25] 200 manuscripts are found in the dead sea scrolls all written before 70 A.D.. 14 scroll manuscripts were discovered in 1963-65 at Masada in Israel. The largest original collection of Hebrew old testament manuscripts in the world is found in the Russian National Library in Saint Petersburg (Second Firkovitch Collection) where is found the oldest <u>dated complete</u> Hebrew "Biblia Hebreica Stuttgartensia which represents the text of the Lenningrad Codex B19ᴬ. [26] These manuscripts are handwritten copy of the original "autographs". Again the study of Biblical manuscripts is important because handwritten copies can contain errors. The science of textual criticism attempts to reconstruct the <u>original</u> text, must be contrasted with an attempt to rewrite that text after the critique's worldview. We will see that an analysis of Theodore Parker and the Harvard Transcendentalists will expose both the liberal church and its theology.

The liberal German Church must have been searching for a replacement for the Word of Creator-God when it incorporated the new and exciting theory's of Julius Wellhausen. He played off the new running "science" of Darwin and what he claims is the "scientific" technique of "higher textual criticism" to claim the book of Genesis was all wrong on dates, times, and authorship. Claiming with the greatest hubris only a proud demigod would conger up, that he Julius Wellhousen had discovered the Bible was not the word of Creator-God, but composed of "mythic materials of primitive world-history…suffused in the Jehovist (one of his 4 imagined authors) with a peculiar somber earnestness, a kind of antique philosophy of history……
Jehovah does not stand high enough, does not feel himself secure enough, to allow the earth-dwellers to come very hear Him". Wellhausen, openly twists the mocks and manipulates the reader into believing his fantasy that Moses did not write the first 5 books of the bible and that at least "…for the most part we have the product of a countless number of narrators, unconsciously modifying each other's work. [27] If Satan is to try to destroy all the Jews, he will have to rewrite and degrade them from the "chosen peoples" to something else, and their Old Testament or at least the key first 5 books that include the promises of Creator-God to them as a covenant that will last forever, the Abrahamic Covenant will have to be degraded to some "mythic" thing. Wellhausen couldn't have come at a better time for this horrendous evil to be perpetrated by the German Nation. I repeat, if you take the time

to read Wellhousen's many works (mostly still in German and not translated), you will note that to apply the ideas of Darwin to the Old Testament that religion goes from crude polydemonism, totemism, animism, ancestor worship, and fetishism getting "better and better" or "evolving" has not historically been found. Instead, far more often the earliest were monotheistic or in most cases the number of gods/idols increased with time, not the other way around. [28]

What happened as a result of this proud "higher criticism" by adding this degraded bible to the German academic school of Rationalism by the proud Professor of Oriental language at Halle University near Leipzig, many writers see a very significant change in the German attitude of "doubt, distrust of God, and spiritual disquiet, and it has continued to blow from then until now".[29]

As C. S. Lewis put it, "There used to be English scholars who were prepared to cut up *Henry VI* between half a dozen authors and assign his share to each. We don't do that now... Everywhere, except in theology, there has been a vigorous growth of skepticism about skepticism itself." [30]

The work of the Biblical scholar should be the text itself, and not hypothetical sources. Enough time has been wasted chasing shadows; may scholarship regain its taste for substance. There is much work to do to assemble all the texts and clarify the differences as well as identify the earliest. We know that the original autographs were without error, but today we only have copies. This is true of all ancient writings. A modernist could claim this as a weakness of the bible, even though Creator-God speaks in it as He was there, the modernist somehow misses the point as he claims we should believe only "modern" stuff or words he has decided are true.

Liberalism-Modernism: the root of the problem

The root of the movement is one; the many varieties of modern liberal religion are rooted in naturalism--that is, in the denial of any entrance of the creative power of God (as distinguished from the ordinary course of nature) in connection with the origin of Christianity. The word "naturalism" is here used in a sense somewhat different from its philosophical meaning. In this non-philosophical sense it describes with fair accuracy the real root of what is called, by what may turn out to be a degradation of an originally noble word, [31] Machen observed in 1923 that with the great and wonderful expansion of science and industry "So many convictions have had to be abandoned that men have sometimes come to believe that all convictions must go."No department of knowledge can maintain its isolation from the modern lust of scientific conquest; treaties of inviolability, though hallowed by all the sanctions of age-long tradition, are being flung ruthlessly to the winds. In such an age, it is obvious that every inheritance from the past must be subject to searching criticism; and as a matter of fact some convictions of the human race have crumbled to pieces in the test. Indeed, dependence of any institution upon the past is now sometimes even regarded as furnishing a presumption, not in favor of it, but against it. So many convictions have had to be abandoned that men have sometimes come to believe that all convictions must go.[32]

If such an attitude be justifiable, then no institution is faced by a stronger hostile presumption than the institution of the Christian religion, for no institution has based itself more squarely upon the authority of a by-gone age.

The question:

> What is the relationship between Christianity and modern culture and the Bible? ....this is the problem which modern liberalism attempts to solve (also within the liberal church).
>
> Admitting that scientific objections may arise against the particularities of the Christian religion... against the Christian doctrines of the person of Christ, and of redemption through His death and resurrection....the liberal theologian seeks to rescue certain of the general principles of religion, of which these particularities are thought to be mere temporary symbols, and thee general principles

he regards as constitution "the essence of Christianity"....Modern materialism especially in the realm of psychology, is not content with occupying the lower quarters of the Christian City, but pushes its way into all the higher reaches of life .....in the intellectual battle of the present day in which there can be no "peace without victory"; one side or the other must win. [33].....Two lines of criticism, then, are possible with respect to the liberal attempt at reconciling science and Christianity. Modern liberalism may be criticized:
(1) on the ground that it is un-Christian and
(2) on the ground that it is unscientific.

......despite the liberal use of traditional phraseology, modern liberalism not only is a different religion from Christianity but belongs in a totally different class of religions.

In trying to remove from Christianity everything that could possibly be objected to in the name of science, in trying to bribe off the enemy by those concessions which the enemy most desires, the apologist has really abandoned what he started out to defend ....it may appear incidentally.... that it is not the Christianity of the New Testament which is in conflict with science, but the supposed Christianity of the modern liberal Church, and that the real city of God, and that city alone, has defenses which are capable of warding off the assaults of modern unbelief.[34]

Before "modern liberal man" can finally walk away from the answer to death, the power of the Holy Spirit, and the incredible Grace of Creator-God toward the humans which He has individually knit together in the womb, modern man must have his individualism removed, his liberty removed... as well as his power to question the existence of the Holy Spirit and consider the acceptance/rejection of the gift of eternal life by his Creator! Machen in 1929 suggested the whole development of modern society has tended mightily toward the limitation of the realm of freedom of modern man. The tendency is most clearly seen in socialism; a socialist state would mean the reduction to a minimum of the sphere of individual choice. Labor and recreation, (and medical care) under a socialistic government, would both be prescribed, and individual liberty would be gone......When once the majority has determined that a certain regime is beneficial, that regime without further hesitation is forced ruthlessly upon the individual man" ie. welfare may be good, forced welfare may be bad and is certainly controlling). "In other words, utilitarianism is being carried out to its logical conclusions; in the interest of physical well-being the great principles of liberty are being thrown ruthlessly to the winds.....the result is an unparalleled impoverishment of human life. Personality can only be developed in the realm of individual choice....it is especially felt in the realm of education. The liberal object of education is the greatest happiness for the greatest number...but the greatest happiness for the greatest number, it is assumed further, can be defined only by the will of the majority (perhaps a strange coalition of bedfellows). Idiosyncrasies in education, therefore, it is said, must be avoided, and the choice of schools must be taken away from the individual parent or family and placed in the hands of the state. The state then exercises its authority through the instruments that are ready at hand, and at once, therefore, the child is placed under the control of psychological experts, themselves without the slightest acquaintance with the higher realms of human life, who proceed to prevent any such acquaintance being gained by those who come under there care."[35] A public school system,..once it is allowed to become monopolistic, is the most perfect instrument of tyranny which has been devised. Freedom of thought in the middle ages was combated by the Inquisition, but the modern method is far more effective. Place the lives of children in their formative years, despite the convictions of their parents, under the intimate control of experts appointed by the state, force them then to attend schools where the higher aspiration of humanity are crushed out, and where the mind is filled with the materialism of the day, and it is difficult to see how even the remnants of liberty can subsist....Such a tyranny, supported as it is by a perverse technique used as the instrument in destroying human souls, is certainly far more dangerous than the crude tyrannies of the past, which despite their weapons of fire and sword permitted thought at least to be free. " [36]

Since our freedoms are given by the Creator-God [Declaration of Independence] this teaching is clearly against the very freedoms granted to us by our constitution.....so the documents as they are written must be set aside by the liberal-progressive so as to proceed with a socialist agenda. So as in America in 1929 as in pre Nazi Germany(National Socialist Parti), we see this beat of the drum attack on Christianity and the Bible. Imagine those hundreds of Lutheran student Pastors that attacked Professor Tholuck graduating in Germany's churches...teaching the liberal theology.".... it may appear that what the liberal theologian has retained after abandoning to the enemy one Christian doctrine after another is not Christianity at all, but a religion which is so entirely different from Christianity as to belong in a distinct category." [37] If you review the nature of the weak German church Hitler inherited you will understand how easy it was for him to destroy the objection to replacing one Messiah with another.

Part 3. America

Formation of American Colleges and Universities

Alvin Schmidt has written an excellent summary of Christianity's imprint on education, especially the university which he notes as follows:

"Most colleges and universities that are well known began as Christian schools. Harvard College established a 1636 now known as Harvard University was founded by the Congregational Church as a theological institution; the college of William and Mary started as an Episcopalian school, also primarily to train clergy; Yale University began mostly as a Congregational institution to "educate Ministers in our own way." The Methodists founded Northwestern university in Evanston, Illinois; Columbia university (first known as King's College) began as an Episcopalian bench; Princeton University started as a Presbytery and school and Brown University had Baptist origins.

Even some state universities, for example, the University of Kentucky, the University of California (Berkeley), and the University of Tennessee, had their origins as church schools. But today these institutions of higher learning have abandoned their one time Christian foundations. Other colleges, which still have some tenuous ties to their founding denominations, also have largely deserted their Christian allegiance... The fact remains that many universities would not be in existence today had it not been for their Christian forbears. Similarly, most of the present state universities in Europe - - for example, Oxford, Paris, Cambridge, Heidelberg, and basal …..had Christian origins."[38]

While the catholic–protestant battle greatly affected the university it probably drove the secular mechanism as a compromise. "Every school you see (today) public or private, religious or secular …..is a visible reminder of the religion of Jesus Christ. So is every college and university."[39]

Usa: Attacks continue in America stem from Europe…we must be "Modern"!

To follow the process of the weakening of the German theology and church to America will require a short study of two men who went from being Christian accepting the authority of the Bible and the risen Christ to a so-called "liberal Christian" who saw the German textual criticism and bought it "hook and sinker" allowing them to even become the leaders of Anti-Semitic transcendentalism in America with almost nothing to claim "true Christianity". Theodore Parker's biographer had no bones calling him an "American Heretic".

Parker's views began to change when Convers Francis, the Unitarian minister at Watertown Massachusetts introduced him to the new field of historical Biblical criticism, then being developed in Germany.… In 1834 Parker is seen interpreting some Old Testament miracle naturalistically . While by 1836 in an article for the "Interpreter" he denied the traditional view - - accepted by most Unitarians at that time--- that Isaiah had predicted the coming of Christ.

Parker was so taken by German Higher Criticism that he then spent seven years translating from German the works of WML De Wette's "Critical and Historical Introduction to the Old Testament (1817)". De Wette claims the old testament miracles are myths. [40]

One of the ways we know that Creator–God wrote the bible is, in more than1000 places, He tells us what will happen before it happens! For some reason these people who walk away from Creator–God's word ignore this fact. De Witte, Wellhausen, and other German rationalists as well as Parker, Emerson, and the American Transcendentalists, failed to address the 1850 discovery by Henry Layard of the great library of Ashurbanipal and the meaning of these texts. It is without excuse that they continued to minimize the history of the Jews, there antiquity, and the amazing fact that they were the chosen people. The enemy of man has his hands all over this. Jesus said "I am telling you this now, before it happens so when it happens you may believe that I am He." [John 13:19, Gal. 5:12]$_{NET}$

The Lexington church was organized in 1691 with the famous grand-father who signed our constitution, John Hancock filling the pulpit from 1697 to 1752 followed by Jonas Clark from 1755 to 1805. The town of Lexington (population 700) is the place where pastor Hancock was challenged by "The Great Awakening" religious renewal by the famous preacher George Whitefield. Who was not liked by both the Congregational Clergy and Harvard College (who didn't like his informal education and demonstrative style). But Whitefield's great message stirred all the churches he preached in up and down the Colonies. In 1741 Whitefield's published his first "New England Tour Journal". In this journal he called Harvard and Yale a 'seminary's of paganism' whose 'light is darkness'. Whitefield saw a Harvard and Yale filled with the rational direction (emphasizing the Humanism of man and not the Spirit of God) he condemned ministers for no longer requiring the "born again" conversion experience for ministry, emphasizing that they were "..fraud hiding their lack of conversion behind worthless educations". [41] The reader should recall that Jesus said, "…Except a man be born again, he cannot see the Kingdom of God" [John 3:3 KJVS, first Peter 1:23]. Whitefield and these new pastors he supported were called "New Light" and followed traditional Christian doctrine while accusing some "Old Light" pastors as leaning to the liberal Armenianism; that is, "good behavior" improved one's chances of salvation - - sort of like buying your way into heaven by doing works which was repugnant to Whitefield. Orthodox Calvinist new light ministers did not believe human control had anything to do with Creator–God's grace which is His free gift of salvation by "faith alone" in Jesus' atoning sacrifices on the cross of Calvary ….. a once and for all complete atonement for all, for all time. The big opponents of the "New Light" great awakening, where the so-called Armenians, led by mostly Harvard trained ministers of wealthy churches in and around Boston; although not all Armenians were of the local elite, most of the local elite were Armenian. [42]

The liberal Christianity of leaders such as William Ellery Channing, "Abandons original sin and predestination, arguing that these doctrines made God, not humans, responsible for evil. In contrast, they emphasize God's benevolence, which led a few of them by the end of the century (1890's) to abandon eternal damnation (hell).[43] Hell is something Jesus warned us about more often then he described heaven because man wasn't apparently made to handle it at all, since it was made for Satan and his angels.

Hancock and his successor Jonas Clarke were "Old Calvinists" initially but Clarke ordained pastors without the requirement of a "born again" experience and most all of Clarke's children and students "turned out to be liberal as did his parishioner John Parker. It was Clarke's son-in-law Henry Ware's appointment to the Hollis Professor of Divinity at Harvard in 1805 and Samuel Webber as Harvard's president in 1806 that constituted the liberals take over of Harvard for the first time leading to the liberal American Unitarian Association 20 years later. [44]

Once the liberals walked away from the Christian definition of sin, the very reason Creator–God sent himself to the atonement on the cross, they walk away from the true Gospel of Christ. Grodzins notes, "… Because they did not believe sin was infinite, they did not see the necessity of an infinite sacrificed to atone for it; God no longer needed to be crucified, so Christ no longer had to be God."[45] This is a product of rational thinking of man not Creator-God. So the final emptying out of their liberal church of "the Christ" was their leaving the central issue of the Trinity". By making Creator–God not Creator–God they walked into full idolatry! When we study the history of the Lexington church, we see a church moving from the stable ministry with the conservative John Hancock through Clark and Avery Williams to the liberal rationalist John Parker and Theodore Parker. Parker's ambition was Unitarianism, which he embraced as did Lexington and the elite of Harvard and Boston. He saw this as progress in leaving the role of the laboring class of orthodox believers - - - fitting in the evolutionary ideas of Darwin and the German rationalists that "man is getting better and better" as the so-called progress of man and in so doing walked away from the "Christ" of the bible and his words, "behold the Lamb of God who takes away the sin of the world" [John 1:29]$_{\text{NET, KJV}}$

The liberal Christianity of William Ellery Channing can be seen in Covers Francis whom greatly influenced Parker. Francis showed Parker the Unitarian bible critic Andrews Norton who gave the accepted view of Unitarians at the time. In 1813 Norton's introductory lectures at Harvard "deride as the worst error the interpretations that scriptural passages could be interpreted literally, apart from its historical context." [46] To claim the plain meaning of the words of scripture are not the real meaning is a bizarre approach to the "Word of Creator–God". That means he thought the words could mean whatever someone wanted them to mean. We are told that Parker even believed that, "if a man leads a 'good' and 'pure' life he will be accepted with God.[47] Of course good and pure seem to be self-defined and places these beliefs with the idea that you can buy eternal life by a works trip, which has no place in new testament theology based on:

"For by grace you are saved through faith; and not of yourselves: it is the gift of God: not of works, lest any one should boast" [Eph 2:8-9]$_{\text{NKJV}}$

Harvard's Hollis Professor of Divinity Dr. Henry Ware taught many young Harvard trained pastors natural and revealed religion, church history, and dogmatic theology. A system of apologetics that undergirded orthodox Congregationalist opinion, and that modern scholars identify as 'supernatural rationalism'... In which people could with their unaided 'natural' reason discover certain basic religious truths. We find in Professor Ware's writing that he taught that Jesus does not reconcile God to us. [48] Again, teaching of a false Christ who was too weak to do what He said is a real problem. "For God did not send his Son into the world to condemn [or judge] the world, but in order that the world might be saved through Him" [John 3:16-17]$_{\text{ESV, NET}}$

The plain meaning of the text is not part of liberal theology and does give us to accept calling their "liberal Christianity" as another religion made from whole cloth. Especially when they change the meaning of the direct words of Jesus Christ!

While there are 309 prophecies clearly describing the Jesus Christ of the bible before he arrived on earth Parker stated, "..That he was the subject of inspired prophecy I very much doubt". [49]

The clear linkage between pre-NAZI German Humanist rationalism and the Unitarian –Transcendentalism of New England can be seen when Theodore Parker travels to Europe in 1844 carefully visiting Wittenberg and Halle University where Parker met with anti-rationalist Professor Frederick Tholuck in an attempt to convince him that American Unitarians had not become pantheist (were God is everything). While we don't know Tholuck's opinion of Parker we are given a clear description of his meeting with the famous liberal professor Wilhelm Leberech De Wette who held a reception for his American translator. De Wette conversed with Parker about the liberal state of German theology. We know Parker considered the old testament stories of Noah, Baal, and Balaam as myths of the Jews and absurd. It's hard to read parker's transcendentalist hostility to the Jews and his generally low estimate of the Jewish character. Amazing when you look at the effect of humanist liberalism and so-called "Rational Christianity" in preparing Germany for the holocaust, we see the same threads holding on to the liberal church in America today.

Theodore Parker's biographer Dean Grodzins notes that when Parker was translating the German work of De Witt that De Witt had convinced him that the Hebrew books were largely inauthentic and mostly mythological". [50] Key of course was Parker's claim that "science" is contradicted in the bible and creation took "millions of years". So Parker claimed that "evolution", man's reasoning was correct and that Gods words in Genesis was a myth, following the German De Wette's thinking. The idea that only Creator–God could have observed and known what He did; did not occur to Parker for some reason.

On the other hand Parker's preaching and writing against social ills, the right of women, and the "evils" of the community and his call for reform are admirable. However, his understanding of the doctrine that undergirds a man's life had radically changed from trusting Creator–God and His power to teach us with His Own Word (the Bible) to accepting the power of man's own reason and man's own facilities as the focus… An incredible mistake reflected in the path of the German liberal church and the American liberal denominations.

There was a two pronged attack on the "old" theology, that included both a theological component and an educational component. Both the Transcendentalists that took over Harvard and the three most important men in the American progressive education movement – John Dewey, James McKeen Cattell, and G. Stanley Hall –(which were all at Johns Hopkins at the same time). Hall, who was trained by Wilhelm Wundt at Leipzig, taught Dewey and Cattell the new psychology. Psychology at the University of Leipzig, Germany, can be traced as far back as late 17th century. The works of Gottfried Wilhelm Leibniz (1646), Christian Thomasius (1655-1728) and Christian Wolff (1679-1754) are closely linked to this history. Whereas Thomasius was appointed to a professorship in Leipzig, however Leibniz and Wolff left town. Leibniz was refused a professorship after his dissertation and Wolf habilitated in Leipzig in 1703 and was appointed to a professorship in Halle four years later. Central to Wolff's practical philosophy is its autonomy from theological doctrine. Although maintaining that universal ethics is certainly compatible with the teachings of Sacred Scripture, Wolff is adamant that morality does not depend on revelation or God's divine commands. Advocating the separation of philosophy and religion is a theme that Wolff developed and defended throughout his entire career and it is a feature of his thought that secures him a place among other philosophers of Europe's Enlightenment.[51]

It was also at Johns Hopkins that Dewey was introduced to Hegelianism. James McKeen Cattell later studied under Wundt in Leipzig and went on to become America's leading educational psychologist at Teachers College,

Columbia University. Dewey went on to create the new progressive curriculum for the public schools, which downgraded literacy and emphasized socialization. Cattell's experiments in Wundt's laboratory were to become the scientific basis for using the look-say, whole word method in teaching reading in the primary schools.[52]

Reaction to strict Calvanism and the Battle of Boston Churches for the heart of Americans.

Boston's churches influence on Harvard was quite profound. The town supported the college development and to a large degree, the theology and Christology of the campus. The Pious church of the puritans and the strict Calvinist came under a direct attack that would soon be a battle for the heart of the American People, which continues today. The wonderful Constitution of the United States is owed primarily to the understanding that 3 co-equal branches of government will deal with the man's depraved black heart, that is "who knows it?" Checks and balances are built into the Constitution so that no one branch can run over the others and no President can practice the tyranny seen in the English crown. Somehow, the idea that man is getting "better and better" as in "Evolving" entered into the heads of certain individuals and they walked away from the clear teaching of the Bible and Christianity in general. There is a grave penalty to any nation that walks away from the word of Creator-God. Let's look at the movement of the liberal church in Boston that invaded almost all colleges and universities of America.

You could say that the clear words of the bible describe man as a depraved and fallen soul needing redemption and salvation from hell. This salvation is by faith alone not from any works one could do. This was the clear statement of the Reformation in which many lives were lost by those who spoke the truth of scripture. One such speaker of this truth was, beside Luther, John Calvin. Many rejected this clear understanding of the plain words of the bible. If you look at history and wars and deprivation, you don't have a leg to stand on to claim man is basically good. The reader will only understand if he looks at what Jesus said of the Decalogue....the 10 commandments. You need to understand that only one that did not break these 10 commands was the Hebrew Messiah himself. If you understand what the writer of this sentence has noted of Idolatry in this book, you will probably see that we all have committed some form of idolatry, a violation of the 1ˢᵗ commandments to have "no other gods before Him". And that doesn't yet list lying, stealing, adultery (lust of the heart), desiring that you have something others have and they not have it anymore (10ᵗʰ commandment). Who among us has not demeaned another's reputation when it is not or not likely true....that's murder (it's the heart that counts).

"The Unitarians also rejected the Calvinist view of man as being innately depraved. Man, they were convinced, was not only basically good, but perfectible. For this reason, social action became the principal mode in which Unitarians practiced their religion. They were convinced that evil was caused not by man's sinful nature, but by ignorance, poverty, and social injustice. Thus, by eliminating ignorance (through universal public education), they would eliminate poverty and thereby eliminate social injustice. Once this was done and the happy results observed by all, the Unitarians would have proven that they were right and the Calvinists were wrong." [53]

Boston became a University center and not surprisingly started out somewhat like Halle University, actually Halle-Wurtenberg University, containing the very name where Martin Luther began the Reformation. Boston was a center of strict Calvinist Churches that did what seems to also have happened in Europe, and stimulated church splits aplenty. Looking at early American church history, even though there is disagreement by some of the Christian and non-Christian institutions, should allow us to see the development of the Idolatry of which we continually refer.

"The underground churches in England and exiles from Holland provided about 35 out of the 102 passengers on the Mayflower, which sailed from London in July 1620. They became known in history as the Pilgrim Fathers. The early Congregationalists sought to separate themselves from the Anglican church in every possible way and even eschewed having church buildings. They met in homes for many years...... The Pilgrims sought to establish at Plymouth Colony a Christian fellowship like that which gathered around Jesus himself. [54]

Congregationalists include the Pilgrims of Plymouth, and the Puritans of the Massachusetts Bay Colony, which were organized in union by the Cambridge Platform in 1648. These settlers had John Cotton as their most influential leader, beginning in 1633. Cotton's writings persuaded the Calvinist theologian John Owen to separate from the Presbyterian church. He became very influential in the development of Congregationalist theology and ideas of church government. Jonathan Edwards was also a Congregationalist.[55]

The history of Congregational churches in the United States is closely intertwined with that of American Presbyterianism, especially in New England where Congregationalist influence spilled over into Presbyterian churches farther west. Some of the first colleges and universities in America, including Harvard, Yale, Dartmouth, Williams, Bowdoin, Middlebury, and Amherst, all were founded by the Congregationalists, as were later Carleton, Grinnell, Oberlin, Beloit, and Pomona.

Without higher courts to ensure doctrinal uniformity among the congregations, Congregationalists have been more diverse than other Reformed churches. Despite the efforts of Calvinists to maintain the dominance of their system, some Congregational churches, especially in the older settlements of New England, gradually developed leanings toward Armenianism, Unitarianism, Deism, and Transcendentalism.

By the 1750s, several Congregational preachers were teaching the possibility of universal salvation, an issue that caused considerable conflict among its adherents on the one side and hard-line

Calvinists and sympathizers of the First Great Awakening on the other. In another strain of change, the first church in the United States with an openly Unitarian theology, the belief in the single personality of God, was established in Boston, Massachusetts in 1785 (in a former <u>Anglican</u> parish.) By 1800, all but one Congregational church in Boston had Unitarian preachers teaching the strict unity of God, the subordinate nature of Christ, and salvation by character."[56]

Harvard University,(1636-) founded by Puritan Congregationalists, became a center of Unitarian training. It's initial motto was *Veritas Christo et Ecclesiae* (Truth for Christ and the Church). That later had little to do with the Truth of Christ. Prompted by a controversy over an appointment in the theology school at Harvard, the Unitarian churches separated from Congregationalism in 1825. Most of the Unitarian "descendants" hold membership in the Unitarian Universalist Association, founded in the 1960s by a merger with the theologically similar Universalists. This group had dissented from Calvinist orthodoxy on the basis of their belief that all persons could find salvation (as opposed to the Calvinist idea of double predestination, excluding some from salvation.) (Of course the important question is what does the Bible clearly say.) Congregational churches were at the same time the first example of the American theocratic ideal and may be considered the seedbed from which American liberal religion and society arose. Many Congregationalists in the several successor denominations to the original tradition consider themselves to be Reformed first, whether of traditional or neo-orthodox persuasion.[57]

So my first understanding that Germany and Europe was filled with ministers that first bought Julius Wellhausen's higher textual criticism in 1878, Is incorrect. It is obvious that Halle Lutheran graduates had filled the state churches of Germany long before this and thus were easily swayed by Wellhausen's idolatry..... And the German church fell before Hitler. It seems that liberal university teaching precedes the destruction of a nation as "when pride comes, then comes disgrace"[Prov. 11:2]$_{NET}$.

So, I will make my case of the same attack on the Church in America. Will there be Bonhoffers not in need of the holy spirit standing beside their liberal professors at the seminars? It seems the enemy of man (Satan) is not so creative, he just repeats the same process over and over until he meets his final fate. His first words were, as you remember, "god hath not said" …..a lie and a misquote of the Word of Creator–God.

The University run's to idolatry and away from it's Christian beginnings
I will use America's first College/University as an example but the process seems to run deep in America's schools.

This is my plan in this book, to demonstrate how we got to a situation where the treasurer at Harvard University in 1866 was able to convince the board that had become predominately Unitarian that the treasure's son should be appointed to the head of Harvard University . (those Unitarians did not recognize Jesus as God and therefore worshipped something else and so did not trust God, the Trinity). At one time, matriculation from a freshman to a sophomore required the translation of one of the Gospels from Greek to English . After this new head of Harvard took over, He decided to "modernized" the University by hiring evolutionists as the new head of law and the sciences. So the head of the law school and the sciences were both dedicated evolutionists both trying to remove the influence of Christianity from the Campus, replacing it with a "new religion" (deceptively disguised) and drove the university deep into their way of thinking.

These events served to move America away from the biblical morality that created it. That new president was a chemist just like the Brit who donated the initial monies and is considered the father of the Smithsonian Institution. Smithson performed an "experiment" on his laboratory tabletops in which he did a "flood" and noticed that everything was covered with "muck" after the mock flood……his conclusion was that there was no flood because nothing would work due to the muck he found. And the logical thing is that God is lying in Genesis and the Bible is not true. So we see the founder of the Smithsonian Institution, the prototype of all our museums is this failed individual named Smithson, a chemist. What is the relationship between Smithson's story as a Chemist and the chemist that took over Harvard University for 40 years. The Universities of the U.S. copied the seemingly modern Europeanized Harvard very closely thereafter. If you will look carefully look at a club that was established at Harvard at the time, you will find that the people that come out of that club are the ones who seeded the supreme court, seeded the judgeships of the U.S. , academic leaderships in the U.S., Biology courses, college classrooms and the museums and key popular publications.

There would have been friction between the World Famous Anti-Evolutionist Prof. Louis Agassiz professor of zoology and geology who was instrumental in establishing the Lawrence Scientific School at Harvard University in 1847 . He also founded the Museum of Comparative Zoology in 1859 which he was in charge until his death in 1873. So in 1866 the big move to Darwinian Evolution pushed by the new President would be contrary to Harvard's most famous scientist Louis Agassiz, considered a Paleontologist, Glaciologist, Geologist, and Natural History authority. He is Perhaps the first Glaciologist, and the most highly regarded American Scientist at the time. This speaks strongly of the power of the Univ. Treasurer to convince the board to hire his son and move America's First University in the "Modernization" of Europe's Darwinism when such a anti-Darwinian was on the faculty. One wonders how he pulled it off over Agassiz's head. Lets investigate how this all happened.

When Harvard was first Formed

Before 1870 Harvard trained many of America's greatest leaders. Signers of the Declaration such as John Adams, John Hancock, Samuel Adams, William Ellery, William Hooper, Robert Treat Paine, William Williams, and Elbridge Gerry as well as signers of the constitution William Samuel

Johnson and Rufus King. Other National leaders Fisher Ames (a framer of the bill of rights) William Cushing (an Original Justice of the Supreme Court) and Timothy Pickering (an American General during the Revolution and the Secretary of War for Both George Washington and John Adams.

How Harvard changed: How could the defection of one man "from Christian faith provide a hinge upon which to turn an entire nation"

For 100 years the Congregational Church Controlled the board of Harvard College which was established to produce ministers and leaders of the new America. Harvard was the oldest school of higher learning in America without equal for at least 60 years. It was founded in 1636 just six years after Boston was founded having been dedicated by pastor John Harvard simply to the cause of Christ. Today Harvard would not be recognized even slightly as dedicated to that same cause... Some might say the "Trinity" with Christ as Creator–God incarnate is hard to be found there even in the school of divinity. Notice the course offering on http://div.hds. harvard.edu/adademics/courses/byinstructor.cam?range=all offered today. One might ask how has this happened? Who has taken over the board and driven the university to be in disjunction with its original purpose, leading most all of American universities and staffing with personnel that appear to have spoken little of the "cause of Christ" that John Harvard espoused (at least in these amazing school of Divinity course descriptions)?

The destruction of that cause has been a battle as described by Ruth Nourse in her "hijacking of American education: flip jack turning at Harvard." Pointing to Ralph Waldo Emerson's fall from a form of Christianity to the religion of "transcendentalism" or instrumentalism philosophy... as the hinge upon which to turn the entire nation."[58] Emerson's father was a Unitarian minister which must have greatly affected him and later had much to do with the direction of the Harvard school of divinity's "Unitarian teaching positions". His life was not without great difficulties with the loss of his first wife and his series of "sexually charged" poetry directed to a young male student, Martin Gay attending the College.[59] "Ralph Waldo Emerson had muttered in his journal for 30 years or more about new laws, new religion, the new race, and other things quite enigmatic.

He spoke about spiritual things:" He and his circle of friends were very much into fundamental "social change."

The transcendentalism Religion: Where does it come from?
Herman Melville, who had met Emerson in 1849, originally thought he had "a defect in the region of the heart" and a "self-conceit so intensely intellectual that at first one hesitates to call it by its right name", though he later admitted Emerson was "a great man".[60]

In his book "The American Religion", Harold Bloom repeatedly refers to Emerson as "The prophet of the American Religion," which in the context of the book refers to indigenously American religions such as Mormonism and Christian Science, which arose largely in Emerson's lifetime, but also to Mainline Protestant churches that Bloom says have become in the United States more gnostic than their European counterparts. William Dean Howells set around the table with Harvard professor Oliver Wendell Holmes, William James, Charles S. Peirce, and Oliver Wendel Holmes, Jr. where they would discuss things with William Wordsworth Longfellow, never really understanding Wordsworth's Christianity. Instead they believed that route to truth was related to "purpose" rather than reality. Not a small flaw in thinking.

Emerson discounted Bible miracles and proclaimed that, while Jesus was a great man, he was not God and ...'if there be one lesson more than another which should pierce (the scholar's) ear, it is, The world is nothing, the man is all: in yourself is the law of all nature... In yourself slumbers the whole of Reason: it is for you to know all; it is for you to dare all. A nation of men for the first time exists, because each believes himself inspired by the Divine soul which also inspires all men.'..... Emerson taught as most all relating to him afterwards taught, a new religion rejecting the absolute authority of the bible and against the teachings of the bible arguing that,' Christ did come to teach that God was incarnate in man — all men. He suggested that what man had been unable to find in church may be found in the soul: "in the soul of redemption be sought".[61] for this speech Emerson was banished from Harvard for 30 years. However just 14 years later in 1866 there was the election of a new president William Charles Elliott who within one year turned the university on it's ear, awarded Emerson and L.L.D. degree and got the alumni to elect him to the board of overseers. This is the "flip jack turning" that Ruth Norse describes. Emerson influence on American intellectuals and anti-biblical thinking cannot be emphasized, together with his friends Henry David Thoreau and Henry James his Godson through his extremely well written essays and thousand or so lectures throughout America on the Philosophy of History and many other topics on Transcendentalism and "Nature" were effective proponents of a Utopian ideal, a sort of spiritual or "soulish" ideal with major effects still seen in the university of today in one form or another relating to relative truth.

Ralph Waldo Emerson And The Transcendentalists: Creator-God's Authority, Biblical Authority Vs. Merging With Humanism's Authority

The concept of *Sola Scriptura:* That the Bible is the sole written divine revelation and alone can bind the conscience of the believer absolutely. Is the first of the 5 *Solas* of the Protestant Reformation. Many people gave their lives and their sacred honor to face a monstrous heretical church to give us this understanding. All of a sudden we see in America a small, but intellectually infective group of men with their discovery of what WC Fields calls "looking for loopholes" in the authority of the Word of Creator-God (higher criticism) to create their own Humanist religious institutions within America. Interesting that the need for the Protestant Reformation was similar. The Church had become infiltrated with Humanist ideas, placing the authority of the "creature" (man) over the authority of Creator-God. All five of the *Solas* are about the fifth *Sola, Sola Deo Gloria:* to Creator-God alone belongs the glory. The 4 exist to exalt this fifth *Sola.* What I am attempting to describe as we investigate the crux of Emerson's incredible influence on Harvard's intellectuals as they at first reject him as a Heretic then a few years later when Humanists take over the College, herald him as their Theological leader. The Humanist religion is a slow "creep" through existing institutions by attack on the authority of those institutions ever driving wedges by redefining terms and relationships----between the plain meaning of the Word of Creator-God and supposedly more modern ideas invented out of whole cloth by man's pathetic "water-brain".

Emerson's resignation (from the ministry in Boston) was an act that followed his 'glorious' speech before the Harvard graduating class in which cooler heads identified as the words of a heretic… challenging the very authority of the Bible with his clever inventions. He rejected the authority of the Lord's Supper and resigned because he could not in good conscience preside over the Lords Supper in a congregation. His explanation had to do with what he called "forms …that are inscribed by and the judge of existing religious institutions." Richard A. Grusin has written "Transcendentalist Hermeneutics: Institutional Authority and the Higher Criticism of the Bible" in which he carefully evaluates Emerson, Parker, and Thoreau. [62]Please note, an attack on the personal authority of Jesus and the Lords Supper is a frontal assault on the Gospel of Jesus Christ who tells us in His own words to "Do this in remembrance of Me". This application of European Higher Criticism of the Bible to American Unitarian Congregationalist ministries at the level of Harvard College had an enormous effect. The seeds of the "creature's" attempt to crumble the Body of Christ (the Church) in America. This attempt has been quite effective among those that fail to realize *Sola Scriptura*.

There was a higher criticism influence on Emerson's early career and on Thoreau that Richard Grusin found in Henry David Thoreau's critique of institutionalize religion in the "Sunday" chapter of *"a week on the Concorde and Merrimac Rivers"*. Although Thoreau was less directly affected by the higher criticism than Emerson, he formulates an account of mythological interpretation that ironically has more bearing on the higher criticism than either Emerson's resignation from the ministry or his Divinity School address. Consequently Grusin read the "Week's" "Sunday" chapter in relation to the continental development (and subsequent criticism of the maxim that to interpret Scripture correctly the Biblical interpreter should aim to see through the eyes of its author or intended audience. Taking as my starting point Thoreau's suggestion in

Walden that to look through the eyes of another would constitute the greatest of all possible miracles, Grusin argues that the account of mythological interpretations set forth in the "Week" constitutes the denial of the possibility either of reading the ancient texts through the eyes of their authors or of reading them independently of our own particular historical, institutional situations.[63]

Whatever acquaintance with continental higher criticism Thoreau might have had would likely have come from Theodore Parker, whose view of David Frederick Strauss's infamous "Life of Jesus" Grusen then takes up in relation to Thoreau's mythological interpretation and examines the coupling of material an intuitive authority of Parker's critique of institutionalized religion.

"Although Parker had the most thorough and extensive knowledge of the higher criticism among the Transcendentalists, he makes surprisingly little use of this knowledge in his Sermons and published works relying instead on the internalization of a logical or rhetorical identity between maternal and divine authority. Read in the context of the two autobiographical pieces composed in the year before his death, Parker's attempt to ground religion permanently in our innate intuitive facilities turns out itself to be contingent upon the authority of such transient institutions as marriage and the family. More clearly than either Emerson or Thoreau, Parker reveals the way in which the Transcendentalists appeal to the authority of the heart is an appeal not to a source of authority independent of institutions but to an authority so fundamentally institutional--- in Parker's case the authority of the mother--- that it appears to be innate."[64]

Among the lessons that Emerson, Thoreau, and Parker took from the higher criticism was what in the present critical climate might be characterized as the discovery of history.(Their own ideas of interpretation taken from the Liberal German Humanist influence we saw that invaded Helle University.). ".... the influence of the higher criticism on Emerson, Thoreau, and Parker spawned a recognition that the religious truths set forth in the bible are not

the absolute and unconditional word of God but the product of the historical epochs in which the Bible was written, edited, and collected. One consequence of the collective realization was the perceived need to re-conceptualize
the authority of existing religious institutions...... made' by accommodating
existing institutions to the authority of oneself. ..... For it is only insofar as
"we do not make a world of our own" that The Orphic Poet's injunction to
"build, therefore, your own world" has any force at all. [65] Emerson wrote a
poem called the "Song of the Soul" later published in the Atlantic in 1857
titled "Brahma" referring to the Hindu god of creation (or perhaps Brahman,
the absolute or universal soul). Emerson is quoted as telling his daughter "that
one need not adopt a Hindu perspective to understand the poem that one
could easily substitute "Jehovah" for "Brahma", he explained and not loose the
sense of the verse." [66] Emerson is today celebrated by writers as the iconoclastic
America's first poet. From Unitarian Preacher to America's Preacher of his
own god certainly not one consistent with a lover of the Scripture of the Bible.
A leading intellectual, planting seeds in the new world.

Things changed radically. In the early 1870s, a small group of young men
formed a Harvard Square circle for philosophical discussion. Meeting sometimes in the study of Charles Sanders Peirce and sometimes in the study of
William James, they half-ironically, half-defiantly called themselves The
Metaphysical Club. While they called themselves Pragmatists, they were
merely extending the Hot Idols of ancient Humanism into this country in
a big way. If you read Peirce carefully he was in love with Evolution in any
and every form.

"Three modes of evolution:

1. evolution by fortuitous variation
2. evolution by mechanical necessity
3. and evolution by creative love" [67]

**Agapism (wiki) was Peirce's name for this Unitarian Evolution mock-
ing the Greek word *agape*, that Christians use for the love of Christ......
self-sacrificing love. Also the love we are to have for one another and
our wives.[66]**

In those youthful Harvard Square philosophical discussions, the doctrine
of pragmatism saw the light in 1873. The meaning of an idea could be
known only considering its consequences for practical experience, for actual
or possible action. In writing later to Peirce, William James exclaimed,
"There is no more original thinker than yourself in our generation." The
two had become acquainted when both of them were studying chemistry
in the Lawrence Scientific School. Charles's father, Benjamin Peirce, the
Perkins Professor of Mathematics and Astronomy at Harvard, has been
described as America's most eminent scientist in the nineteenth century.
He was one of the incorporators of the National Academy of Sciences, one
of the founders of the Harvard Observatory, and author of *The History of
Harvard University 1636-1775*. His students included two future presidents
of the university, Charles William Eliot and A. Lawrence Lowell. And they
greatly influenced Louis Agassiz (his father's closest friend), Margaret Fuller,
Judge Story, Henry Wadsworth Longfellow, James Russell Lowell, Daniel
Webster, James Freeman Clarke, William Henry Channing, and sometimes
Ralph Waldo Emerson.

Charles William Eliot was a fearless crusader for educational reform and
the progressive movement, attempted to end football and other sports, calling only rowing and tennis the only clean sports. Eliot is called by Stephen P.
Shoemaker, in the Unitarian History, as the one that eliminated the favored
position of Christianity from the curriculum while opening it to student
self-direction. "While Eliot was the most crucial figure in secularization
of American higher education, he was not motivated by a desire to secu-
larize education, but by Transcendentalist Unitarian convictions. Derived
from William Ellery Channing and Ralph Waldo Emerson, these convictions were focused on the dignity and worth of human nature (not Creator-
God), the right and ability of each person to perceive truth (at the expense

of revealed Biblical Truth), and the 'indwelling God in each person'...." [68] During Eliot's Presidency at Harvard from 1869-1909, Harvard was known as the Unitarian Vatican. Consistent with the takeover by the Unitarians in 1805, the University has not deviated greatly from that period. Today this influence in the School of Divinity is a good example. Under Eliot's 40 year administration, Harvard developed from a small college to a great modern university. From 1848 to 1870 (immediately after Eliot became President) Theophilis Parson was dean of law. Parson was a follower of Emanuel Swedenborg, a man that wrote many volumes but never started a church. Swedenbord was labeled a Spiritist because he claimed "special knowledge" not unlike a group of Heretical individuals in old church history called "Gnostics". Today's critics of Ralph Waldo Emerson note that Emerson did not thoroughly read Swdenborg, and while he praised him in his famous Oration delivered before the Phi Beta Kappa Society at Cambridge Aug 31, 1837, he referred to Swdenbord's muse (no doubt his spirit guides) and saw him as a fellow humanist. Eliot replaced Parson during the first year of his presidency with Christopher Columbus Langdell who still rules the legal classrooms of our law colleges. Langdell saw law as a evolutionary science with a imperfect evolution. He was a Transcendentalist and imbedded American law in Transcendentalist doctrine in a quite deceptive manner. [69] Langdell made all possible efforts to remove "religion" from the law. Which means in 1871, remove the bible and the justice of the Bible leaving no absolute morality but human case-law which is followed to this day by most American Law schools.

"....the reason for longevity of Langdell's pedagogy, as Grey noted more then a quarter century ago, may be the fact that the rejection of Langdell's theory left legal academics with no conceptual scheme with which to revitalize the law school curriculum. [70]"Academics have struggled to find a credible functional analogy ever since legal formalism was targeted by the legal realists in the early twentieth century. In the void, a number of academics have written to defend the watered-down practices of case examination and Socratic-style interrogation, while playing no heed to Langedell's Scientific Theory "....instead the law student learns by the brutal technique of 'Habituating (a physiological term) to the need for reasoned judgments under conditions of maximum moral ambiguity....giving them practice at rendering such judgments themselves"[71] The morality of American law, according to him was that of a deductive law system based on **self-evident** moral axioms......that then, because there was no 5 billion copies of a document with absolute morality to rely on or cite (the Bible), allowed morality to float into judicial decisions today that are on the way to the moral destruction of our country. And making the backward looking *Stare Decisis* rule of honoring older precedents control the future of our country, where the older precedents have removed from them, the absolute morality given by Creator-God. So "the murder" and the "abominations" and much more morality Creator-God teaches us were cleverly removed from all precedents since Langdell and his "Transcendental Nonsense" took over the law of the United States of America. Show me where a top lawyer cites the "Word of Creator-God" to support his position, even where a Federal Court Judge (other than Judge Bork) was brave enough to argue from the absolute truth of Creator-God in a decision. The law "floats" for this very reason, and the results are the end of us all. If a Supreme Court Nominee dared to mention he referenced this, he would be destroyed in the Judicial Committee by such as Senators Joe Biden and Ted Kennedy, to terminate their nomination...... it really happened. [Read congressional Record of Judge Bork before the Senate Judicial Committee hearing]

As a result of these educational decisions we must ask, Are we approaching the "end of law" in America today? The 4th and 9th Circuit Court blocked President Trump's executive travel order on the 6 lawless nations. The travel ban to protect the U.S. on the principle that "Muslim feelings" would be offended. We now suffer from Lawyer/Judges trained without any absolute morality or anchor in the Ethics of the Bible and instead tie the law to "feelings" as if that test is all that is left as a standard. America was saved by the quality of thinking of our Supreme Court who voted 9 to nothing to uphold the ban. But how long will that last? During the 4th Circuit oral argument, the plaintiff admitted if, "anyone except President Trump had signed the order it would be constitutional". Amazing, that should have been the end of the case, but our legal reasoning is now in the toilet. Feelings are the guide of those progressive lawyer-judges? We're in big trouble in the future if this continues. Law schools removal of moral-standards of the Bible and those of our founding fathers are to blame. How solid a basis for a society not on Biblical moral principals but in the solid reproducible limbic expression "feelings". Absurd ! How to take a nation down by demonic forces/thinking. The university's religion… Humanist motives are exposed.

Who was saved in the San Bernardino Massacre when two jihadist murderers who believed in female genital mutilation among other things were given gifts by their co-workers at their baby shower; this future "mom and dad" turned and murdered their "friends". Whose feelings are marred appellate judges? How do you weigh feelings to make a decision? The decision becomes one of simple political expediency and nothing else. This feelings standard becomes a weighing of population estimates: Decision=Islamic Feelings/Americans Feelings(Constitution). This places the power in those who have the evil ability to control and drive population feelings…the media. Out of control, what few media owners can destroy a nation? Propaganda power is a big big deal under those conditions. Its happened before, remember.

While the historian Ruth Nourse in her "Hijacking of American Education: Part 5-Flapjack Turning at Harvard", declares Ralph Waldo Emerson's defection from Christianity provided a hinge upon which to turn an entire nation, the leadership at Harvard Law and Harvard Divinity were deeply into this scheme…..yet, I must admit Emerson did preach the religious script, part of the deconstruction of words such as faith, law of nature (evolution), Reason, Devine Soul seen in the following Emerson quote twisting truth in a sinister unbiblical manner. See if you can identify it for it is hidden in great flowery "spiritual" terms.

"…if there be one lesson more than another which should pierce (the scholar's) ear, it is, The world is nothing, the man is all; in yourself is the law of all nature…..in yourself slumbers the whole of Reason: it is for you to know all; it is for you to dare all. A nation of men for the first time exist, because each believes himself inspired by the Divine Soul which also inspires all men." These were the words of a man who denied Jesus Christ and Creator-God, was a believer of Darwinian Evolution and the leader of American Humanism..a wordsmith hammering out new perverse meanings of key biblical terms. The words he desecrates here are words known by believers by what they do, like "Love", and "Faith", "Reason with Me", "Nature from Creator-God" which are more powerful then Emerson understands as he exalts himself as, along with Poe, the "great poets" of the Darkness, certainly not the light.

No man has kissed the University "scholar" with epethets and feigned glory than Emerson when, in the same speech to the Harvard "glorious <u>August</u> body" with:

"The scholar is that man who must take up into himself all the ability of the time, all the contributions of the past, all the hopes of the future. He must be an university of knowledges".

If you study Emerson, especially his presentation to the Harvard Faculty August 31,1837 you see someone equating academics with gods. He does glorify Emanuel Swdenborg in an interesting manner. And, it appears adopted a great deal of Swdenborg's words and ideas. Those who really know Swdenborg's work complain that he didn't read Swdenborg thoroughly. No matter, Emerson's fails to understand, no matter how witty and cleaver he is with words, the distinction between Creator-God's knowledge and wisdom and man's knowledge and wisdom. In fact the entire failure of those that follow or believe in the enemy of man (Humanist) to separate the written word of Creator-God from their own creative work is amazing. Would you say these are "humble" people who see themselves "like the most high God".....finding divinity in themselves and boasting in it. I'm afraid the academic who feels divine and claims to create divine work is in big trouble! Remember Satan's first communication with man was to misquote the word of Creator-God to Eve, "You will not surely die" (if you disobey God). This, was an enormous lie, as all men know now, but a big surprise to the first man Adam and his wife. How long will man fail to read and understand the Word of God, the " LOGOS"? Indeed how long will our nation fall under this deception. Colleen Walsh, a Harvard staff writer declared in the "Harvard gazette" Feb 16,2012 in a piece labeled "When religion turned inward" notes that in commemoration of Emerson's speech, every July, Divinity School officials give out free Popsicles, in part to celebrate the famous words of Emerson's "landmark speech".[72] She writes as an Emerson apologist, claiming that he offers the idea, "not that we are not like God, but that we are divine, insofar as we act out of this inner, essentially moral or ethical law which is within us".[73] The absolute moral authority of Creator-God and His Word, is mocked again by these statements. So man can find the correct moral behavior in himself? Look around, how great a lie is this! Combine this with the Langdell and Eliot's removal of the Bible's moral standards from the training of all American Lawyers, and you have quite a move on our nation. Then add the mockery of Creation by the Biology Departments, a deception I will discuss in the next chapter. Today, we are reaping what was sewed before 1900.

Once the premier colleges had "modernized" their curriculum with Darwinian Evolution and the Humanist idols, it would spread its idols and its newest of man's invented creator and mankind's most important creator the idol "Chance" or "Random", considered by the evolutionists as what has, by fortuitous circumstances created random mutations that were beneficial in the environment leading from molecular soup to mankind. Most universities copied the Harvard newfound religion and creator in an effort to imitate what some saw as the greater universities of Europe. Never mind the British Banks that financed the revolutionary and civil war and built a morality of slavery into the American economy. A far more deadly insert into American culture was introduced into the very educational blood of America, a new idol, a new god that we have eaten thinking we were wise. As if the lesson of idolatry that destroyed Jerusalem in Ezekiel's day, Jeremiah's day and the city of Sodom or read the two books of Kings where we learn of kings leading the nation to destruction and captivity by idolatry. While we "sometimes" chant "in God we trust" as on our money; is it now "In Chance do we Trust", taking on the chant of the god of Vegus to lead us out of darkness. I think not!

I do not present Harvard University in a very favorable light here, which might not be completely fair for the venerable institution is certainly more then I have described. In 1986, Peter Gomes, Harvard's campus minister helped establish the "*Veritas* Forum" named from the original Harvard motto "*Veritas Christe et Ecclesiae*" or truth for Christ and the Church which he indicated seeks to remind the university community of the centrality of Christ to the founding of the University. The first meeting of the forum was a sharing of the authors of :*Finding God at Harvard*, a compilation of testimonies of 48 people that have related to the institution. The author of :Finding God at Harvard", Kelly Monroe Kullberg, considers Creator-God not very evident at the prestigious campus. But she does demonstrate Christian Faith can survive a rigorous intellectual atmosphere. Truth can and will survive, even the trial of a secular campus onslaught.[74]

Who gains and who loses.

1. There is nothing but destruction that faces an idolatrous nation!
2. Who Loses?
   It is the faculty that teaches Idolatry that is in a bad spot.
   1. Those who know it and are proud of it.
   2. Those who do know it but are not proud of it.
   3. Those who don't know they teach idolatry.
   4. Those who are ashamed that this is happening on campus.

Idolatry will keep us from our preparation for eternity, we will show up for the wedding not clothed in the "Righteousness of Jesus Christ", and un-prepared for eternity.....and most of all, we will be a "unprofitable servant"... thrown into outer darkness where there will be weeping and gnashing of teeth!".[Matthew 22:1-14,25:1-30, 13:24,8:12, Luke 13:22-30, 16:23]$_{NET}$ Knowing these things, why should our teaching institutions teach idolatry to our children, or anyone else for that matter?

Creator-God made man with incredible function and design. Man and women's anatomy are fearfully and wonderfully made with a design clearly to do specific functions and to protect mankind from destruction by the environment. Creator-God has fine-tuned this world so that the fixity of man's internal environment, or the internal *mileau* as far as temperature, pressure, gravitational forces, chemistry, and availability of vitamins, minerals... food, let alone all the physical constants that must be so precise for our existence. Reproduction has been carefully designed. The contrast between two structures is germane to problems we face today, ie. The spread of disease that could wipe us off the earth.

The Degrading of Sex in America
(God invented it initially)

Vaginal structures vs. rectal structures, can this destroy America

The recent work highlighting this is "Unprotected", by Miriam Grossman, M.D. with 12 years on the staff of the UCLA student counseling service. The vagina maintains a low pH, which inactivates HIV/AIDS,. Its mucus has anti-HIV proteins. Its lining is 20 to 45 cells thick, increasing the distance to be traversed by the virus. Under the lining is a layer in which target cells are found: this area is rich in elastic fibers followed by a layer of muscle, then more elastic fibers allowing for stretching without tears or abrasions. Good research shows that HIV is unable to reach target cells in the human vagina under normal circumstances. [75]

The physician then describes the rectum, which as part of the gastrointestinal system, has a lining whose primary function is absorption, "bringing in molecules of food and water. The pH is higher with a barrier of only one cell thickness. Below the delicate lining are blood vessel and target cells. Elastic fibers are absent. No disruption of the 1 cell layer is necessary for HIV infection to occur because specialized cells on the rectal surface were shown to bind to the virus, take it in, and deliver it to the target cells. "M" cells are abundant in a healthy human rectum. Their function is to bring a sample of foreign, "potentially dangerous" particles for identification and response by the body's defense system. "An "M" cell wants to attract microbes, so its surface is sticky, and can fold over a virus or bacteria, engulf it, and bring it inside in a pocket. The pocket moves to the other end of the "M" cell, to immune cells and process the microbe and determine the response to it. HIV subverts the system, turning "M" cells into express lanes for invasion. They deliver the virus to a lymphocyte in 10 minutes data shows, and a person is infected with HIV. There are no "M" cells in the vagina so no infection can occur. The vagina must be weakened by infection, bleeding, an open sore, trauma, or cancerous cells. Many argue that Vaginal transmission is "very rare". [76] The HIV virus is much smaller then the standard pore size of the prophylactic, and a lubricated prophylactic has much larger pore sizes then the un-lubricated.

Social sexual activities or anal intercourse is a practice called *catamitus*. It has an important history. lets look at recent archeological findings from Tall El Hamman in Jordan.

Idolatry of Zeus and Ganymede at Minoah and Tall El Hammam (Sodom). {Catamitus means Ganymede in latin}

Definition: Catamite, entymology: latin *catamitus*, from *catamitus ganymitus*, from Etruscan catmite from greek Ganymedes= a boy kept by a pederast for ritual sex. There is evidence that during the bronze age the Tjeker in Ayvacsk provenance of Troy (Turkey) were probably from Crete where they were most likely the source of the name, Mount Ida, which they took from Mt. Ida Crete.[77] Caesar Nero had a young boy, 12 year old "Sporus" castrated and then married him in the worlds biggest Toga party. This all happened a year after Nero kicked his pregnant wife Sabina to death in 66 A.D. Sporus then appeared publically as Nero's "wife". After Nero's suicide, there was apparently a war between to Roman Generals over "Sporus". Carlin A. Barton in "The sorrows of the Ancient Romans: The gladiators and the Monster" Princeton Univ. Press, 1993, pointed out, "The dissolution of republican ideals of physical integrity in relation to *libertas* contributes to and is reflected by the sexual license and decadence associated with the Roman empire".[78] That Empire is no more.

Cretan Pederasty, background and where it went

In the history of idolatry we find a cultural path leading not just to moral decadence but also to the destruction of nations.

The Idolatry of the Mycine culture of Bronze age Crete is found in the Mycinian's worship of Zeus. A well known myth describes Zeus's abduction of a young male labeled as his "cup bearer" Ganymede. Recall that most all myths of Zeus start with his birth on Mount Ida which is in Crete.

Cretan Pederasty was a form of Pederasty that involved ritual kidnapping (harpagmos) of a boy by an adult male with the consent of the boys father. [79] Various Greek terms were used to describe the homosexual practices such as *philetor* (beriender) and *Kleines* (glorius) relating to battle as *parastates* (sidekick) implying the Zeus-like divine character of these homosexual practices. Strabo implies that it was considered shameful for a youth to not acquire a male lover.[80]

Many archeological findings have documented the Cretan pederastic rites. The homosexual practice appear in Zeus worshipping states. The gifts given the boy after the ritual sex with his abductor and the abductors male friends were a military outfit, an ox or a bull (a sacrifice to Zeus), and a drinking cup (symbolic of a spiritual accomplishment). The boy then sacrifices to Zeus (similar to the Roman Army's Mithras rite) and gives a feast (the Oxen) to those who came down with him from the mountains (high places). Roman historian Cornelius Nepos notes that Cretan boys had more then one homosexual relationship. G. Saflund in "Cretan and Theran Questions" in "Sanctuaries and Cults", pp198-200, notes that two forms of marriage co-existed in Aegean Bronze age culture: a group marriage and a sacred marriage (*hierosgamos*). The "rite of passage" as one graduated from one 'age grade' to another.[81]

From almost 2000BC to 50 AD a period of 2,050 years this Zeus Pagan ritual of homosexuality is found in Rome. An infection documented in one of the most evil individuals, Caesar Nero. I must repeat the description of the abomination when Nero had a young boy "Sporus" castrated before he married him in what was, as I previously mentioned, the biggest Toga party ever. After Nero's suicide and the war between two Roman Generals in which many soldiers died over the battle for Sporus, an event that must have really strengthened the Roman legions and exposed to all the true decadent underbelly of Rome.

For the past 10 years, Dr Stephen Collins has been at work in archaeological digs in Sodom (in Jordan) at a location called Tall El-Hammam. The institutional pederasty of Minoan (Cretan) culture where every single male grew up from twelve years old in a homosexual relationship with an older mentor generation after generation as a fundamental relationship….appears in Sodom and Gomorrah. Dr Collins notes, "…knowing the eventual penchant of the Israelites themselves to what the bible calls 'whoring after the religious and cultural practices of Canaan's inhabitants, God decided they could deal with the Canaanites. Joshua could deal with the Canaanites, but not this. God, I think, decided to excise this Minoan cultural influence, this cancer from the land that He was giving to Abraham's descendents. He wanted it cast out, and he cut it out in a pretty dramatic way."

Dr Collins has clear examples proving that extremely high heat 12,000° – 15,000 ° F. minimum burned the city with fire and "*gophrith* (Lightning) or electromagnetic discharge…..a fireball out of the heavens. Quite comparable material called "Trinitite" has been found at the Bronze age dig level of Sodom. Trinitite is the unique fused desert material found in the Alamogordo desert after the atom bomb blast (called Trinity) exploded at ground zero in New Mexico…..a desert glass that is quite unique. Collins links the Minoan culture to Sodom with two very unique findings. Architecture that is unique to each and statues of Bulls with their horns pointing down. Sodom was less then 20 miles from Creator-God's Holy City Jerusalem. These gross homosexual catamite practices where women even lived in separate quarters, gave birth and raised the children while males did what was called an "abomination" to Creator-God led to the total destruction of the city Sodom which was, at that time, one of the most advanced city of the Bronze age middle east and at least 10 times as large as Jerusalem! Fried in a few seconds.[82]

The archeology shows no rebuilding or inhabitant there in the circle of the best watered land of the middle east (the Circle of the Jordan Valley just above the Dead Sea) for 400 years after its destruction. I would imagine anyone coming near there would be spooked from that area, and the rumors must have been something. Creator-God assembled a unique demonstration of His tolerance of such practices. A clear witness to all (and all nations) who follow after the Cretin-Minoan-Spartan-Roman model! Once a culture adopts such laws and practices it is doomed....unless it repents and recognizes its error.

"Men committed shameful acts with other men, and received in themselves the due penalty for their error".[Romans 1:27]$_{NIV}$ What is unusual when you put the first paper in which the toxoplasm can alter the behavior of the host like in the mouse, we are not so sure of cause effect in populations of humans today. This does raise the question anyway.

I have included the abstract of a paper perhaps relating to this decay of mankind and the world. I don't know if the problem is a great as the authors make it. My old invertebrate Zoology text describes these as a sickle shaped plasmid and you can see it in the brain tissue in the electron microscopy study.

This recent paper may shed light on what is causing this behavior. The research by House PK, Vyas A, Sapolsky R (2011) "Predator Cat Odors Activate Sexual Arousal Pathways in Brains of *Toxoplasma gondii* Infected Rats." [83]. The authors are from the Program in Neuroscience, Stanford University, Stanford, California, United States of America, and School of Biological Science, Nanyang Technology University, Singapore, **3** Departments of Biology, Neurology and Neurological Sciences, and of Neurosurgery, Stanford University, Stanford, California]. The abstract describing their work is as follows:

Cat odors induce rapid, innate and stereotyped defensive behaviors in rats at first exposure, a presumed response to the evolutionary pressures of predation. Bizarrely, rats infected with the brain parasite *Toxoplasma gondii* approach the cat odors they typically avoid. Since the protozoan *Toxoplasma* requires the cat to sexually reproduce, this change in host behavior is thought to be a remarkable example of a parasite manipulating a mammalian host for its own benefit. *Toxoplasma* does not influence host response to non-feline predator odor nor does it alter behavior on olfactory, social, fear or anxiety tests, arguing for specific manipulation in the processing of cat odor. We report that *Toxoplasma* infection alters neural activity in limbic brain areas necessary for innate defensive behavior in response to cat odor. Moreover, *Toxoplasma* increases activity in nearby limbic regions of sexual attraction when the rat is exposed to cat urine and feces, compelling evidence that *Toxoplasma* overwhelms the innate fear response by causing, in its stead, a type of sexual attraction to the normally aversive cat odor. That a microorganism found in the feces has the ability to cause "Amorous feelings" in a host's brain or limbic system resulting in continued transfer of the organism in a host-host cycle is amazing.

Catamitus is Latin for Catamitus Ganymede and from Etruscan Catmite or Greek Ganymedes is a male involved in a behavior that could indeed operate in this manner. Remember that Ganymede is the name of Zeus's boy cup bearer. Perhaps the behavior is not simply due to unnatural attraction but also to a "smart" parasite. I'm not sure. But the culture that practiced it was completely destroyed by Creator-God when Sodom was destroyed.

· Homosexuals take heart, the Messiah Jesus Christ the Creator-God is a forgiving God. To understand this we need to look at the words of Jesus when describing the terrible state of the city of Capernaum near the Sea of Galilee where people saw many of Jesus miracles but rejected Him. "And you, Capernaum, who are exalted to heaven, will be brought down to Hades; for if the mighty works which were done in you had been done in Sodom, it would have remained until this day. But I say to you that it will be more tolerable for the land of Sodom in the day of judgment than for you." [Matt 11:23-24] If the Sodomites had seen His miracles they would have repented and been saved; please don't reject Jesus words.

Part 4. Ill-logic

Where has the admixture of Dialectical thinking and Humanist evolution done to Americans campus : How Did That Happen?

Consider Hegelian synthesis in the materialist world (a world considered without Creator-God) . Marx synthesis of the tension in the worker-owner relationship reduced to the "Means of Production" where the synthesis to move the ownership of the tools of production to what Marx decided was a higher, more evolved situation-location......the "STATE" should or ought to own the means of production. This has historically led to Nation's becoming so enfeebled and destroyed so many economies that it is said:

" The only residence of true Marxist communism today is in the Universities" [RC Sproul}

What in the nature of the university has shielded the Marxian faculty from the reality of economics: The "dream" of the Utopia or the remoteness from reality or both. The deception of the god of the intellect, Baal, where they are the "final" authority, the keeper of "knowledge" without wisdom because they are controlled by their own constructs. "The Bead Game" exposed the folly of their operation, that Nobel Prize winning novel of Hermann Hesse. However the greatness of the University, the production of the "trained" student who can produce value almost immediately, ie the power supply electrical engineer verses the generalist "medical engineer with no specific skill set. As long as robots can produce what can be purchased, the University both size and scope must change and make itself into a value in "reality" not in the imaginary realm....a modern fiction. The Baal's of the

University are a fiction, empty of Creator-God and the language of Creator-God, the Bible. So what future does it have as presently constituted, full of courses and programs such as liberal arts incapable of true value other than producing a student with his head full of idols the danger of which, he doesn't even recognize.

Student Beware!

The Bible tells us to not get involved in "the philosophies and vain deceit of man"

"Beware lest any man spoil (rob) you through philosophy and vain deceit, after the tradition of men, after the rudiments of the world, and not after Christ" [Col 2:8 (KJV)} or from a more modern translation of the Kone Greek "Be careful that you don't let anyone captivate you though an empty deceitful philosophy that is according to human tradition and the elemental spirits of the world and not according to Christ". [NET]

"The people imagine vain things" [Acts 4:25]$_{KJV}$

"...became vain in their imaginations, and their foolish heart was darkened" [Rom 1:21] $_{KJV}$

"..desirous of vainglory"[Gal 5:26]$_{KJV}$

"Let no man deceive you with vain words, for because of these things cometh the wrath of God upon the children of disobedience" [Eph 5:6] $_{KJV}$

The teaching of Paul here is in need of historical explanation for context because the Greek is difficult, lets listen to a description of Paul's work, quite the scholar (with the equivalent of at least 2 PhD's before he was 23). William McDonald gives us the following:

> "Paul is dealing with specific errors that threaten believers in the Lycus Valley where Colosseee was situated.......philosophy means literally 'the love of wisdom'. It is not evil in itself, but becomes so when men seek wisdom apart from the LORD Jesus Christ.
>
> Here the word is used to describe man's attempt to find out by his own intellect and research those things which can only be

known and spiritually discerned [1Cor 2:14] $_{NET}$. It is evil because
it exalts human reason (our water brains) above Creator-God and
worships the creature more than the Creator. It is characteristic
of the liberals of our day, with their boasted intellectualism and
rationalism. Empty deceit refers to false and valueless teaching of
those who profess to offer <u>secret truths</u> to an inner circle of people.
There is really nothing to it. But it gathers a following by catering
to mans curiosity. Also it appeals to their vanity by making them
members of the "select few "…..The traditions of men here means
religious teaching which have been invented by men but which have
no true foundation in the Scriptures (a tradition is a fixation of a
custom which begins as a convenience or suited some particular
circumstance….(ie. Yoga, worship of academic achievements with
its robes and ceremonies and ordinances by which men hoped to
obtain God's favor. Is that not similar to the operation of ancient
paganism?)

More specifically at Colosse:

The law of Moses served its purposes as a type of things to
come. It had been a 'primary school' to prepare the heart for the
coming of Christ. (however the 10 Commandments are still a
schoolmaster today). Paul saw the false teachers using it by conspir-
ing to use a discarded system to displace the Son of God…(an effort
to reverse time) [Daily notes of the Scripture Union] Paul would
have the Colossians test all teaching by whether or not it agreed
with the doctrines of Christ. Phillips' translation of this verse is
helpful:"Be careful that nobody spoils your faith through intellectualism or high sounding nonsense. Such stuff is at best founded
on men's ideas of the nature of the world, and disregards Christ!".[84]

Why must I write these things? The solemn fact of bloodguiltiness taught
in both the O.T. and the New Testament (Ecc 3:18-20 and Acts 20:26)
to witness only at God-given opportunities, sensitive to his leading, only
sometimes silent.

The false Hegelian logic of the dialectic is rampant throughout many departments of the university. Beware of the Marxist, and the products of Marxism such as the teaching that Jesus was a Marxist, "Liberation Theology", Evolutionary Humanism or any derivative of these. Why these faculty will seek to defile you is only for us to wonder at. But protect yourself by the reading of the Word of Creator-God

Problems with truth....what is truth verses the truth of human knowledge?
I must include a wonderful note from Dr Ray Steadman in his monumental work "Adventuring Through the Bible", 1997, on Colossians 2:8:

"The Gospel is not anti-intellectual, it is not against knowledge. Rather it is against knowledge that does not come under the judgment of Creator-God's word. Certainly not all of the knowledge of this world and reality is false knowledge. Much of it is good and true and cannot be found in scripture----medical knowledge such as the secret of penicillin and techniques of surgery; technical knowledge such as how to build a fast computer or a space shuttle; historical knowledge such as the defeat of Napoleon at Waterloo or events of the Civil War. All of this is human knowledge and is valuable. But Paul wants us to understand there is a deceptive knowledge that comes from false sources-----tradition and philosophies that have built up idea upon idea, over the centuries. Many of these philosophies mingle truth and error in such a way that the two become indistinguishable. Those that accept these ideas are bound to accept as much error as they do truth. It will lead them therefore into mistaken concepts and erroneous and injurious ideas---- ideas such as these. 'The human spirit is recycled again and again and again through reincarnation. ' or, 'As a human being you have totally unlimited power and potential to be your own god, to make up your own morality. 'or, 'A human being is just a mound of molecules that is born, lives, and dies... there is not afterlife, no purpose for living, so enjoy yourself, forget faith and morality, eat, drink, and be merry for this moment, for that is all there is.' (All of these are false and completely contrary to the true knowledge of scripture) Therefore "Human knowledge:, is rudimentary, elementary, and basic to the fallen nature of this world. (As if we see only through dark glasses a weak subset of reality). It never gets at the real heart of spiritual reality. That is why our nation's university community, its entertainment community, its information and news community, and its political establishment have become so saturated with those who profess the highest levels of human knowledge yet are filled with vileness, corruption, immorality, lawlessness, drug abuse, suicide, and every evidence of moral decay and spiritual deterioration. All of these institutions are permeated---if not dominated by a philosophy called deconstructionism, a worldly philosophy that teaches that: Words have no objective content and therefore words have no truth. (Derrida's philosophy) [85]

The Philosophy of Deconstructionism

A key note is while Creator-God tells us that He is "Truth", the religions of Humanism teaches truth cannot be assigned to words. If humanist claim they can deconstruct the "Word", God's LOGOS, then they claim they can make Creator-God meaningless or anything anybody wants the word to mean. This is a deceptive but direct idol of Humanism. the chaos and destruction of thought-communication between and among men and between men and their Creator-God is complete with this presupposition. During Derrida's life he was rewarded, lauded and praised by many of our great universities. While Derrida's philosophy is not simple and in part very confusing, it is answered by attempts at clarification such as the disambiguation attempt by the wiki team, and the lexicographers of languages to maintain or improve communication between and among humans.

Deconstruction is a method that relies on subverting the surface appearance of a text, in order to reveal (supposed) hidden layers of articulation and contradictory logic that traditionally are overlooked. He claims to amplify the elusive nature of language by looking at what he refers to as the self-referential character of a text to nullify the idea the words refer to particular things in the world---an open threat to truth and falsity, playing into the eastern concept of the Buddha excluded middle.

Derrida's work has severely been criticized by Richard Wolin, that along with Heidegger, and Nietzsche, leads to corrosive nihilism. ie. Applying deconstruction to Nazism blurs the distinction between Nazism and non-Nazism. [86]

An academic protest by knowledgeable writers claiming that Derrida's work, "does not meet acceptable standards of clarity and rigor, and that his philosophy is composed of "Tricks and gimmicks similar to those of the Dadasts...a semi-intelligible attack on reason, truth, and scholarship" .[87]

Once you remove the true objective meaning of the Bible you have no words that occupy our libraries or airways that are confidently truth or "mean what they mean and say what they say". Along with the words of Julius Wellhausen who set up the Transcendentalist to walk away from Jesus as God and eventually muddle the bible through their followers greatly contributing to the darkness in academia today. An infection that leads to the end of philosophy, and the end of reason....Nihilism in its ugly face, no hope, no reason for existence, just die: to add to the trillions of evolutionary deaths to progress and protect or improve the human genome. (remember, Hitler said he was protecting the German gene). What a bunch of hogwash. Cooler heads must prevail by asking the question "what of sin and the grave?" Stop trying to gain the pseudo-intellectual upper hand by using the power of position and pomp to further our destruction as a nation!!

The final result of all this stupidity of dialectical materialism and deconstruction of Creator-God's word is the Idolatry of "Liberation Theology", which, while completely false is coming at the world on a much larger scale then even the University can cope with. ie. (search on "Jesus is a Socialist".)What of Sin and the grave?

v

What does the God of creation say about how we got here and why we are here

The problem

The first human being on this earth lived in a perfect environment in which only Creator-God's will was known and done. There was only one path and there was only one rule. Law was simple. When Eve went into the middle of the garden and broke the one law Creator-God had made following another will, the will of Satan who had told her, by misquoting the bible or the word of Creator-God, that "she would surely not die". (when Creator-God had told them that they would die if they broke the law). By following the will of Satan rather than Creator-God they then had knowledge of good (the will of Creator-God and his path) and evil or bad (the will of Satan and his path...Which is death) . So Satan who initially had no real power (or just the value of 1/3 of God's fallen angles that followed his authority which can't be much) because he had been kicked out of heaven for his pride; claiming he could be like "the Most-High God" which is the ultimate in pride (and Idolatry), who gains his power by lying about the word of Creator–God, and getting people to follow his path of evil. So missing the mark, or sin, is Satan's path that leads to eternal death (or hell which must be the same thing). Missing the mark set by Creator-God is an infinite error, that requires his Justice. It is so great a crime against Him that only He Himself can pay the fine for us by the terrible death of His only Son, Jesus, the Hebrew Messiah. Therefore His great wrath comes together with His great sacrificial Love (agape Love) for each of us. So we look at the 10 commandments as the will of Creator–God. And Because Jesus, "Immanuel, Creator-God with us", was able to keep those 10 commandments, Creator–God has provided a path for us at great cost to Himself by the Sacrifice of the unblemished lamb Jesus. Creator-God told us of the horribleness of sin and its great importance to this existence that blood ("life is in the blood") must be shed in atonement for sin. This once-and-for all sacrifice altered the entire universe, and the opacity that we have "through a glass darkly" will soon be removed when the Great Conqueror-King returns to this earth. He already maintains at His cost, the space the universe occupies every instant, which is a greater energy cost then we can ever imagine. Poor John Lennon, if he could only imagine which you probably can now… what makes more sense than his stupid song. Because he can't imagine,,… it may be too late for him. Those of us that are alive have a chance. Start your physics with Creator-God's word. Creator –God "holds everything together". Get an idea of how much energy it takes to do that for each cubic meter of space. America's greatest physicists in this century was Richard Feynman. Feynman was quoted as saying that the energy density of empty space is the same as the energy density within an atom.[1] To get a feeling of that energy density look at the energy released when 19 kg or so of uranium explodes in the atom bomb. Very likely only a few of those atoms were ripped apart. And Einstein told us that $E=MC^2$ so only 1kg would release 8.519 x10^{13} or about 850 trillion BTU. That gives us an idea of the energy density within the tiny atom. We know how tiny an atom is. So cram all these atoms into the space of a cubic meter at absolute zero, and calculate the energy required to be input into the cubic meter every instant. Some say that value is equal to the radiant energy of all the suns in our Milky Way galaxy every instant. That's a billion suns radiant output every instant. If you're really big and you occupy a cubic meter that's how much energy Creator–God is expending every Instant just to maintain the space you occupy let alone the keep the matter functioning which you are made of. There is evidence of this background energy. We're unable to tap it because we know very little about it and we cannot sync it from one source to a location that has less content so it's never really been directly measured. In fact the electron undergoes 10^{20} hits per second from the photons of the background or vacuum energy (ZPE) causing it to change direction slightly each hit making for the "Heisenberg Indeterminacy and what is called the Compton Frequency.

The permittivity and permeability of free space is also a function of this background energy as well. If it is as great a value as Feyman suggests we have no instruments with that capacity. Perhaps the Casimir effect which has been measured reflects something of it's existence. The Casimir effect is measured, by placing two plates so close together that they exclude what appears to be many frequencies of this background energy. At that point the plates are shoved together by a force which has been measured…a force somewhat mysterious seems to come from every direction as if it didn't have the properties of locality and is certainly related to photons.(one position is the plates are attracted together, its quite controversial). If this energy is there it would exert a gravitational effect and would be the so called "dark" energy posited by the "Big Bang theorists. I've already mentioned that we have cell phones but we are not entirely sure what a photon is or what an electron is. However, most scientists agree light is complex, not simple. I would argue that there is a light that is not created…the light of Creator-God is not created, it always is! The <u>Larmor</u> radiation is the energy released when an electron is accelerated, any charge that is accelerated must cause a release in energy or radiation and the ground state electron of hydrogen is assumed to emit Larmor radiation which causes it to spiral inward, but this does not lead to collapse of the orbit because the electron also absorbs background zero-point energy.

Footnote: [the Bohr orbit of hydrogen could arise without a quantum law. In the latter case, the ground state electron is assumed to emit <u>Larmor</u> radiation which causes it to spiral inward, but this does not lead to collapse of the orbit because the electron also absorbs zero-point energy from the 10^{20} interactions. The calculation of the absorption was done by Boyer and later by Puthoff by treating the electron as undergoing harmonic oscillation rather than true motion in a Coulomb potential. This is a weakness in the analysis but nonetheless it is striking that the Larmor emission and harmonic-oscillator-type absorption prove to be in balance exactly at the Bohr radius. The fact that the orbital angular momentum is zero in the quantum ground state is mirrored in the SED (Stochastic electrodynamics) orbiting-electron interpretation by random changes in the orbital plane (due to the zero-point fluctuations) yielding a time averaged zero net angular momentum. [see: the 465 page "Cosmology and Zero Point Energy" National Philosophy Alliance Monograph #1, 2013][23]

If you carefully read the bible we get the impression that Creator-God is "Omnipresent" which is awfully close to the same definition.

It is hard to believe that the LORD's presence does not have energetic ramifications! So His face may shine from all directions but somehow if men were to see his face they would die. We're not sure that's because man who was alive and full of Sin cannot look at one who is incredibly Holy! Or Creator–God has released so much energy at creation that the zero–point–energy (ZPE) or something like it for all we know continues from all directions as an echo of creation. How can an "echo of the big bang" have continuous input? Or it could be that we don't have what is needed to make out his face because of the opacity in the universe due to sin. Making fools out of us as we claim a crude claim about the background microwave radiation that we see from our vantage point. Our vantage point is strangely unique in that we can make measurements and observe the universe from our location from this segment of the Milky Way galaxy. But we've made absolutely no measurements of how the clock ticks outside of our little solar system except with our little nuclear powered satellite Voyager 1. Don Gurnett, University of Iowa's James Van Allen Professor of Physics and the principal investigator for the Plasma Wave experiment, tells us it is more than 11 billion miles distant 37 years since it was launched.

In graduate school I studied physiology and biophysics a great deal. So I know something of the physics of life and living things and their control systems. But as I finished gathering data for my dissertation I was allowed to analyze my data on NASA's wonderful ubiquitous spectrum analyzers in Dr. James Van Allen's lab. Because I knew how to run the 70 MM rear screen projection equipment called Oscar, the engineer in charge Roger Anderson called me and let me listen to the ping-pong sound that I had heard from our earth satellites when they recorded a lightning hit. Over the phone I heard a very powerful "ping-pong" and

Roger told me that I was a second man on earth to know there was lightning on Jupiter. Dr. Van Allen's group had powerful instruments on Voyager 1 to look at plasma and magnetic fields. So I feel close or at least have some personal interest in the continued data coming to us from beyond our solar system as it relates to the tick of the clock or how the clock ticks far far away from us. All evolution requires that the clock tick the same in those far out galaxies as it ticks here so evolutionists can claim the billions and billions of years they require for these impossible processes to evolve to where we are now, and explain how it happened without Creator-God as he has told us in His wonderful book called the bible. And yet we know that the tick of the clock at sea level is different in the tick of the clock at Denver 5000 feet above sea level. Does the data and the signals coming from Voyager One give us a hint at how the tick is changing?

(**Speciationists** unsubstantiated conjecture about the past.)

John 1:3 ...all things have been made by Him... (Creator-God can't lie, that's His nature)[_KJV_]

Colossians 1:17 [Jesus] is the image of the invisible God, the first-born [*prototokos*] of all creation, for in Him were all things created, in heaven and on earth, visible and invisible......all things were created through Him and for Him. He is before all things, **and in Him all things hold together.** [ESV]

(**note: we are house guests in someone else's universe**)

2Peter 3:10 Heaven shall pass away with a great noise and the elements shall melt with a fervent heat.[KJV] (elements=original constituents or atoms)

So what does a faculty do that has offended the Creator of the universe by teaching false gods to the students?

First, this Creator-God would that no one would be lost. All of us need answer the question, "are we a good person?" And the answer is, "no one is good but Creator God". Next, we need to realize that a god of mercy and love only, is a false god and completely idolatrous. But the true creator of the universe has something called, "The law of the LORD"; Ten little items that determined if we're good or not. If any of us have ever stolen anything, we are and will continue to be forever a thief; if any of us have ever hated a brother or one of our colleagues we have committed murder in our hearts; if any of us have ever lusted after someone that is not our spouse we have committed adultery in our hearts; if any of us have ever wished that something belonged to us and not to the person it actually belongs to; we have offended the Creator. And right up front if we have worshiped or taught or instilled in others a false god, one that is not the creator the universe, we have offended him in his first law. For we are to love the Creator with all our heart, mind, and soul; and to love our neighbors as ourselves.

So the law of the LORD is perfect, converting the soul. We all know that sin, missing the mark that He has set, is transgression of a law. So the real schoolmaster is the law of the LORD. It's not about happiness but it's proportional to righteousness. If we seek heaven we must realize that to live before the face of almighty God we cannot have offended him with our sin.

We must read and understand Creator-God's word....the bible he has written through others to us. "...if you can't understand me in my speech, how can you understand me in my silence."

It doesn't take a rocket scientist to understand the finite cannot contain the infinite!

There is a remedy that the creator of the universe has made for all of us. A single remedy, published more than 5 billion times throughout the earth, exceptionally well disseminated among us all. That lets us know why we're here and how precious we are to him. The creator of the universe is like a wonderful father who loved you so much he sent His only Son Himself to die on the cross for your sin and mine! And we will want to please that Father. It is so simple. To please him, we need to accept His gift and not reject it. So that the one who has paid the price for our sin (violating the law of the LORD, and missing the mark), is identified for who He really is, the Creator and ruler of the cosmos, the God of justice; of laws that work, that identifies what offends Him and is not permitted before Him. The writer of this paragraph is not judging you, you're judged already, just as I was. Us professors proclaimed to ourselves our own goodness like most humans. We are proud! Once we know something and have special knowledge, at least more than the students in front of us, we become puffed up and we hide ourselves from our self and we don't allow ourselves to see the truth. We even pretend the truth is relative to cover up our sin.

Do all men seek to live forever? All men have offended the King who's perfection we cannot even imagine, and either we must pay the price or someone must pay the price for that offense. An offense so grave that we don't have what it takes to pay the price and continue to exist. It is not by accident that you are standing where you are today, reading this paragraph. The Creator is a father to us and has protected us in many impossible situations with his angels many many times to the point where we find ourselves, if we are honest, standing, looking up at the stars at night and wondering what we're doing here.....how we got here..... with that key question....... Why? As we reach our hands to the heavens, are we aware of a mighty Father reaching down to us with this incredible gift for us. We're here at the good pleasure of the King. And all the pain and sorrow of this life are but a tiny instant of the eternity of the existence of our spirit and soul. We know we didn't create ourselves. And we know we've done wrong. And for some reason we seem to be blinded by science, or invented explanations that hide our nakedness...... Or some man-created gospel that's without repentance, confusing what really is. If God is willing to die for us, this horrible death on the cross, he is defining what love truly is! That is the gospel of love, destroying the barrier of pride between us and our Father..... acceptance on our part through repentance of our sins and then trusting in the One He sent for our salvation, a complete and final act of our Creator. We are not to rely on any work we could do to buy our way to Him, so we could boast and regenerate our pride before Him. That is the good news for faculty, teachers, students, and all of us! That is the Gospel of Jesus Christ, the Hebrew Messiah!

Timeline of History

Isaac Newton worked 40 years on a history timeline that we should pay attention to. He taught us the following:

"We need not then wonder that the Egyptians have made the king and the dynasty of the monarchy, which was located at Thebes (Egyptian) in the days of David, Solomon, and Rehoboam, so very ancient and so long lived. The Persians have done the same with their Kings, who began to reign in this area 200 years after the death of Solomon. Assyrians of Damascus have done likewise to their Kings Hadar and Hazael, who reigned for a hundred years after the death of Solomon. They worshipped them as gods and boasted of their antiquity, ignorant that they were of recent origin as Josephus states. 'while all these nations have exaggerated their antiquity so much, we'd need not wonder that the Greeks and Latins have made their first Kings a little older than the truth!'. Cicero reminds is that the first law to be an author must be to not dare to tell anything but the truth and the second that he must be bold to tell the whole truth that there must be no suggestion of partiality anywhere in his writing nor of malice.[4]. So what do we make of the invention of a stone age to permit such an ancient man as to contrive time for his "frequency of beneficial mutations" to create what speciationists claim exists today. Their whole time frame must approach ancient timing of such antiquity that it supports their unsubstantiated conjecture about the past.

Darwins "Origin" Ch 6 laid out the principle that seems to drive all Progressives and their Idolatrous progressivism that "formation and perfection of the new form."Where Darwin was explaining how species should become extinct so that this "new form" would become perfect, a Darwinian pipe dream that would find itself the "deep" thought basis at the very bottom supporting the idolatrous religion of "evolution".

"Evolutionists have recently been resurrecting Darwin's old 'struggle for survival' explanation for the origin of species. How would a struggle for survival increase the mutational rates which would supposedly produce new genetic material for new species to emerge? It wouldn't. A "Struggle for survival would only decrease species variety not increase it, unless you subscribe to the old Lamarkian theory, which Darwinists supposedly abhor. Also in what way did the humble artichoke arrive on planet earth through a struggle for survival in which it beat out its competitors into extinction? Artichokes survive very well but a struggle for survival in no way answers the question. How did artichokes get here in the first place? The same question might be asked of every other species that supposedly arrived here through this mysterious struggle for survival. The very idea of a "struggle for survival" produced all of the wondrous forms of life that we see today on this earth is ludicrous."

This is the theoretical basis for future race wars as we see in Germany 1933-45 and Obama's race war 2008-. " I endeavored, also, to show that intermediate varieties, from existing in lesser numbers than the forms which they connect, *will generally be beaten out and exterminated during the course of further modification and improvement.*" [5]

There is however a problem with this, for Darwin plainly stated that *all* species, including the races of man, in some respect are transitional forms: "As Sir J. Lubbock has remarked, 'Every species is a link between other allied forms.'" [6]

This is why, on the very first page of his *Descent of Man,* Darwin advocated a race war among human beings, believing that this would produce "beneficial" results with one of the races of man being exterminated (ie. Sanger, Margaret Higgins (1879-1966) Founder of Planned Parenthood Fed. Of America), since all species of life in Darwin's struggle for existence are prey to being "beaten out and exterminated during the course of further modification and improvement."

The whole thing, along with his second work pseudo-documenting man's "evolution", is nothing but a plea for warfare, violence and extinction as necessary components for the improvement of our existence[7]

The correct summation of all this is the plain Word of Creator-God:

"For God so loved the world, that he gave His only Son, that whoever believes in Him will not perish but have eternal life". [John 3:16]$_{ESV}$

vi

Science and God vs. the gods of the campus

Part 1. Philosophical Background

"For as the heavens are higher than the earth, so are my ways and my thoughts higher than yours" [Creator-God, (Isaiah 55:9$_{KJV}$)] Do scientists have a problem with pride?

While Science is a great profession. Proverbs 25:2 tells us, "It is the glory of God to conceal a thing but the honor of kings is to search out a matter"[KJV]. I would argue that Historical Science is in most cases not of the observable and rarely "falsifiable", as required by good science. If you presuppose materialism is all there is and reject the teaching of the word of Creator-God who was there and did it, you start with false presuppositions and can never arrive at the truth.

True science is reality and Creator-God is reality, therefore true science is not man's feeble imagination or his vain theories and philosophy but is a description of the knowledge of reality.

"Shall the one who contends with the Almighty correct Him?"[Job 40:2 KJV]

Dear student, listen to your science professor/teacher carefully. Is what is presented representative of his training or is the teaching a question of theology where he has little or no training? The claim of secularism is that it has no Theology. You will find by asking simple questions that that is not true! Are his/her comments about creation misquotations or out of context quotations from the Bible? The professor's world-view should be clearly presented so that bias can be understood. If bias is hidden, why is that occurring. The major struggle with scientific studies and statistics in scientific studies concerns removing

bias. Your hearing should do the same. The next major problem in science is understanding all the presuppositions in the hypothesis or model under study. And finally all in the classroom should concern themselves with the solid rock of science, Logic. Is the logic clear and correct? Consider the following contrast of what is a question of science:

Humanist Bias(Michael Ruse)

1. Guided by "natural" law;
2. It has to be explanatory any hypothesis can be reference to "natural" law;
10. Is it testable against the Empirical world?
11. Its conclusions are tentative?
12. It is falsifiable? [1]

Straight forward demarcation without Humanist Theology

1. An assertion must be made.
2. Clearly state the criteria whereby verified and/or falsified.

3. Follow the evidence wherever it leads.

> When a Humanist plays the "natural" card he is saying only man can know…man was not a witness of creation, and man's information about reality is far from complete.

Even pure logic has a problem. Robert B. Laughlin, who shares the Nobel Prize for his work on the quantum hall effect, points out that the all the fundamental laws of the Universe are not known. We thought that Newton's laws explained the universe but soon found that Newton's laws are wrong for what is happening on the micro scale and in condensed matter. Laughlin notes that .."Human beings reason by analogy…when we say something is unreasonable we usually mean it is not suitably analogous to things we already know. Pure logic is a superstructure built on top of this more primitive reasoning facility and is thus inherently fallible."[2] Strangely Laughlin only identifies two scientists that were most logical when they were dealing with the unknown without analogy but these two Newton and Einstein believe in Creator-God so their reasoning from analogy began with Him, and therefore started without error.[3]

What is good science? Is evolution good science?
Dr Michael Ruse (ACLU & Florida State Prof. of Philosophy), probably the most eloquent evolutionist today says:

"Evolution is promoted by its practitioners as more then mere science. Evolution is promulgated as an ideology, a secular religion—a full fledged alternative to Christianity, with meaning and morality....Evolution is a religion. This was true of evolution in the beginning, and it is true of evolution still today. [4]

The following statements are [Modified from Warner Gitt's paper: "In the beginning was information" [5]

The University is a place for an "Enterprise of ideas"

...where the student is free to select and reject from an entire spectrum when it is presented to him/her.

Lets look at another perspective in your training! Hopefully it will challenge your thinking.

"Men Occasionally stumble over the truth, but most of them pick themselves up and hurry off as if nothing had happened" (Winston Churchill).

THE <u>ONLY Absolute</u> BARRIER TO THE TRUTH IS THE PRESUMPTION THAT YOU ALLREADY HAVE IT!!

If you start out with A false presupposition!!!!!

1. There are an INFINITE (∞) number of FALSE conjectures that can explain the spaces in the datum.

2. These probably only describe our ignorance to describe reality.
3. There is only <u>one</u> conjecture that describes TRUTH.

I repeat:

There is only <u>one</u> conjecture that describes TRUTH!

1. That is: The probability that man, with a false presupposition would arrive at the truth approaches ZERO or $1/\infty$
2. Therefore false presuppositions lead to false conjectures.

Is Science Based on Facts? Facts are REAL not imaginary.

YET is the SCIENCE taught on campus based on propositions that have evidence to support them?

FAITH-BASED propositions that can in no way be supported by evidence (suggested by Dinesh D'Suza)

A. 1. The Universe is Rational
B. 2. The Universe Obeys LAWS or the operations of the universe are describable in lawful terms.
C. 3. That the rationality of the external universe is mirrored within the rationality of our own minds (it matches).

Speaking only to the Christians

A. Christians see God as Rational …our answer to presupposition 1
B. Christians see God as the "Law Giver" so we understand Presupposition 2
C. Christians see man as made in God's image so that is our "spark of rationality"
D. BUT if you are a secularists you can't make any of these 3 assumptions

E. You have to take the presuppositions on 100% FAITH. Without that faith, modern Secular science would be completely impossible. That means Secularists have their feet firmly planted in mid-air!

F. THEREFORE: Atheist /secular Science must be completely Faith Based at the level of First Cause

G. FAITH is amazingly big in Physics:: Max Plank, the reluctant originator of quantum mechanics observed that "Over the entrance to the gates of the temple of science are written the words: Ye must have faith".[6] Of course in the quantum mechanical world, only populations of particle statistics works. (ie. The three body problem is unstable and fails miserably.)

No doubt the reason many of us arrive at "all truth is relative" as students:

A. Is related to the large number of empty conjectures we are told or taught

B. that come from a myriad of false presuppositions

C. Does that explain the disconnect between what we are often taught and our concern for the truth as well as our common sense?

It is never good science to ignore anomalous data or to eliminate a conclusion because of some presupposition.

1. Sir Henry Dale, one-time President of the Royal Society of London, made an important comment in his retirement speech: *"Science should not tolerate any lapse of precision, or neglect any anomaly, but give Nature's answers to the world humbly and with courage."* To do so may not place one in the mainstream of modern science, but at least we will be searching for truth and moving ahead rather than maintaining the scientific status quo.[7]

2.

Begin with some simple questions......What? Why? How?

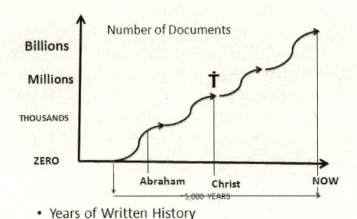

Fig 3. Paleontologists say we have 5,000 years of Written History. {Fig. redrawn from Gitt, Warner. "In the beginning was information"] [8] What are the limits of mans knowledge discovered in this short period of time?

What is Science?

1. Is science a search for real truth or true reality?
2. Can real truth be known?
3. Can science determine reality?
4. Science is a middle English term (about AD 1660) from the Latin *scientia*, knowledge

The stuff of science is information.

1. The first researcher who tried to define information mathematically was Claude E Shannon
2. Shannon's theory of information has the advantage that different methods of communicating knowledge could be evaluated.

3. He was the first to describe the unit of information as a bit.
4. Disadvantage was that content and impact were not investigated

Today we are essentially taught: RANDOM = INFORMATION

Look at that equation carefully and think what it says......isn't it clearly a contradiction?

For RANDOM by definition does not contain information! That is it is without informational content!

No one Can understand a contradiction. So it can be made a god (little g).

*   So it can be made the creator of a Self-Created Nature----AN IDOL
*   Just as Self-Creation ...also a CONTRADICTION.

THE FIRST PRECEPT OF LOGIC AND SCIENCE IS:

*   THE LAW OF NON-CONTRADICTION
*   Something can't BE and NOT BE at the same time

Think of The Theology of the Campus as an American Positivism philosophy turned into a religion which follows the logic of a Bill Maher, Pseudo intellectuals who call themselves rational on the one hand

Yet call Christians as believing myths
The Truth...*VERITAS*.... Is
Good science is a picture of the LORDS creative works and His Design

Semantic Tricks of the Campus.
The word EVOLUTION.
From a Biologists Perspective, the word should be two terms:

3) Genetic Adaptation + 2. Speciation (or creation of new Forms or Families)

Great Evidence exists for Genetic Adaptation, No Evidence for Speciation (that scientists agreed upon)

We should not allow such a poor term (evolution) to gum up good SCIENCE!

I have tried to lay out the interesting History that exposes both this Term and the concept of Secularisms to our America.

QUESTIONS THAT AREN'T PROPERLY ANSWERED DON'T GO AWAY

"Let not the wise man boast of his wisdom or the strong man boast of his strength or the rich man boast of his riches, but let him who boasts boast about this: <u>that he understands and knows me, that I am the LORD, who exercises kindness, justice and righteousness on earth, for in these I delight</u>," Jeremiah 9:23-24

Share your questions about God with the unbelievers.

Remember in Jeremiah 51:7 that the gold cup had something in it that made the nations mad (halal #1984Strongs)[9] ...to make a show to boast clamorously and foolishly, to rave, to celebrate, mad---to be against, to rage).

What is it that Babylon had that all nations drank.....Nimrod's humanism, his false gods and idols, there everywhere if you look, and they are the gods of your campus.

There are, in a very real sense, two natures within us, each warring with the other! And all the battles and conflicts we see in the world are just extensions of that inner struggle playing itself out in seven billion human beings.

"The Cosmos is all that is, or was, or ever will be." Carl Sagan and Neil deGrasse Tyson.

SCIENCE
Pantheist god in a box
Can Reality be found there?

Only within Sagan's box

Or, instead of "the Force", "the Moon god", or any other of Nimrod's inventions inside the cosmic cube of Carl Sagan, please find:

The transcendent holy and pure Creator – God within and without the boundaries of time and dimensions who tells us "… That I am the LORD, who exercises kindness, justice, and righteousness on the earth, and for in these I delight," [Jeremiah 9:23-24, KJV]

Lets define what we mean by "Science"

For the Creator, who is the very source of geometry and, as Plato wrote, "practices eternal geometry," does not stray from his own archetype. [JOHNNES KEPLER, p1018."*Harmonies of the World*", by Johannes Kepler, tr. Charles Glenn Wallis] [10]

None of the processes of Nature, since the time when Nature began, have produced the slightest difference in the properties of any molecule. We are therefore unable to ascribe either the existence of the molecules of the identity of their properties to the operation of any of the causes which we call natural.[11]

Maxwell later said "What I thought of was not so much that uniformity of result which is due to uniformity of result which is due to uniformity in the process of formation, as a uniformity intended and accomplished by the same wisdom and power of which uniformity, accuracy, symmetry, consistency, and continuity of plan are....important attributes. [12] [Garber, E., et al (Eds.) Maxwell on Molecules and Gases (1986) MIT press, Cambridge Massachusetts.]

Remember the laws of nature are originated by Creator-God and subsequently formulated by man by building models, speculations, hypothesis, and theories. The laws of nature can and will refute the formulations built by man. There is a very large gap between the laws of nature and all the scientific work of man. Physicists know a lot about matter, but the knowledge of information is relatively new. And the knowledge about life rests and interacts with both the knowledge of matter and information as Warner Gitt draws:

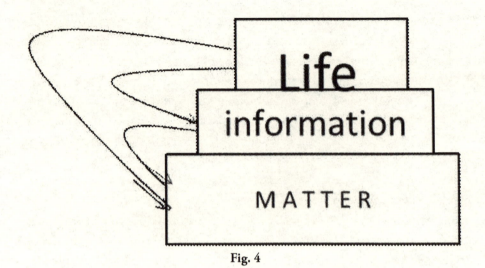

Fig. 4

Only one law of nature about life is known it is the one Louis Pasteur pointed out. "Life only comes from life". Is that what you are being taught. Man's weak formulations will not last when they violate the laws of nature.

A CD full of 700 MB of data doesn't weigh any more then an empty CD. Information doesn't weigh anything or occupy any space and therefore is quite separate from matter or energy.

Science today works for us because we are cognitively wired to be able to base our judgments on what has transpired during mans short-time here on earth. Our brain seems to be wired so that we quickly identify causal events and relate them to objects and create meaningful word symbols to manipulate our reality. The apparent structure of our brains matches the apparent structure of our environment so things work well during the period of time that we are allowed to observe. However, we are given the "Word of God" that tells us that our experience in the "universe of Creator God" is incredibly limited and therefore our ordered reasoning facilities are not so valuable <u>in God's time frame</u>. This is why the big bang and Darwinian speciation, the "rocks of pagan humanism" are of no value to us because we actually have no information on creation other than what is found in the bible. .....no observation of explosions that created order; no logic of "particles-two-man" reasoning, and no agreed on observation of one species (of the millions that we see today) becoming an other species. We know that once "El Nino" occurred in the Galapagos islands and extra food was available, Darwin's finches interbred and were therefore not newly created species. This was just foolish thinking from too short and observation period. There is no way around Creator God!

Science and those engaged honestly in the enterprise of Science deal exclusively with questions that are falsifiable, ie. They are capable of being disproved. While science contains or seeks to contain a reasonable description of reality, it is a "moving train" that is always subject to alterations..... usually by small increments. It tends to be the science of the local because the far events require un-provable assumptions (presuppositions) about light and time. At its very fundamental we do not know beyond question what a photon is or even what an electron is even though we know enough to build smart phones.

Causality in science is a search for relationships and the ultimate understanding of the world about us. When we say a real truth that these must be a "first cause" we are clearly defining Creator-God. Many many scientists would agree with this statement, in fact it is the "default position" rather than the position suggested by your Prof. When we assign the origins to any other we are practicing idolatry; attributing to honoring other things than the one true Creator.

Even Carl Sagan, with his excellent imagination and exploration encouragement refused to identify the miracles of the creation of space and time. The idea that "nothing" exploded and created the order we observe is absurd on its face and to call this event a "singularity" and therefore not reproducible, not observable, and only a matter of inference is amazing. Hopefully the reader will note the misdirection of the ancient term "miracle" even found in Shakespeare (1564-1616) and Chaucer (1343-1400) and replace it as a pseudo-scientific term "singularity" may work for the mathematician but smacks of the ancient gods of Babylon.

No other cosmogony explains the creation of time or the creation of space itself ("stretched out like a curtain by the Creator-God) as we have been notified by the more than 5 billion copies of His publication. Why is That? Because the question of creation is not falsifiable and clearly not a question of science. The scientific method requires falsifiability, otherwise a professor can claim there are no limits to what "science" contains and the word totally loses its meaning. Science then becomes a tool of soothsayers and liars which is repugnant to all men and women of science.

Steven Hawking wrote in "God created the Integers" that Pierre Simon Laplace explains the formation of planets and galaxies with his so-called "accretion" theory where:

If a group of urns arranged in a circle each containing a random collection of white and black balls are mixed or randomized, one ball removed and placed in the neighboring urn and this continues over and over so that the random order of the balls (particles) will "eventually" approach an ordered collection of particles. Laplace proves his theory mathematically and Hawking argues this proves the creation of the galaxies etc. Hawking then points out that Christians should take note of Laplace's work as if he believes this is the answer to galaxy formation....(ie. Gravity replaced Creator-God). [13]

That the one doing the mixing and moving to the next urn <u>in the same direction</u> has a purpose in his action as if he is an "agent" is obvious. It describes what kind of actor . "Direction and purpose" are key terms of any underlying intelligent control system and are required descriptors of all physiological functions of life.....all under feedback control of some kind for stability. The full argument that random is responsible for order is clearly false. In fact, the simple relationship:

Random=Information is a direct contradiction as pointed out earlier, for random is without order and therefore without informational content other than the statement that no information is contained within its boundaries. Remember, a contradiction cannot be understood by anyone and therefore can be worshipped and embraced as the campus creator or creator-force.

Watch a room full of physicist's eyes glass over when equations with this contradiction is given representation in their reality. Random is key to the tools we use in statistics to identify probabilistic events with large populations so we can predict events as a likelihood or to describe population with mean and variance from that mean so we know location within a population.

Mankind has developed very impressive statistics for risk, description, sorting, noise control, information processing, and much more, but none of these would infer that information is random. Stochastic events are real but to equate their random components as unique "information" as defined by the information scientist would be a fallacy.

<u>Origin Science. Vs. Operational Science</u>
<u>Historical Science vs. Observational Science</u>

"Science of the past" creates many major problems. They are often so "fuzzy" that any process of refutation is difficult, and no one can revisit the conditions of the past to find a definitive solution or retest the problem in the precise previous conditions leaving the mass media to decide the popular view. Popper's tests of science doesn't work either. It can still have value, it is just not capable of the same level of confidence as "observational Science". When we deal with Big Bang cosmology and Evolution conjectures we are clearly working in the arena of "Science of the Past". Williams and Harnett point out that human nature will place most scientists on projects that require funding approval by those Senior scientists of the "ruling paradigm". (ie. Big Bang, Global Warming, Evolution). So, "researchers will tend to try to refute conjectures within their favored paradigm itself.....conjectures within this framework will be subjected to experimental testing, but the framework itself will not be. Readers beware!" [14]

Naturalism as god?
Suppression of Truth disguised as Freedom on the campus
Relative Truth: Science and Sanity, what is truth?
The universe was created with truth not lies. Lies don't work! What is written in Creator-God's Word is the truth that created both the universe and man. Lies did not create anything, they only destroy! Reality is composed only of truth! Is that so hard to grasp? Error doesn't work.

Part 2. Why it matters.

[1 Corin 2:14]_{NKJV} "But the natural man does not receive the things of the Spirit of God, for they are foolishness to him; nor can he know then, because they are spiritually discerned."[15]

If deception wins out over truth, our wonderful science, our very understanding of reality is destroyed and truth is slayed in the streets. We are not only in the dark ages, but also find the Word of Creator-God taught as of no import......no effect resulting in the diminishing of the enormous power of bible prophecy, truth, and agape love. An enormous problem is pointed out by Paul in 1Corin 2:14 that our teachers may be incapable of discerning the truth. So how to we respect them and the material they teach and still stay true to our Creator-God and His teachings?

The next 3 parts of the book are for your consideration. Always place the Word of Creator-God first. Any additional consideration I mention here should be weighed in the scope of where you are. The university classroom should be a place where the "enterprise of ideas are presented for your consideration".

Part 3. Logic

The problem of Demarcation: what isn't science

Karl Popper in pointing out that science is a process of "conjecture and refutation", noted that we cannot prove something is "true", but we can prove something is "false". Therefore only falsifiable conjectures are questions of science. Conjectures are to be informed by our original observations and then tested by experiment or further observations.

Logic of Isaac Watts and the Low level of Induction called "Abduction"

Issac Watts, the man who wrote "Joy to the World" for Christmas singers, was a brilliant writer. His work on "Logic, the Right use of Reason in the Inquiry after Truth" (1724) was a standard textbook at Oxford, Cambridge, Harvard, and Yale for nearly 200 years.[16]

Logic: How science Works
Fallacies of Logic
Science is a "moving Train": not an entity to be worshipped

Steven Hawking says that, "...a well constructed model creates a reality of its own"; exposing his idea of reality or that there are multiple realities like the model of multiple universes. There is no evidence for this at all. If a mathematical model or thought experiment can create "true reality", then man's mind, according to this thinking is god. Look carefully at theories of science, they are always being modified once we find out a way to make measurements; they are a moving train. They are not "reality". I find those that place their thoughts above those of Creator-God troublesome. The whim of science theory at a given time is little more then an addition to the historical path we take in our searching. Not all scientists as they approach the end of their lives, claim they have evidence there is no Creator-God based on a thought model......Newton, Faraday, Maxwell, and Einstein were not so silly.[17]

Chance as Creator? Impossible!
Remember, chance can't happen when it is not possible to happen.

The limits of man's imagination-guessing-"abduction" to describe creation
R.C. Sproul on the most <u>impotent</u> University Idol,"Chance".[18]

"The ABCs of Biblical faith are almost gone in our culture. We are taught from kindergarten on that we live in a closed universe that came into being by a cosmic accident and operates according to the <u>fortuitous circumstances of chance</u>. But the word of Creator-God says:

"…..by which He upholds with his hands heaven, earth, and all creatures".

Providence begins with the understanding of Creator-God's preserving, nurturing, providing his creation. The new testament says it is in him we live and move and have our being. We do not live in a closed mechanical universe that operates by its own power.

Arthur Koestler has written, "As long as chance rules, God is an anachronism." [19]

What's wrong with this statement? Whatever rules has to be Creator–God. A god who doesn't rule is not worthy of the title. Certainly not worthy of honor, glory, power, your worship, and your praise.

R.C. Sproul's thesis is that as long as chance "is" god is an anachronism. That if there is one thing that happens in this universe by chance, than god doesn't rule. He is not sovereign! If one thing in this universe happens by chance god isn't. Yet we are accustomed to thinking today that all kinds of things happen by chance. Sproul was speaking with a Harvard professor who told him he believed the universe came about by chance. So Sproul took out his 50¢ piece, and ask him if he flipped the 50¢ piece what are the chances of it coming up heads or tails. He asked the professor how much influence chance has on its coming up heads or tails? Let's say we have an absolutely closed experiment were we have the coins in a position in which we will control the force how high it goes how far it falls and how it starts out, the density of the atmosphere which it's moving. If you could get rid of all those variables, could you predict with greater than a 50% accuracy, the outcome? The professors answer was, yes. Sproul said what I want to know is how much influenced chance has on whether it comes up heads or tails. Sproul reiterated how much power does chance have? Assess the question of what is chance? It is a perfectly legitimate and meaningful word to use for mathematical possibilities.

But what about its ontology? What is the structure of its being? What is it... It's 'is Nis'. How much does weigh? Where does it live? The professor answered, well, it's not a thing!

Sproul responded, "it's no thing, right!". He said right it's no thing. Sproul said let's say it a little faster no thing no thing no thing….. <u>nothing</u>. Sproul said how much power does no thing manifest? Sproul points out that if it has no being, it has no influence! That which has no being cannot possibly have power to do anything. That means if they're such a situation where things can come into being in this world from nothing, than there is no god, is no reason there's no science there's nothing left. In fact that's all there is, is nothing and we can even say there is nothing because we can say nothing is because if it were something that wouldn't be nothing. So we have to say that nothing is not. Sproul is not playing games, this is very serious. Because as a substitute for god we have enshrined as the god of our age... a thinly veiled concept of nothing. And generated a thing we call "chance" with a capital "C".

"The most impotent idol man as ever invented." "Chance"!

In reality all things come to us by the hand of Creator–God! Our idolatry is an abomination! Because Creator-God is sovereign over history.

Aristotle's god is not sovereign, in fact he doesn't deserve the title. He does not rule over his creation. The IDOLATRY of the campus is to claim Aristotle's god as some kind of creator and "CHANCE" as the Sovereign of the universe, allowing equations and probability and likelihood to be predictive in front of the students, so tabletop experiments in the classroom give the false guise of truth of this false Sovereign-god called Chance. How deceptive can you be? The Stoichiometry of the Chemistry class is not driven by the god Chance but by the concentrations of the substances, the temperature and the pressure surrounding the experiment. Equations do not describe the god Chance! Nothing happens by chance, because the order in the universe, the energy flow in the universe, and the casual mechanisms in the universe while not apparent, and not in the simple equations on the board before the student, the Prof. can be politically correct by inserting the nothing term "Chance" and move on because he doesn't understand the ontology of Chance, that it is not an operator, or he refuses to discuss the deception of the use of the term as an operator. This harkens back to my discussion of the Pagan Idols of Babylon where the god Chaos was described… making up the substance of Nimrod's universe. How we have descended from the glory of science to the base, lowly, pit.

The new math of "Chaos" extols the power of the "Sensitivity to initial conditions" as definitive in those unpredictable outcomes like the weather and so many unexplainable events in science. Never once suggesting that a Creator-God who knows and controls every atom and molecule is not surprised by any outcome…..indeed is the One who moves the butterfly's wings over the ocean to alter the entire weather pattern. This must be to much for the classroom scientist to address because of the moral consequences for both him and his students. In all truth the statement, "Chaos is an agent of order" we hear from the Prof. is an example of linguistic confusion. It may be the problem between classical physics and quantum physics. "Linguistic problems will continue to plague us as anomalies continue to appear that do not fit existing paradigms. Until the paradigm is revised or expanded to accommodate the anomalies, we will tend to attempt to squeeze or force the anomalies into old categories giving rise to linguistic confusion and even nonsense statements". [20]

For the Creator, who is the very source of geometry and, as Plato wrote, "practices eternal geometry," does not stray from his own archetype. [21]

If we recognize that questions of science must be falsifiable if "necessarily true". The so-called sacred rocks of human paganism that are worshipped in modern secular universities are not falsifiable propositions/conjectures and therefore not questions of science, even though Faculty positions are created, entire departments have been formed, and large course requirements have been developed at great expense to the society. "They exchanged the truth of God for a lie and worshiped and served the creation rather than the Creator..." [Romans 1:25] seems quite prophetic in the scheme of things.

Science and Reality: Einstein on Reality

"The whole of science is nothing more than a refinement of everyday thinking... (the physicist) cannot proceed without considering critically a much more difficult problem, (than the field of physics) the problem of analyzing the nature of everyday thinking." [22]

"... The real extra world of everyday thinking rests exclusively on sense impressions."

(first comes) a "bodily object" and next we attribute to the object a significance (independent of the sense impression which gives rise to it).... A "real existence" (that makes the object) a free mental creation appear to us stronger and more unalterable than the sense experience itself... (In which we are not completely guaranteed) are not illusions or hallucinations... On the other hand, these concepts and relations, and indeed the postulations of real objects and, generally speaking, of existence of ' the real world' have justification only in so far as they are connected with sense impressions between which they form a mental connection... That can be put in order.

"this fact is one which leaves us in awe, but one in which we shall never understand. One may say the eternal mystery of the world is its comprehensibility." (Kant) "... The fact that it is comprehensible is a <u>miracle</u>. The totality of the connection... Is the only thing which differentiates the great building which is science from a logical but empty scheme of concepts."

Note that Einstein believes in miracles.

Einstein says everyday thinking (the sense experience) is, "utterly lacking in logical unity. We (theoretical scientists) build layers of systems that become remote from the complex experiences to arrive at a system 'of the greatest conceivable unity which is still compatible with the observations made by our own senses." (he has hope that someday we will arrive at such a system)

"These layers of ours are not like soup is to beef but of check numbers to overcoats. (i.e. pointers)... In a way similar to a man in solving a well designed word puzzle. He may propose any word as the solution; but, there is only <u>one</u> word which really solves the puzzle in all its parts." [23]

Why Science is incompetent in both structure and function when it comes to addressing and trying to manipulate Creator-God

Imagine if you were to create a painting on a wall behind you, and you gave that painting senses and consciousness. It would only detect your brushes coming on it. It would not have the dimensionality to detect you. You have to be dimensionally above or greater than something to create it. So Creator-God is way above us dimensionally and knows we were not given the power to picture Him or grasp what His thoughts are. When we imagine Him we are moving close to the Idolatry He warns against at least 8 times. He gives us one of His names, YHVH which we don't know how to pronounce because the vowels are not there in the writing. He describes Himself with a number of our descriptors but language is quite weak in describing Him. So how could a scientist turn Him into an equation of sorts. So many of them just punt. What results are in effect attacks to exclude Him, which is senseless in the reality of things.

Edward O. Wilson in a book on human nature cleverly describes science as a continual oscillation between expansion and compression. The cycle begins when a scientist ----a "system building" more specifically -----comes along and claims he can compress a large body of information into a small theoretical package (or smaller set of principles or equations).[24] Wilson sees most scientists as bookkeepers filling in the Blanks in a theory (compressed statement). Isn't it obvious how impossible it would be for a scientist to take the infinite Creator-God and his multi-dimensionality (perhaps infinite dimensions) and compress Him to a thing of science. Because the enterprise of the scientist is to walk away from infinity's; because no one can grasp the concept, and it would be a contradiction to shrink infinity. The scientist is at a loss to work with Creator-God in this (theory). But he needs a job, money, and recognition so he invades the domain anyway. But doesn't this compression and this oscillation as Wilson has it appear as foolishness! [25]

Yet scientists functioning in a "compression of information" process can learn something on the efficiency of Creator-God. If the purpose of the psychiatry and psychology profession in our society is "mental hygiene", listen to a secular psychiatrist J. T. Fisher M.D.:

"If you were to take the sum total of all the authoritative articles ever written by the most qualified psychologists and psychiatrists on the subject of mental hygiene – if you are to confine them and refine them and cleave out the excess verbiage --- if you are to take the whole of the meat, and none of the parsley, and if you are to have these unadulterated bits of pure scientific knowledge concisely expressed by the most capable of living poets, you would have an awkward and incomplete summation of a Sermon on the Mount. And, it would suffer immeasurably through comparison.

For nearly 2,000 years the Christian world has been holding in its hand the complete answer to its restless and fruitless yearnings. Here rests the blueprint for successful human life with optimum mental health and contentment."[26]

Part 4. Physics: The Physics of Creation vs. the Physics of maintaining the Universe.

Let us ask if the only Physics we can observe today is the Physics involved in the maintenance of the Universe today. Is it possible that there is a creation Physics we can't observe? How can a modern physicists know (and with what confidence) he is observing Creation Physics? I enjoy my telescope and all fine astrophotography of the wonderful NASA Hubble telescope, but I keep my thinking cap on when some artist labels a picture of beautifully colored (usually false colored) gas and dust as a "stellar nursery" while someone waxes eloquent describing what he sees......just as what he presupposes is present. Is this Maintenance Physics or true creation and how does he know. Similar to the fellow that finds water in space or amino acids and immediately says, "that is the beginning of life there". Quite silly, wouldn't you say. I think we should ask for a little more "rigor" in their teaching. What has he measured, what does his data mean? What are other reasonable explanations when you drop his presupposition?

Proof of the truth of the Bible

Victor J. Stenger, an emeritus professor of physics and astronomy at the university of Hawaii in his book "Has Science found God" sadly represents a number of faculty that have no idea what the bible is about. Stenger claims that the bible tells us, "When they look in the mirror in the light of faith. It reflects an image of themselves as fallen angels, set on this planet with the divine purpose of rehabilitating themselves so they may rejoin their fellow angels in paradise."[27] His mockery unfortunately describes incredible ignorance of the Bible. Fallen angels are demons, and Christianity has nothing to do with Christians saving themselves. If your professor is critical of the Bible, caution, he/she may be speaking from abject ignorance.

All the documented events in the bible have never been shown to be false even though the bible has been attacked more than any writing. Creator-God tells us we will know His writing is True by the fact that He tells us what will happen before it will happen. The precision of the more then 1,000 prophecies of the bible are amazing. Only a Creator-God outside of time could write it as "God-breathed" through the 40 authors, in which the theme of the Gospel of salvation possible for each of us, is the theme throughout. The more you study it the more you see Jesus Christ on every page. There is much we know and much ignorance still abounds:

> Manuscript evidence. We have more early manuscripts of the bible to compare than any other book. For the New Testament: It has not been changed throughout time. The New Testament dwarfs all other ancient works with respect to the total number of manuscripts that still exists. Together the 121 papyri fragments, 2813 Minuscules (Cursives) writings, 2281 Lectionaries, and 25,000 to 30,000 ancient translations from the original Greek, and many Thousands of references to the Original Text in letters by the early church fathers mean there is so much textual material that there is little question of the original Kone Greek writing. There are however variant readings of small parts of the text of the New Testament that have little or nothing to do with doctrine. Shakespeare's plays, though written after the invention of the printing press, are in much poorer textual shape with gaps in every play in which we do not know what was originally written...we have to guess even though it was written sixteen centuries later than the New Testament. [28]

> Probability and likelihood- Nearly one fourth of scripture was prophetic when it was written. Of more than a Thousand or so

major prophecies, there are at least 500 prophecies completed with great precision and 500 yet to be completed or fulfilled. [29] The likelihood of just the 456 prophecies about Jesus of Nazareth serially occurring by chance is a number greater than the number of particles in the universe. The probability that 456 prophecies would be fulfilled in one man by chance is vastly improbable. According to Emile Borel, once one goes past one chance in 10^{50}, the probabilities are so small that it is impossible to think that they will ever occur.

The apparent stability of the universe is impossible without the First Mover because motion stabilizes both the atomic level, the macro level, and apparently the spiritual level.

Water's properties....Hydrogen bonding theory is way beyond our grasp. Water is unlike any other substance! H_2O has a slight polarity and we have to study 3 inch thick books to learn biochemistry. We do not know these rules. Creator-God has made water very special, its properties and interactions show great intelligence in its design as it relates to life. Google "DNA hydration" and see how complex water behavior is just in the structure and function of DNA and DNA relationship to proteins. My first textbook of Biochemistry "Lerninger" noted in the first chapter that the bioactive structure of biological molecules depends upon water's complex attraction for itself (ie. Hydrogen bonding) far exceeds the weak bonds of the biomolecule so that its specific bioactive conformation is due to water shoving the biomolecule into the conformation that works. Our biochemistry books would be thin or certainly not so thick if we only understood water's behavior completely! But we don't. X-ray diffraction and other tools haven't yet revealed the answer so we can predict complex structure of the molecules of life.....they may never explain it all. Indeed, DNA has at least 4 different hydration structures. [30] And of course the fact that no two snow flakes are alike is a quiet suggestion of the amazing characteristics of water which, added to the fact that water at 4 degrees is heaver means bodies of water don't freeze solid. Thereby protecting aquatic life.

Plasma Physics are also way beyond our grasp. Over 98% of the universe is made of plasma yet our knowledge of all properties and interactions of plasma are miniscule. My copy of a recent textbook "Introduction to Plasma Physics" by Donald A. Gurnett (James A. Van Allen Professor of Physics at the University of Iowa), and Amitava Bhattacharjee (University of New Hampshire) is a remarkable 452 page book based on Applied Physics courses taught at Iowa and Columbia University. The book only deals with the classical regime not the quantum regime for plasma. A complete mathematical model of plasma is difficult consisting of three basic elements: "….first, the motion of all particles must be determined for some assumed electric and magnetic field configuration; second, the current and charge densities must be computed from the particle trajectories; and third, the electric and magnetic fields must be self-consistently determined from the currents and charges, taking into account both internal and external sources." The electric and magnetic fields used in last step must be the same as those used in the first step. [31] Even though this book is a remarkable introduction, it is apparent the complexity of a plasma is quite remarkable. I believe we can say that we don't know much about what most of what the universe is made of. We haven't solved how to contain plasmas in a breeder reactor magnetic bottle yet, because of the interaction between surfaces. The complexity of the problems boggles the mind.

Embryology. My copy of Harvey and Rosenthal "Heart Development" notes that we are just beginning to understand some of the genetic pathways, cellular interactions, and control systems involved in heart development (let alone the human brain). This text brings 65 of the experts together…..but just a beginning in complete understanding. While the plight of the plasma physicists is evident as they deal with 98% of the universe, the complexity of the development of a human being within its mother is of a far higher complexity, perhaps the equations for embryology will someday be written, but I doubt it. Who could grasp it. Is man's water brain capable of design like that? What have we designed in which the plans were not stolen from what Creator-God already made?[32]

Gravity: A force that seems to be a property of mass yet seems to have no force carriers (no Boson?) Job, the oldest book of the bible thought to be written at the time of the patriarchs 2000 to 1800 BC noted that the Pleiades are a group of stars that not only lie close together but travel in the same direction...are gravitationally linked, unlike most other constellations."Can you **bind** the beautiful Pleiades? Can you loose the **cords** of Orion?"[Job 38:31] How is it the writer knew this at that time, who told him? So far we have arrived that the universe is very close to the borderline between a closed and a open universe, ie it is a "flat" universe or not so much matter as to collapse or to little so that it flies apart. "Out of the infinite range of possible densities, the flat universe is a unique case and couldn't be chosen at random. As all of the theoretical universes age they "diverge" from the flat unique case. "Like a pencil balanced on its point; it might stay upright for a fraction of a second, but to make it stand up for what is claimed "billions" of years is to all limits and purposes impossible." Of course Alan Guth's idea of "Inflation" is designed to miraculously force the universe, no matter how it started out into the flat one we think we see now, at least until we have another perspective to make measurements.[33] [Lindley, David."The End of Physics: the myth of a unified theory". Basic Books.N.Y.1993.pp167-169]

The Three interacting Particle problem: Steven Hawking points out in his recent book, "We cannot even solve exactly the equations for three or more particles interacting with each other."[34]

Cosmological Constant. While its value has enormous implications, there is no agreement as to it value or whether it is a small or huge number.

Dark energy, dark matter If all the mass of the universe is estimated at 10^{54} kg then using Einstein's equation $E=MC^2$ the energy content of this mass is 10^{60} MWh (Mega Watt Hour). If we look at the largest generating plant on earth as 10^6 MWh per year, the ratio of the two is a incomprehensibly large number. The Big Bang theorists teach our children that this energy and matter came about by what Carl Sagan calls, "The biggest mystery we know".[35] This Primordial Singularity somehow allowed the universe to escape the grip of great gravity far exceeding that of any black hole by what some theorize as a "fluctuation in quantum gravity". Except that an acceptable theory of quantum gravity is apparently mostly at present in man's imagination. What evidence is there of such a beginning? Presupposing that the universe is expanding and can be theoretically taken backward in time, and call all it "Inflation Theory". And since our water brains are limited by what we can imagine, if we claim we understand time and wind it back from now backwards, we can imagine matter and energy and light in space-time wound backwards on a "world line" to a point where there is nowhere left in space or time for it to go.....we have a "singularity". Not a scientific event because it is by definition one that only occurs once and can never be studied or reproduced so it could be a "Emperor has no clothes" but more like a "suppose". That is a model for physicists to work on to keep them funded and off the streets. Since energy has the property of gravity as well how did all the stuff of the universe escape the gravity present in this primordial dot? How do the big bangers escape their own creator-god "Gravity"?

Momentum

Richard Feyman tells the story of his Father (a tailor) showing him how the brick in his "Red Flyer" wagon stayed put when he suddenly pulled it forward. When he sent his son to college he asked him to find out why. Just after Feyman received the Nobel Prize, His father sat down with him to lunch in Pasadena and asked his son "Why the brick sat still?". The new Nobel winner replied " I still don't know dad". We still don't know what momentum is or why it occurs. Einstein writes that he incorporated his friend Mach's Principle in his "General Theory of Relativity". Mach suggested the value for Momentum is a function of the Mass of the universe.[36] That is the damage your car would incur when it hit a brick wall would be half as much if there were half as many stars in the heavens. How do you prove that? So Momentum continues to be a real problem for Physics and science in general, even though it is so very basic a question because it is a fundamental property of matter.

Electron. We know a lot of description of this, but exactly what it is and why is a mystery that is what is it's "substance" isn't known. When it is so around us in that we live in an electrified world and the electromagnetic force is so incredibly greater than the miniscule gravity force, it is highly unlikely that gravity created us, but the electron participates in most all of our chemistry, and all plasma which makes up 98% of the universe we know.

Proton. Seems the counterpart of the electron caries the positive charge but as Newton would ask, "What is its substance?" We know a lot of description as well of this, but exactly what it is and why is a mystery.

The explanation of all these are not statistical!!

If man creates anything with probabilities or stats imbedded in the process, he creates with significant error imbedded within. The universe can't function with such a level of error-for the error would multiply when coupled together into interacting control systems to multiply into problems of enormous proportions. Truth cannot contain such errors, or reality will recede from us and insanity will approach....we need Creator-God for correction and direction! Notice what our control has led to as we "progress from World War to World War and Greater weapons to greater weapons! Also notice the progressive movement to greater morality in the world and less violence in the world, even our "Evolution" is nothing short of Devolution on its face. (Remember we have 200 or more genetic errors with each generation). The accumulated errors in the "Y" chromosome alone affects an enormous number of men. Will man continue to a point where we cannot comprehend our Creator? Absurd!

Einstein sees nature as a well formulated puzzle on the way to physics that is logically as uniform as possible.

The Fine-Tuned Universe

Who among our fine physicists have struggled with the incredible "Fine-Tuned Universe"?

Paul Davies physicist, starting to see that somebody has fine-tuned the universe is impressed with data on constants.

George Greenstein also finds a supreme being?

Arnold Penzias identifies supernatural event.

Stephen Hawking suggests, it's hard to explain without Creator-God.

This fine-tuning would be One chance in 10^{215} by random chance.... (never happen).

200 scientist have found 800 parameters discovered that have to be precisely fine-tuned for man to exist.

That 10 billion trillion stars needed or it wouldn't work. That's a stack of dimes 4 round trips to Alpha Centauri. Fewer stars would mean inefficient fusion in which only hydrogen and helium would form.

More stars than the 10 billion-trillion in the universe would mean all elements would be heavier than iron....no carbon, nitrogen, or oxygen would form. [37]

Only in our cosmos can the life-essential elements be produced.

The Reason Creator-God is a personal God.

Precision:

Precision in 1 part in 10 trillion trillion for several physics constants.

Many physicists claim Dark energy makes up 72% of the universe. If you expand the universe too quickly gas and dust would never be collected by gravity to make stars and galaxies.

If too slowly then gravity will collapse everything into black holes and neutron stars. So dark energy must be fine tuned precisely according to their equations-model. Man's best fine-tuned construction is the gravity wave LIGO instrument can only resolve 1 part in 10^{23}.[38] On the other hand when compared to a precision of 1 in 10^{122} means that God's fine-tuning is

10 to 99 Thousand trillion, trillion, trillion, trillion, trillion, trillion, trillion, trillion, trillion, (x9) More precise than the Caltech people who built the instrument.

And at least that level better funded.

Famous Physicists that are seeing the light

Netterfield et al in the Measurement by boomerang of multiple....microwave background called the "Boomerang project" which is the speeding up expansion due to space energy density. If it varied more than 1 part in 10^{120} or mass density if it varied more than 1 part in 10^{60}, life would be impossible anywhere and anytime in the universe!

Person-like qualities:

The reason Creator-God is not an impersonal entity but is instead a person is because he expresses Intellect, Knowledge, Creativity, Power, Care, and Love. Attributes only a person can manifest.

This matches only the God of the bible. Forcing people to think like never before about the theological implications.....only the bible speaks for many thousands of years about the beginning of space, time, and energy!

Isaiah 42:5[NET] Under constant laws...I have established....the fixed laws of heaven and earth.

Jeremiah 33:25 [NET] While the universe today is dominated by the "law of decay"

"The whole creation groans...subject to its bondage to decay." [Romans 8:20-22][NET] The 2nd law of thermodynamics Our measurements over cosmic history is exactly what the bible predicts In fact ....Creator-God.[39]

Famous Scientists of the Past

A number of our finest scientists who we could call "truth seekers" have addressed the understanding that we need. Sir Isaac Newton, Johannes

Kepler, Galileo, Copernicus, Sir Robert Boyle, Michael Faraday, Blaise Pascal, and James Clerk Maxwell to name a few.

This understanding enabled them to unlock many of the secrets of the universe and to usher in the scientific revolution. Said Albert Einstein: "Let no one suppose, however, that the mighty work of Newton can really be superseded by relativity or any other theory. His great and lucid ideas will retain their unique significance for all time as the foundation of our whole modern conceptual structure in the sphere of natural philosophy" [40] Einstein felt that Newton's genius had effected scientific thought, research and practice "... to an extent that nobody before or since his time can touch." Three portraits of scientists adorned the walls of Einstein's study—Isaac Newton, Michael Faraday and James Clerk Maxwell.

All three of these men, as well as the others mentioned above (except Darwin) were able to unlock the basic laws of the physical universe. All firmly believed that the universe was constructed in a reasonable (logical and "lawful") way, since a reasonable Creator-God who created man in His image, would only create a reasonable (logical) universe.

The Greeks, Chinese, and Egyptians, however, all eventually failed because they either believed in a "random" universe where things happened entirely by chance (as do the followers of Darwin), or that things happened by the whim of unknowable gods or forces.

The eight scientists mentioned in the first paragraph were men of facts and knowledge. They understood reality more clearly than most of us ever will. They were not superstitious men, nor were they seeking to escape from the hard facts of reality by blind faith in a "fantasy" of religion. Higher mathematics requires the most logical thinking. It would be nearly impossible to find eight other men who have affected the world as they have, and who also have their reasoning capabilities.

Yet each of these eight scientific geniuses understood that Jesus is the only Messiah of the world, and that He would physically return someday on the clouds, receiving those who believe in Him, and judge the living and raise the dead for judgment.

Einstein admired Sir Isaac Newton above all scientists. Newton spent the last 40 years of his life studying the timeline and endtime prophecies of the bible. His dedication to Creator-God shows in the following quote which is characteristic of his writing:[41]

Sir Isaac Newton (1642-1727)

"... the motions which the planets now have could not spring from any natural cause alone, but were impressed by an intelligent Agent." "... the diurnal rotations of the planets could not be derived from gravity.""... and though gravity might give the planets a motion of descent toward the sun, either directly or with some little obliquity, yet the transverse motions by which they revolve in their several orbs required the divine arm to impress them according to the tangents of their orbs." "I would now add that the hypothesis of matter being at first evenly spread through the heavens, is, in my opinion, inconsistent with the hypothesis of innate gravity (today a scientific law) without a supernatural power to reconcile them, and therefore it infers a Deity." "For while comets move in very eccentric orbs, in all manner of positions. Blind fate (chance) could never make all the planets move one and the same way in orbs concentric." "Did blind chance know that there was light and what was its refraction, and fit the eyes of all creatures after the most curious manner to make use of it?" "Was the eye contrived without skill in optics and the ear without knowledge of sounds?"

Before Newton, Kepler, the father of Astronomy wrote:

Johannes Kepler (1571-1630)

I strive to publish them (his discoveries)in God's honor who wishes to be recognized from the book of nature. This I pledged to God, this is my decision. I had the intention of becoming a theologian. For a long time, I was restless, but now see how God is by my endeavors, also glorified in astronomy."

While The Catholic Church expelled Kepler from his home country where he saw their false teachings for what they were. He wrote his friend Galileo, "All this is rather hard. But I should not have believed that in the communion of brethren it is so sweet to suffer loss or insult for our faith and Messiah's honor, and to abandon home, fields, friends and country. If it is the same with real martyrdom and the sacrifice of life, if the joy is the greater, the greater the loss, then it must also be an easy thing to die for faith." "I am in earnest with my religion, I don't play with it."

Michael Faraday's last words: "I shall be with Christ, and that is enough." [42]

While it was the great Blaise Pascal (1623-1662) before Faraday who wrote: "I look for God, therefore I have found Him. ....in science, in contrast to theology, one should never be guided by authority but by experiment. We can only know 'some' of the effects of nature because nature is ever active. One can only falsify, not prove ...and so that it appears in those who follow it [true religion] that it is grace and not reason, which makes them follow it; and in those who shun it, that it is lust, not reason, which, makes them shun it." He also wrote:, "It is the nature of self esteem and of the human self to love only oneself alone. But what can a man do? He wants to be great and finds that he is small; he wants to be happy and finds that he is unhappy, he wants to be perfect and finds that he is riddled with imperfections, he wants to be the object of men's affections and esteem and sees that his faults deserve only their dislike and contempt. The embarrassing position in which he finds himself produces in him the most unjust and criminal passion that can possibly be imagined; he conceives a mortal hatred of the truth which brings him down to earth and convinces him of his faults. He would like to be able to annihilate it, and, not being able to destroy it in himself, he destroys it in the minds of other people. That is to say, he concentrates all his efforts on concealing his faults both from others and from himself, and cannot stand being made to see them or their being seen by other people."

The task of science, therefore, is not to attack the objects of faith, but to establish the limits beyond which knowledge cannot go and find a unified self-consciousness within these limits.

James Clerk Maxwell (1831-1879)

"But we have no right to think thus of the unsearchable riches of creation, or of the untried fertility of those fresh minds into which these riches will continue to be poured."[43]

".... I have the capacity of being more wicked than any example that man could set me, and that if I escape, it is only by God's grace helping me to get rid of myself, partially in science, more completely in society, — but not perfectly except by committing myself to God as the instrument of His will, not doubtfully, but in the certain hope that that will be plain enough at the proper time."[44]

These scientists echo the writing of the old testament: . "All we like sheep have gone astray; we have turned everyone to his own way and the Lord hath laid on him the iniquity of us all." (~700 B.C.—Isaiah 53:6).

Charles Darwin (1809-1882) Charles Darwin, however, wrote in a letter to Asa Gray (May 22, 1860) at the age of 51, "I am inclined to look at everything as resulting from designed laws, with the details whether good or bad, left to the working out of what we may call chance. Not that this notion at all satisfies me. I feel most deeply that the whole subject is too profound for the human intellect. A dog might as well speculate on the mind of Newton. Let each man hope and believe what he can. Certainly I agree with you that my views are not at all necessarily atheistical... A child (who may turn out an idiot) is born by the action of even more complex laws, and I can see no reason why a man, or other animal, may not have been aboriginally produced by other laws, and that all these laws may have been expressly designed by an omniscient Creator, who foresaw every future event and consequence. But the more I think the more bewildered I become, as indeed I have probably shown by this letter."

Darwin's own confusion as to the existence of a personal God is clearly shown above. Interestingly, Darwin uses Isaac Newton's name as an example of the highest human intellect, yet Newton had no problem, after much thought, seeing that Jesus Christ Is the Truth. The use of "aboriginal" is curious. Darwin's grandfather is said to have stuffed a aborigine and placed him in the British Museum implying a subhuman status, an amazingly repugnant act against one of Creator-God's people.

> "During the three years which I spent at Cambridge my time was wasted, as far as the academical studies were concerned... The work was repugnant to me chiefly from my not being able to see any meaning in the early steps in algebra. This impatience was very foolish, and in after years I have deeply regretted that I did not proceed far enough at least to understand something of the great principles of mathematics, for men thus endowed seem to have an extra sense, but I do not believe that I should ever have succeeded beyond a very low grade." [45]

While Darwin was a excellent observer, but as far as Mathematical rigor, Darwin was unable to master early algebra he declares. He was far below such men as Newton and Maxwell. His education was for the purpose of becoming a Unitarian pastor but failed to materialize.

(Note: Perhaps the thought and work of his grandfather's book "Transmutation" did not take hold on Darwin until John Gould, a bird expert, told him the finches with different beaks he sent from Galapagos qualified as different species (they didn't) but Darwin accepted Guild's authority to all of Science's hurt.)

Prominent evolutionist Professor Richard Lewontin (1929-) made an amazing admission about this bias:

We take the side of science *in spite* of the patent absurdity of some of its constructs, *in spite* of its failure to fulfill many of its extravagant promises of health and life, *in spite* of the tolerance of the scientific community for unsubstantiated 'just-so stories', because we have a prior commitment, a commitment to materialism. It is not that the methods and institutions of science somehow compel us to accept a material explanation of the phenomenal world, but, on the contrary, that we are forced by our *a priori* adherence to material causes to create an apparatus of investigation and a set of concepts that produce material explanations, no matter how counter-intuitive, no matter how mystifying to the uninitiated. Moreover, that materialism is an absolute, for we cannot allow a Divine Foot in the door.[46]

The Good Scientists: What is he like who is not an Idolater?
"Newton wasn't the last magician. But he was the last one who know who he was."[John Maynard Keynes]

When Newton wrote the "Principia" he created a scientific work that is far and above all other scientific works. Newton became the leading authority in mathematics, optics, mechanics and alchemy/chemistry. Who else was given such talents? Newton, like Aristotle had the desire to piece together everything ----he truly sought reality...truth in to an "understanding" not just a simple description, some definitions and some rhetoric. A real scientists seeks to construct a <u>coherent</u> story of reality. It requires study of history, math, physics, chemistry, and theology. Leave out one of these disciplines and you have not honestly arrived at a truthful "world-view".

What was unique about Newton's definition of holiness and authority of scripture that placed an emphasis on "industriousness, self-discipline, and a constant guarding against vanity of pride. But more than that, his belief system was personal, a relationship with Creator-God. "Newton's God was not aloof and impersonal....Newton recognized that Creator-God was his father, which was something he was born without." Those who read his notebooks note his lifelong desire to please his heavenly Father.[47] What we see is the greatest scientists worldview. He refused to operate in a reality where his feet were firmly planted in mid-air!

Scientists who try to teach our children that creation just happened, the children are just grown-up worms, that the student himself is sovereign over their own little world with relative truth and relative morality are so remote from Newton as can be imagined. The success of their "world view" is "Slouching toward Gomorrah" and an incoherent position that doesn't hold water.

Newton understood and may be the first to grasp the mystery of "action at a distance" (as opposed to the Jesuit teaching) that both light and gravity were quite mystical. Steven Hawking, who sits in Newton's Chair of Physics at Cambridge sees that gravity and chance created everything, planting the start of his thinking firmly in "mid-air". No doubt the "action at a distance" for light and gravity came from Newton's deep study of alchemy---the basis of modern chemistry. [48]

My point is that Newton's love for Creator-God and his love for truth and understanding without compromise is in contrast to the Professor who teaches the copout "it must only be 'Natural' explanation and without Creator-God", condemns a man and his followers-students to, "always learning but never coming to the knowledge of the truth.[2 Tim3:7]. The context of the reference to 2nd Timothy in the Bible is to the "last days" when men will be lovers of themselves and lovers of pleasure rather than lovers of God, just the idolatry of the end times. We are there!

Newton grew up at a time and place where acceptance of Creator-God and Jesus Christ was part of the culture----a presupposition.

Scientific Hypocrisy and self-deception

"Most modern scientists pride themselves on having purged themselves of thoughts of mystery and magic (it won't fit in with their equations and notations) while unwittingly using theories that are as "mystical" as they are scientific---scientific hypocrisy. Newton, believing the world is full of magic, found that it is full of magic. He, in turn, revealed some of his discoveries to us.

But probably not all of them. In later years, he burned boxes of his own writings. Perhaps he was afraid of them falling into the wrong hands." [49]

Newton and Hooke knocked down the "ether" theory but it keeps reappearing as dark energy and dark matter (as 95% of the universe) from the Heisenberg to Ort and Zwicky. There is no evidence of the Ort clouds existence other than hypothesis, identical to the state of Darwin's hypothesis arrived at by the logic of "best guess" or "abduction logic".

Picture man stumbling through the void. If he has no lantern to let him see what is there, he is lost. That lantern is the Word of God. You must pick it up---grasp it in your hands, open it and seek to understand its works or you are sure to wonder from "nowhere" to "nowhere".

Missing the Mark

Today, many professors believe in Creator-God? The problem with them as well as this professor (myself), is we do not see ourselves as Creator-God sees us!

If we have stuff; if we have titles; we all commit the sin of "covetousness". If we teach a Creator-God that is not the ultimate righteousness, who gives us the moral law and reject any of Creator-God's teaching.....that he is Holy, full of Justice and Mercy; so loving that He has given himself in the form of His Son on the Cross for all our sins against Him we have missed the mark. We need to all fall on our knees before Him in repentance, realizing that these offenses block our entry into eternal life (as He has told us)! If we teach our students anything otherwise then the "truth" we miss the mark as well. We are held to a higher standard because we are teachers!

Part 5. Narration, Conjecture & attempts to contradict the Bible

Time is way beyond our grasp. When we say Creator-God is omni-present, apparently meaning he has the property of non-locality (perhaps). And when we say He is outside of Time, we lose the understanding that comes from our senses. I'm fairly sure we can imagine the truths that describe these properties…certainly we know he is infinite and that infinity is not within man's capacity to imagine, in spite of John Lennon's song to pretend such an absur-dity of the non-existence of Creator-God (or no heaven or hell). We know gravity effects time, yet we don't know what gravity is or what carries its force. Chance can only occur if it is possible to occur. A miracle or "singularity" as physicists call it; a space in the datum or their equation that goes to infinity and means they haven't any hon-est idea. Man cannot conceive of infinity or relate it to any sense or feeling he has outside of theology, certainly not science. The begin-ning of time is not a physics concept….yet men play with the idea knowing they are instructing our children in their vain idolatry.

Consciousness; what is it? No one knows convincingly. Guilt, shame, morality; while it makes for a better world, it is found less and less in our population. The pagan world attempts to redefine or suppress all of these or use drugs to omit them. We have them for a reason, a truth! Will it be our downfall to loose them?

Blue Stars Confirm Recent Creation

Recent work by Jason Lisle, Ph.D. noted that "…Orion is one of the most well-known and easily recognized constellations of the winter sky. The three bright blue stars in Orion's belt seem to draw our attention instantly.[50] Such stars are a strong confirmation of the biblical timescale.

Most stars generate energy by the process of nuclear fusion of hydrogen into helium in the stellar core. This is a very efficient power source. Theoretically, a star like the sun has enough hydrogen in its core to keep it burning for ten billion years. But that's not the case with blue stars.

Blue stars are always more massive than the sun. This means they have more hydrogen available as fuel. Yet, blue stars are much brighter than the sun; some are over 200,000 times brighter![2] They are "burning" their fuel much more quickly than the sun, and therefore cannot last billions of years. Based on their observed luminosity, the most massive blue stars cannot last even one million years before running out of fuel.

None of this is a problem for the biblical timescale of about 6,000 years for the age of the universe. But if the universe were 13.7 billion years old, as secularists allege, then it really shouldn't have blue stars. Yet blue stars abound in every known spiral galaxy. It seems that these galaxies cannot be even one million years old.

Secular astronomers must assume that new blue stars have formed recently to replace all those that have burned out over deep time. They claim that some nebulae (clouds of hydrogen gas) eventually collapse under their own gravity to form a new star. Some astronomy textbooks even have pictures of nebulae labeled as "star-forming regions" or "stellar nurseries," as if star formation were an observed fact. But it is not. Star formation has never been observed and the physics behind this alleged process is riddled with difficulties.[51]

Starlight and time

Dr Russell Humphreys explains why the Doppler shift explanation of the so-called "ancient age of starlight" is not likely the truth. He also explains why the temperature of the microwave background radiation does not declare the age of the universe and the earth. In fact the genesis account is a clear explanation of what we see today. [52]

Dr John Baumgardner and Dr D. Russell Humphries describe a fascinating possibility for why the stars seem to be "billions and billions" of years away from us relating to the "tick of the clock". We know mass and it's gravity affects the "tick of the clock"…. that a caesium133 atomic clock at the bottom of a mountain ticks faster than an identical clock at the top of the mountain. Dr Baumgardner, referring to an article in the Journal Nature [53] that describes a fractal analysis of galaxy distribution to large distances in the cosmos contradicts the assumption of the big bang that there is no edge boundary or center… that is the cosmological principle assumption is incorrect. Rather if instead the cosmos had a center, "Then its early history is different than all of the big bang models". He suggests a massive black hole containing the entire mass of the known universe. And center to his argument is such a mass distribution would have a "whooping gradient in gravitational potential which affects the local physics including the speed of the clocks. Clocks near the center where we are would run more slowly or even be stopped during the earliest portion of cosmic history.[54] Since the heavens appear" isotropic" (the same value from different directions) from the vantage point of earth, the earth must be near the center of such a cosmos." So light from the far reaches would reach earth in a "very brief time" as measured by clocks on earth.[55] Scientists are amazed that the stars of the universe seem to be accelerating apart more and more. But that is clearly explained in the Bible in Ps 104:1-2 and Isaiah 42::5,44:24 and Isaiah 45:12. Where the LORD tells us he created the heavens, ordained them, and stretched them out with his hands. If he could create 2 trillion galaxies with 5 words and name all the stars in them, He created the universe in 6 days and rested on the 7th! How He did it is for Him to know and us to find out. But if we start with His words we arrive at a coherent explanation. Remember, If you start out with A <u>false</u> presupposition, there are an INFINITE (∞) number of FALSE conjectures that can explain the spaces in the datum. These probably only describe our ignorance to describe reality! In contrast there is only one conjecture that describes TRUTH. I repeat. There is only one conjecture that describes TRUTH![56]

I have attempted to describe something of the equation of Creator-God and Science. We do see His work in Nature, and that helps us understand Him if we begin with presuppositions He presents us in His Word. I pointed out the emptiness of "naturalists presuppositions" causing very large regions of error in many modern extrapolations and conjectures from Neo-Darwinian evolution, the Big Bang, and the age of the earth. We have no observers of these events other than Creator-God, who loves us so much that He tells us what He did and what He must do, due to His very nature! The work of a scientists, to search out a matter, is also the work of kings. Shouldn't the level of logic employed be greater than "best guess"?

Other positions by Reputable Scientists:
While these positions on Evolution and the Big Bang seem far more reasonable to me there is another position to consider by a person I respect. The present head of the Institutes of Health and our top M.D., Dr Francis Collins. Dr Collins was a Physical Chemist before medical school many years ago so I assume he has a limited grasp of theoretical physical chemistry in contrast to the Theoretical Physical Chemist Dr Ed Bordeaux I discussed. I did see Dr Collins at the Veritas Forum at Cal Tech present his case for accepting both Darwinian Evolution and the Big Bang, what he called the "Majority View" We need to be reminded that majority views fall all the time in science, that is why it is a moving train. Dr Collins questions the literal interpretation of Genesis (which would allow about any interpretation of the written words). He follows a statement of St. Augustan who wrote in 400 AD which Collins argues is against literal interpretation of Genesis 1 and 2. Collins has founded the "BioLogos" foundation, which means "God speaking life into being". Collins doesn't battle the scientific community on "Billions of years" or the Big Bang, and just declares God "Outside of Time" is his answer.[57]

Creation vs. Big Bang
True Science and the Big Bang

True science begins with an understanding of Creator-God, His Word, and His testaments old and new to us. Remember with a false presupposition there are an infinite number of false conjectures that can explain the spaces in the datum and that these result primarily in our ignorance in describing reality.

A reasonable theory that begins with the words of Genesis:

Students, Consider: Boudreaux-Baxter theory of Aquo-nucleosynthesis of the Chemical Elements and accelerated beta decay rates

Present theories of creation of the earth and their failures are described by what I consider a reasonable scientists who begins with the Word of Creator-God. Dr Edward A. Bordeaux, specialist in quantum/computational chemistry, magneto chemistry and chemical physics with more than 54 papers in pear reviewed journals. Co-author/editor of 4 technical books with some 97 presentations, forty invited lectures to local national and international conferences has written what I consider a definitive book, "God Created the Earth; Genesis of Creation Chemistry" (2012, 2nd ed.) He presents the Boudreaux-Baxter theories of 1. Aquo-Nucleosynthesis of the Chemical Elements and 2. Accelerated Radioactive decay rates.

I first heard Dr Boudreaux ten years ago and I was suspect because his whole idea depended on what was really written in the Bible, in fact a word that needs clarification. My King James Bible translates the text of Genesis 1:2:

"And the earth was without form, and void; and darkness was upon the face of the deep.

And the Spirit of God <u>moved</u> upon the face of the waters" [KJV]

I was dumb-founded that this early translation of the ancient Hebrew of "moved" was not informative. 10 years later I did what I am supposed to do and pursued the Word (like a Berean) and found out that "'moved" is not the word but "rachaph" (Strong#7363) is a primitive root meaning to "brood". My grandmother kept Road Island Red Hens and had a "brooding" house. I knew what she did with those eggs----she "<u>incubated</u>" them in the brooding house. Low and behold the ancient Syriac cognate term translated means "to brood over; to incubate". Realizing that the hen heated the egg with her body, I started to grasp Ed Boudreaux's point.

Read Genesis 1:1 and 1:2 and note the "Waters" that are mentioned as the precursor to the elements. Where the simple meaning of the Word is clear, any other meaning is without bounds.....if you walk from literal, it could mean anything which, I would argue is not what Creator-God speaks to us.

Once the Holy Spirit heats the water to 1×10^{10} + degrees Kelvin (a billion or more degrees) the ".. 6.02×10^{24} kg of water was used to produce the elements and provide 2.013×10^{50} oxygen atoms (O) and 4.02×10^{50} hydrogen atoms (H), each H atom ionizes its electrons to produce 13.5eV and each Oxygen atom produces 871.4eV if all eight of the electrons are ionized. The atoms providing 1.754×10^{53} eV plus 5.44×1051 eV from the H atoms, yield a total of 1.08×10^{53} eV or 1.808×10^{47} MeV." Boudreaux gives us the work done equation that includes the plasma decomposition energy parameters, recombination energy of solid earth, mass of water converted to non-aqueous earth, Boltzmann's constant, the temperature change in going from the plasma state to a solid earth yielding work=2.0 MeV in which the temperature equivalent of the energy is 2.3×10^{10} confirming the condition of the high temperature plasma. " The pressure to drive nuclear collisions is a property of the plasma." [58]

So if the Boudreaux-Baxter theory of Aquo-nucleosynthesis of chemicals is true, it appears that the "waters" of the bible were turned to water plasma at a temperature of 2.3×10^{10}-2.3×10^{14} K^0 or more than a billion degrees plasma where he next argues, the <u>collisions become non-elastic</u> and, because of the application of the standard collision theory of hard spheres, the collision rate between unlike particles. He then calculates the nuclear collision energy for effective fusion as a function of the reaction utilizing

the nuclear activation energy (critical energy) for the collision-fusion process modeled after the rate equation addressing chemical activation energy
where the actual collision rate is clearly dependent on the total number of
effective collisions. [please read the equations directly in his book].

The presuppositions/assumptions of this data Boudreaux gives as
follows:

1. "Conventional nucleosynthesis theory as applied in the production
    of chemical elements in the evolution of <u>star</u> formation is not con-
    sidered in this model.
2. All nucleosynthesis processes are treated in terms of the energy
    transferred according to inelastic classical collision theory of hard
    spheres. In this model, collision cross sections are not a function of
    energy but are confined to particle dimensions.
3. The total energy provided for each fusion processes is a function of
    the masses of pertinent nuclides and the Q (excess energy) of each
    reaction. (see the following section on rate production p27)
4. For purposes of simplicity and time constraints, this study has
    completed thus far, is limited to the production of only the most
    stable abundant isotopes of product elements. An extension to vari-
    ous other isotopes, particularly for heavier elements, is planned in a
    continued extension of this study.
5. Although more then one process may be applicable for the produc-
    tion of a specific element, for purposes of consistency, only the most
    energy efficient options have been selected.
6. Because of the limitations of this present work, no comments can be
    made about relative elemental abundances in the earth, much less
    in the solar system or universe." [59]

"Is the Nuclear Collision Reaction Model Scientifically Rational?
The question of whether or not collision processes provide an adequate mechanism for producing fusion products, has been criticized in terms of the follow-
ing- 'although at high pressure temperatures the thermal energy and collision

frequency is greatly increased, it is natural to presume that the nuclide (hard sphere) collisions will be increased. However, at close inter-nuclear collision distances and high charges, the repulsive energy will be substantially in excess of the collision energy required for fusion. Consequently, such collisions cannot allow for a fusion product to be realized.' This premise can be tested using a selected example of one of the specific collisions listed in Table 3 (Part 1). On the last page of Table 3 the two nuclides bearing the highest charges are Pd^{+46}/ Nd^{+60}. Application of equation (9) in Part II at a collision distance of 1.75 x 10^{-14}m and an effective charge of Ze= +45.2, yields a repulsion energy of 3.46 MeV. This is slightly less than twice the 1.55 MeV required to produce the fusion product. If this were the only factor involved, then indeed the repulsion energy would prohibit any fusion from taking place. But fortunately, this is not the case, because, as shown in Part II, there is a plasma kinetic energy of 5.6 MeV imparted to each nuclide contained within the plasma. This is more than sufficient to overcome the repulsive energy and still provide the 1.55 MeV required for the Pd/Nd collision to be effective.

Hence, the objection to nuclear collisions being effective at high charges is nullified and the collision process for nuclear fusion is vindicated for all nuclear reactions forming all elements."[60]

Boudreaux's work is remarkable to say the least, while I'm not trained enough to do more than present their work, I encourage you to read their publication and communicate with them directly.

Plasma Physics, apparently in its infancy, should be able to describe 90-98% of the Universe since it is plasma. Our ignorance can be seen in the billions of dollars spent trying to imitate the environment of the "Big Bang" (which never happened) because the leaders of our scientific-university complex used what S.A. Adamenko called the so called "Force" method which posits the problem of controlled nucleosynthesis can only be solved by...

".. using more and more powerful technical means (accelerators with maximally high energy, neutron sources with maximally high energy, systems of controlled synthesis of the 'tokamak' type etc.), which requires high cash investments measured in billions of dollars (with subsequent high salaries) However, this way is erroneous in principle because the technical resources of our civilizations are bounded, and the force-based attempts to reproduce the process which occurs in abnormal astrophysical objects of the type of pulsars or neutron stars, under lab. Conditions are unrealistic". [61] Perhaps, taking a clue from Ed Boudreaux's concern for high electric charge blocking the processes to be studies, the giant projects fail because of the simple reason they are working with too great a charge density or some such problem due to the very enormous scale they are attempting.

At the **Proton-21 Electrodynamics Laboratory** (Kiev) where the method is basically explained in US Patent US20050200256A1 published Sept. 15, 2005, Stanislav Adamenko basically has provided the data that totally supports the Boudreaux-Baxter Theory and totally wiping out the "Big Bang" Theory (which required 18 Billion years followed by the accretion of stellar dust by gravity) which no mechanism of this type has ever been validated. Adamenko has produced all known chemical elements instantaneously in the Protein-21 Electrodynamics lab in the Ukraine using relatively low energy but in a micro scale. Where a solid target substance (pure metal, alloy, plastic) is subjected to explosive induced compression, transforming it into plasma, whereby all the elements are produced. [62]

Boudreaux and Baxter describe with their equations how all the elements of the earth are shown to be produced in amounts currently accepted to be in the earth within the time period of 2 ½ days and the plasma earth is rapidly cooled within a minimum of 47 hours (59-63 hours) via thermal conduction based on a maximum thermal diffusivity of the plasma particles. This totally supports Creator-God's Word as written down by Moses some 3,400 years ago! If you start your equations with truthful propositions you will more likely be able to explain the gaps in the data truthfully.

Does this make as much sense to you as it does to me?

The Death of Accretion: Elapsed "Time"
The key mechanism for the "Big Bang theory" to create the galaxies, the planets, and the earth is a random process requiring "Billions and Billions" of years and much magic called accretion. When the Holy Spirit heated the

waters to super-hot plasma, an event occurred during the cool down phase that has support in the literature (as opposed to no data proving accretion. (Accretion is only a "best" guess-hypothesis).

The first paper by Takahashi et al suggested an atom with its electron shells stripped away would be able to emit a beta particle (beta-decay) at a much faster rate allowing the beta particle to fill up the empty shells rather then the much higher threshold requiring much more kinetic energy to jump past filled shells into empty space.[63] [Shortly after the theory was presented experimental data was forthcoming proving accelerated beta decay rates.][64]

The newer system of rock dating uses Lutetium-Hafnium (^{176}Lu-^{176}Hf) in which a normal half-life of 40 billion years becomes a 3.68 hours in one study and 8 days in a second study.[65] Another system ^{187}Rhenuim-^{187}Osmium Beta decay with traditional half-life of 43 Billion years dropped to 33 years when fully ionized in the lab.[66]

So when these elements are heated to 15.4 billion degrees Kelvin, Uranium 283 half-life becomes 2 minutes, Thorium 232's half-life of 14 billion years becomes 15.6 minutes, Samarium 147's half-life of 106 billion years becomes 2.46 minutes, Rubidium87 half-life of 47 billion years becomes 2.46 minutes, and potassium 40's half-life of 102 billion years becomes 5.87 minutes—etc. The point is that when today's evolutionist brag about "Billions and Billions" of years "proven" for his theory he is looking at the "appearance" of enormous age generated by ignorance of hot plasma accelerated decay------a more reasonable scientific explanation disavowing any "accretion" theory or other "Billions of Billions"; fanciful thought so necessary to those claiming Creator-God and His Word are not true.

Notice the Billions necessary for Darwinian Evolution falls apart, thus the frequency of beneficial mutations necessary for dead "molecules-to-man" evolution so controlling our biology texts and departments melts away to silence. What happened is "knowledge increased" and data of the Physics that describes 98% of the universe, plasma, came to light.

To further support Boudreaux and Baxter's theories Dr Stanislav Adamenko of the Proton-21 Electrodynamics Lab in Kiev wrote a letter that "water could indeed be used as a target substance, if the equipment were provided with a means of keeping the water frozen when it is subjected to the explosion induced compression" (used in his lab) [67]

It's darkness when you or your teacher are not seeing the world from Creator-God's point of view. It has been a 400 year artificial separation of the supposedly morally "neutral" science claiming a neutral position on "good and bad". What a cop-out as we see the potential evil use of science and pseudo-science to destroy and kill all humans (H-bomb) and murder human spirits and souls in our universities and schools (clearly evil-bad stuff). As noted in Matt 6:22:

"When your eye is bad your whole body is filled with darkness and if the light you think you have is actually darkness, how deep that darkness is!" [Matt 6:22, New Living Translation]

Students Consider: Death of the Big-Bang Theory

The Inflation mechanism proposed to save the whole big bang model may have no supporting data. Paul J. Steinhardt in the Scientific American noted there are much simpler explanations for the cosmic microwave background. [68] The headline article in Sky and Telescope June 2,2014 "Big Bang Inflation Evidence Inconclusive", written after the BICEP2 (Background Imaging of Cosmic Extragalactic Polarization) of the Cosmic Microwave Background (CMB) at the south pole. As scientists struggle to validate the Cobe2 picture of the cosmic microwave background and it's finding of a tiny microwave temperature differences from one area to the other of one part in 100,000 which, with false coloring appears significant and which Big Bangers claim represents their miraculous/singularity. These scientists cannot yet separate the amount of polarized emissions coming from their glorious "signal that proves the Big Bang" and the signal "noise" coming from the plain anatomy of the galactic dust of our "Milky Way" which is known to be polarized. They must correctly separate the E and B modes (Electric and Magnetic). Its as if they assume the universe is a gigantic cavity resonator and they can look at it or sample the signal from it and, with a long string of pre-suppositions make sense of it. I assume some unique phase-shifting is being used but the whole enterprise seems misdirected. There is a much simpler explanation for the CMB then the Big Bang Model. Since we are looking at a 95% plasma universe that is quite heterogeneous (look up at the night sky) and since we know there is a electromagnetic wave-plasma interaction and its oblique propagation cross polarized field components are induced within the plasma medium when the plasma medium is moving (it is) with respect to the observer (expansion).[69] Or the very "bumps" they claim as signal could be due to the very presence of electric and B mode separating in the signal at extreme distances and includes microwaves projected from other galaxies leading to a "best guess" for creation rather than a the Word of a Book that tells us more than 1000 key events before they happen, the Bible.

Also key data was presented in the Astrophysical Journal in 1970 that all but kills the Big Bang's idea of galaxy formation when Vera C. Rubin and the highly respected Ford W. Kent Jr. published "Rotation of the Andromeda Nebula from a Spectroscopic Survey of Emissions Regions" .[70] They studied 67 bright stars in this beautiful galaxy (the only one moving toward us) with a DTM image tube spectrograph (now seen at the Smithsonian Nat. Air and Space Museum) The velocity profile as you moved from far in to far out regions of the galaxy showed an effective "flat" velocity profile which doesn't allow the accretion mechanism according to La Place's mechanism or other mechanism (no agreement). Because of this failure to prove the bible wrong, they had to invent out of whole cloth that more than 90% of the universe is missing and is strangely "dark", for the necessary gravity to hold it together, that is "Dark matter" and "Dark" energy. Just to hold their theory together...for they claim Creator-God, the only observer of these events, must be wrong.

Our major point about Science and the study of science is that it is a "moving train", always changing with new findings and not something to rest your theology and certainly not your kids morality on. Not for a minute discouraging the study of science, for to search out a thing God has concealed is an honor of Kings (Proverbs 25:2). Indeed a scientists that conducts a true search for knowledge and truth is an "honor of Kings" and is to be respected.

In dismantling the Big Bang, Williams and Harnett gave us 4 reasons to reject the Big Bang Theory.

1. "It doesn't work...It only produces a expanding cloud of gas"(and gas clouds don't make-up what we see is here today)
2. "The theory lacks a credible and consistent mechanism." (infinite density point containing all energy and matter we now see in the universe?) (what started the expansion, no equations exist for this) " It requires a hypothetical period of stupendous inflation to stop the universe from (early) re-collapsing. It further requires incredible fine-tuning to maintain stability. (miraculous, It's mechanism would produce equal amounts of matter-anti-matter but we only see matter. It violates physical laws with appeal to "dark" matter and energy to explain what is observed.
3. "Chemical evolution (eventually leading to intelligent life, an essential ingredient in any evolutionary cosmology) is clearly excluded by the evidence."
4. "Science cannot produce any final answer on the subject of origins."

   (because science works in the present. If scientists claim they are looking back "Billions of Billions" of years of elapsed time but they know a light year is a distance not a time. We have no measures of how the clock "ticks" in deep space.)

   William and Harnett point out correctly that "The honor and glory of God are revealed in His work of Creation".[71]

   How can a product such as man who is so dimensionally below the Creator imagine a observer that has the correct information and the correct operator (ie. Hamiltonian) to describe his Creator?

   Because these parameters have infinite possibilities with 0 (zero) or $1/\infty$ chance of nailing down the truth, I choose to go with what the only Observer of these events, Creator-God who tells us simply How it was done, when it was done and why it was done, thereby explaining to this poor man who he (me) is and what he is doing with respect to his Creator.

Just saying the beginning must have low low entropy (order) and to create humans, must have precise "initial conditions" is as bad a contradiction as "random=information". Poincare Recurrences require waiting a "sufficiently" long time----presumes the invention of time. What observer can our "water brains" imagine in such impossible unnatural conditions pushes the understanding of "naturalism" beyond credulity. Someone is pulling our leg to get grant money! Herman Hesse's "Bead Game or Magister Ludi" is somewhere operating here. We see the breakdown of these thoughts are inevitable.....they collapse with the weight of their own propositions! The irony is they build structure of their pretend universe on the power and precision of "unable to know" (ignorance) from the Heisenberg picture. [72]

I repeat, picture man stumbling through the void, if he has no lantern to let him see what is there he is lost. That lantern is the Word of Creator-God. You must pick it up---grasp it in your hands, open it and seek to understand the words (and ask your Creator to explain it to you) or you are sure to wonder from "nowhere to nowhere". Otherwise you are always learning but never coming to the knowledge of the truth.

Students Consider: The Worldwide Flood of Noah: How did Pangaea become today's continents
The Flood of Noah's Day
The layers of sedimentary rock throughout the world and the fossils among those layers present a challenge to science like no other. Einstein tells us that, " Science is not and never will be a closed book. Every important advance brings new questions. Every development reveals,

in the long run, new and deeper difficulties…..Without a belief that it is possible to grasp the reality with our theoretical constructions, without the belief in the inner harmony of our world, there could be no science."[73] Scientists have constructed a false science based on a clever lie that the earth's past must be viewed in terms of present day processes acting at present day rates, a rapidly failing theory called "uniformitarianism". And that material processes by themselves can give life to all the living things we see today. These old assumptions and presuppositions are collapsing as we open our minds to the "Days of Noah " and what new understanding will help us with reality.

One of Creator-God's great works was restarting man's relationship with Him when perhaps 7 billion or more people turned from Him. While He would that none would be lost, all but 8 souls were destroyed! Obviously this is the greatest catastrophic event in the history of the world. The LORD has an incredible history with man's. Having to deal with the tendency of man to initially come to Him then to re-emerge grossly sinning against Him. Even a time after the Great Flood when Creator-God had given the 10 commandments to Moses and the surviving kingdom of Judah and Jerusalem was created we see it soon falling away from the LORD. This happened over and over, king after king. A young 18 year old King of Judah named Josiah (640 BC) was read a "Book of the Law" that had been found in the temple by the high priest Hilkiah and subsequently the people were lead back to the LORD (for a time only). "Josiah put away all those who consulted mediums and spiritists, the household gods and idols, all the abominations that were seen in the land of Judah and Jerusalem, that he might perform the words of the law which were written in the book that Hilkiah the priest found in the house of the LORD."[2Kings 22-23]

Man's tendency to drift away from sin against his Creator continues even today as you must be aware. What is happening as you read this is of great meaning. Jesus Christ said of the end of time:

"As in the days of Noah were, so also will the coming of the Son of Man be."[Matt 24:37]

The best way for our enemy to hide the understanding and wisdom of this event is to deny the "Days of Noah" and the world wide catastrophic flood. Especially hide the description of the pre-flood culture as never existing with a false science......so as to create the environment " My people are destroyed for a lack of knowledge, I will also reject thee, that thou shall be no priest to me: seeing thou hast forgotten the law of thy God, I will also forget thy children" [Hosea 4:6]$_{KJV}$

The ungodly multiply, giants in the earth, such wickedness of man that Creator-God said: " I shall not strive with man forever," and limited man's life to 120 years.

Man's intent and thoughts of his heart was only evil (or violence) continually so the LORD was "grieved in his heart" and had to destroy all ungodly except the 8 that found <u>grace</u> in the eyes of the LORD. [Gen 6] **A godly life in an ungodly world is no simple assignment.**

For the earth was corrupt before God, and the earth was filled with violence.

In Genesis 6:11 the Hebrew word for "violence" refers elsewhere to a broad range of crimes that include unjust treatment, cruelty, cruel hatred, injurious legal testimony, deadly assault, murder, and rape"[74]

Evidence for the 8 and the world wide flood:

1. The ancient Chinese ideograph for the word "boat" is a boat with 8 souls. **Meaning the ancient person that founded the Chinese language knew Genesis 6.**

Sedimentary Data support for the Global Flood
Sedimentary rock is formed when sediment is deposited by water flows, air, ice, wind, or gravity. Most often when materials settle out of suspension. **For example, the Grand Canyon's Coconino sandstone alone continues across Arizona, New Mexico, Texas, Oklahoma, Colorado, and Kansas**

covering 200,000 square miles with a volume of aprox. 10,000 cubic miles. Adding that on the European, Asian Continent, and seafloor, sedimentary rock covering 70% of the earth's surface. How did it get there?

Note: 73% of earth's current land surface is covered with sedimentary rock.

2. Rock formation exposed in the Grand Canyon shows a <u>Sedimentary "Permian Coconino Sandstone that extends laterally for hundred to thousands of miles in both directions with amazing uniform microscopic and macroscopic properties.</u> [75]

3. Global Sedimentary Rock formations. German Triassic: Keuper, Muschelkalk, and Bunter, also found across Europe from England to Bulgaria and in North America on the eastern seaboard as well as across Texas, New Mexico, and Arizona. **We are referring to both the Paleozoic and Mesozoic formations.** .

4. The absence of erosional channels at boundaries between these sedimentary units suggest a single continuous cataclysm. [76][77]

In 1983 a young astrophysics graduate student at UCLA named John R. Baumgardner choose to do his PhD dissertation on 3 dimensional modeling of the thermal flow, heat flow in the mantel of the earth. It so happens that this study would lead to a **reasonable** scientific explanation of the deep opening up to initiate the flood of Noah. **An explanation that includes the columns and layers deposited catastrophically in 1 year not over billions of years. Mocking sir Charles Lyell's "columns" of Neo-Darwinian uniformitarianism. As well explaining a mechanism for the movement of a united "Pangaea" continent moving in perhaps as short as one year to the continents we see today.** A good dissertation question is a life-long problem for most of us. Baumgardner subsequently published is work in 1985 in the Journal of Statistical Physics 39:(5) 501-511 as a model of 3 dimensional <u>convective</u> flow in the earth's mantle. "The earth's mantle is modeled as a thick spherical shell with isothermal (constant temperature) and free slip boundaries." The definition of "Convective Flow" is the movement caused within a fluid by the tendency of hotter and thereby less dense material to rise and colder, denser material to sink under the influence of gravity, which consequently results in the transfer of heat. Many definitions say it's a circular motion.

Then in August 9, 2003 Baumgardner presented his "Catastrophic Plate Tectonics: The Physics Behind the Genesis Flood.[78] He reported new computational results from 2-D and 3-D simulations of the catastrophic process during the most extreme part of the runaway causing the global flood. To understand this paper, 5 key concepts must be grasped.

1. Denser (heaver) rocks sinks
2. Gravitational body forces acting on the slab lead to high stresses
3. As the slab sinks, gravitational potential energy is released in the form of heat
4. Greater heating = weakening of the rock can lead to increased sinking rate that leads to increased heating and so on in a positive feedback mechanism driving a runaway condition. **The sinking rate increases from a finger nail growth rate of inches per year to the velocity of 5 MPH!**
5. Olivine is a reasonable representative of the mantle rock. A group of silicate rock-forming minerals of olive-like colors (green to black), with a name that reminds us of "the place of Olive Crushing" or Gethsemane.

Baumgardner tells us in a wonderful essay, part of essays collected from 50 scientists "In Six Days"[79] "Just as there has been glaring fraud in things biological for the past century, there has been fraud in things geological. The error in a word, is uniformitarianism. The outlook assumes that the earth's past can be correctly understood purely in terms of present day processes acting at more or less present day rates.....they have ignored that the planet has suffered major catastrophe on a global scale"

Baumgardner tells us, "The reason most researchers in the mainstream geophysics community didn't see the dramatic runaway solutions is because "a deformation law that accommodates realistic levels of weakening has yet to be included in their models".[80] This thermal runaway of, "with more heat we get more heat and with more weakening we get more weakening" follows from recent data on the properties of silicate rock. A key paper supporting this is work by Kirby, 1983 where he shows reduced silicate rock strength by 10 or more orders of magnitude (a billion times) without the material ever reaching its melting temperature.[81] The Gravity of the earth is enough to do the heating **once the runaway starts**.

While the **computer** model that the U.N. decided to move the world into "Global Warming" could be run on your X-Box, Baumgardner's models used his own famous Fortran Finite element analysis program called "Terra" that has 1,377,000 cells in a mesh that defined the relationship of the elements and nodes representing the entire mantle of the earth. Elements must capture the dominant actions of the actual system both logically and globally. When nodes move or displace they drag the elements along in a certain manner. The system could only run on a Cray X or faster system.

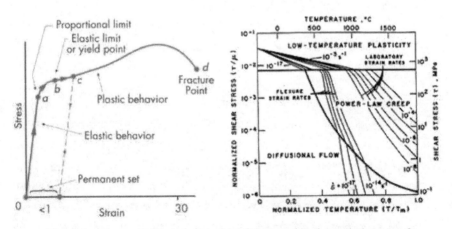

Fig. 5,6: 1.Stress strain relationship showing the plastic behavior of Silicate rock and 2. Deformational map for Olivine, Absolute temperature T normalized to the melting temperature T_m (after Kirby, 1983)

Today Baumgardner's "Terra" is used in many applications. The French and Germans use it to forecast the weather.

What is driving this thermal runaway-slab sinking process that opens up the rapid water channels of the deep? Unique "plastic yield" properties plus deformation rate weakening, combined with temperature weakening of Olivine minerals of slabs of crust.

Scott D. King tells us that the flow **Rheology** of the mantle depends on grain size of the mantel materials and that in the upper mantle with grain sizes greater than 1mm, power-law creep should dominate at st**resses greater than 1MPa; other**wise diffusion dominates. Usually olivine is treated with grain size of 0.1mm noting the stress and depth.[82]

What follows is an outline supporting the proposed scientific explanation of the processes of the world wide flood:

- **The 5 key steps noted above began causing the "thermal Runaway" collapse of the rocky surface on the floor of the oceans. The Bible tells us <u>All</u> the fountains of the great deep were broken up, and the windows of heaven were opened"[Gen 7:11] Great stores of water in deep channels of the earth were opened likely by the process Baumgardner describes. It was likely initiated by Creator-God Himself. Baumgardner suggests a 400 degree lower temperature in the lithosphere surrounding Pangaea (the early combined continents) could begin the process of slabs of lithosphere sinking unleashing enormous forces, enormous water and steam geysers (its hot so superheated steam forces) that would be driven up to the stratosphere at high velocities and then immediately fall as rain....to the point that the water would cover all land mass. Since Sir Edmond Hillary found closed sea shells and petrified clams by the millions on Mt Everest with the sedimentary rock in 1953. There are many pictures of them on the internet (search for Flood Fossils). We** all know that clam shell mussels relax and open when they die so they were caught rather suddenly,, this was an amazing event. Note: for a living animal to fossilize, it has to die suddenly and be covered and preserved somehow. Otherwise it is a food for others or exposed to rapid decay and dissolution

- Catastrophism is evident in the Paleozoic, Mesozoic and Cenozoic portion of the geological record.
- Paleozoic and Mesozoic sedimentary formation with internal evidence of high energy water transport represents the catastrophic processes. We have discovered in 1990 when the Magellan spacecraft's high res. Mapping showed our sister planet Venus was recently resurfaced.
- Crossbeds present in the sandstone and limestone of Paleozoic, Mesozoic, and Cenozoic rock is strong testimony of high energy water transport.[83]
- When sandstones in the Grand Canyon show sand waves of tens of meters in height and hydrostatically transported boulders tens of feed in diameter you know enormous water forces have been applied.[84]
- Water currents at a velocity of tens of meters/second are analogous to planetary waves in the atmosphere driven by 1000 MPH earth rotation and fits with a incredible and chaotic earth motion that would uplift much of the earth's surface into the waters....explaining subsequent extreme sediment rock formation we find today with the fossil record.
- Fossil record documents a brief intense destruction of life, not an evolutionary history1
- The opposite of the Darwinian illusion we hear from many teachers today merely teaching what they have been taught and missing the exciting truth of Creator-God's work.
- Notice, the Bible tells us "All" the fountains of the deep were broken up, so there is no record of any left today. Our faith in Him is tested
- But faith in non-catastrophic science must be a religion of its own.

Students Consider: The problems of Evolution?
Evolution, the Anti-Science: Naturalism as god?

My Biology professor at Cornell was an amazing scientists. His passion was the embryology of Rotifera that was not classed as particularly unique. He was kind and truthful to tell us that there were many things in evolution that didn't quite add up. The Rotifers he obtained from the University of Iowa's pond water displayed an embryology called spiral indeterminate cleavage as I recall which, he argued, was so unique that they deserve a totally separate phyla (unique body plan). This was 1962 and Dr Pray was a very wise scientist. Would that all Biology Professors were so truthful today!!

Mix a little religious Humanism with a pet theory and you arrive at what is taught totally as a totally untenable and un-testable theory with a mixture of the following: Darwinian Evolution, "argument from homology", phylogenetic inference, convergent evolution, punctuated equilibrium, allopathic speciation, species selection of complex intricate structure, "word salad" explanation of unobserved events with a gain of genetic information, and the roadblock for it all "the Cambrian Explosion", all coming from the doubting mind of Charles Darwin who got us in this mess, no doubt holding back good science for the last 100 years. [85]

Stephen Meyer, a Cambridge Ph.D. has written eloquently of "Darwin's Doubt". By joining Meyer with the work of a Physical Chemist from Australia and New Zealand, Johnathan Sarfati in the not so gentle "The Greatest Hoax on Earth" you will find they have denuded the arguments of evolutionist Richard Dawkins. I will use Meyer and Sarfati together with a excellent collection of authors edited by William A. Dembsky in "Mere Creation" in an analysis of where we are with evolution today. Reminding you that to claim Creator-God did not create but "Nature" and random created is directly taking the honor and glory due Creator-God and direction it to something else...establishing an Idol.

To draw a contrast the rubric of the idolatrous system being taught today requires a definition of evolution:

A.

New more complex body types have been created by successive changes due to mutations of less complex and simpler body types by a process called neo-darwinian evolution producing life from the first simple life form all the way to homo sapiens man. A "tree" pathway exist that describes this true one path of history of the evolution from molecules to man.

B.

The process of small successive changes has an operator causing increased information in more complex body types. That operator is chance or successive fortuitous events called beneficial mutation operating with the <u>agent</u> called natural selection that refined or optimizes the process.

Either A and B are true or false. A and B cannot be disproved.

The frequency of beneficial mutations is such that:

1. Information is increasing

Or 2. Devolution is occurring, just the opposite of the claim.

The Presuppositions of Modern Darwinism

1. Life came to be without Devine intervention instead by "natural means".
2. Life arose from non-life ie. Dead molecules and atoms.
3. All life on earth can be traced back to the first primitive form(s).
4. Life began with a simple cell(s) and changed by chance mutation in which the mutated form had an advantage over the previous form in that it was more suited to survive and propagate others like itself.
5. Natural selection or "survival of the fittest" from this advantage means it had enhanced capacity for survival.
6. This whole process is without purpose and direction, mindless and without need for intelligent direction (Creator-God).[86]

If you believe these 6 presuppositions are true your mind is the mind of the naturalist-materialist. Lets take a look at what some call "The Greatest Hoax on Earth"

What is the Mechanism Evolution Proposes that created what we see today?

On Genetic Mutation, its rate, adaptation, and problems.
Eric F. Wieschaus, 1995 Nobel Prize in Medicine and Physiology found in fruit flies (Drosophila Melanogaster) all or most all of the mutations that effect the essential patterning genes that are used throughout development. Wieschaus was asked about the implications of his finding for evolutionary theory. And, wondering aloud about whether his collection of mutants offered any insight into how the evolutionary process could have constructed "novel body parts" responded:

"The problem is, we think we've hit all the genes required to specify the body plan of Drosophila, and yet these results are obviously <u>not</u> promising as raw material for macroevolution.

The next question then, I guess, is what are—or what would be---the right mutation for major evolutionary change? And we don't know." (the mutants always died). [87]

Even today genes involved in body plans embryology are expressed so early with so many precise events to follow in development, that animals don't survive mutations in these locations. How did new genes appear... Those required for new body plans? No Darwinian mechanism has been able to explain distinctive new structures, cell types and new organs. Indeed we don't yet completely understand embryogenesis. If we did, we would have probably conquered cancer by now, but we haven't. Wieschaus and Nusslein-Volhard of the European Molecular Biology Lab at Heidelberg used the mutagen ethyl-methane sulphonate (mutates by guanine alkalation) to identify the key body plan genes and showed that development of an embryo is so tightly controlled and integrated in which everything produced later is highly dependent on what is produced earlier. If mutated you get crippled and dead bodies not more fit bodies.

Stephen Meyer summarizes findings as:

"… The kind of mutations the evolutionary process would need to produce a new animal

body plan…..namely beneficial regulatory changes expressed early in development …..don't occur (or are fatal). While, the kind it doesn't need …..viable (survivable) genetic mutations in DNA generally expressed late and development – do occur. Or put more succinctly, the kind of mutation we need for major evolutionary changes we don't get, the kind we get we don't need."[88]

I repeat these body plan mutations never have been tolerated in any animals that developmental biologist have studied.[89]

Michael Behe's book "the heads of evolution" discussing the malarial resistance to the anti malarial drug chloroquine strongly suggests evidence that multiple coordinated mutations are often necessary to produce even minor genetic adaptations. The frequency he reports is only one in 10^{20} mutations causing cells called a complex of the cluster. This cluster if two with an incidence of 10^{20} had to happen together coordinated would require 10^{40} organisms. The problem Behe points out is that there have only been 10^{40} organisms existing in the entire history of the earth. [90]

The conclusions are that if coordinated mutations are required to generate new body plans, that even the math of the Darwinians make Darwinian mechanisms implausible in even the enormous time scale they claim to have. [91]

So I conclude that the frequency of "beneficial mutations" required that would lead to a new body plan is a negative number. Genetic adaptation to the environment within body types is occurring but new "kinds" theory is a hoax!

What evidence do Evolutionists claim to show that evolution occurred?
Background of "Tree of Life" claims: Argument from Homology
Universal Common Ancestry Darwin held the "tree of life" as critical for his theory. He even sketched in one of his notebooks the "tree of life" that a BBC radio program labeled the "Darwinian Sistine chapel" while the University of Edinburg Archives of Natural History journal said the tree celebrates "Darwinian evolution secular science and reason".[92] Darwin's key argument for his theory was that all life had a universal common ancestor.

We all came from the same "simple beginning". There is no data to support this contention. The idea that body plans (phyla) all developed by increasing complexity is without support or without even and agreed theoretical mechanism. Steven Meyer does an excellent job discussing all sides of the "tree" argument in his 500 page monumental work "Darwin's doubt", he documents with almost 3000 notes and references (on 71 pages). Notably one of the finest academic books on the subject that helps us see why evolutionary biology is crumbling with its feet planted firmly in mid air! He contrasts the evidence of genetic and anatomic similarity. Molecular studies suggest widely different "trees" than anatomical similarities and the gene group locations don't suggest a vertical inheritance but a horizontal "net" which fits too closely to the simple understanding that all life comes from one intelligence.. I remember them.... File cabinets full of successful cellular and hormonal procedures in the lab where I learned radioimmunoassay while I worked on my doctorate. Once a successful procedure was developed, you didn't reinvent the wheel but built on that finding. Our Creator–God who knows the end from the beginning, knows for example that mitochondria are and will be successful as power houses so we find them throughout. The same is true for chloroplasts to capture sun energy. The fact that we find butterflies with both (while amazing) is evidence of remarkable intelligence not "stupid, non-directed evolution" hidden by millions of years of untraceable history. I'm forced to agree with philosophers of science that suggests "biology may not be a pure science and should be found among the historical sciences", especially when we see its modern teaching full of idolatry and anti Biblical theology. This should change. And that change would require the improved training of our lawyer judges to be able to understand statistical and research design so that they can identify truth/faults claims in original research work. At least to be able to determine an expert witnesses anti-Christianity is their religion and bias when it exists.

The "tree of life" farce continues in our children's textbooks with clever artist's drawings of the relentless "progress" of the genes. Molecular systematists Anonis Rokas concedes that, "a century and half after the Origin of this Species, a complete and accurate tree of life remains an elusive goal".[93] It appears the "tree of life" people are using "best guess" abduction logic while beginning with a false presupposition. Their puzzle will never fit if they are honest. Meyer makes the point:

"In reality, however, the technical literature tells a different story (from common ancestry).

Studies of molecular homologies often <u>fail</u> to confirm evolutionary trees depicting the history of animal phyla derived from studies of comparative anatomy... Often showing that phylogenetic trees derived from anatomy and those derived from molecules often contradict each other."[94]

If multiple genes or traits are considered, the phylogenetic reconstruction doesn't result in a single tree. But as Meyer notes, "... The history of animal life only happened once".

We know that if these were pre-Cambrian animal forms and comparative sequence analysis should "converge" around a single tree of life." That is not what is found. So, just like the inability to question these false presuppositions and abandon the neo-Darwinism religion, there is an effort to construct a "Tower of Babel" and tree of life studies rather than a "Sistine chapel". Convergent evolution (and other related mechanisms) only add to the doubt of the logic of the argument from homology. That is when nearly identical traits or structures are found in animals with very different body plans.... Completely against evolution from a common ancestor.[95]

Do these family relationships exist at all? With each pressing year the argument on the "tree of life" would converge rather than crumble into something that doesn't belong in our children's textbook except as a failed "guess" that negates the word of Creator-God.

Optimization of Living Things
There are four (4) possibilities for the incredible variety of living things we see today.

1. Genetic Adaptation within body kinds
2. Evolution by successive fortuitous occurrences were random has added information and complexity (like a god)

3. Hand of Creator-God designed change (ie. Potential to do with changing environments to increase Survival)
4. Yet unknown

Can we pick and choose the truth or at least discard some of these from hard data? Which contain a fallacy in logic?

We know Darwin was worried that the transitional or intermediate forms would not be found in the fossil layers… And they have not been found. To fill this enormous problem of the second optimization plan we just mentioned… Evolution, a new hypothesis was proposed to save evolution called "punctuated equilibrium" that rejects Darwinian gradualism. Steven Gould and Niles Eldridge had what can be called a "scientific epiphany" where absence of change or "stasis" was the most important pattern. He then continued to reject its Darwinian presupposition, decided this means that his "fast" change mechanisms within small groups called "allopathic speciation" which selects the most fit species among a group of competing species with large changes occurring suddenly and therefore leaving no hard data…. Allowing them to use "best guess" logic. Through clever popular writing the theory and it's salesman Stephen J. Gould achieved considerable celebrity in biology approaching that of Carl Sagan in physics.

The Problem of the Cambrian Explosion
Darwin believed that small differences that distinguished one species from another would "accumulate" and until it produced organisms that were different, progressing from genera all the way to phyla. However within the Cambrian later was found forms that were different enough to be classified as separate subphyla and phyla "from their first appearance in the fossil record".[96] This fact totally negates traditional Darwinism, neo-Darwinism, and punctuated equilibrium evolution. "The Precambrian fossil record does not document however, the existence of such a large diverse pool of competing precambrian species upon which species selection (via allopatric speciation) might operate.[97] Other paleontologist support this. For example see the key paper by Erwin & Valentine.[98]

Gregor Mendel (in 1860s) and his classical Mendellian genetics we use today, replaced Darwin's blending theory of inheritance while suggesting limitations on the amount of genetic variability to natural selection.[99] Mendel's work did not support Darwin's extension of natural selection to whole populations. It was a small group of the evolutionary biologists and physiologists who formed a sub-discipline of "population genetics" who tried to synthesize Mendel's work with Darwin to form "Neo–Darwinism". The short list of these men include Sewall, Wright, Ernst Mayr, Theodosius Dobzhansky, J. B.S. Haldane, and George Gaylord Simpson. Limited math models were used in which best guess logic seem to be so convincing (even though DNA structures had not been elucidated) that Huxley proclaimed at the Darwinian centennial celebration that, "… Indeed all reality is a single process of evolution".[100] "Just as a few typological errors in an English sentence might alter the meaning of a few words or even the whole sentence, so too might a change in the sequential arrangement of the bases in the genetic 'text' in DNA produce new proteins or morphological traits".[101]

From a sponge with only a few cell types to a fly with the genome of 140,000,000 base pairs give us a hint to the enormous increase an informational content with increasing complexity. Of course all living things have amazing complexity. Carrots have half the genome we have for example. But Meyer reasonably ranks increasing complexity with increasing number of cell types after the works of Valentine. [102]

"… The realization that specificity of arrangement, rather than mere improbability, characterizes the genetic text has raised some challenging questions about the adequacy of the Neo-Darwinian mechanism".[103]

So where did the vast amount of new information that suddenly appeared in new body plans that appeared fully formed come from? It is not even likely that random mutations in DNA within the scheme of natural selection could do new novel forms of life. The Neo-Darwinians find themselves again with their feet planted firmly in mid air! The specificity of a DNA of three billion base pairs and it's informational content…. What reduction in uncertainty it provides is the power of 2^N where N is the sequence length, equals a number at least larger than the number of particles in the universe.

Open a textbook like the text used to teach California's high school and elementary teachers "Life, the Science of Biology" with over 200 reviewing faculty for many colleges and universities. In the book we find in chapter 21 "the history of life on earth" page 465, a representative misrepresentation... the statement under the heading "how do scientists date ancient events?"[104]

"Many 'evolutionary' changes happen rapidly enough to be studied directly and manipulated experimentally." The term 'evolutionary' tells the future teachers the "Truth" of evolution yet the misdirection from the truth of the accepted term 'genetic adaptation', has little or nothing to do with Darwinian or neo Darwinian evolution. This Text grandly uses the term 'evolutionary' without distinction, mulling together an unproven theory with the accepted term "micro-evolution' or what I call 'Genetic Adaptation' for the purposes to muddle the minds of the uninitiated who would not detect the error, and I might add teach what they hear/read as fact. This 1200 page text book has almost no references to it's misleading statements, given the impression to the future teacher that the statements are not highly controversy at all. But they are! "The Neo-Darwinism predicts that desperate adult structures should be produced by different genes. However, the Pax-6 gene called "eyeless" helps regulate the development of fruit flies [Arthropods}, squid (cephalopods) and mice (vertebrate) eyes. But the fly eye is compound with hundreds of separate lenses while squid and mice have a camera like a eye with a retinal surface. Squid and mice focus very differently. "They undergo completely different patterns of development and utilize different internal structures and nerve connections to the visual cortex of the brain."[105] So the finding of "same genes, different anatomy" is a contradiction of the textbook teachings that can be called nothing more than misleading. The theology the biology texts imparting to these future teachers is what I would call a state of the art of misdirection.

The Epigenetic Revolution: an example of inadequate or incomplete knowledge of science

There is new information that out strips the whole neo-Darwinian mechanism foundation.

Steven Meyer[106] points out in his explanation of the epigenetic revolution, non-gene contributions to embryo building by: cytoskeletal arrays and microtubules built by tubulin; membrane patterns; ion channels interacting with electromagnetic-fields; sugar surface codes; and induction from cell to cell contact. Enormous amounts of non-genetic information contributes to the formation of life. We have so much to learn, and Darwin's ideas are so inadequate and misleading. Presupposing neo-Darwinian as the underlying theory of life is silly and will lead you down a false science path. Recent studies by C.J. McGann found the protein from the endplate of severed amphibian newt limbs could signal mouse myotubes to start a regeneration process similar to that seen in the newt.....an amazing point that the mouse and probably humans have dedifferentiation and regenerating capacity but not the signal to make limb regeneration work.[107] Since cancers are mostly undifferentiated or dedifferentiated cells, future research should be directed at first understanding the basic science involved in cell induction and molecular embryology where our knowledge is woefully inadequate. We are quite primitive in our understanding of these things....ie. we have incomplete knowledge.

Evolution and Time problems
Implied Millions and Millions of years plus Random Changes equals man.

The oldest document we know dated with carbon 14 is less than 6000 years old. If we reject the evolution that has clearly been thrust on us with the fact that the ages of rocks were fossil layers are found cannot be reliably dated if accelerated beta decay and completely ionized elements at 10^{10} degrees Kelvin can make in 2 minutes, the appearance of 40 billion year old rocks. Evolutionist–materialists "science" hasn't the time to even process with a lie "evolution plus billions and billions equals man".

Cave wall Painting Dating

And honest question that should be answered today is what is the age of primitive paint on the cave walls? Why are the evolutionary sociologists not forthcoming with data for the age of that paint is because when they make honest measures they can't publish in the evolutionary journals. Remember the more ancient a "result" the more notoriety is received in an academic publication.

If we really question evidence of how long the age of man has been on this planet. We must look at the reliable and accurate techniques measuring cave drawings. Just how convincing are the data the evolutionists have of man's presence on this earth of hundreds of thousands and some claim "millions" of years? Cave art absolute dating might be of considerable value. But we mentioned that accelerated beta decay of such long half-life dating elements as uranium and thorium cause one to select ^{14}C radiodating as the method of choice. Charcoal is predominately the dated archaeological material, but it dates the death of the plant from which it was made, not the time of the painting on the rock,,,,,so old wood and old charcoal problems should be eliminated.

"It is sad, however, to note that over a decade on, careful analysis has not become a routine precursor for cave art dating....Sadly, Watchman's understandable call has gone unheeded, and the simple problem remains, at present, no direct radiocarbon dates exist that can unproblematically be linked directly to the act of painting." [108]

Apparently there are no standards at this time for sample preparation and dating, although in 2009 Marvin Rowe published a impressive work in the journal "Analytical Chemistry" on radiocarbon dating of ancient art which was honored by the Archaeology Magazine for top 10 discoveries of 2010.....which uses an assay for ^{14}C of a sample as small as .05 micrograms of carbon (50 specks of dust). A two step method that first cleans the sample with a supercritical fluid (pressurized slightly heated CO_2 similar to commercial dry cleaning) then treating the sample with low-temperature argon plasma to remove absorbed CO_2 (reduced to < 1ug Carbon) then oxygen extraction of organic carbon with 1 mTorr, 50-100 watt Oxygen plasma with a bulk temperature of < 150⁰. The CO2 produced was collected by freezing it in a 6 mm glass tube under liquid nitrogen then re-sealing the tube. The resulting sample was then sent to an accelerator mass spectrograph (AMS) laboratory for radiocarbon measurement. He calls it "plasma-chemical extraction and AMS radiocarbon dating of Rock Art".[109] This method shows remarkable agreement with widely different kinds of organic archeological artifacts.

The 1960 Nobel Prize was awarded to Willard Libby for radiocarbon dating work he did in the 1940's. Carbon 14 is produced when cosmic ray neutrons strike ^{14}Nitrogen in the upper atmosphere with rapid oxidation of the ^{14}C to ^{14}CO2. The ^{14}CO2 then becomes incorporated in living organisms. When that plant or organism dies it is assumed to have a very similar ^{14}Carbon/^{12}Carbon level and the ^{14}C decays to half the original amount in 5,730 years…..so the date of death can be estimated by comparison with the constant level in living material. This is the "gold standard" in archeology. Older methods used a strong-acid wash followed by a strong base then again a final acid wash which destroys as much as 1/3 up to all of the organic material in the paint. There was also a large contaminant from the inorganic carbon in the rock independent of the paint (but part of the scrapings). The radiocarbon date Rowe reports are 11,000years or less B.P. (Before the Present). [110]

Questionable evidence for Cave Drawings many thousands of years old
Where 3 pictographs from a Myan cave were radio-carbon dated ABS and compared to the Myan calander dates the following was concluded: The plasma-chemical extraction and AMS radio- carbon dating of charcoal from three Maya hieroglyphic texts has been shown to be accurate to within about 110 — 140 years of the calendrical dates contained in the inscriptions. But the radiocarbon dates agree with the Maya dates within the statistics of the AMS determinations only at the extreme end of ±2S.D. This work underscores the care that must be taken when interpreting radiocarbon

ages of rock paintings. There are numerous caveats that must be examined in the specific context of the particular dates that have been measured. The "old wood" and "old charcoal" problems can be serious and must be carefully considered if the dates are to be taken as accurate and reliable. Contamination is an ever-present problem in view of the small amounts of carbon typically extracted from a rock painting. It is essential to apply careful checks of the technique being used to date rock paintings. Without verification of the veracity of a given technique, rock art ages should be viewed with caution. Consideration of the consistency of a rock painting date with archaeological information is important. Archaeological evidence could show that a given date is suspect-or even wrong in some cases. As mentioned earlier, high-oxalate samples can be problematic with techniques that utilize high-temperature combustion after a-a-a pretreatments for dating rock paintings. Radiocarbon dates obtained with plasma-chemical extraction are not seriously affected by the presence of other carbonates or oxalates.

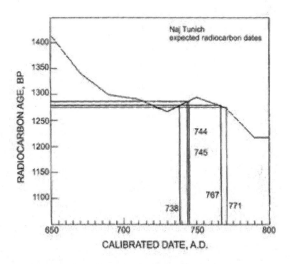

Fig. 7. Expected radiocarbon ages (calculated with CALIB Stuiver and Reimer 1995) corresponding to calendar ages AD 738,744,745,767, and 771, the ages of the Maya glyph text (Stone 1995).[111]

Accuracy was only within ±2 S.D. and that was a date of about 1700 years…what if you are extrapolating to 100,000 years. Absurd!

The era of direct dating of cave art began with *applications*. It has yet to undergo a demonstrable developmental phase. As such, *all* results that are published without detailed supporting data on context, contamination, pre-treatment, measurement and interpretation should be regarded as provisional at best and potentially misleading.

One cannot but conclude by re-emphasizing the calls by Watchman (1999) and Rowe (2001) for the development of universal protocols *both* for sample collection, pre-treatment and measurement, *and* for full and objective publication of all results, whether or not they have been deemed to be a "success" or "failure."[112] [113]

Despite numerous problems and in many cases the experimental nature of the methods, the ongoing application and research into the dating of rock art is a testament to its potential as an archaeological resource. Unfortunately the need to provide archaeological chronologies sometimes outweighs the need for scientific rigor, and we perceive a number of problems that have yet to be addressed.

Utmost care must be taken to demonstrate the stratigraphic relationship between the flowstones and the engravings. There are many cases (as yet undated by this method) where engraving or painting is directly on flowstone, which has been covered subsequently by further flowstone analysis. In this case it is theoretically possible to provide both maximum and minimum ages for the art, but it may prove difficult without overly destructive sampling to identify which of the usually thin flowstone layers overlay and which underlay the art. While U-series methods are perhaps the least controversial of the dating methods applied to rock art, the provision of archaeologically meaningful dates is fortuitous. Flowstones continue to form in caves today, some newly over Palaeolithic rock art, and large scale dating programs are required if we are to by-chance sample flowstones that formed shortly after a figure was painted or engraved. [114]

So far, the very ancient cave-man is unconfirmed. The accuracy of the very old dates is only within ±2 Standard Deviations (in the ages of the Maya Glyph)(in a range which could be considered 'outliers' and ignored as valid data) so extrapolating to 100,000 years is absurd. Apparently the need to provide older and older (Who's 1st!) archaeological chronologies sometimes outweighs the need for scientific rigor! Using mineral coverings that drip over the art is useful but merely saying stalactites nearby prove the very ancient is not reasonable. If you open the bottom doors of the Washington Monument you will see stalactites from the limestone above.

How Old?

In 1913 Arthur Holms published the first book on the age of the earth by radioactive dating claiming that the age of the earth rocks to be at least 1.6 billion years old. Later in 1956 Claire Patterson measured the ratio of isotopes in meteorites claiming a 4.55±0.07 billion years. The problem with these dates is that isotope dating must be interpreted ….within the framework of stratigraphy or the fossil record in the layers of rock, their order, and the location of the fossil. The assumption of a slow constant rate of sedimentation does not fit with the data of rapid deposition, "….meaning the isotope ratios are not an accurate measure of time at all---they are simply reflecting an inextricable tangle of radioactive decay and geochemistry."[115] I have observed the layers of pyroclastic flow at the Mt. Saint Helen's volcano site that occurred in 24 hours that, if a photo were shown to an evolution geologist would be labeled an event taking "millions of years". That convinced me. "Accelerated Nuclear Decay" is an ad hock conjecture that has considerable supporting data that include: Heat effects, daughter products, visible tracks and halos in surrounding rocks, and helium gas. For example Humphreys, Austin, Baumgardner, and Snelling report 1.5 billion years of nuclear decay took place in from 6,000 to 14,000 years in rock crystals.[116] An additional observation that the total energy stored in the earth's magnetic field has decreased 14% since 1829 supports the free decay conjecture over the "dynamo" conjecture of the evolutionists. Study of bricks and pottery "Archaeomagnetism" shows 40% loss since 1000 A.D. strongly suggesting a younger earth, at least not the "millions and millions" evolutionists claim.

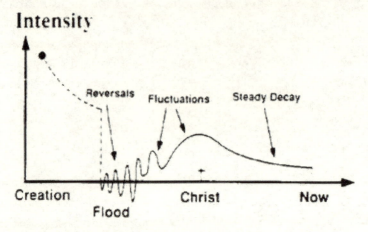

Figure 1. Magnetic field intensity at the earth's surface, from creation to now.

Fig. 8. See:[117]

Logic Fallacies: Examples in Evolution teaching

The biology classroom in particular is filled with illogical arguments and logically offensive statements in support of "Evolution". All designed to deceive the student into believing that Evolution is a science when that is far from the truth. An astrophysicists named Dr Jason Lisle has outlined the errors in evolutionary arguments in "Discerning Truth", Master Books July 2010 in which I have excerpted below by permission.

The following are examples of statements Dr Lisle selected that are errors in logic often presented in support of so-called "evolutionary science":

1. Formal Fallacies of Equivocation (Switching from one meaning of a word to another within an argument in error) "We can see evolution

happening all the time. Organisms are constantly changing and adapting to their environment". [the fact that animals adapt does not demonstrate they have a common ancestor.][118]

2. <u>The Strawman Fallacy of irrelevant thesis</u> (misrepresenting an opponent's position and proceeding to refute the misrepresentation rather than what the opponent actually claims)"The creationists teach that God created all the species we see on earth as they are now and in their current locations. But scientists have discovered that species have diversified and lived in different locations in the past." [119]

3. <u>Faulty appeal to authority</u> (endorsing a claim simply based on the person making it) "Dr. Bill, who has a Ph.D. in biology, taught us that these animals evolved from a simple one-celled creature". Biologists have knowledge about how organisms function today. However, how things came to be, is a history question. He has not made direct observations of the ancient past anymore than anyone else. That makes his position an opinion. [120]

4. <u>Ad Hominem Fallacy</u> (directing the argument against the person making the claim rather than the claim itself) "Creationists are really uneducated; you shouldn't bother listening to their arguments." [121]

5. <u>Fallacy of Bifurcation</u> (claiming there are only two mutually exclusive possibilities when there may actually be three or more options) "Do you believe the universe is governed by natural laws, or do you believe it is upheld by the hand of God?" [122]

6. <u>Reification errors</u>(Attributing a concrete characteristic to something abstract.) ie."Nature has designed some amazing creatures." Nature does not have a mind and therefore cannot design anything.[123]

7. <u>Begging the question.</u> *petition principia* (Circular Reasoning, merely assuming what one is attempting to prove)"We actually don't need evidence for evolution because it is a fact." [124]

8. <u>Question-Begging Epithet</u> :"...creationism vs. evolution" [subtle attempt to label creation as a mere belief while evolution as not.][125]

9. <u>Complex Question Fallacy</u>: *plurium interrogationum* (attempting to persuade by asking a loaded question) "How did life arise from random chemicals and diversify into all the species we see on earth today?" [126]

Additional Errors of Logic

a. <u>The Genetic Fallacy</u> (Dismissing an argument because one objects to the source of the argument) Disregard the source as unreliable only if that can be established. [127]

b. <u>The Fallacy of Composition</u> (arguing that what is true of the parts must also be true of the whole, or what is true of the members of a group is also true of the group) "Everything within the universe has a cause. Therefore, the universe must have a cause." [128]

c. <u>Begging the Question</u>."The creation of a new species from a pre-existing species generally requires thousands of years, so over a life-time a single human usually can witness only a tiny part of the speciation process." "It doesn't occur to the author that perhaps the reason we do not observe evolution (in the particles-to-people sense) today is because it is not true. Instead, he argues that this must be because evolution happens far too slowly to be observed today. He has assumed evolution in his argument for evolution. [129]

d. <u>The Fallacy of Affirming the Consequent</u> (Formal Deductive error where the second premise affirms the consequent of the first premise) and Begging the Question. "For example,..... comparisons of the differences in DNA sequences among organisms provides evidence for many evolutionary events that cannot be found in the fossil record." "That the similarities in DNA are due to evolution rather than a common creator/common purpose is the very claim at issue. In standard form, this argument commits the fallacy of affirming the consequent." [130].

e. <u>Special Pleading, Irrelevant Thesis, and Appeal to Authority</u>."Because creationism is based on specific sets of religious convictions, teaching it in science classes would mean imposing a particular religious view on students and thus is unconstitutional according to several major rulings in federal district courts and the Supreme Court of the United States." "Whether or not creation is based on religious beliefs or is unconstitutional are both irrelevant to the truth of the position---so this is an irrelevant thesis. Also, evolution is also based on a religious/philosophical view: naturalism. So the author has exempted himself from the same standard (special pleading). The reference to the Supreme Court is an irrelevant appeal to authority."[131].

The No True Scotsman Fallacy (when an arguer defines a term in a biased way to protect his arguments from rebuttals) "No real scientist believes that God created everything in six days." [132]

f. Special Pleading Fallacy (double standard)"The arguments of creationists reverse the scientific process. They begin with an explanation that they are unwilling to alter---that supernatural forces have shaped biological or earth systems---rejecting the basic requirements of science that hypothesis must be restricted to testable natural explanations." "So creationists are unwilling to give up their basic interpretive framework (the Bible) in light of which they interpret the evidence. However, evolutionists are also not willing to give up their basic interpretive framework (naturalism) regardless of any evidence to the contrary. A double standard.[133]

g. False Analogy ."Science has boosted living standards, has enabled humans to travel into earth's orbit and to the moon, and has given us new ways of thinking about ourselves and the universe. Evolutionary biology has been and continues to be the cornerstone of modern science." "Science which is testable and repeatable operational science in the present is equated with evolution which is non-testable, non-repeatable belief in molecules-to-man." [134]

h. Fallacy of False Cause ."The rapid advances now being made in the life sciences and in medicine rest on principles derived from an understanding of evolution." "The advances in life sciences are due to scientists studying the continued predicable behavior of the universe and not by a belief in evolution in a molecules-to-man sense.[135]

i. <u>Slippery slope fallacy.</u>"If intelligent design creationism were to be discussed in public schools, then Hindu, Islamic, Native American, and other non-Christian creationists views, as well as mainstream religious views that are compatible with science, also should be discussed." "Discussing intelligent design or creation in schools will lead to a chain of events whereby the creation views of many other religions must be discussed as well. This isn't likely since most other religions embrace some form of evolution anyway. So there is a false analogy and question begging also that creation is not compatible with science---but no argument is made.[136]

<u>Why has "the lie" made it this far in history?</u>
The demand that you must promote some 19th century science of metaphysical Naturalism mechanism or you can't be in the game....that is what keeps the lie of Evolution standing! That fails to see the whole of Naturalism theology as bogus and the point in question.....everyone should use this bogus theology for their ethics?

<u>Natural Selection in human practice:</u>
Adolph Eichman recorded the words of the organizer of the Wannsee Conference
 SS-Obergruppenführer Reinhard Heydrich for the final solution:

"The possible final remnant will, since it will undoubtedly consist of the most resistant portion, have to be treated accordingly, because it is the <u>product of natural selection</u> and would, if released, act as the seed of a new Jewish revival".[137]

The use of the cosmic microwave background (CMB) to declare the age of the Universe is not by any means the complete answer. The point that the Ultra High Energy Cosmic Ray (UHECR) project has measured energies that are quite inconsistent with these UHECR's travelling across the cosmos at nearly the speed of light which would be drained of energy as it constantly interacted with Cosmic microwave background photons, which can't be reconciled leads to the conclusion that the great weight placed upon the CMB to claim "billions and billions" of years is a fallacy.

The great invented theories of physics of the 70's like the symmetry SU(5) theory have fallen in disarray since the finding that protons do not decay at the predicted rate.......ending the incredible understanding that came from Gauge Theory and symmetry breaking.[138] Smolin is somewhat unique in that he is willing to suggest that the strings of "string theory" are made of "nothing". And we know that Creator-God made the things that are from nothing...*Ex Nilo,* is not to be taken lightly. I am convinced, that the emission of Larmor radiation by a ground state electron would lead to collapse of the orbit of the electron causing it to tunnel into the nucleus of the atom, but this does not lead to collapse of the orbit because the electron also absorbs zero-point energy (ZPE). "It is striking that the Larmor emission and harmonic-oscillator-type absorption prove to be in balance exactly at the Bohr radius."[139] Repeating Richard Feynman's suggestion of a background energy, one constantly pumped into all of the universe every instant," that the energy density within the atom is the same as the energy density in empty space". And the failure of the theoretical physicists finding Protons decay into its 3 parts supports the existence of "*Corum Deo*" support of all matter and space. That the face of Creator-God is present (omnipresent) shining from all directions at all points maintaining the universe in the state He chooses from all possible states that would be possible from symmetry splitting. It would certainly support the point He makes that He will not always strive with his creation but will at some time in the future, turn his face (His presence) away from his creation and "The heavens will pass away with a great noise, and the elements will be dissolved with fervent heat, and the earth also and the works that are therein shall be burned up". A "fervent heat" as $MC^2 = E$ predicts.[Ps 19:6, 2Peter 3:10, Isaiah 34:4]

I repeat, the ground state electron is assumed to emit Larmor radiation which causes it to spiral inward, but this does not lead to collapse of the orbit because the electron also absorbs zero-point energy. The calculation of the absorption was done by Boyer and later by Puthoff by treating the electron as undergoing harmonic oscillation rather than true motion in a Coulomb potential. This is a weakness in the analysis but nonetheless it is striking that the Larmor emission and harmonic-oscillator-type absorption prove to be in balance exactly at the Bohr radius. The fact that the orbital angular momentum is zero in the quantum ground state is mirrored in the SED orbiting-electron interpretation by random changes in the orbital plane (due to the zero-point fluctuations) yielding a time averaged zero net angular momentum.[140] [141]

Why, would a man recognizing that we don't know what an electron, a photon, or a proton and neutron are and what inertia is or why we weigh anything at all; if "Science" can't clearly explain these, understand that "Science" hasn't the capacity to declare anything theologically valid. I have no confidence that the perspective of the theoretical physicists who is without understanding of an Infinite Creator-God can truly describe to our children the universe about us. How could the scientist blind to the truth ever arrive at the equations responsible for creation or even the maintenance of creation? If He began with the word of Creator-God, perhaps those equations might follow, but so far Creator-God's thoughts are higher than our thoughts than the heavens are from the earth as He has told us.

The Problems of Unified Theory of Everything: Man the know it all:
The case has been made that Naturalism is a belief system imbedded with many of the false gods of the campus. This is the belief system that many instructors and educational associations claim as a pure science. This appeal is without merit and contains a doctrine full of fallacies when arguments are made and logically analyzed.

3 propositions we understand to be true in science because there is such regularity in the universe. There are many instances where scientists are able to make successful predictions about the future:

1. The Universe is Rational
2. The Universe Obeys LAWS or the operations of the universe are describable in lawful terms.
3. That the rationality of the external universe is mirrored within the rationality of our own minds (it matches). [142]

The argument can be made that to the secularist, there is no basis for induction.[143] Induction suggest truth but does not ensure it.[144] Inductive reasoning is PROBABILISTIC; it only states that, given the premises, the conclusion is *probable*. Inductive reasoning allows for the possibility that the conclusion is false, even if all of the premises are true.[145] Hume argued that it is impossible to justify inductive reasoning: specifically, that it cannot be justified deductively, so our only option is to justify it inductively. Since this is circular he concluded that it is impossible to justify induction.[146] Induction logic usually relies on convenient information around the observer, not the necessary data or observation needed for the argument, creating a significant bias in many situations, such as speciation and the presumed early geologic information. The confirmation bias is based on the natural tendency to confirm rather than to deny a current hypothesis. Research has demonstrated that people are inclined to seek solutions to problems that are more consistent with known hypotheses rather than attempt to refute those hypotheses. The predictable-world bias revolves around the inclination to perceive order where it has not been proved to exist. A major aspect of this bias is superstition, which is derived from the inability to acknowledge that coincidences are merely coincidences.[147] [148]

vii
Implications of a Godless Campus

"There is a cry in the heart of every man that says, "I don't want to die!"
[Kirk Cameron]

Part 1.. The Godless Campus

"According to Christianity, what Creator-God values above all is relationship. But for relationship to be meaningful, it must be freely chosen; for relationship to be freely chosen there must be the possibility of it being rejected; and wherever there is the possibility of rejecting relationship, there is also the possibility of pain and suffering" [1]

Please remember I don't consider Christianity as a religion like the others, but rather, a "relationship" with the one who made you and me.

"What kind of world Creator-God would have made depends on what Creator-God Values".[2] Wouldn't it be valuable to know what our Creator values? He comes in the volume of a book, the Bible. He sent his Son into the world not to reform the world but to "save" us. If man is indeed a 3-fold creature with a body, soul, and spirit, and we have the capacity to live forever with Creator-God. And, if eternity is the period of our possibility; this present life is so small and insignificant a part of that eternity that even when we are alive and without the Spirit of Christ within us (ie. Not born-again) we are for all intents and purposes dead even though our physical body is alive for this infinitesimal period of time.(85/Infinity=0) Continually rejecting our Creator's gift of His Son as payment for our transgressions against Him and Him only until we die is not wise, and a great tragedy! For even if we conquer the whole world but reject Jesus Christ, we have nothing at the end of the race. We are told that the Angels are learning just as we are learning. Creator-God is so incredible in the first place plus the fact that the Church, the Bride of Christ, was a mystery to the Old Testament prophets. (see: 1Peter 1:12) There is no such thing as secular vs. sacred. There is no such

division because there is only one "reality" and "secular" is really nothing
al all. The things invented by man will fall by man and are nothing more
then very very short-lived things or words or whatever. What is real is all
things that are "to the Glory of Creator-God". You are certainly free to bow
down to any god you choose, but in the end the "manner of our heart will
be found out." 1Corin 10:3 tells us to "do all to the Glory of God". Without
Christ, our hearts are deceitful, desperately wicked, who can know it?". The
"flesh" refers to human nature apart from Jesus. And the "World" refers
to all people apart from Jesus. We have a "living Hope" and the "world" a
"dying hope" that is fading. Shadrack, Meshach and Abed-Nego didn't bow
to the Idol of Nebuchadnezzar and they didn't burn and the Son of God was
standing beside them in the fiery furnace. [3]

The point I am trying to make bears repeating. Creator-God does not
want to reform the world. It is in a state He knows completely. He instead
seeks to save us by His Grace through Faith, according to his Word. His nature
requires Justice first!! But He Himself provides the Justice by paying the price
of our "missing the mark" with His life by sacrificing Himself on the Cross----
showing us the "eternalness" of our "missing the mark". So His Grace gives
us eternal life with Him if we accept His gift freely given. The promises of
Creator-God live eternally. Even in the Old Testament the Spirit of Christ
spoke to those author's hearts and they wrote it all down. He has preserved
those words for all....those Words will never perish! You can count on His
promises. But we must remain patient, all things happen in His time, not ours.

Again, Creator-God will forgive us, no matter what we have done. The
greater the forgiveness, the greater the love! Nobody gets away with sin,
nobody! James tells us if you can live in sin and enjoy it, you are not of the
LORD---you need repentance before the LORD [Ironsides] Trials are for
spiritual instruction.

The Deception of Trials: "the problem of pain"
People get deceived because they are in trials or one they love is allowed to
go through cancer, death, divorce, or similar trials. We are told in Luke:

"You are the one that remained with me in my trials. Thus I grant to you a kingdom just as my Father granted to me, that you may eat and drink at my table in my Kingdom…"

This is what Jesus said at the Last Supper to his disciples the night before His sacrifice on the cross. Note: He is with us in our trials and we are not to abandon Him and He will not abandon us. The trials gave great meaning as a partaker in Christ's suffering. Probably a great spiritual event in our lives if we have learned to recognize it!! Trials test our perseverance with Jesus!

Why trials? Satan has demanded to have you all to sift you like wheat, but I (Jesus) have prayed for you" [Luke 22:31]$_{NET}$ An error on our part is misunderstanding Creator-God in the trials that befall us. We all fall short of the Glory of the LORD, and sin directly against Him. Payment has been made and Justice must be satisfied. The work has been completed in Jesus Christ!

Once justice is satisfied we have access to the Love and Bounty of Creator-God. His Holy Spirit lives in us for our bodies have been prepared a tabernacle for Him. We then continue in the flesh and imperfect but continue forgiven though we have refining fire trials to strengthen our faith and reliance upon the LORD.

As a warning against Idols and Idolatry consider Zechariah 10:2[RKJV]

"For the idols speak delusion; the diviners envision lies, and tell false dreams; They comfort in vain.

Therefore the people wend their way like sheep; They are in trouble because there is no shepherd."

The Bankruptcy of the gods of the campus

Without a correct view of God, the gospel seems foolish and unnecessary to relativists. There is no Absolute. With no belief in the one true Creator-God there is no absolute. How can a student learn about the Gospel and the Grace of Jesus Christ without the understanding that prepares him for that opening of faith?

What happens when man follows the dictates of Our Creator's enemies:

When the woman Eve, listened to the serpent and accepted his lies that God didn't say we would die if we disobeyed his Word, mankind found himself forfeiting the Deed of the earth to the enemy of man and we are now subject to death.

When the woman Mary, listened to the Angel of God that she was to bear a Child, God himself, she finally listened to the Word and replied, "Behold the maidservant of the Lord! Let it be to me according to your word". Thereby setting the stage to reverse the terrible event that happened with the first Man/Woman. We finally did something right 2000 years ago.

Why is it that we haven't listened? Why is it that we have fallen into all kinds of Idolatry failing to understand the truth? Why are most of the teachers of mankind continuing to believe a lie rather than open their eyes to the truth? Once you accept one enormous lie you are open to a cacophony of lies! Lets look at a careful work describing the direction of a nation after it secularized, just like the Universities are advocating. A brilliant writer Dr Erwin W. Lutzer in "When A Nation Forgets God: 7 lessons we must learn from Nazi Germany (Lutzer, 2010), carefully analyzed the exclusion of church from state, resulting in:

(1) economic meltdown
(2) laws that circumvent justice
(3) laws that circumvent morality
(4) systematic secularization of media, education, workplace and German culture
(5) experience trumping reason
(6) revision of history to serve special interests
(7) the erosion and breakdown of family systems[4]

If you don't think these seven are occurring today in the world you are not a careful observer. Please consider the following:

Richard Terrell wrote, "Create a critical mass of people who cannot discern meaning and truth from nonsense, and you will have a society ready to fall for the first charismatic leader to come along".[5]

Many are held captive by the Power of Darkness, in which we were all once captive slaves. [Eph 2:1-3] Be "partakers of the inheritance of the saints in the light" [Col 1:12]$_{NKJV}$

James Clerk Maxwell Presented a paper to the British Association for the Advancement of Science in 1873, he said: "No theory of evolution can be formed to account for the similarity of molecules, for evolution necessarily implies continuous change....The exact equality of each molecule to all others of the same kind gives it....the essential character of a manufactured article, and precludes the idea of its being eternal and self-existent.[6]

Maxwell also noted in the above paper with regard to Evolution:

"........But in the heavens we discover by their light, and by their light alone, stars so distant from each other that no material thing can ever have passed from one to another, and yet this light, which is to us the sole evidence of the existence of these distant worlds, tells us also that each of them is built up of molecules of the same kinds as those which we find on earth. A molecule of hydrogen, for example, whether in Sirius or in Arcturus, executes its vibrations in precisely the same time.

Each molecule, therefore, throughout the universe, bears impressed on it the stamp of a metric system as distinctly as does the metre of the Archives at Paris, or the double royal cubit of the Temple of Karnac.

No theory of evolution can be formed to account for the similarity of molecules, for evolution necessarily implies continuous change, and the molecule is incapable of growth or decay, of generation or destruction.

None of the processes of Nature, since the time when Nature began, have produced the slightest difference in the properties of any molecule. We are therefore unable to ascribe either the existence of the molecules or the identity of their properties to the operation of any of the causes which we call natural.

On the other hand, the exact equality of each molecule to all others of the same kind gives it, as Sir John Herschel has well said, the essential character of a manufactured article, and precludes the idea of its being eternal and self existent.

Thus we have been led, along a strictly scientific path, very near to the point at which Science must stop. Not that Science is debarred from studying the internal mechanism of a molecule which she cannot take to pieces, any more than from investigating an organism which she cannot put together. But in tracing back the history of matter Science is arrested when she assures herself, on the one hand, that the molecule has been made, and on the other that it has not been made by any of the processes we call natural.

Science is incompetent to reason upon the creation of matter itself out of nothing. We have reached the utmost limit of our thinking faculties when we have admitted that because matter cannot be eternal and self-existent it must have been created.

It is only when we contemplate, not matter in itself, but the form in which it actually exists, that our mind finds something on which it can lay hold.

That matter, as such, should have certain fundamental properties — that it should exist in space and be capable of motion, that its motion should be persistent, and so on, are truths which may, for anything we know, be of the kind which metaphysicians call necessary. We may use our knowledge of such truths for purposes of deduction but we have no data for speculating as to their origin.

But that there should be exactly so much matter and no more in every molecule of hydrogen is a fact of a very different order. We have here a particular distribution of matter — a *collocation* — to use the expression of Dr. Chalmers, of things which we have no difficulty in imagining to have been arranged otherwise.

The form and dimensions of the orbits of the planets, for instance, are not determined by any law of nature, but depend upon a particular collocation of matter. The same is the case with respect to the size of the earth, from which the standard of what is called the metrical system has been derived. But these astronomical and terrestrial magnitudes are far inferior in scientific importance to that most fundamental of all standards which forms the base of the molecular system. Natural causes, as we know, are at work, which tend to modify, if they do not at length destroy, all the arrangements and dimensions of the earth and the whole solar system. But though in the course of ages catastrophes have occurred and may yet occur in the heavens, though ancient systems may be dissolved and new systems evolved out of their ruins, the molecules out of which these systems are built — the foundation stones of the material universe — remain unbroken and unworn.

They continue this day as they were created, perfect in number and measure and weight, and from the ineffaceable characters impressed on them we may learn that those aspirations after accuracy in measurement, truth in statement, and justice in action, which we reckon among our noblest attributes as men, are ours because they are essential constituents of the image of Him Who in the beginning created, not only the heaven and the earth, but the materials of which heaven and earth consist.

It is not because we happen to be chemists or physicists or specialists of any kind that we are attracted towards this centre of all material existence, but because we all belong to a race endowed with faculties which urge us on to search deep and ever deeper into the nature of things.

......though the statements in our own elementary text-books may be so neatly expressed that they appear almost self-evident, their true interpretation may involve some principle so profound that, till the right man has laid hold of it, no one ever suspects that anything is left to be discovered." [Maxwell][5]

—◊—

"If my people, which are called by my name, shall humble themselves, and pray, and seek my face, and turn from their wicked ways; then will I hear from heaven, and will forgive their sin, and will heal their land." (2 Chron 7:14 KJV) (my people=those whom His name is called=ownership by Creator God) NET bible note)

—◊—

James Clerk Maxwell when asked to tie a scientific hypothesis of his day (1896) to the bible responded...."I think that each individual man should do all he can to impress his own mind with the extent, the order, and the unity of the universe, and should carry these ideas with him as he reads such passages as the 1st chapter of the Epistle to the Colossians......"

"Giving thanks unto the Father, which hath made us meet to be a partakers of the inheritance of the saints and light: who have delivered us from the power of darkness, and have translated us into the kingdom of his dear Son: in whom we have redemption through his blood, even the forgiveness of sins:

Who is the image of the invisible God, the first born of every creature: Four by him were all things created, that are in heaven, and that are in earth, visible and invisible, whether they be thrones, or dominions, or principalities, or powers: all things were created by him, and for him: And he is before all things, and by him all things consist. And he is the head of the body, the church: who is the beginning, the firstborn from the dead; that in all things he might have the preeminence. For it pleased the Father that in

Him should all fullness dwell; And having made peace through the blood of his cross, by him to reconcile all things unto himself; by him, I say, whether they be things in earth or things in heaven.

> *"And you, that were some time alienated and enemies in your mind by wicked works, yet now hath he reconciled in the body of his flesh through death, to present you holy and unblameable and unreprovable in his sight: If you continue in the faith grounded and settled and be not moved away from the hope of the gospel, which ye have heard, and which was preached to every creature which is under heaven; whereof I Paul am made a minister;.......Whom we preach, warning every man, and teaching every man in all wisdom; that we may present every man perfect in Christ Jesus."* [Colossians 1:12-23,28]$_{KJV}$

Maxwell died of severely painful abdominal cancer (of which he did not complain) on November 5, 1879, aged 48. One of his close colleagues at Cambridge wrote: "We his contemporaries at college, have seen in him high powers of mind and great capacity and original views, conjoined with deep humility before his God, reverent submission to His will, and hearty belief in the love and atonement of that Divine Savior Who was his portion and comforter in trouble and sickness."[7] [8]

Bankrupting the Western Democracies

"The average age of the world's greatest civilizations from the beginning of history has been about 200 years. During those 200 years, these nations always progressed through the following sequence: From bondage to spiritual faith; From spiritual faith to great courage; From courage to liberty; From liberty to abundance; From abundance to selfishness; From selfishness to complacency; From complacency to apathy; From apathy to dependence; From dependence back into bondage. [9] Nevertheless the wisdom of the deterioration path of civilizations is of value here.

The Ideologies of sex, the politics of sex, hating masculinity, and the sexual militant's destructive work on the family is having its result. "These social pathologies in turn rationalize most all domestic public spending, which is now bankrupting the Western democracies. Virtually the entire domestic budget of every government from Italy to Missouri is justified by problems proceeding from single-parent homes and connected forms of family dissolution." [10]

Marxism and all attempts to control economic behavior, are constrained by the simple problem that good economic systems requires both "trust" and "good faith" especially at the one-on one level (micro) and thus has a great moral factor overriding. There must be understanding between trading partners that permits monetary policies to work. That means agreement on "right" and "wrong" as it relates to the social-value of things. Marx objectified most all of society rejecting the requirement of a moral standard (he rejected) mainly the 10 commandments of the Hebrew scriptures. The basis of harmony in economic relations at all levels. Note this Absolute standard is unknown at our educational institutions and rejected by our highest courts.....leading to economic collapse regardless if your professor is a Marxist or not.

What Historically happens to Nations and Cities that Reject Creator-God and fall into idolatry?

I have already discussed Sodom, it's idolatry and demise. Not a pretty picture. In a nation with organizations such as NAMBLA and many other such organizations driving the nations agenda to the nation's detriment; the concern of a similar fate befalling America should be understood.

> "Son of man, these men have set up their idols in their hearts; and put before them that which causes then to stumble into iniquity" [Eze 14:3]
>
> "Son of man, when a land sins against Me by persistent unfaithfulness, I will stretch out My hand against it; I will cut off its supply of bread, send famine on it, and cut off man and beast from it." [Eze 14:13]

We also know that the end of time will be like the days of Noah, when men only had violence in their hearts. The director of the movie "Alien" complained in an interview may 2017 that it is much harder to scare people today, the people have become desensitized to VIOLENCE! Does that mean that violence is so prevalent that it hardly registers today? We need to be very careful not to allow the violence that is all around us to enter our hearts.

We know that the idolatry of Israel lead to the Dispersion of the Jews all over the world, away from their promised land. What modern nation that worships a false god has continued to this day. Perhaps the oldest city in the world that has been continuously inhabited is Damascus Syria. This very day it is under siege. The Bible tells us it will be completely destroyed and never be rebuilt. Keep your eye on Damascus [Isa 17 and Jer 49:23-27] which will not be rebuilt…."cease being a city". What are the false-gods of these cities and nations. USA is the longest present nation and free government driving by idolatrous teaching institutions that change our culture into something not imagined by our founders! They cryout with the word "Rights", forgetting that our Declaration of Independence informed all of us that our "Rights" were given by Creator-God! Many in the teaching institutions call a Constitutional right that which Creator-God tells us is an abomination to him. [Leviticus 18]. What nation continues that murders 60 million of its children by passing them through the "osmotic file" (as performed in Planned Parenthood Clinics) to Molech, the god of sensuality or as Milton describes him as the greatest warrior of the fallen angels (demons), or as Winston Churchill in "The Gathering Storm" described Hitler as one who "…had conjured up the fearful idol of an all-devouring Moloch of which he was the priest and incarnation".[11]

A treatise was written in 1947 by the noted Harvard sociologist and historian Carle C. Zimmerman "Family and Civilization". Zimmerman traces the decline of the unit of all civilizations the nuclear family. The Book has been updated and republished in 2008 with summaries and addendum by recent scholars reiterating the astounding collapse of the family unit in Greek, Roman, and all once great civilizations studied. These multiple civilizations and empires had eight patterns of domestic behavior that signaled the decline of that civilization. 1) Marriage loses its sacredness; is frequently broken by divorce. 2) Traditional meaning of the marriage ceremony is lost. 3) Feminist movements abound. 4)Increased public disrespect for parents and authority in general. 5) Acceleration of juvenile delinquency, Promiscuity, and rebellion. 6) Refusal of people with traditional marriages to accept family responsibilities. 7)Growing desire for acceptance of adultery. 8) Increasing interest in and spread of sexual perversions and sex-related crimes.[12]

It turns out that the marriage is a core symbol of the bible…where the "bride" is presented as the very body of the Christ seen as in a harmonious union at the end of time. The Hebrew wedding ceremony where the groom, after building a new addition on his father's house for the bride, suddenly appears without warning for the wedding, a preview of the coming Messiah for his bride, the Church. Marriage is treated as a sacred and honored covenant by Creator-God and civilizations that destroy its very symbolic meaning have ceased to exist or collapsed into insignificance.

Billy Graham tells us about a statement from his wife given in despair:

"Some years ago, my wife, Ruth, was reading the draft of a book I was writing. When she finished a section describing the terrible downward spiral of our nation's moral standards and the idolatry of worshiping false gods such as technology and sex, she startled me by exclaiming, "If God doesn't punish America, He'll have to apologize to Sodom and Gomorrah."

She was probably thinking of a passage in Ezekiel where God tells why He brought those cities to ruin. "Now this was the sin of … Sodom: She and her daughters were arrogant, overfed and unconcerned; they did not help the poor and needy. They were haughty and did detestable things before me. Therefore I did away with them as you have seen" (Ezekiel 16:49–50, NIV).

I wonder what Ruth would think of America if she were alive today. In the years since she made that remark, millions of babies have been aborted and our nation seems largely unconcerned. Self-centered indulgence, pride, and a lack of shame over sin are now emblems of the American lifestyle. Just a few weeks ago in a prominent city in the South, Christian chaplains who serve the police department were ordered to no longer mention the Name of Jesus in prayer. It was reported that during a recent police-sponsored event, the only person allowed to pray was someone who addressed "the being in the room." Similar scenarios are now commonplace in towns across America. Our society strives to avoid any possibility of offending anyone—except God.

Yet the farther we get from God, the more the world spirals out of control.

My heart aches for America and its deceived people". [13]

Hope for Skeptics

Christian chaplains have identified three major hurdles that keep people from trusting in Christ for salvation. These three barriers are 1) Your doubting you are important enough for Creator-God's attention. 2)As your own worst critic, you believe you are unworthy of His forgiveness. And 3) You wonder why Creator-God is not communicating with you if He is there. (for He is totally accessible, He comes in the volume of a book) Find at least one of the 5 billion available.

> "So shall My word be that goes forth from My mouth; it shall not return to Me void, but it shall accomplish what I please." [Isaiah 55:11]

Randy Kilgore helps us understand these barriers:

"God doesn't play head games. He promises that if we read His Word, He will make sure it accomplishes His purpose. In other words, if we read it we will discover that God is communicating with us. This is precisely why the Bible speaks so often of His grace and mercy toward all. His willingness to forgive surpasses our own. Once we learn that we can hear God in the Bible and once we see the emphasis on His mercy, it becomes easier to believe we have His attention when we cry out to Him. Creator-God's story is amazing. It can give hope for all of us.[14]

Mankind has a choice:

"...love the LORD thy God, to walk in His ways, and to keep His commandments and His statutes and His judgments, that thou mayest live and multiply: and the LORD thy God shall bless thee in the land... But if thine heart turn away, so that thou wilt not hear, but shall be drawn away, and worship other gods, and serve them...... I call heaven and earth to record this day against you, that I have set before you life and death, blessing and cursing: therefore choose life, that both thou and thy seed may live....". [Deuteronomy 30: 15 – 19]KJV

> **"There is a cry in the heart of every man that says, "I don't want to die!"**
>
> **[Kirk Cameron]**

Part 2. Effects of what is being taught on the campus today

What does it mean when a nation's educational institutions teach it's children to give honor and glory and reverence to false gods; to walk away from the Word of Creator-God and to remove Him from the public square? Instead of "One Nation Under Creator-God", :This Nation is not a Christian Nation"[President Obama]. Fill all children with multiculturalism instead. Learn of many gods and relative ethics so that what is an abomination to Creator-God, that which is bad and evil is instead good and acceptable. Are there consequences: What has happened to other peoples that have embraced idolatry?

British Astronomer Sir James Jeans declared, "We are not yet in touch with ultimate reality." The science we have cannot tell us what life is; cannot teach us the reality we find in Creator-God's word, our scientists, while they impress us with their learning are often empty when it comes to "ultimate reality", denying the power of Creator-God leading to abject Nihilism. Children who are taught they are grown up worms in a universe without purpose and direction are doomed to the void of outer-darkness, an eternity without the love of Creator-God whom they are taught to ignore by people who have no real life within them. They cannot understand the trials of life all of us face, especially death and rampant deception.

Information can originate <u>only</u> from a conscious intelligence, a quality found in personal beings". The reader knows there is a non-physical side to man. "Words and the conceptual ideas they express (including those imprinted on DNA) are <u>not</u> a part of the dimensional, physical universe. The idea of "Justice" for example has nothing to do with and cannot be described in terms of any of the five senses. It lies in another realm…".[15]

What is true is what reality is about. Walk away from truth and invent word-symbols that are not reality and use these to think with and you have a society-culture losing its sanity.

"Intelligence is non-physical because it conceives of and uses non-physical constructs that do not originate in the material of the brain or body…. this takes us beyond the physical universe into the realm of spirit. We do not know what a soul or a spirit is, or what it means that God is Spirit [John 4:24]$_{NKJV}$ who created man in His own image"[Gen 1:27]$_{NKJV}$".[16]

Teach our children they were knit together lovingly in the womb by Creator-God who is outside of time; that they are very special to Him and He has written a book through 40 different Authors to instruct them in the path to eternal life.

> "God has given us sufficient proof in what we can verify to cause us to trust completely whatever His word declares concerning things we cannot fully comprehend. That is where faith enters. While seeking to unravel the secrets of the universe, science neglects the Creator. The universe can lead man only to a dead end, since ultimate knowledge is hidden in the God who brought all into existence.
>
> Though not idol worshippers in the primitive sense, scientists, university professors, business executives, and political leaders, no matter how brilliant, who do not know Christ fit the description in Romans 1 of those who reject the witness of the Universe and worship the Creation instead of the Creator. It is possible for Christians also to be caught up in this same materialistic ambition and to miss what God offers us in Himself." [17]

Secularism tries to teach us a great lie. That it has the truth and there is no mystery that the secular professors do not know. This entire book documents the lack of true understanding in the secular world. Just like Newton understood that "action at a distance is a mystery" (and it still is) there continues to be a great deal that is a mystery....that we know but cannot comprehend. Probably the greatest of these is the fact that most of us believe in Creator-God but few have made the effort to take into themselves His Word.

"The concept of one true God who exists eternally in three Persons (Father, Son, and Holy Spirit) is rejected by some who claim to be Christian. Yet it is taught all through scripture, in the Old Testament as well as the New. Consider: "I have not spoken in secret from the beginning, from the time that it was, there am I.." Surely the speaker who has been in existence forever must be God Himself. Yet He declares, "the LORD God, and His Spirit, hath sent me" [Isaiah 48:16] We cannot comprehend the mystery of the Trinity, yet that is no more reason to doubt it than to doubt anything else we know is real but cannot comprehend."[18]

We all know we sin against Creator-God, we just don't admit it to ourselves. We sometimes hide that our hearts are dark and there was no light in us. "the penalty for our sins is infinite because Creator-God in his justice is infinite. Consequently, those who reject Christ's payment (on the cross) on their behalf of will be separated from God forever." [19]

This mystery, the mystery that means that what was that sense of how evil could arise in Creator–Gods "good" universe is unclear. Except to note that what Creator–God's enemies intend for evil, Creator–God will turn to good. As in Genesis 50:20 as Joseph spoke to his brothers who had sold him into slavery "as for you, you meant to harm me, but God intended it for a good purpose, so he could preserve the lives of many people, as you can see this day".[Net bible]

Creator–God teaches us to have an excellent spirit in the face of evil, to learn of Him, and to render good for evil. Joseph comforted them, and, to banish their fears, he spoke kindly to his brothers. Broken spirits who have participated in evil must be bound up and encouraged. We must not only love and forgive those that are in offense but we do well to also speak kindly to him. But at all times respect them as created in the image of Creator–God, even if they are in prison. Especially those in prison, for they have the unique understanding of their offense. Yet all mankind except one has offended Creator–God. There is only one unforgettable and unforgivable offense against Creator–God and that is to claim that Creator–God is evil or gets his power from evil....called "blaspheming of the holy spirit". Although even this definition is incomplete. If one calls the "Christ" evil or claims He is not Creator-God and, knowingly rejects His salvation and then subsequently died in this without repentance, they have committed an unpardonable sin as well, I think.

What this all means is we all have a loving Creator who forgives us all of our sins (except the one noted) if only we repent and admit we have sinned against him and accept His gift of forgiveness. He wins us and we win Him!

Obviously the universe was created for a "win win" scenario. It's your free choice!

This is why he is the Word, the Bible matters greatly; why it should be read aloud in our homes each day; that what He values becomes what we and our children, and our communities also value. Then we understand what is "biggest" for us and what is "good" and what is "bad" not allowing those values to "float" becoming whatever seems right at the moment..... produces trouble, big trouble!

Everyone reading this has to deal with the part of reality that is a misery, pain, suffering, and death. Creator–God has everything to do with these because 1) He knows all three of these and tells us he will go through each with us. 2) At the cross we see the absolute uniqueness of the Christian response to suffering. In Islam, the idea of God suffering is nonsense—it is thought to make God week. In Buddhism, to reach divinity is precisely to move beyond the possibility of suffering. Only in Christ do we have a God who is loving enough to suffer with us."[20]

3) ".. each of us is going to deal with significant suffering in our lives. And, one day, each of us is going to have to deal with the reality of death. When suffering comes, and when death comes, who will bear it with us? Who will see us through it?" [21] Who will answer?

Does the teacher or professor teaching you idolatry really help you with what really counts? Is he filling the void in us with emptiness and non–reality. Is he/she stealing your children's salvation? What has been taken from you, how much have you lost if you lose eternal life. We are told "What profit does the person have if he gains the whole world, but destroys himself or is lost forever? "[Luke 9:25]

Inoculate yourself and your children from false instruction!

While the "Science of the Bible, ie. begin with Creator-God" suggested in this book in place of "Evolution and the Big Bang" and "Global Warming" are reasonable alternatives, they are merely presented to suggest we have not arrived with man's best guess theories. That Creator–Gods thought is indeed higher than our thought than the heavens are above the earth is a true statement from Him.

"For my thoughts are not your thoughts, neither are your ways my ways, declares the LORD

(Yahweh). For as the heavens are higher than the earth, so are my ways higher than your ways and my thoughts, than your thoughts".[Isaiah 55:8-9]$_{ESV}$

Another False Science example.

Global Warming; not a Scientific Theory, not a Scientific Model, but a Scenario/narrative (Best Guess/"abduction logic")
The science of "Global Warming" is not economic but a question of the the Physics of "The Greenhouse effect of CO2?". Misdirection is quite common in false science.

"Faculty teaching "Global Warming Proofs" as true incontrovertible science are generating a false "molded image in your mind". It is not a carved idol but generated by word strings creating a False Science. Habakkuk 2:18 "….The molded image, a teacher of lies, that the maker of its mold should trust in it". Do they know they are building an Idol that will give that idol economic and global power and control …."Rank Globalism"! The Physicists who destroy the scientific underpinning of Global Warming, "Greenhouse effect of CO2" say the following:

The point discussed here was to answer the question, whether the supposed atmospheric effect has a physical basis. This is not the case. In summary, there is no atmospheric greenhouse effect, in particular CO_2-greenhouse effect, in theoretical physics and engineering thermodynamics. Thus it is illegitimate to deduce predictions which provide a consulting solution for economics and intergovernmental policy."

After you read Gerlich and Tscheuschner paper I think you will say like I did that True science is awesome.

See: Gerlich, G. And Tscheuschner, R.D. (2009) "Falsefication of The Atmospheric CO2 Greenhouse Effects Within the Frame of Physics", arXiv:0707.1161v4 [physics.ao-pg] 4 Mar 2009. 115 PAGES[22]

Gerhrd Gerlich:Institut für Mathematische Physik, Technische Universität Carolo-Wilhelmina, Mendelssohnstraße 3, D-38106 Braunschweig, Federal Republic of, Germany. Ralf D. Tscheuschner Postfach 602762, D-22377 Hamburg, Federal Republic of, Germany. Received: 12 March 2010

"A thorough discussion of the planetary heat transfer problem in the framework of theoretical physics and engineering thermodynamics leads to the following results:

1. There are no common physical laws between the warming phenomenon in glass houses and the fictitious atmospheric greenhouse effect, which explains the relevant physical phenomena. The terms "greenhouse effect" and "greenhouse gases" are deliberate misnomers.
2. There are no calculations to determinate an average surface temperature of a planet
    *   with or without an atmosphere,
    *   with or without rotation,
    *   with or without infrared light absorbing gases.

The frequently mentioned difference of 33 ºC for the fictitious greenhouse effect of the atmosphere is therefore a meaningless number.

3. Any radiation balance for the average radiant flux is completely irrelevant for the determination of the ground level air temperatures and thus for the average value as well.

4. Average temperature values cannot be identified with the fourth root of average values of the absolute temperature's fourth power.

5. Radiation and heat flows do not determine the temperature distributions and their average values.

6. Re-emission is not reflection and can in no way heat up the ground-level air against the actual heat flow without mechanical work.

7. The temperature rises in the climate model computations are made plausible by a perpetuum mobile of the second kind. This is possible by setting the thermal conductivity in the atmospheric models to zero, an unphysical assumption. It would be no longer a perpetuum mobile of the second kind, if the "average" fictitious radiation balance, which has no physical justification anyway, was given up.

8. After Schack 1972 water vapor is responsible for most of the absorption of the infrared radiation in the Earth's atmosphere. The wavelength of the part of radiation, which is absorbed by carbon dioxide is only a small part of the full infrared spectrum and does not change considerably by raising its partial pressure.

9. Infrared absorption does not imply "backwarming". Rather it may lead to a drop of the temperature of the illuminated surface.

10. In radiation transport models with the assumption of local thermal equilibrium, it is assumed that the absorbed radiation is transformed into the thermal movement of all gas molecules. There is no increased selective re-emission of infrared radiation at the low temperatures of the Earth's atmosphere.

11. In climate models, planetary or astrophysical mechanisms are not accounted for properly. The time dependency of the gravity acceleration by the Moon and the Sun (high tide and low tide) and the

local geographic situation, which is important for the local climate, cannot be taken into account.

12. Detection and attribution studies, predictions from computer models in chaotic systems, and the concept of scenario analysis lie outside the framework of exact sciences, in particular theoretical physics.

13. The choice of an appropriate discretization method and the definition of appropriate dynamical constraints (flux control) having become a part of computer modeling is nothing but another form of data curve fitting. The mathematical physicist V.Neumann once said to his young collaborators: "If you allow me four free parameters I can build a mathematical model that describes exactly everything that an elephant can do. If you allow me a fifth free parameter, the model I build will forecast that the elephant will fly." [23]

14. Higher derivative operators(e.g. the Laplacian)can never be represented on grids with wide meshes. Therefore a description of heat conduction in global computer models is impossible. The heat conduction equation is not and cannot properly be represented on grids with wide meshes.

15. Computer models of higher dimensional chaotic systems, best described by non-linear partial differential equations (i.e. Navier-Stokes equations), fundamentally differ from calculations where perturbation theory is applicable and successive improvements of the predictions - by raising the computing power - are possible. At best, these computer models may be regarded as a heuristic game.

16. Climatology misinterprets unpredictability of chaos known as butterfly phenomenon as another threat to the health of the Earth.

In other words: Already the natural greenhouse effect is a myth beyond physical reality. The CO_2-greenhouse effect, however is a "mirage" [24]

"...Advocators of the greenhouse thesis claim that the discussion is closed, and others are discrediting justified arguments as a discussion of "questions of yesterday and the day before yesterday"[25]. In exact sciences, in particular in theoretical physics, the discussion is never closed and is to be continued ad infinitum, even if there are proofs of theorems available. Regardless of the specific field of studies a minimal basic rule should be fulfilled in natural science, though, even if the scientific fields are methodically as far apart as physics and meteorology: At least among experts, the results and conclusions should be understandable or reproducible. And it should be strictly distinguished between a theory and a model on the one hand, and between a model and a scenario on the other hand, as clarified in the philosophy of science."

The above paper was severely criticized by Halpern et al. Gerlich and Tscheuschner responded to their critiques with the following:

International Journal of Modern Physics B, April 2010, Vol. 24, No. 10 : pp. 1333-1359
"Reply to "comment on 'falsification of the atmospheric CO2 greenhouse effects within the frame of physics' by Joshua B. Halpern, Christopher M. Colose, Chris Ho-Stuart, Joel D. Shore, Arthur P. Smith, Jörg Zimmermann https://doi.org/10.1142/S0217979210055573
Received: 12 March 2010

It is shown that the notorious claim by Halpern et al. recently repeated in their comment that the method, logic, and conclusions of our "Falsification Of The CO2 Greenhouse Effects Within The Frame Of Physics" would be in error has no foundation. Since Halpern et al. communicate our arguments incorrectly, their comment is scientifically vacuous. In particular, it is not true that we are "trying to apply the Clausius statement of the Second Law of Thermodynamics to only one side of a heat transfer process rather than the entire process" and that we are "systematically ignoring most non-radiative heat flows applicable to Earth's surface and atmosphere". Rather, our falsification paper discusses the violation of fundamental physical and mathematical principles in 14 examples of common pseudo-derivations of fictitious greenhouse effects that are all based on simplistic pictures of radiative transfer and their obscure relation to thermodynamics, including but not limited to those descriptions (a) that define a "Perpetuum Mobile Of The 2nd Kind", (b) that rely on incorrectly calculated averages of global temperatures, (c) that refer to incorrectly normalized spectra of electromagnetic radiation. Halpern et al. completely missed an exceptional chance to formulate a scientifically well-founded antithesis. They do not even define a greenhouse effect that they wish to defend. We take the opportunity to clarify some misunderstandings, which are communicated in the current discussion on the non-measurable, i.e., physically non-existing influence of the trace gas CO_2 on the climates of the Earth.[26] If we look at the GreenHouse Co_2 pseudo-science we will find a amazing attempt to predict or prophecy the future with a very weak scientific analysis tool for prophecy. Let us look at the data that has been gathered before it is "adjusted" or fudged where "weighing factors" are applied to the data points in an arbitrary and capricious manner. (view the Easterbrook YouTube referenced in the next section for graphs of the original data points.)

𝒮𝒸𝑒𝓃𝒶𝓇𝒾𝑜 𝒶𝓃𝒶𝓁𝓎𝓈𝒾𝓈 𝒶𝓈 𝒻𝒶𝓁𝓈𝑒 𝒫𝓇𝑜𝓅𝒽𝑒𝒸𝓎

Isaiah 25:1 "...Your councils of old are faithfulness and truth.
   What Creator-God creates he maintains....were in this too.

A fine scientists, Dr Don Easterbrook, in discussion the false science of CO_2 and the Global Warming hoax said:

Editorial Boards of the world will not even read a paper critical of CO_2 as a Cause of Global Warming".........like it is a "Religion of Climate". [https://www.YouTube.com/watch?v=ofXQdl1FDGk]

- From 1915 to 1945 there was global warming but no CO_2 increase. Conclude that warming can occur without an increase in CO_2.
- The model maximum effect just due to CO_2 is 0.1%..not meaningful.
- CO_2 is the result of global warming, not the cause.

- CO2 increase always follows an increase in temperature, it does not precede it.
- CO2 has risen eight 1/1000 of one percent, miniscule increases have a miniscule effect.
- CO2 rise is not correlated with changes in global temperature.
- Sea has risen about 6 inches in the past century, and continues at that slow rate probably due to increased volume of the 300 million cubic miles of ocean when it happens to warm.
- Only the south pole has an Ice cap and it is not melting. The average temp of Antarctica would have to rise 100 degrees to melt the ice cap....impossible.
- There is no ice cap on the north pole, the ice is about 3 to 4 feet thick.

Scenario analysis is from gaming theory. It has some mathematical underpinnings but it is essentially used as "curve fitting". We should ask how do the global weather people control errors, indeed how do they know they have committed an error. The assumption of uniformitarianism...things will be as they have been, which is a fallacy.

In the critique "The Fallacies of Scenario analysis"[27], the author tries to define the process as one of analyzing possible future events or series of actions by considering alternative possible outcomes (scenarios) The analysis is designed to allow:

".....rehearsing the future" sometimes to model the uncertain factors in the analysis. There is often ambiguous and ill-defined factors with little consensus about what the problem is.[28] In the last sense,.. it is a compromise between computational complex stochastic models and overly simplistic and often unrealistic deterministic models. Each scenario is a limited representation of the uncertain elements and one sub-problem is generated for each scenario." Often best case/worst case decision making for the purpose of investment... which ends up plotting two lines on a graph. The authors note that when you have a large number of correlated and non-correlated variables there is no way of finding out where you are on the probability distribution-unless you do a complete Monte Carlo simulation (start with a truly random position). "It is like being out in the woods at night without a map and compass-you know you are in the woods but not where." What I would like to see is a calculation of risk and cost. Is it being completely wrong, since the Paris agreement would cost the U.S. Trillions?

The biggest error in the modeling is the false assumption or presupposition that if CO2 increases therefore water vapor will increase with that increase. We know that CO2 only contributes 3% or 4% to "global warming". And the rest is mostly water vapor. So the greatest effect by far has nothing to do with CO2!!!

Is this an APPEAL FROM IGNORANCE (*argumentum ad ignorantiam*) assuming a claim is true because it has not been or cannot be proven false? Or is it a ECOLOGICAL FALLACY –inferences about a specific (WATER VAPOR) are based solely upon aggregate statistics collected for the group (Atmospheric gasses) to which those individuals belong. Or are they committing a LUDIC fallacy- the belief that the outcomes of non-regulated random occurrences can be encapsulated by a statistic; a failure to take into account unknown unknowns in determining the probability of events taking place.

In spite of these likely fallacious errors the most damning problem the modeling has is <u>it is not predictive</u>. The curve the models draw the past 15 years are not at all the path of reality. The satellite measures of temperature have not risen significantly.[29]

Imbedded false correlations and disinformation…their best guess is hidden so well that attempts to defend it fall short. For example:

Matthew Hudson's Washington Post review or Nov. 13, 2015. :Jamie Holms "The Power of Not Thinking" (Crown Books) "Holms might have mentioned, say, the documentary "Merchants of Doubt", which explored the strategy of equating the weather with the repair manual of an airplane."[30] The weather is a chaotic system which is compared to "an airplane", a non-chaotic system in which the physics is almost completely understood. This comparison is completely absurd on its face.

Most recent global warming studies are economic or financial cost studies that assume that we really know how to measure the average temperature of the globe accurately, which we don't. Satellite data is probably the best, but it changes minute to minute. The models are so crude. Bayesian logic requires a accurate database that shows an associated accurate prediction of future events. While it begins with some belief about the weather, the likelihoods or inferences are completely tied to the input data. If you cannot get an accurate average global temp, and there is no proven correlation between CO_2 and Warming, you look pretty foolish.

A British House of Lords member Lord Moncton provides the identification of a significant error in the IPCC (UN Intergovernmental Panel on Climate Change) climate modeling of greenhouse gas interaction with light photons. It turns out that the physics equation (initiated by Boltzman) for the molecular-photon interaction between CO_2 gas and infrared photons has a key parameter time constant of 1.6 picoseconds that is ignored in the small local model of a lab gas, but cannot be ignored in a column from the troposphere to the ground....the flaw in the atmosphere chemists model. The Error according to Lord Moncton is 40% or more in the sensitivity of earth's temperature to the increase in CO_2 atmospheric gas. This is supported by the fact that CO_2 concentration has increased the past 15 years but world mean temperature has not. (why they call it global "climate change" not 'warming' today). Since the Error is the radiative forcing function, it is a multiplier, increasing the equilibrium sensitivity way out of proportion to reality. If the atmosphere chemists do it correctly, they don't get the grant dollars and loose the power to be part of a one world government.(see https://www.youtube.com/watch?v=Ebokc6z82cg).

Moncton concluded at the Climate Conference at hartland.com " It's very easy to find excuses to depart from freedom and that is why the totalitarians have made up this "nonsense" (clever ruse of global warming).[31]

Monckton said at the Ideacity Conference in Toronto Canada June 18, 2014 ." The breaching the Berlin wall and the melting down the iron curtain marked not the end of totalitarianism, but the end of its confinement. The new menace to liberty is groupthink gone global. The globalization of groupthink is guilefully disguised under the green fig leaf of pietistic environmentalism. From behind that fig leaf, emerges today's tumescent totem of totalitarianism tyranny [32] of climate change."

The Future and the Hope in a Dark World

Winston Churchill teaching hope to a very distraught world on and August 24, 1941 afternoon by describing the British soldiers and American soldiers accompanying President Roosevelt at a critical meeting in World War II:

> "We had a church parade on the Sunday in our Atlantic bay. The President came on to the quarterdeck of the *Prince of Wales* where there were mingled together many hundreds of American and British sailors and marines. The warm misty sunshine plays on great ships which carry the white ensign or the stars and stripes. ... Human life is contrasted with the immutability of Him to whom a thousand ages past are but as yesterday and as a watch that is past in the night. We sang the sailors' hymn "For Those in Peril," and there are very many in peril on the sea. We sang "Onward, Christian Soldiers," and indeed I felt that this was no vain presumption, but that we had the right to feel that we were serving a cause for the sake of which a trumpet has sounded from on high.
>
> When I looked upon that densely packed congregation of the fighting men of the same language, of the same faith, of the same fundamental laws, of the same ideals and to a large extent of the same interests and certainly in different degrees facing the same dangers, it swept across me that here was the only hope, but also the sure hope, of saving the world from merciless degradation.

And so we came back across the ocean waves uplifted in spirit, fortified in resolve. Some American destroyers, which were carrying mails to the United States marines in Iceland, happened to be going the same way too, so we made a goodly company at sea together.

And when we were right out in mid-passage one afternoon a noble sight broke on the view. We overtook one of the convoys which carry the munitions and supplies of the New World to sustain the champions of freedom in the Old. The whole horizon-the whole broad horizon—seemed filled with ships. Seventy or eighty ships of all kinds and sizes, arrayed in fourteen lines, each of which could have been drawn with a ruler, hardly a wisp of smoke, not a straggler, but all bristling with cannon and other precautions on which I will not dwell, and all surrounded by their British escorting vessels, while overhead the far-ranging Catalina airboats soared, vigilant, protecting eagles in the sky.

And then I felt that hard and terrible and long-drawn-out as this struggle may be, we shall not be denied the strength to do our duty to the end." [33]

You cannot deny that the USA has enjoyed unprecedented blessing as a result of our past obedience to Creator-God. We called ourselves a "Judeo-Christian Nation" and told the world our civil rights came from God. That was the benefit we have enjoyed. We have never been conquered and do not speak German or Japanese or Italian or any foreign language or are required to bow to a foreign god our fathers did not know. Do we want Creator-God's continued blessings or will our nation go the way of all others who lost their sovereignty, their borders, and their freedom to tyrants.

Part 3. What this means in Education

Paul Blanchard (1923 – 2011), a signer of the A humanist Manifesto and a NEA (National Education Association) advocate notes:

"Johnie may not be able to read properly from high school but at least 12 years of public school education has divested his mind of religious superstition."

What has happened is truth has been replaced with cleverly devised fables, mystical terms like "Dark Matter", and "Dark Energy" and "Billions of Billions" to replace the Creator–God and his Word with another stealth religion .....that clever lawyers can argue and with certain expert witnesses to judges with no scientific research training (ie. No statistics or research design education to determine good/bad studies) allowing them to pass off this false idolatrous religion as "science" when there is no scientific support for Humanism as a science.

When Jesus said 2,000 years ago, "Father forgive them for they know not what they do!" That, in most cases is who the university Humanists/ Naturalists are today. They just don't understand. They are somewhere on the fringes of reality and afraid to look carefully at the Word of Creator-God. The "Physics of Creation" may be beyond our finding out because the "physics of maintaining this universe" is all we can observe today!! Strangely, many suspect this is so. But they do what they do because there is sin (offence to Creator-God) in their lives like all of us but they refuse to recognize it and its importance to their eternal life.... or even recognize eternal life. Sadness! Dear Student, do not follow their theology, please.

To be a religion, Humanism has to have been recognized as such. It has in the dicta of the supreme court case Torcaso v. Watkins in 1961. It must have a doctrine like that of the "Humanist Manifesto I and II" and the doctrine espoused by the NEA. To be hidden in a free society it must be miss-labeled and miss-filed under "secular" or non–religious and it must have institutions where it is taught. Mother–churches would be each misappropriated classroom we all pay for where even Christian, Jews, and others teach the doctrine deceived into believing it is both non–religious and not doctrine. Just who is violating the constitution? Humanism is a cult, defined "a doctrine that is completely exclusive" and is so big a lie that most of us did not believe anyone would front such a "non–truth" that is too big for us to see the forest for the trees, a mind– boggling blending of sacred and secular using a set of descriptors that no judge or jury could separate from truth or fictions...... "the encouragement of sensuality and sexual exploitation and of all things Creator–God tells us is an abomination". Not really different from those at the foot of Mount Sinai when Moses was away talking with Creator–God for 40 days. They worshipped the god Baal(the god of the intellect), as a golden calf and had some sort of orgy celebration near the beginning of the Exodus. Any moral absolutes and any Judeo-Christian ethic is banished from the schoolyard and replaced with secular Humanism, America's new religion.

The Bible points out in Roman 11:1-8 what happens to those who bow to idols. In the day of the Prophet Elijah, when King Ahab and his evil wife Jezebel were trying to take over Israel, Creator-God tells a fearful Elijah who feels alone that He has preserved 7,000 people for Himself, those that had not bent the knee to Baal. The judgment of those into idolatry was to loose their ability to hear, see, and turn from sin as a consequence of their own stubbornness. In short their hearts were hardened. Resisting Creator-God is like saying to Him "leave me alone". We should pray asking Creator-God for ears to hear and eyes to see with more openness and sensitivity to His calling and his Word......that is sensitivity training that has true value.

It's for the parent to teach this for our far-gone secular schools don't have the capacity for such meaningful instruction it seems.

Motive of the Public Education System of today: Political Correctness
"To achieve World Government, it is necessary to remove from the minds of men their individualism, loyalty to family traditions, national patriotism, and religious dogmas!" [34]

Conclusion

"Their sorrows shall be multiplied who hasten after another god..."[Ps 16:4]

The teaching of a nation that brings the nation into idolatry, creates a nation in bondage. And a nation in bondage no longer has the protection of Creator-God or "God shedding his grace on thee", as we sing the anthem. Are we forgetting that today we live in a very spiritually hostile world?.

Once your teacher has pounded "multiculturalism" in to your head *ad nausium*, and defined morality and ethics as culturally based, you find yourself or your child with no sense of "ought"...unable to see that for oughtness to exist, there must be what Ravi Zacharias calls an ontic reference (factual reference", or an ultimate authority from which oughtness is referenced or grounded. Secularism thinkers operate in a void, and lead the world down a path to the destruction of moral relativism. It is worth repeating the statements of Robert Fitch in "The Obsolescence of Ethics: Christianity and Crisis":

"Ours is an age where ethics has become obsolete. It is superseded by science, deleted by philosophy and dismissed as emotive by psychology. It is drowned in compassion, evaporates into aesthetics and retreats before relativism. The usual moral distinctions between good and bad are simply drowned in a maudlin emotion in which we feel more sympathy for the murderer than for the murdered, for the adulterer then for the betrayed, and in which we have actually begun to believe that the real guilty party, the one who somehow caused it all, is the victim, and not the perpetrator of the crime.[35]

This book was an attempt to identify those gods. Their identity is enormously deceptive but they have plagued mankind since day one. You may be surprised where they may be found; we even hide them in our heart and fail to recognize them. Who of you, dear reader wants his sorrows to be multiplied? Walk away from them! Open the bible at the book of John, and as you read it, ask the Holy Spirit to teach you the one true Creator-God. Eternity is staring you in the face!

Our universities and their faculty have the potential to save this nation. Is there any more wonderful potential for anything as that? While in the past it has created such havoc in the spiritual universe, there is hope for the future. I pray this book is not seen as a gauntlet or a empty slap in the face but instead an "eye opening" for the potential to raise up a generation in love with the One that knit them together in the womb, maker of the stars to shine, and maintainer of the very space we occupy, One who has a special place for each one of us with a new perfect body, mind, and spirit that can live into eternity with Him. Remember, He would that none would be lost!

Division in our world, our nation and the campus

Why do we have such division between the Christian and so many teachers and faculty? Why such division in out nation and among the nations. Vince Vitalii has found the answer and its simple.[36] When we sing, " the LORD is a strong tower," we are describing reality. Only in Jesus Christ reside both Truth and Agape-Love...only in Him, our Maker. Not 'truth is greater than love.' Not 'love is greater than truth. .Creator-God is Love (1John 4:8), and Creator-God is Truth (John 14:6). Therefore, Love is Truth and Truth is Love. Jesus teaches us there is no choice between Love and Truth. And He is the only One. And that, " love that is not truth is not love. And truth that is not love is not truth".[37] Any distance from Him is a separation from the two; so many claim they have the truth but show no agape-love; those who claim they have love but are without the truth. If man is always in this universe with only partial knowledge....partial truth as we have shown, and he knows that is true he must seek coherent understanding that he is somewhat remote from the center of truth and agape-love, Creator-God Himself.

If you have accepted Jesus Christ as your savior and trust in Him as the only <u>locus </u>of truth and agape-love, you need not fear evil. As a co-inheritor of the universe there is no need to strive against anyone or any concept. Begin at the center, remain at the center and be comforted.

To repeat my position from the prolog, This nation needs a mighty educational system....and a mighty academy of its universities and colleges that can train our children to think logically, to seek the truth, and learn in environments where the "enterprise of ideas campus " includes the words and ideas given to us by Creator-God...one that respects and does not denigrate the Bible. Respects true science and identifies what is not known by man. After all, who founded the universities in the first place? One thing is for sure, Creator-God is in the business of forgiveness. Asking Him for forgiveness is a start!

The New Atheism-Humanism

Robert Morey speaks to us in his work "The new atheism and erosion of freedom". When we battle with the new atheism we will come across 7 false suppositions that are absurd on their face:

1. Everything ultimately came from nothing (absurd)
2. Order came from Chaos (impossible by 2nd law of thermodynamics)
3. Harmony came from disorder (..   ..   ..)
4. Life came from non-life.   (..   ..   ..)
5. Reason came from irrationality. (impossible)
6. Personality came from non-personality (impossible)
7. Morality came from amorality.[38]

Remember the nexus of Truth and Agape-love reside only in One location. (all science, all good, all joy, all peace, all Love) Our Creator-God. Resolution Awaits!. Eternity Awaits!

Dear student, if you are a careful listener, you should be able now to hear the idolatry preached from the lectern, identify it as idolatry and protect your heart and mind from it.

Awake "O Sleeper
May You Participate in the Devine Nature of
Creator-God
Our Death is His, His Life is Ours
(Why would anyone seek another god)[39]

—⚭—

George Washington wrote in a circular letter to the states June 14, 1783 when he was ready to resign his commission:

"I now make it my upmost prayer, that God would have you, and the State over which you preside, in his holy protection, that he would incline the hearts of the Citizen to cultivate a spirit of subordination and obedience to Government, to entertain a brotherly affection and love for one another, for their fellow Citizens of the United States at large, and particularly for their brethren who have served in the Field, and finally, that he would most graciously be pleased to dispose us to do Justice, to love mercy, and to demean ourselves with the Charity, humility and pacific temper of mind, which were Characteristics of the Divine Author of our blessed Religion, and without a humble imitation of whose example in these things, we can never hope to be a happy Nation."

- **Acceptance-**Embracing people for who they are, not necessarily for what they say or do. (**NOT** the postmodern definition: Endorsing and even praising others for their beliefs and lifestyle choices.) [1]
- **Agape-**Greek for self-sacrificing Love. The love a husband is to have for his wife, willing to die for her and to give up what is important to him for her. Notice love is not a " mere feeling" but ACTIONS. The kind of love Creator-God has for man in giving up the life of his only begotten Son (Himself) so that man can live forever by accepting this incredible gift. Christ's love for his Bride, the Church. Once you understand the Agape Creator-God has for you, you will agape Him and become a child of the "most high God".
- **Angels-**Angelic Creatures individually created by God for his service.
- **Arian Controversy-** First occurred when the theological teaching of Arius of Alexandria Egypt claimed that Jesus was not God but a created being. Resolved at the Council of Nicaea in 325AD, which affirmed that Jesus is God of the Father-Son-Holy Spirit Trinity. All religions that deny this (ie. Unitarian, Jehovah Witness, Islam, etc.) therefore are worshipping an idol that is not the one true Creator-God but a god man has invented.
- **Babylonianism-**They involve a seeking of earthly power or status gained by religious authority. That is Babylonianism. That is what first arose in the city by the Euphrates -- a search for earthly power and glory by religious means. The Tower of Babel was built unto heaven, and the people said, "We will make a name for ourselves." That is Babylonianism. (Ray Steadman)
- **Christianity-**Begins with a relationship with Creator-God with those He has created through their acceptance of his gift of Himself, His Son Jesus Christ, sacrificed for their sin (missed the mark) against Him. His word is the Bible that is God-breathed through the 40 writers of these 66 books that is an integrated message

system from outside of time published in more than 5 billion copies throughout the world. We are without excuse when we walk away from His Gift of Himself for our redemption. Christians recognize that Jesus Christ is Creator-God, a Trinity of Father-Son-Holy Spirit.....The One and only God.

- **Cosmos-** Organized System, a cosmos is an orderly or harmonious system. It originates from the Greek term κόσμος (*kosmos*), meaning "order".

- **Creator-God-**The One who created time, space, the heavens, the earth and all things. Who loves us so much He has written the Bible as "God Breathed" through 60 authors to describe himself to us. He validates His word by telling us what will happen before it happens, showing us He exists outside of time. He has published His word throughout a dark world 5 Billion times at least. He tells us we are in three parts, a body, spirit and soul and his word is food for our spirit We are here for knowledge and understanding, His good pleasure, realizing we must turn from our self-centered wicked ways and worship Him in spirit and in truth....to be redeemed from death by the complete work of His only Son Jesus (the one called the Messiah). He demands we turn from our wicked ways, accept the incredible gift He has given us for complete payment for our sins by Messiah and worship and serve no other gods. He said He has searched heaven and found no other God. (If we could completely understand Him with our water based brains He would not be Creator God.) If we don't know why we weigh anything or what an electron and a photon are we are most likely at the early beginning of understanding what he has created.

- **Culture-** a meaning system that tells us what to do. Science does not give value systems or tell us what to do so beliefs are central... explicit value system. Once we wake up and put our feet on the floor, the grand descriptive science has nothing to say to tell us what to do, while our cultural beliefs do.

- **Deconstructionism**-A philosophy that has infected most of our institutions. It teaches that words have no objective content and therefore words have no truth. Therefore, if truth cannot be assigned to words, then we can make words mean anything we want them to. We no longer have to be concerned with objective truth, with true truth. Each of us can invent our own truth, our own reality; I can lie and call it truth if it gets me what I want. We can deconstruct the Word or Logos of Creator-God (the Bible) and empty it of all truth....so the words of Jesus would make no sense to deconstructionists......they say the wisdom of this world cancels out the Logos of God, portraying the Word of God as empty and meaningless. "You have your truth," says the wisdom of this world, "and I have my truth.....so don't you dare impose your truth on me!".[2]

- **Devolution**Negative evolution seems to be occurring in which many species are losing in their fitness. There is no evidence that mankind is not losing some of his smarts either. Notice how few Newton's and Einstein's are appearing. It now seems it takes a group not an individual to see new things that others have not seen. If as some speculate, we have 200 errors/generation in the Human genome one can wonder how long the devolution will continue. It is obvious to a Christian that our Creator-God would not allow things to continue that long...the point where we could no longer comprehend Him with our water-based brain.

- **Demon**-Behind every False-god is a Demon, one of the third of the angles of heaven who fell with the Father of Lies, Lucifer. Part of the Principalities and Powers mankind is at war with that the Jewish Messiah will remove at his coming.

- **Dewey, John**-rejected both Creator-God and the Bible in favor of Darwinian Evolution and pragmatic Humanism. He may have written a significant part of the Humanist Manifesto. Many (and the NEA) see him as the father of public education in the USA. He did all he could to remove the idea of the "good and moral" behavior prescribed by Creator-God for an "Experimental method that treats norms as hypothesis to be tested, in light of their widest consequences for everyone."[see:http:plato.stanford.edu/entries/dewey-moral/] Refusing to recognize that man and Dewey himself had a black heart with dark intent against the Word of Creator-God, he opened up American Society to such totally bogus works as the "Kinsey Report of the sexual practices" (disseminated by Playboy Magazine) of what he claimed was the American Population when Kinsey had in fact studied a most bizarre and non-representative population. One is reminded of Dave Kerouac's "On The Road: the Beat Generation" of the late fifties where we were encouraged to experiment to find the path. However experimental education never finds peace anymore than discontent. Dewey can be quoted on both side of key educational arguments. For him nothing was constant, given, or finally true (an enemy of true science). Instead " all things were pragmatic, adaptable, and subject to whatever reinterpretation seemed appropriate for the day and the hour". [Breese, Dave. Seven men who ruled the world from the grave". Moody publishers, Chicago, 1990, p157] Dewey said schools were for the production of "social change". They have obviously adopted his teaching! He implied he would move the world away from the supernatural or Creator-God. Dewey, the preacher of this strange religion has indeed done that.

- **Evolution**- a unstable theory or better an unsubstantiated conjecture about the past treated incorrectly as a theory of everything best characterized as containing 2 hidden terms; 1) Genetic Adaptation-which best fits the data as slow changes over time within species. and 2) Speciation-the creation of all species from one species after the spontaneous generation of life from dead matter, requiring the contradiction that:

RANDOM = INFORMATION, which cannot be understood by anybody and is therefore the basis of many belief systems or religions invented by humans since the time of Nimrod in Babylon.

- **Evolutionary Conservation**- about 200 genetic errors occur spontaneously in each generation, randomly changing the amino acid sequences of proteins. Individuals with mutations that impair critical functions of proteins may have resulting problems that make them less able to reproduce. Harmful mutations are lost from the gene pool because the individuals carrying them reproduce less effectively. Over time, only harmless (or very rare beneficial) mutations are maintained in the gene pool. This is evolution (actually devolution). However the frequency of beneficial mutations has always been observed to be 0 or negative, creating a very big problem for the 19th century humanistic theory. Truth is slain in the streets!

- **Epistemology of TRUTH**-The concern is regards truth and lies or something masquerading as truth that is not. We must begin with the identification of truth to have any truth at all. Truth had a beginning as did Lies.

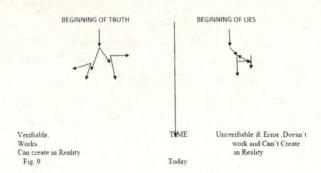

BEGINNING OF TRUTH   BEGINNING OF LIES

Verifiable,   TIME   Unverifiable & Error ,Doesn't
Works   work and Can't Create
Can create in Reality   in Reality
Fig. 9   Today

- **False-gods**-idols that steal the honor and glory due Creator-God causing us to face the destruction of both out souls and bodies. Will find their fate in the bottomless pit and the lake of fire.
- **Fallen Angels**- about 1/3 of Creator-God's individually created angels chose to follow Lucifer-Satan. They are angels of the darkness, demonic forces in ranks called principalities and powers directed by their leader Satan and behind all false gods and idols. Will find the fate in the bottomless pit and the lake of fire.
- **Final Reality**-Either 1. An infinite Creator-God.

  Or 2. Material and energy which has always existed, shaped into its present form only by pure chance. Where there is no meaning for life, no value system, and no basis for law and therefore man must be the measure of all things leading to Humanist idolatry.
- **First Cause**- What initiated the beginning. First motion of creation.
- **Freedom**- Being free to do what you know you ought to do. (**NOT** the postmodern definition: Being able to do anything you want to do.) [1]
- **gene regulatory sequence**-A part of a DNA molecule that binds a gene regulatory protein.

- **Genetic adaptation** –Long term within species genetic changes in response to the environment. Complete agreement with the data exists. The accepted half of the theory of evolution. See: speciation
- **Genotype**-The fundamental genetic constitution of an organism comprising genes from both parents.
- **highly conserved**-Term used to characterize proteins that has little differences within the animal kingdom. Presumably because of their fundamental importance for the life of cells.
- **homeostasis**-The maintenance of uniformity or stability in the organism by coordinated physiological processes (usually negative feedback control systems).It appears 800 or more constants, and parameters are operating here.
- **Humanism**-The man is the measure of all things. If the Final Reality is "Material and energy" always existing, shaped into its present form only by pure chance. Contrast with a Final Reality in which there is an infinite Creator-God (as in Christianity). [Francis A. Schaeffer]
- **Humanist Idolatry**- Where the final Reality is material and energy which has always existed, shaped into its present form only by pure chance. Where there is no meaning for life, no value system, and no basis for law and therefore man must be the measure of all things.
- **Idolatry**-Anything that removes or detracts from the glory of the one true God----the Creator of everything. More specifically, Paying obeisance to or worshipping in any way or attributing to something else that which is due God.
- **Information**-something that people can learn, know about, and understand. It does not occupy space or weight anything and is thus outside of time, yet may be time-stamped or time-limited somehow. The key to the value of information is its veracity or truth. Note that a empty DVD and a DVD with gigabytes of information weigh the same yet the information has changed the disk. Creator-God tells us that heaven and earth will pass away but His (Jesus)

Word will exist forever.[Matt 24:35] Indicating the staying power of the Truth.

- **Intron**-segment of a non-coding DNA in a eukaryotic gene that is transcribed but is then excised from the primary transcript. Also called intervening sequence.
- **Junk DNA**-an evolutionary term referring to a region of DNA for which no known function has been found. However Embryologically active segments are starting to be discovered raising doubts on the empty evolutionary term.
- **Lie**-a known falsehood, usually given to deceive.
- **Love** The word "love" as taught usually has a deceptive meaning similar to that described by the Oxford Universal Dictionary (1933) "in the U.S. a frequent vulgarism for "like". That we should use the same word for ice cream that we use for our wife or child or Creator-God demonstrates a major weakness in the English language. Look at the definition above of "**Agape**" and see what we mean. Jesus taught us that the entire law is based on 2 "loves". The love of Creator-God and the love of our neighbor. However the word is best represented by the Greek word Agape. That love is not "feelings" but ACTIONS.
- **Materialism**-The doctrine that material reality is the ONLY reality. As defined by California's Willie Brown, "If I can't eat it, wear it, drive it, or make love to it I'm not interested it". In essence noting that if I can't actually see it, touch it, or make use of it in some way then it doesn't exist. It's all just neurons firing in your cortex and spinal column and there is no "mystery" to life, "its all basic and scientific." A manner of expression indicating a total lack of spiritual understanding or concern. The doctrine of Materialism cannot be proven. Unfortunately it is not a scientific conclusion but a scientific presupposition not discovered in nature but imposed upon nature and therefore an article of FAITH! Apparently because there is no math yet invented to represent something non-material,

scientists are afraid to address it. Yet most humans believe non-material exists.

- **Moral Judgments**-Certain things are morally right and wrong as determined by Creator-God. (**NOT** the postmodern definition: We have no right to judge another person's view or behavior.) [1]

- **Nature**- The physical component of Creator-God's Creation comprising the entire universe and its physical makeup and the laws that govern its physical operation along with its imbedded control systems. It is below or inferior to His spiritual Creation, which is not immediately discernible by our water based brains.

- **Natural Selection**- Implying a "selector" as a deception designed to replace the creationists "Divine Watchmaker" with what is supposed to be an impersonal force like a ghost that is an external agency of some type that disintegrates under scrutiny...unless Darwin gave "selection" omnipotent power embarrassing evolutionists in the process.

- **Naturalism**- The doctrine that nature is all there is. The doctrine of Naturalism cannot be proven. Unfortunately, it is not a scientific conclusion but a scientific presupposition not discovered in nature but imposed upon nature and therefore an article of FAITH! ! Apparently because there is no math yet invented to represent something non-material, scientists are afraid to address it. Yet most humans believe non-material exists.

- **NIMROD**- Noah's grandson, Ham's son. First man given the title king or Moleck and deified as Marduk which degenerated to many pagan god names ie. Enki, Apsu, Astalluhii, Acsculapius, Chinon/Centar, Tital/Atlas, Bel/Baal, Nabul/Nebo, Apollo/Nabul, Hermes, Mars, Orion, Ninus, was claimed to be reincarnated in Astarte's (Semiramis) womb to Tammuz.

- **Noah**- A man, who along with his wife and three sons and their wives are the progenitors of all living today. Chosen by Creator-God to perpetuate mankind and witness to those that follow of His marvelous work. The world no doubt had many millions, perhaps billions of people and a culture that had willfully walked away from their Creator filling the earth with "violence". Creator-God hit the reset button and the enormous reserves of water hidden in the earth as well as 40 days of deluge flooded the entire earth such that we find sea shells on Mt. Everest. The mass of water greatly interacted with plate tectonics and magnetic phenomena to change the world to the form we see today.[Google John Baumgardner PhD, noted in the US News and World Report as "the world's preeminent expert in the design of computer models for geophysical convection". [Burr, Chandler. 8 June, 1997 "The geophysics of God: a scientists embraces plate tectonics-and Noah's flood" pp55-58]]

- **Pantheism-** The belief that God is everything or all things are God! Identified as a Heresy and contrary to the Bible.
- **Personal Preference-**Preferences of color, food, clothing style, hobbies, etc., are personally determined.(**NOT** the postmodern definition: Preferences of sexual behaviors, value systems, and beliefs are personally determined.) [1]
- **Personal Rights-**Everyone has the right to be treated justly under the law.(NOT the postmodern definition: Everyone has the right to do what he or she believes is best for himself.) [1]
- **Progress-**(A) improved quality of life through scientific discovery and application. Does not involve, and may indeed interfere with soul and spirit progress and peace. Wealth can possibly cause a person mistakenly to rely upon his resources rather then commune with his Maker, leading to his complete destruction in the end.(B) in terms of evolutionary progress, falsely labeled scientific progress, a religious Humanistic belief that organisms trend toward improvement or "better" above their given genetic capacity to adapt to a environment through "evolution". That mankind is getting "better and better" is not supported on moral terms at all. War, strife, and conflict is not changing since the beginning of time. If a man or woman finds himself with Creator-God at the end of time then he/

she has indeed progressed toward eternal life, something that can be known assuredly in this life if He becomes "Born Again" by the action of the Holy Spirit of Creator-God [John 3:5].

- **Question of Science**-a question that is or can be falsifiable by objective evidence, observable, with non-contradiction in its logic of inquiry. True Science describes reality and is not a part of the description of the Creation of Creator-God. These questions are limited to physical reality, with no tools to describe non-physical reality or unobservable events. If events are unobservable, then only "best guess" or Abduction the lowest level of logic can be applied and testing will be nonexistent, leading to error or a high probability of misleading statements and description.

- **Question of Theology**-inquiring about Creator-God (*Theos*) or the study of His writings. Christianity describes the Word or the Logos as The Christ. For the Word became flesh and dwelt among us. (John 1:1) The Creator of the universe can get the ink on the page correct. ie. The original writing of the Bible is without error and is timeless for "He comes in the volume of a book" and is not to be taken lightly.

- **Random**- without informational content. Helpful in working with probability as a reference for no relationship, pattern, predictability, or purpose. In random selection, equal probability of being selected is considered random assignment.

- **REALITY**- Things as they actually exist. Especially as described by one in a position to describe things as they are, namely Creator-God.

- **Respect**-Giving due consideration to others beliefs and lifestyle choices without necessarily approving them. (**Not** the postmodern definition: Wholeheartedly approving of others' beliefs or lifestyle choices) [1]

- **Relative Truth**-Denies that the human mind has the capacity to arrive at Real Truth or absolute truth. Since Jesus Christ said he "was the Truth", relative truth denies Him, and thereby prevents accepting Him and His gift of eternal life. A fatal flaw in life...a very fatal flaw in thinking leading to moral relativism and the acceptance of things that are an abomination to Creator-God who defines what is right and good and moral for all mankind. Relative truth is given many descriptors by anthropologists and sociologists in a blind attempt to remain neutral when describing a culture, leading to the false conclusion that what is true depends on the culture or the person, a fatal flaw in logic. An individual believing he can make up his own good and morality, believes himself a god.

- **Religion-** A set of beliefs, actions, and emotions, both personal and corporate, organized around the concept of an <u>Ultimate Reality</u>. This Reality may be understood as a unity or a plurality, personal or non-personal, divine or not, and so forth, differing from religion to religion. [Peterson, Michael William Hasker, Bruce Reichenbach, and David Basinger. "Reason and Religious Belief: An Introduction to the Philosophy of Religion", NY: Oxford Univ. Press, 1991, p4 Italics removed]

- **Satan-Lucifer-**Lucifer, the name given to the angel second only to Creator-God, and initially head angel "lightbearer", son of the morning in Isaiah 14:12 who said he will be "like the Most High "endowed with the privilege and responsibility of self-determination---Creator-Gods gift of "free will" changed through Pride in himself by centering his wisdom and understanding on himself and not Creator-God.... is called Satan and the Devil (and 40 other titles) becoming Creator-God's Adversary who will face final judgment and be destroyed in the end along with about 1/3 of the angels created initially. It appears there is a demon, a servant of Satan's, behind each idol. In contrast, "Holy" Angles are "ministering spirits to the Heirs of Salvation (Heb 1:14)" of Creator-God that interact so wonderfully with man and the children. Much of this operation in the spiritual realm is veiled to us but the fact is that Satan endeavors to defeat Christ's earthly ministry but Jesus Triumphed over him and over the darkness of this world will play out as we come to the end of time or end of the age. When we live our lives in pain and suffering and what seems with few gifts from Creator-God yet still honor and Love Him, we are as Job, executing the greatest Honor of our Maker and proving Satan a lier.

- **Secular-**(A) of this world (not of Creator-God)
  (B) excluding religion. If religion refers to all theology in which the god worshipped requires man to do acts and rituals to gain his/her favor and thereby win heaven as a consolation; but if it includes Christianity as a non-religion but a "relationship" with Creator-God then this form of secular has value to mankind! Originally a religious word, "secular" priests lived outside the convent.

- **Speciation** – generation of new species from an original species. No agreement on this process exists. No observations and no convincing data to support. An unsubstantiated conjecture about the past. The first half of the so called theory of evolution. See: genetic adaptation

- **Theistic Religion-**Man's attempt to reach up to God by various means ie. rites, sacrifices, etc. Contrast with Christianity: Creator-God reaching down to man by offering His only Son Jesus as payment for our sins against Him…therefore Christianity is a <u>relationship</u> and to be distinguished from all other religions. It could be that it is misclassified as a religion intentionally by those misdirecting their students or as a administrative convenience

- **TOLERANCE-** Accepting others without agreeing with or sharing their belief or lifestyle choices. (**not** the postmodern definition: Accepting that each individual's beliefs, values, lifestyles, and truth claims are equal)[1]

- **TRUTH-** An absolute standard of right and wrong, correct and incorrect. (NOT the postmodern definition: Whatever is right for you) [1]

- **Violence of today and Noah's day.** Genesis 6:11 the Hebrew word for "violence" refers elsewhere to a broad range of crimes that include unjust treatment, injurious legal testimony, cruelty, cruel hatred, deadly assault, murder, and rape.

- **World View**-consists of our most basic assumptions or presuppositions about reality. They cannot be proved by something else because they are the most foundational. We usually hold them to be unquestionable.

- **Worship**-"worship" To honor or revere as a supernatural being or power or as a holy thing; to adore with appropriate acts, rites, or ceremonies…to regard with extreme respect or devotion (1720). To salute, bow down to −(1737). To invest with or raise to honor or repute; to confer honor or dignity upon-(1601)[Universal Oxford dictionary 1933]

- **Zarathustra**-Friedrich Nietzsche's name for the first Zoroaster or Nimrod who introduced the concept of the Ubermensch or "superman" in his book "Thus Spake Zarathustra" considered the forerunner of modern existential thought.

- **ZPE**-Background energy or "zwitterbewegung" Zero Point Energy found once all heat is removed from space. Suggested by Richard Feynman as equal to the *Energy Density within an atom 10^{98}-10^{114} ergs per cubic centimeter.* Say our sun radiates energy at the rate of 3.8×10^{20} watts. Our galaxy has > 100 billion stars that may average the size of our sun, so the total radiant energy expended by our galaxy for 1 million years is the energy somehow locked up in 1cc of space. Continuously input into the 1 cc of space from what source? How many cc' s do you occupy? Here we are operating before the face of Creator-God? If a identical signal is coming from ALL directions, a sensor will report no signal.

Appendix

Candlelight on the campus: written the evening of 9/11/01

The students met today on campus for the candlelight vigil. The electronic mails and the emergency notices in the student paper had called the ones in pain together. All over America the campuses were slowly responding. As I scanned my inbox quickly there was the note from Scotty calling the members of the faculty and staff Christian group to attend. Of the 5 members I spotted 4 quickly from my vantage point beside the University president. A man ever so sensitive to those under his care. His face was very glum and he was feeling the deep pain from the students as they spoke into the outdoor loudspeaker system, holding a small votive candle in a paper bowl.

The students came to the mike slowly, some eagerly, some haltingly, but always with a sensitivity to the enormous event that had just happened. One after the other they expressed feelings and deep, deep signs of the pain, vulnerability, and outrage that the world they had been taught to know was now in question. Many mentioned God, but all realized this title was to be spoken at but not spoken to. This was after all the property of the State of California and we have laws here and a campus street named after the Chief Justice Earl Warren, the man who presided over the Smithsonian Institution and Museum so many years, over Roe v. Wade, and the removal of this title (God) from the American public schools. Never mind that the first of the week, the notice came from the TV networks, in order to compete with cable, they will blaspheme of the name of God and Jesus Christ in their programming, clearly a financial decision.

My heart raced, my throat grew dry, was any faculty secure enough with tenure and retirement to speak out….. more so then the University Faculty in Germany in 1935. Was truth held hostage in America in 2001? Student after student spoke. The word I heard over and over, could it possibly be Hitler Speak…… " Tolerance", we must be tolerant and 'don't be hateful'. If there was so much tolerance why was I afraid to speak what I felt was the truth.

My thoughts jumped to my own classroom where the class came to me that afternoon and asked, "We want to know what you think professor?" The previous lecture and discussion on the Scientific method in clinical research, included a discussion of the difference between coherent truth and correspondent truth. Coherent truth, where reality is not a requirement but coherent thought only, so it all sticks together with a theory and excludes any mystery such as grandma knew all about, that is God. I rattled off the greatest scientists from Kepler, Newton, Mendel, and Virchow all the way down to C. Everet Koop as teachers of the Correspondence theory of truth, where truth must correspond to reality and no invented global theory (or gigantic lie) is allowed to fill in the unknown. We showed how the Kinsey Report as representative of a global lie, not anything of science, but a paper with a false hidden agenda. So now, in the middle of the campus, I was stuck. I had to speak to this crowd, I must lay out my thoughts.

Suddenly a giant Bowing 767 Fed-X Jet flew right over the campus, very low but straight, very straight thank you God. My thoughts raced....... prepare your thoughts....speak your heart! So I planned:

1. Do I start with Abraham, whose name is <u>Great</u> for all Jews, Moslems, and Christians?
2. Do I lay out the spiritual reality of Paul's writings in Ephesians 6, after all he was an academic, held the equivalent of 2 PhD's before he was 23. Gamaliel, the greatest teacher of his time couldn't find enough books for him to read. I'll give the intro from _____ We wrestle not against flesh and blood but against principalities and powers_____against dark forces in high places. The facts I had to speak from were that my country was confronted with 4 fiery darts from hell. Will they see that a 767 flying full throttle with thousands of tons of fuel guided by Satan himself as a fiery dart. The twin towers already had burned that into all our minds so I'll go with it.

3. Point out that Abraham's faith was attributed to him as righteousness. Ephesians 6 lays out how to protect ourselves. A nation and a people that has a 'Shield of Faith", a righteous people, will be protected from the fiery darts of hell it says. It seems that 3 or more brave men dropped one of those fiery darts but the other 3 struck deep into the heart and mind of America. We all died a whole lot. Are we only 25% righteous and 25% faithful. We must raise the shield, one American at a time. The moral standard up to 1962 and the Warren court must be reintroduced...but those I am about to speak to have benefited (they think) so greatly from this deception. They are comfortable pursuing pleasure, Roe v. Wade will save them. They believe in relative truth...the coherent type that makes them the judge of morality. Jesus himself called judges 'gods' with a little g. They are responsible to which authority? Only the ones that don't know what the student is doing and thinking as a mighty God would and does. America suggests by its images that they pursue all that is pleasurable and fun, sex is good, lust is even better. We can flood our conscious discerning mind with vision of all sorts of input, 70,000 murders, 1,000,000 adulteries and endless food for my flesh. But, my unconscious mind is NOT discerning in the least. It feeds at night and all times probably on every latent thought and image without discernment. It drives my neuroendocrine center and the sympathetic fibers that can send my heart into such disorder that I die of sudden death. Susceptibility to disease of all sorts is clearly affected, especially chronic ones.

4. Man is driven to find a cure for a disease that is destroying him and mankind. What hides this disease from our laboratories, the Earl Warren court's rulings, I doubt it. The deception is almost complete. The lie is protected by the law of the land.....shields down to 25%... will the rapture, the "snatching up" remove the 25%? (don't tell Bin Laden) I can't say this, these students live with their feelings, half their professors' notes were written by the deceiver himself. Many of the fathers of disciplines on campus believed that

God will not be needed once man discovers everything and man in essence will be master of his destiny, man will become god (at least till he dies, since he is just a animal). Pardon me but isn't that a quote from Satan's words. Sin as a word has been erased from the campus because recognition that we are all sinners and in great need of a savior is the first part of becoming a Christian. Spiritual things to the natural man are foolishness. Is that true while our nation lies prostrate, or will this be different?

5. How do I convey to the students my surprise that one who stays so hidden would be willing to expose himself to detection with such a bold act as the September 11th attack. Satan is bold because his time is short. How do I convey the Gospel of a loving savior? That all of us have lied let alone violated his first precept to love Him with all their heart mind and soul....they know his title but don't even know his name. Have all these students demeaned a man (sworn in his name) Jesus Christ whom even the Koran says is without sin and therefore by the words of Jesus, committed murder. Have we lusted in a way that commits adultery. Hay, forget all the sensational sin's, we all deserve the fiery darts of destruction and 100 zillion years in a place we aren't even designed to be. Hell wasn't made for *homo sapiens* it won't be nice even for Bin Laden. The Lord would that no one would perish.

6. Time to bring out the word that begins John's teachings.
    He wrote, In the beginning was the Word and the Word was God.......and the word became flesh and blood and dwelt with us. Isn't that referring to the Hebrew Messiah?
    Even the Qur'an calls him the Messiah, naming Him (Isa) 94 times (while Mohammad is only named 4 times). We all agree!

7. I don't know why a life must pay for violating his precepts, it's one of his laws, like gravity, but in the dimensions of our motivator (our R2 unit doesn't just have a broken motivator, it's not been born yet....it's still pre-natal). What part of the student do I speak to

about this. Will it just be me, all proud because I know something they don't know, the professors cross.

8. But if the Holy Spirit (that Jesus sent to comfort us when he moved to the throne of the universe) is blanketing America now, they already know this and my words are only confirming to their conscious mind.

The mike is free, this is my chance God willing, to speak. But wait professor, I don't believe it… the Indian funeral drum chant just began. A hymn that will not offend the university has taken center stage. I have failed, like so many of the German Professors in 1933, Global amnesia will set in and I will be forever silent on campus. As the smoke rises.

Introduction

1. RC Sproul Jr [R.C. Sproul, Jr.]

2. Sproul,RC "Right Now Counts Forever: Our story" in TableTalk, The Heart of the Gospel April,2017.p4.

3. Ibid p5

4. Peck, M. Scott ."People of the Lie:The hope for healing human evil". P78,NewYork: Touchstone Simon and Schuster, 1983

5. Peck, M. Scott ."People of the Lie:The hope for healing human evil". P78,NewYork: Touchstone Simon and Schuster, 1983

6. Barna Research, Sept 11, 2006. https://www/barna.org/research

7. Romans 1:22 New King James Version. Thomas Nelson. Nashville, 1994

8. Sproul, RC.Tabletalk 38(3)p4].

9. Sproul, RC.Tabletalk 38(3)p4].

10. 10 Sproul, R.C. Tabletalk 38:(3) pp4-5

11. [2Timothy 4:3 New Living translation]

12. Ravi Zacharias "The end of Reason" , p16, Zondervan 2008 Grand Rapids.

13. Habakkuk 2:18

14. Courson, Jon. Application Commentary Vol. 2:Psalms-Malachi;p543. Nelson Ref. and electronics, 2006 Copyright© 2006 by Jon Coursen. Used by permission of Thomas Nelson. www.thomasnelson.com.All rights reserved.

Chapter 1: The Creator-God of the Bible vs Ancient gods

1. Sproul, RC Jr.

2. NASA. https:// jwst.nasa.gov [accessed 6/23/17]

3. Craig, William Lane . (answers given by William Lane Craig ,Talbot school of Theology on John Ankerberg show on 3/13/2016)

4. Sproul, RC, *The Holiness of God (Scripture Press Foundation, 1986), 38.*

5. Putoff, H.E. "Physics Review D." Vol 35⊗10), May 10, 1987.

6. Owen, John." The Works of John Owen 1669", edited by William H Goold, first published by Johnstone and Hunter 1850–1853. Reprinted by The Banner of Truth Trust, Edinburgh 1965. ." [for a full copy of John Owen's book see: http://www.ntslibrary.com/PDF%20Books/John%20Owen%20Vindication%20Doctrine%20of%20Trinity.pdf

7. Ironsides, H.A. "Revelation" p31, Kregel reprint 2004. Grand Rapids.

8. Barnhouse, Donald Grey, "The invisible War", pp207-208,Zondervan, Grand Rapids

9. Einstein, Albert .The Expanded Quotable Einstein, Princeton University Press, 2000 p. 208

10. Morris, Henry M." The Genesis Record", p31

11. Schaeffer, Francis A. "Genesis in Space and Time: the flow of biblical history"Regal Books & intervarsity press, Glendale 1972, p152.

12. Schaeffer, Francis A. "Genesis in Space and Time: the flow of biblical history"Regal Books & intervarsity press, Glendale 1972, p121.

13. Homer.(Pope's), corrected by Parkhust. See: *Ilead,Lib V/ II, 339,340, pp198,199.*

14. Hislop, Alexander."The Two Babylons". Neptune,New Jersey:Loizeaux Brothers, 1916.

15. Bruce, FF, "Babylon and Rome". The Evanglical Quarterly 13: (Oct 15th, 1941) 241-261.

16. Ironside,H.A.." Babylonian Religion" p2

17. Pascal Chronicale vol I,p245

18. Ironside,H.A.." Babylonian Religion" p3

19. Morris, Henry, "The Genesis Record",p274

20. Morris, Henry, "The Genesis Record".p268

21. Morris,Henry, The Genesis Record,pp269-271

22. Jones, Dr Gloyd Nolen. The Chronology of the Old Testament (Accompaning James Usher (1581-1656) Chronology) Masterbooks, 1993 Green Forest, p211.

23. Wilkinson, Sir J Gardiner, :Manners and Customs of the Ancient Egyptians" Vol 1 V. (London: 1821))p405.

24. Langdon p326

25. Custance, Arthur C. "Primitive Monotheism and the Origin of Polytheism"(www.theapricity.com/from/showthread.php?t=26537)

26. *Ibid*

27. Langdon, Stephen H. "The Scotsman, Nov 18, 1936.

28. Meek, T.J. Primitive Monotheism and the religion of Moses, U. of Toronto Quarterly 8, (Jan 1939):189-197.

29. Custance Dorway Papers, Part I "The past played by Shem,Ham, and Japetyh in subsequent world history: Part IV "The technology of the Hamitic People; and Part V, "A Christian World View:The framework of History,"

30. *Ibid* p4

31. Custance p4

32. Muller, Max :Lectures on the Science of Language, 1st series, Scribner's, Armstrong, N.Y. 1875,pp21,22.

33. McCrady, Edard "Genesis and Pagan Cosmogonies," Tran.Vict. Instit. 72:55, (1940)

34. Hays, William "Daily life in ancient Egypt," National Geographic Magazine, Oct. 1941, pp425-428, and the Rhind Papyrus

35. Morris, Henry" Commentary on Gen 10:9-10".

36. Schaeffer,F.S. p159

37. Schaeffer, F.S. p157.

38. Bunsen" Egypt", vol I, p419. London, 1848

39. Hislop, Alexander. Two Babylons" p305

40. Hislop, Alexander. "Two Babylons ".pp190-191

41. ibid p164

42. Ulansey, David. The Origins of the Mithraic Mysteries, Oxford University Press, 1989 pp4-5, 50

43. Comfort, Ray, "Hitler God and the Bible". P114

44. Wilkinson, Sir J Gardiner, :Manners and Customs of the Ancient Egyptians" Vol 1 V. (London: 1821))p405

45. Barker, William Burckhardt "Lares and Penates", ch 8, "Magi and Monks"

46. Heroditus,1,101

47. Diogenes Laertius [1,6,seqq].

48. Bidez and Cumont, II, 9ff Clemen p42

49. Muller. "Theopompi Fragmenta" in Muller, vol 1, p280. Paris 1846-51

50. Plato. "De Republica" lib x vol ii, p614

51. Clericus, De CHaldaeis vol 2, p195

52. Wilson, The Parsee Religion ,Bombay 1843

53. Hislop, Alexander.," Two Babylons", p314

54. Plutarch. "The Symposiaca", Quad 5, vol ii, p670,B

55. Hislop, Alexander. "The Two Babylons" p317

56. Heroditus, 3,65

57. Ramsey, William Mitchell, "Asiatic elements in Greek Civilization", p89, 1915. 2nd ed New Haven, Yale U. Press, 1929

58. Ovid, Tristia iii,I,29

59. Hammerston's Universal History of the World vol ii, p1159 see the famous bronze liver of Piacenza and the similarity to models in Anatolia and Babylon

60. Anderson, Sir Robert. "The Bible or the Church" p. 42. [also see G.H. Pember "The Church, The Churches and the Mysteries and Mystery Babylon the Great ed by G.H. Lang Oliphants Ltd.]

61. Ulansey,David. " Mithraic mysteries". Scientific American 261(6):130-135 Dec 1989

62. Clauss, M."The Roman cult of Mithras" pp26-27

63. Barker, William Burckhardt "Lares and Penates", p106

64. Ulansey, David. The Origins of the Mithraic Mysteries, Oxford University Press, 1989 p134

65. Cicero. "De Natura Deorum". 2.51;Cicero, Nature of the Gods, pp143-44

66. Ulansky, David. The Origins of the Mithraic Mysteries, Oxford University Press, 1989 ,p74 referencing Arnold, *Roman Stoicism* p30.

67. Vermaseren, *M.J. Corpus Inscroptionum et Monumentorum Religionis Mithriace*, vol I, and II (CIRM 860).

68. Dally, Stephanie. Sennacherib at Tarsus, Univ. of Oxford, Fourth Anatolian Iron Ages Symposium, May 1997

69. Goldman, H 1940,"The Sandon Monument of Tarsus" Journal of the American Oriental Society 60:544-57

70. Edzard et al 1987-1990:s.v. Marduk; Kammenhuber 1990.

71. Godlman 1940 p544. Gardner 1878 "Catalogue of the Greek Coins:The Selecuid Kings of Syria. London (reprinted 1963 Bologna), Houghton 1983,"Coins of the Selecuid Empire in the Collection of Arthur Houghton) Ancient Coins in North American Collections 4, N.Y. nos 479,486-497.

72. Strabo 14.5.13-15

73. Sax, 1992,"A system of nomenclature for quaretz" [Archaeometry 34:11-20]

74. Dalley Anatolian Studies 1999

75. Griffith, Alison. "Mithraism in the private and public lives of 4th-c. senators in Rome". *EJMS*. http://www.uhu.es/ejms/Papers/Volume1Papers/ABGMS.DOC

76. Clauss, M., *The Roman cult of Mithras*, p.171

77. Meyer, Marvin (2006). "The Mithras Liturgy". In A.J. Levine, Dale C. Allison, Jr., and John Dominic Crossan. . New Jersey: Princeton University Press. pp. 179–180.

78. Ulansey, David (1989). *The Origins of the Mithraic Mysteries*. Oxford University Press. (1991 revised edition)

79. Porphyry, *De Antro nympharum* 10: "Since, however, a cavern is an image and symbol of the world..."

80. Porphyry, *De antro nympharum* 2: "For, as Eubulus says, Zoroaster was the first who consecrated in the neighbouring mountains of Persia, a spontaneously produced cave, florid, and having fountains, in honour of Mithra, the maker and father of all things; |12 a cave, according to Zoroaster, bearing a resemblance of the world, which was fabricated by Mithra. But the things contained in the cavern being arranged according to commensurate intervals, were symbols of the mundane elements and climates."

81. Hopfe, Lewis M., "Archaeological indications on the origins of Roman Mithraism", in Lewis M. Hopfe (ed). *Uncovering ancient stones: essays in memory of H. Neil Richardson*, Eisenbrauns (1994), pp. 147-158, p.154

82. Dager, A.J. "Vengenance is Ours:The Church in Dominion"

83. Plutarch *Numa* 14, 6-7

84. Bunsen, vol. I,pp. 273, 472

85. Hislop, Alexander. Page 256

86. David, F.A, *Antiquites Etrusques* vol. v. plate 57

87. Ovid, Metam.,mxv ll.558-9,760.

88. Salverte, p37 and Flories Ser. P391

89. Martyr, Justin volume II page 193

90. Wilkerson, vol iv. P239

91. Hislop, Alexander, p320

92. Pontifex, Encyclopædia Britannica, 1911 Ed

93. Livy, VI.41: *auspiciis hanc urbem conditam esse, auspiciis bello ac pace domi militiaeque omnia geri, quis est qui ignoret?*

94. Lintott, Andrew. *The Constitution of the Roman Republic* (Oxford University Press, 1999), pp. 183–184

95. *Dictionary of Classical Antiquities*, page 221

96. Custance p12

97. Custance p1

98. Schmidt, Wilhelm. "The Origin and Growth of Religion:Facts and theories. H.J. Rose, Methuen p71 London, 1931, xvi and p71

99. Custance, Arthur C. p10

100. Robbins, John W., The Trinity Review, Feb.March 1996 p2

Chapter 2: How are these ancient gods still with us on the campus

1. The New Criterion [June 2013, p1]

2. IVP NT Commentary on Romans 8

3. ibid

4. Ibid (New Testament Commentary)

5. Lane, Pastor Daniel [http://www.armstronginternational.com/node/56765

6. Easton bible Commentary on Zeph 1:6

7. Barnhouse, Donald Grey,"The invisible War", Zondervan, Grand Rapids, 1965

8. [source WPEC-TV and MSN.com radio.foxnews.com/toddstarnes/ top-stories/university-apologizes-for-stomping-jesus.html]

9. Jeremiah, David. on Daniel 11

10. Custance, Arthur C. "Monotheism and the origin of Polytheism"

11. Langdon, Stephen H, "Semitic Mythologym Mythology of all races, Vol V, Archaeol. Inst. AMer, 1931, p.xviii. And The Scotsman, November 18, 1936.

12. Wiseman, P.J.,Third Preliminary Report on Excavations at Tell Asmar (Eshhunna): quoted by P.J. Wiseman in New Discoveries in Bablylonia agout Genesis, Marshall, Morgan and Scott, London, 1936,p.24.

13. Delitzsch, Friedrich, Babel and Bible, Williams and Norgate, London, 1903, pp. 144f.

14. Rawlinson, George, ed., Herodotus, appendix to Book 11, p. 250.

15. [checkout Realists vs. Nominalists and the internecine struggle..Univ. Mainz manual of logic=Nominalistic principals.]

16. Marx, Karl. "Reflections of a young man on the choice of a profession"

17. Wurmbrand, Richard, "Marx and Satan", Crossway Books, 1986./p12

18. Wurmbrand, p34

19. Marx, Karl and Moses Hess, Sidney Hook Dec 1934, see New International, vol 1.No 55 December 1934, pp140-144.

20. Hess, Moses.(Holy History of Mankind) "Die Heilige Geschichte der Menschheit" ed. by Shlomo Avineri. Cambridge Univ. Press, 2005

21. Hess, Moses. see:http://www.zionismontheweb.org/Moses_Hess_Rome_and_Jerusalem.htm "Rome and Jerusalem", Book 12. Moses Hess, translator Meyer Waxman. Bloch Publishing Company. 1918

22. Hess, Moses, "Religion und Sittlichkeit" pp115-116

23. Zacharias, Ravi. vol 21.4 R. Zacharias Ministeries. Morality, p4-5

24. Zacharias, Ravi. vol 21.4 R. Zacharias Ministeries. Morality, p8

25. Zacharias, Ravi. vol 21.4 R. Zacharias Ministeries. Morality, p13

26. Gianelli,Diane M. "Shock-tactic ads target late term abortion procedure," American Medical News, July 5, 1993, p3

27. Bork, Robert H.,"Slouching Towards Gomorrah", p202
    [also see: "Feminism and the Christian God, Naomi Goldenberg"]
    [Also:"10 lies of Feminism", Sue Bohlin]

28. Russel, Letty. "Human Liberation in a Feminist Perspective: A Theology",Philadelphia, Westminster Press, 1974, pp50-55

29. Russel,Letty. 1997, pp43-57

30. Kassian, p169

31. Bloesch, Doald. "the battle for the Trinity: The debate over Inclusive God – Language", Ann Arbor, Mi, Servent Books, 1985 p xviii,p54.

32. Mollenkott,Virginia. "The divine feminine",p113.

33. Kaissian. P117

34. Kassian. P175

35. Daly, "Beyond God the Father". p 29

36. Adler,Margo. "Drawing down the Moon: witches, druids, goddess – worshippers, and other pagans". [in <u>America Today</u> (Boston, To beacon Press, 1986 pp204-205

37. Bork, Robert. "Slouching Towards Gomorrah". p193

38. Bork, Robert .p194

39. Pati,Daphne and Noretta Koertge. "Professing Feminism: cautionary tales from the Strange world of Women's studies",New York: Basic Books, 1994, p183

40. Bork, Robert. P197

41. Bork, Robert, p197

42. Spiro,Milford. "And gender in culture: kibbutz women revisited"(Durham North Carolina, duke university press. 1979 page 106

43. Hite, Shere. N.Y. Grove press, 1994pp 352-60

44. Bork, Robert.p204

45. Faludi, Susan, "Backlash: the undeclared war against American Women"(N.Y. Crown, 1981

46. Bork, Robert. P209.

47. Bork,Robert. P209

48. Bork,Robert. P209

49. Bork, Robert. P210

50. Bork, Robert. P210

51. Sommers, Christian Hoff," Who stole if Feminism: How women have betrayed women"(N.Y. Simon and Schuster, 1994

52. Bork, Robert. P217

53. Gallagher, Maggie. "Enemies of Arrow's: Hollow the sexual revolution is killing family, and sex and what we can do about it" Chicago bonus books, 1989p 270

54. Bork, Robert. P224

55. Barnhouse, Donald Grey. "The Invisible War". Zondervan, Grand Rapids.. 1965. P232

56. Bork, Robert. P339].

57. Fitch,Robert E. "The Obsolescence of Ethics", in Christanity and Crisis: A Journal of Opinion, 19(19)(November 16, 1959),pp163-65. cited by Ravi Zacharis in "The Real Face of Atheism",Baker Books, 2013. pp65-66.

Chapter 3: How the Humanist have developed: the ones who teach us, the answers are only from man

1. Pascal, Blaise. "Pensees" No.72

2. Pascal, Blaise."The Thoughts of Blaise Pascal". Translated from the text of M. Auguste Molinier by C. Kegan Paul (London:George Bell and Sons, 1901,p89. (PDF Free online) at http://oll.liberty.fund.org. PLL v6.0 (generated September, 2011)

3. Pascal, Blaise. "The Thoughts of Blaise Pascal". Translated from the text of M. Auguste Molinier by C. Kegan Paul (London:George Bell and Sons, 1901.p93.

4. Toynbee, Arnold. "Reconsiderations VOL 12 of the study of history". New York. Oxford University Press. 1961, page 488].

5. Comte, August. . [1851, VOL 1, 127; E., VOL, 100]

6. Encyclopedia Britannica, 1911 volume six, p818

7. Hess, Moses. 12th letter: Rome and Jerusalem the last National Question

8. Schlossberg, Herbert. "Idols for Destruction", P40

9. Schlossberg, Herbert, page 28

10. Schlossberg page 28

11. Schaler, Max." Ressentiment" ed. Louis A. Coser Tran. William W. Holdhime, Glencoe, Illinois .Free Press 1961 [1915], p451

12. Schlossberg, page 52

13. Schlossberg page 52 -3.

14. Scheler, "Ressentiment",p 96. As quoted and Schlossberg p53

15. Schlossberg. p 53.

16. Monroe, Kelly,ed., "Finding God at Harvard. Grand Rapids, Zondervan, 1991,p15.

17. Schoeck, Helmut." Envy". p 209 cf.Ellul, "Betrayal of the West",p 78 "When the gospel of the poor is preached today, the purpose is to rouse the poor to rebellion, violence, and hatred."

18. Schlossberg. p55

19. Bastiat, Federic. "The Law".p 56.BN Publishing 2008.

20. Obama, Barack H. #13489 section three, and John Contrubis, "Executive Orders and Proclamations. CRS Report for Congress #95-722 A, March 9, 1999 pp1-2.

21. Schlossberg. p58

22. Haeckel, Ernst, reported in *Fortnightly Review*, London, vol.39, 1886, p.35.

23. Hitler,Adolf. "Mein Kampf". From the first section of Vol. 1, Chapter 11: Nation and Race

24. Schlossberg. p 70.

25. Schlossberg p 71.

26. Schlossberg p87.

27. Schlossberg p 87.

28. Lewis, C.S. "Miracles" .N.Y. Macmillan, 1978, 27-28

29. Bastiat p 63

30. Noebel, David A. "Clergy in the Classroom: The Religion of Secular Humanism" 2nd Ed. Summit Press, Manitou Springs,2001,p14

31. Potter, Charles Francis, (a Unitarian Minister), "Humanism: A New Religion", Simon and Schuster, NY, 1930

32. Muggeridge, Malcom. In: "The Magazine of Ravi Zacharias International Ministries" 21:4,p6,www.rzim.org

33. Stenger, Victor J. "Has Science Found God: the latest results in the search for purpose in the universe", (p188)

34. Missler, Chuck

35. Missler, Chuck

36. Schwitzer, Mary H. et al. <u>Science,</u> 2005 report: "Tyrannosaurus Rex fossil yields flexible tissue" Mary H. Schweitzer et al Science (March 25, 2005)Vol. 307 no. 5717 p.1852 DOI: 10.1126/science.307.5717.1852b

37. Sanford, J. and John Baumgartner, Mendel's Accountant. http://www.mendelsaccountant.info/ Also see:SCPE 2007. 8:147-165. (supports parallel cluster computers. Software available free online. http:www.sourceforge.net/progects/mendelsaccount)

38. Silander , O.K, O Tenaillon and L. Chao. "Understanding the evolutionary fate of populations: the dynamics of mutational effects": 2007 Plos Biol 5:922-931

39. Teotonio H. et al J. Evol. Biol. 15:608-617.

40. Thomas Pappas, director of Analysis and Production/Threat for the U.S. Arming Training and Doctrine Command G-2. In a War College report May 2011

41. Rubin, Jerry. "Do it!" (New York, Simon and Schuster, 1970), p143

42. Rousas, John Rushdoony, in *"Gold is Money"* by Hans F. Steinholdz, p177

43. Henry M. Morris . *The Long War Against God*: the History and Impact of the Creation/Evolution. Used with permission of the Publisher. Conflict. Baker Books, 1989, pp257-260. Grand Rapids.

44. Henry M. Morris . *The Long War Against God*: the History and Impact of the Creation/Evolution Conflict. Baker Books, 1989, pp257-260. Grand Rapids.

45. Henry M. Morris . *The Long War Against God*: the History and Impact of the Creation/Evolution. Used with permission of the Publisher. Conflict. Baker Books, 1989, p260. Grand Rapids.

46. Einstein, Albert. As quoted in "Time", December 1940, p38, and documented in a youtube video: http://www.youtube.com/watch?feature=player_detailpage&v=Sk_-0UiiauU]

47. Van Valen, L. 1989. Three Paradigms of Evolution. *Evolutionary Theory*. 9: 2.

48. Guliuzza, R. 2011. Darwin's Sacred Imposter: Recognizing Missed Warning Signs. *Acts & Facts*. 40 (5): 12-15; and Guliuzza, R. 2011. Darwin's Sacred Imposter: How Natural Selection Is Given Credit for Design in Nature. *Acts & Facts*. 40 (7): 12-15; Guliuzza, R. 2011. Darwin's Sacred Imposter: The Illusion That Natural Selection Operates on Organisms. *Acts & Facts*. 40 (9): 12-15.

49. Fodor, J. and M. Piattelli-Palmarini. 2010. *What Darwin Got Wrong*. New York: Farrar, Straus and Giroux, 162-163. as cited in Guliuzza

50. Weinrich, Max. "Hitler's Professors". Yale University Press, 1946. 2nd ed. p25. note:We will find in the intellectual circles of Germany in the 1920's the use of the term Ausmerze appearing. [also see: Rosenberg's Myths of the 20th Century. Lulu.com, 2012]

51. Johnson, Phillip A, "Evolution and Christian Faith" p1.A message delivered at the Evangelical Free Church of Hershey PA, May 13, 2001. SEE: www.ldolphin.org/ntcreation.html.

52. Johnson p3

53. Johnson p3

54. Johnson p4.

55. Baskerville, Stephen. WND.com . "Whistleblower", Oct 2013, p22-25.

56. Johnson p7

57. Johnson p7

58. Johnson. P9

59. Jastrow, Robert. Los Angeles Times, June 25, 1978, Part IV, PP. 1,6., As quoted in Hunt, Dave. "in defense of the faith: Biblical answers to challenging questions Harvest House Publishers. Eugene 1996

60. Deewar, Douglas and EL Davies". See:"Science and the BBC", in the 19th century and after, 1943, page 167.

61. Hoyle, Sir Frederick. [from an interview by AP pundit George W. Cornel, quoted from "Times – Advocate", Escondido, California, December 10, 1982, pp. A10-11.

62. Hunt, Dave. pp6-7

63. Kagan, Don. Yale College final address. "The New Criterion" June 2013.

64. Bunyan, John. "Fear of God", London: Printed for N. Ponder, at the Peacock in the Poultry, over against the Stocks market: 1679. http://www.chapelli-brary.org/files/2713/7642/2833/bun-fear.pdf . and Batzig, Nicholas T. "Fear of Men", <u>Tabletalk</u>, Oct 2013,p12-13

65. Dembski, William A. "Mere Creation". Intervarsity Press, Downers Grove. 1998 p450-1

66. Dembski p 450

67. Bunyan,John. "The Works of John Bunyan:A Treatise of The Fear of God",p12

68. Breese, Dave. "7 Men Who Rule the World from the Grave.",Moody Publications, 1990, Chicago. P121

69. Korzybski, Alfred "Science and Sanity", International Non-Aristotelian Library Pub. Co. distributed by the Institute of General Semantics, 1958.

70. Aiken, Henry David, "The Journal of Philosophy 49:25)789-791, Dec 4, 1952

71. [from Wiki on Durkehiim, accessed Jan 2013]

72. [from Wiki on Robert Merton: Anomie Theory..sometimes termed means-ends theory, accessed 1/11/14]

73. Anonymous M.D., Penguin Group, N.Y. 2006, p68-75

74. Owen,Robert L.,"Uptake and transport of Intestinal macromolecules and microorganisms by "M" cells in Peyer's Patches". Seminars in Immunology 11:154-163, 1999

75. Green, John C. "The Death of Adam" The Iowa State University Press, 1959 p311

76. Lyell, Principles of Geology, 1932

77. Kimball, Roger. "The New Criterion". 32: (9) p3, May 2014. See:"The left's exalted are the left's hierarchy of victims " National Review's Charles Coke

78. Kimball, Roger. from: Kimball's notes, "Who's Next? (you)

79. Bork, Robert H. p125.

Chapter 4: From Nimrod to Harvard : how these foreign gods entered America's Universities

1. NAAL April 2002, National Center for education statistics, retrieved 2011 -01-12

2. Ignatius. "The epistle of Ignatius to the Philadelphians, and ante-Nicene fathers, ed. Alexander Roberts and James Donaldson. Grand Rapids, Wm. Erdmans, 1981 1:81

3. Schmidt, Alvin J. "How Christianity Changed the World", Grand Rapids, Zondervan pub. 2001, p172.

4. Freeman, Kenneth J. "Schools of Hellas", London Macmillan, 1922, p46.

5. McGarry, D.D., "Mediaeval Education ", New Catholic Encyclopedia, San Francisco; Mcgraw – Hill, 1967, five: 113.

6. McGarry p175.

7. Rasdall, H. "Universities of Europe in the Middle Ages",vol. i,part 3, p.82

8. Durant, Will. "Caesar and Christ: A History of Roman Civilization and of Christianity from their Beginning to A.D. 325.N.Y. Simon and Schuster, 1972, P602.

9. Noll, Mark. "The Scandal of the Evangelical Mind". Grand Rapids:Wm. B. Erdman's, 1994, p.37.

10. Schmidt, Alvin. P.177

11. Luther, Martin. "A sermon on keeping children in school", and "Luther's Works," 46:256, Charles M. Jacobs, ed. Robert Schultz (Phil. Fortress press, 1967

12. Good and, Harry and James Teller. "A History of Western Education". London, Macmillan, 1969, p.153.

13. Schmidt, Alvin. "How Christianity Changed the World". P. 181

14. Tan, Paul Lee. "And Encyclopedia of 7700 The Illustrations: Signs of the Times". Rockville, Assurance Pub. 1984, p.157.

15. Tewksbury, Donald. "The Founding of American Colleges and Universities Before the Cival War", Teachers College Record. 34(2) 143-145, 1932.

16. Keller, Timothy. "Counterfit Gods" p98

17. Benvenuti, Richard. , "The Ninth of Thermidor: the fall of Robespierre", ed. Richard Benvenuti. Oxford University Press, 1970, PP. 32 to – 49.

18. Keller, Timothy p98.

19. Keller, Timothy. "Counterfeit gods" p98

20. Bonhoffer, Detrich."Creation and Fall: Theological exposition of Genesis 1-3". Fortress Press, Minneapolis (vol 3 of Bonhoffer's works)

21. Hagenbach, Dr. K.R. "German Rationalism, it's rise, progress, and decline". NY, Charles Soribner 1865. Rurnbull and Spears printers (available on Google Books) p.xxix 285-86.

22. Hagenbach, K.R. "German Rationalism, it's rise, progress, and decline" page xix p285-86 written by his translators Wm. Leonhakd Gage. J. H. W. Stuckenberg.]New York: Charles Soribner. MDCCCLXV. (1865)

23. Heinish, Paul. "Theology of the Old Testament"Translated by William G. Heidt St. Paul Liturgical, 1955 page 34

24. Stewart, Don. Class notes on the Veracity of the Bible. and Stewart, Don. "The Case For Christianity", Ch.4 (Calvary Chapel Costa Mesa) not (Don Lee Stewart)

25. Sinclair, David, "An Overview on the Bible". 2006.

26. see http://jewishpub.org, and the eight extant Tanakh manuscripts are the Hebrew, Aramaic, and Greek Dead Sea Scrolls (composed 150 BC -70AD), the Greek Septuagant (300 – 100 BC), the Syriac Peshitta (400AD), the Latin Vulgate (400- 780AD), the Hebrew Masoretic (100 A D, oldest copy 900AD), the Samaritan Pentateuch (200-100 BC, old is copy 1000AD – 1500AD), Aramaic Targum, (500-1000 AD, oldest copy fifth century AD), Coptic Codex (third or fourth century AD).

27. all quotes above are from Wellhausen, Juius "Prolegomena to the History of Israel",Wipf and Stock Publishers, 2003, p280, p269.

28. Paul Heinish, Paul. "Theology of the Old Testament" . St Paul, Minn. Liturgical, 1955, p34 and notes in this book Chapter 1

29. Breese, Dave. "7 Men Who Rule the World from the Grave"p92

30. Lewis, C.S., "Modern Theology and Biblical Criticism" (originally titled "Fern-seed and Elephants"), <u>The Seeing Eye</u> (New York: Ballantine Books, 1992), p. 217.

31. Machen, J. Gresham. "Christanity and Liberalism", p5-6, 1929. text is free from http://www.christuslibrary.com/

32. Machen, J. Gresham "Christianity & Liberalism"*p6*

33. Machen, J Gresham . p9

34. Machen, J. Gresham. p10

35. Machen . J.Gresham. p13

36. [Machen, J Gresham p17].

37. [Machen.,J. Gresham p13-17]

38. Schmidt, Alvin. "How Christianity Changed the World"Zondervan, 2004, p190-1

39. Kennedy, D.J. And J. Newcomb. "What if Jesus Had Never Been Born?"Nashville: Thomas Nelson, 1994. P.40

40. Parker, Theodore. " Dictionary of Unitarian Universalist Biography". http://uudb.org/articles/theodoreparker.html accessed 3/8/<u>14</u> 2:45PMT.

41. Kellen, Richard. "Lexington's Rev. John Hancock" . in www.Lexington history.org accesses 3/8/14.

42. Grodzins, Dean. "An American Heretic: Theodore Parker and Transcendentalism".

43. Grodzins. P14

44. Grodzins. P15

45. Grodzins, p15

46. Francis, Covers. "The Value of Enlightened Views of Religion" the Harvard archives p 73-74.

47. Parker, Theodore. "letter from Theodore Parker to Greene", 2 April 1834. Mass. Historical Society.

48. Ware, Henry. "Inquiry" to: 166, 197, 202 as cited in Grodzins, "American Heretic".

49. Parker, Theodore. Journal F. (1835-36 reconstituted, pp 190–191, May 1836) quoted in Weiss, John. "The Life and Correspondence of Theodore Parker". 2 vol. ,N.Y. Appleton, 1864 1:82

50. Harvard Crimson" March 18, 2005. "Fascism's Flaming motor", and Grodzins, Dean. "An American Heretic" p.150. Parker's journal C. 1836-38. Page 172

51. Hettche, Matt, "Christian Wolff", *The Stanford Encyclopedia of Philosophy* (Spring 2014 Edition), Edward N. Zalta (ed.), forthcoming URL = <http://plato.stanford.edu/archives/spr2014/entries/wolff-christian/>.

52. [in part from "A Brief History of Christian Influence in U.S. Colleges". *By Editorial Staff* Published April **Reprinted by permission from: The Forerunner International, P.O. Box 362173, Melbourne FL 32936-2173**]

53. **The Forerunner International, by Permission. P.O. Box 362173, Melbourne FL see: 32936-2173.** http://www.forerunner.com/forerunner/X0100_Christianity_in_U.S..html

54. Olmstead, Clifton E. (1960), History of Religion in the United States, Prentice-Hall, Englewood Cliffs, N.J., pp. 67-69

55. Olmstead, Clifton E. (1960), History of Religion in the United States, Prentice-Hall, Englewood Cliffs, N.J., p163

56. Olmstead, Clifton E. (1960), History of Religion in the United States, Prentice-Hall, Englewood Cliffs, N.J., pp. 67-69

57. Bushman (1970). *From Puritan to Yankee: Character and the Social Order in Connecticut, 1690-1765.* p. 151.]

58. Nourse, Ruth. "Hijacking of American education: flip jack turning at Harvard." Part 4:Ralph Waldo EmersonJune 1, 1989. **Reprinted by permission from: The Forerunner International, P.O. Box 362173, Melbourne FL 32936-2173**].. See: http://www.forerunner.com/forerunner/x0285_Hijacking_American_L.html

59. Richardson,Robert D. Jr. (1995) Emerson: The Mind on Fire. Berkeley, California: University of California Press. ISBN 0-520-08808-5), p.9,

60. Sullivan, Wilson (1972). New England Men of Letters. New York: The Macmillan Company. ISBN 0-02-788680-8

61. Nourse, Ruth Part 5 Reprinted by permission from: The Forerunner International, P.O. Box 362173, Melbourne FL 32936-2173]

62. Grusin, Richard A. "Transcendentalist Hermeneutics". Duke University Press, Durham 1991

63. Grusin, Richard A. "Transcendentalist Hermeneutics: Institutional Authority and the Higher Criticism of the Bible". Duke University Press, Durham, 1991,pp1-7

64. Grusin, Richard A. "Transcendentalist Hermeneutics: Institutional Authority and the Higher Criticism of the Bible". Duke University Press, Durham, 1991,pp1-7

65. Grusin, p6-7]

66. See: [www.PoetryFoundation.org/bio/Ralph-waldo-emerson]

67. Peirce, C. S. (1893), "Evolutionary Love", *The Monist,* v. III, n. 1, pp. 176–200, for "agapism" see p. 188, *Arisbe* Eprint. Reprinted in *Collected Papers* v. 6, paragraphs 287–317, for the word "agapism" see 302. Reprinted also in *Chance, Love, and Logic* pp. 267–300, *Philosophical Writings of Peirce* pp. 361–74, and *The Essential Peirce* v.1, pp. 352–72.

68. Shoemaker, Stephen P, "The Theological Roots of Charles W. Eliot's Educational Reforms," Journal of Unitarian Universalist History 2006-2007 31:30-45

69. Cohen, Felix S., "Transcendental Nonsense and the Functional Approach" 35 COLUM. L. Rev. 809,821 (1935)

70. Grey, note 49, in" Langdell.

71. Langdell cites 100-101

72. Walsh, Colleen, "When religion turned inward" . "Harvard gazette" Feb 16,2012

73. Walsh, Colleen . "HARVARD gazette" Feb 16,2012.

74. Monron, Kelly. *Finding God at Harvard*, Zondervan, 1997.

75. Anonymous M.D., "Unprotected", Sentinal, N.Y.N.Y, 2006, p68-69] [JAMA 267:1917-18,1992.Molecular Human Reproduction 5:656-61, 1999.Histology for Pathologists pp881-92,1992. Journal of Virology, June 2000, pp5577-86

76. Anonymous M.D.,"Unprotected", Sentinal,N.Y.N.Y, 2006, p68-69

77. Coban, Ramazan. Balikesir, 2012. "Ida's research in comparable mythology"

78. Barton, Carlin A. "The sorrows of the Ancient Romans: The gladiators and the Monster" Princeton Univ. Press, 1993

79. Ephorus of Cyme in Strabo's "Geography 10.21.4

80. Ibid x.4.12

81. Saflund, G. in "Cretan and Theran Questions" in "Sanctuaries and Cults", pp198-200

82. Collins, Steven. "Tall el-Hammam is Sodom: Billington's Hesbon Identification Suffers from Numerous Fatal Flaws with 64 references". "Artifax Magazine", summer 2012.

83. House PK, Vyas A, Sapolsky R (2011) "Predator Cat Odors Activate Sexual Arousal Pathways in Brains of *Toxoplasma gondii* Infected Rats." [see: PLoS ONE 6(8): e23277. doi:10.1371/journal.pone.0023277.

84. MacDonald, William.(ed. Wm Farstad). "Believers Bible Commentary: A complete Commentary in one Volume". Thomas Nelson, Nashville. 1995. P2002

85. Steadman, Ray C. "Adventuring Through the Bible". Discovery House Publishers. Grand Rapids,1997,pp633-34

86. Wolin, Richard. "Preface to MIT press edition: Note on missing text. "The Heidegger controversy. Critical reader MIT press, 1993, p xiii.

87. Derrida "Interviews. 1st ed. Stanford Univ. Press. ISBN 0810103974. pp409-413

Chapter 5: What does the God of creation say about how we got here and why we are here

1. Feynman, Richard. Science Editor, "New Scientists", 2 Dec 1989, p14.

2. Setterfield, Barry. Cosmology and Zero Point Energy" National Philosophy Alliance Monograph #1

3. Larmor Radiation http://www.calphysics.org/zpe.html

4. Cicero, De Oratore, 1.2. c. 15. 3:243,254

5.   Darwin, Charles. "On the *Origin of Species*",, Chapter Ten: "On the Imperfection of the Geologic Record: On the absence of intermediate varieties at the present day)"

6.   Darwin, Charles. On the *Origin of Species*, Chapter Ten: "On the absence of intermediate varieties in any one formation"

7.   Darwin, Charles. The Darwin Papers volume1. Number XIV "Darwin at Nuremberg Part III Thomas Malthus and The Struggle for Survival or W.W.D.D. -In His Tracks What Would Darwin Do? [From "The Nebulous Hypothesis: A Study of the Philosophical and Historical Implications of Darwinian Theory. Editor and Publisher James M. Foard.]

Chapter 6
1.   Ruse, Michael. "But Is It Science?" Prometheus Books, Amherst, 2009. pp538-9

2.   Laughlin, Robert B. "A Different Universe: Reinventing Physics from the Bottom Down". Basic Books, N.Y., N.Y. 2006, p25-26.

3.   Laughlin, Robert B. "A Different Universe: Reinventing Physics from the Bottom Down". Basic Books, N.Y., N.Y. 2006, p25-26.

4.   Ruse, Michael. "Saving Darwinism from the Darwinians". National Post, May 13, 2000,B-3.

5.   Gitt, Warner, Dr. Professor. "In the beginning was information". Master Books, 2006

6.   Plank, Max. "Where is Science Going?". Woodbridge, Conn: Ox Bow Press. 1981, p214

7. *Setterfiel, Barry.* Physicists/Astronomer

8. Gitt, Warner. "In the beginning was information"

9. Strong, James."The New Strong's Exhaustive Concordance of the Bible" (every word of the Bible). Thomas Nelson. Nashville. 1984 . see: (halal , p33 of the Hebrew and Chaldee Dictionary, in Strong's, 1984.)

10. KEPLER, JOHNNES., *"Harmonies of the World"*, tr. Charles Glenn Wallis. p1018.

11. Maxwell,James Clerk. <u>Nature</u>, 8:437-442, 1873

12. Garber, E., et al (Eds.) <u>Maxwell on Molecules and Gases</u> (1986) MIT press, Cambridge Massachusetts.

13. Hawking, Steven."God Created the Integers: The Mathematical Breakthroughs that Changed History". Running Press, Phila. 2005 pp425-426

14. Williams, Alex. John Harnett."Dismantling the Big Bang: God's universe rediscovered". Master Books, Green Forest,2005.pp68-69

15. Paul of Tarsus. 1Corinthians 2:14 "..The Natural Man….."

16. Watts,Issac. "Logic, the Right use of Reason in the Inquiry after Truth" (1724)

17. Hawking, Steven."The Grand Design" Bantam Books. 2009,p172 and Ch.8

18. Sproul, R.C. "Not a Chance"

19. Koestler, Arthur. "Darkness at Noon, trans. Daphne Hardy (N.Y. Bantum, 1941), p149 translated as "As long as chaos dominates the world…"

20. Sproul, R.C."Not a Chance", p50

21. KEPLER, JOHNNES. *"Harmonies of the World,* by Johannes Kepler", tr. Charles Glenn Wallis. P1018

22. Einstein, A. From The Journal of the Franklin Institute Vol221 no. 3, March 1936, pp290-292

23. Einstein, A. From The Journal of the Franklin Institute Vol221 no. 3, March 1936, p292.

24. Wilson, Edward O., "On Human Nature", Cambridge Mass. Harvard U. Press (1978)

25. Einstein, A. From The Journal of the Franklin Institute Vol221 no. 3, March 1936, pp290-292

26. Fisher, J.T. and L.S. Hawley," A few Buttons Missing". Philadelphia; Lippincott, 1951,p.273.

27. Stenger, Victor J. "Has Science found God" ,Promethus Books, Amherst, 2003,p348

28. Stewart, Don. "The Case For Christianity", Ch.4 (Calvary Chapel Costa Mesa) not (Don Lee Stewart)

29. Walvoord, John F. "Every Prophecy of the Bible" , Chariot Victor Publishing, Colorado Springs, 1990, p7

30. Chaplin, Martin. "Water Structures and Science". ww1.isbu.ac.uk/water

31. Gurnett D.A., and A. Bhattacharjee. "Introduction to Plasma Physics". Cambridge University Press. Cambridge, 2005 p23

32. Harvey, RP and N. Rosenthal. "Heart Development" Academic Press. London. 1999

33. Lindley, David. "The End of Physics: the myth of a unified theory", Basic Books. N.Y. 1993, pp167-169.

34. Hawking, Steven. And Leonard Mlodinow. "The Grand Design". Bantam Books.N.Y.2012,p178.

35. Sagan, Carl."Cosmos", London, Macdonald & Co, 1980, p246.

36. Dicke, R.H. "Dirac's Cosmology and Mach's Principle". In:Leslie, John.ed. "Modern Cosmology and Philosophy". Prometheus Books, Amherst.1998, p129.

37. (Hugh Ross)

38. Netterfield, C.B. et al, "A Measurement by Boomerang of Microwave Peaks of the Angular Power Spectrum of the Cosmic Microwave Background ". The Astrophysical Journal, 571:604-614, 2003,Jume 1.

39. [above from Physicists Hugh Ross interview by John Ankerberg 6/23/13]

40. Einstein,Albert .(on Science). (The Times of London 11/28/19).

41. [excerpted from WWW.TRUTHSEEKERS.WS]

42. The Speakers Quotebook (1997) ed. By Roy B. Zuck, p108

43. Maxwell, James Clerk. *Introductory Lecture on Experimental Physics* held at Cambridge in October 1871, re-edited by W. D. Niven (2003) in Volume 2 of *The Scientific Papers of James Clerk Maxwell,* Courier Dover Publications, p. 241

44. Maxwell, James Clerk. Letter to Rev. C. B. Tayler (8 July 1853) in Ch. 6 : Undergraduate Life At Cambridge October 1850 to January 1854 — ÆT. 19-22, p. 189

45. Darwin, Charles. "Autobiography" 1887 p18 and Parkyn, Ernest A. "Darwin, His work and influence: A lecture delivered in the Hall of Christ College Cambridge.Methen and Co., London 1894. P12.

46. Richard Lewontin,Richard. "Billions and Billions of Demons," *The New York Review*, January 9, 1997, p. 31.

47. Stokes, Mitch. "Isaac Newton", Thomas Nelson, Nashville, 2010,p14

48. Westfall, R.S. "Never At Rest: a biography of Isaac Newton" Cambridge. Cambridge U. Press, 1980, p377

49. Stokes, Mitch. P103

50. Lisle, Jason Ph.D "Taking Back Astronomy", Master Books Green Forest.2001,p85

51. Lisle, Jason. "Taking Back Astronomy", Master Books Green Forest.2001,p85-86

52. Humphries pp1120-126] "Starlight and Time" Master Books, Green Forest, 1994

53. Coles, P. "An Unprincipled Universe?" Nature, 391:120-121, 1998.

54. Humphreys, D.R. "New Vistas of Space-Time Rebut The Critics" Creation *Ex Nihilo* Technical Journal, 12:195-212,1998.

55. Baumgardner, John R. "In Six Days". John F. Ashton ed. Master Books . Green Forrest Arkansas. 2001.

56. Missler, Chuck

57. Collins, Francis M.D., https://youtu.be/EGu_VtbpWhE (accessed 4/24/15)

58. Boudreaux Edward A. and Eric C. Baxter. "God Created The Earth".2nd Ed. Rocky Mountain Creation Fellowship. PO box 3451, Littleton, CO 80161-3451,pp22-53

59. Boudreaux Edward A. and Eric C. Baxter. "God Created The Earth".2nd Ed. Rocky Mountain Creation Fellowship. PO box 3451, Littleton, CO 80161-3451,p26

60. Boudreaux Edward A. and Eric C. Baxter. "God Created The Earth".2nd Ed. Rocky Mountain Creation Fellowship. PO box 3451, Littleton, CO 80161-3451,p29

61. Adamenko S.V. "A low energy method of controlled Nucleosynthesis"

62. Adamenko, S. Selleri F. and van der Merwe A. Editors, "Nucleosynthesis-Breakthroughs in Experiment and Theory, Fundamental Theories of Physics, vol 156, Springer-Verlog, The Netherlands, 2007

63. Mendez, Arnold C. Sr. "Accelerated Radioactive Decay-see www.amendez.com

64. Takahashi K. et al "Bound-state beta decay of highly ionized atoms", Physical Review C36(4):1522-1527 Shortly after the theory was presented experimental data was forthcoming proving accelerated beta decay rates.

65. Kapperler F. and H. Beer. ""S-Process nucleosynthesis Nuclear Physics and the Classical Model", Report on Progress in Physics 52:1006-1008, 1989. And Klay. N. et al "Nuclear structure of ^{176}Lu and its astrophysical consequences", Physical Review C44(6):2847-2848, 1991. And Jung M. et al "First observation of bound-state Beta decay", Physical Reviews Letters 69(15) 2164-2167,1987

66. Bosch, F. et al "Observation of bound-date Bea-decay of fully ionized187Re." Physical Review Letters 77(26):5190-5193,1966. And Geochronology Encyclopedia vol 19,p783,1985 and Prantzos N, Harissopals S.
Proc. Nuclei in the Cosmos pp181-186, 1999

67. Boudreaux, Ed. Dec. 28 2009 person communication (email) noted p53. See: computations, tables and fine detail of a master Physical chemist are to be found in Boudreaux and Baxter Book "God Created the Earth"

68. Steinhardt, Paul J. Sci Am 304:36-43 (2011)

69. Yeh, C. J. Appll. Phys. 5066,1969. And Raychaudhuri S. "Microwave-generated low frequency plasma wave excited in the periphery of the evanescent layer". Physics of Plasma Vol 11number10:4634-4640, October 2004.

70. Rubin V, and F.W. Kent. Astrophysical Journal 159:379, Feb.1970.

71. William, Alex and John Harnett. "Dismantling the Big Bang" Master Books, Green Forest, 2005, pp14-15

72. Dyson, L., M. Kleban, and L. Susskind, "Disturbing Implications of a Cosmological Constant", MIT-CTP-3295.hep-th/0208013, 14 Nov2002. Attp://arxiv.org/pdf/hep-th/0208013.pdf

73. Einstein, Albert and Leopold Infeld. "The Evolution of Physics". Cambridge U. Press.1961, pp292,296.

74. NET Bible, note on Genesis 6:11 Biblical Studies Press, L.L.C. version 5.830. 1996 p21.

75. Austin, S.A.(Ed.). "The Grand Canyon: Monument to catastrophe. El Cajon, California: Institute for Creation Research. 1994.

76. Austin, S.A. ibid pp42-51

77. Ager, D.V. "The Nature of the Stratigraphical record. 1973. London: MacMillaln.pp4-6.

78. Baumgardner, John R. Catastrophic Plate Tectonics :The Physics Behind the Genesis Flood.Proceedings of the Fifth International Conference on Creationism. R.L. Ivey Jr. (Ed.) pp113-126, 2003.

79. Baumgardner, John R. in "In Six Days", John F. Ashton (Ed) Master Books, Green Forrest ,Ak., 2001, p230-231.

80. Ibid p116

81. Kirby, S.H. "Rheology of the lithosphere". Reviews of Geophysics and Space Physics, 25:1219-1244, 1983.

82. King, Scott D, "Models of Mantle Viscosity",pp227,1995 in Mineral Physics and Crystallography. A Handbook of Physical Constants. AGU reference shelf 2.

83. Baumgardner, John R. in "In Six Days", John F. Ashton (Ed) Master Books, Green Forrest ,Ak., 2001, p232-233.

84. Austin, S.A.(Ed.). "The Grand Canyon: Monument to catastrophe. El Cajon, California: Institute for Creation Research. 1994.pp46-47,32-36.

85. Meyer, Stephen C. "Darwin's Doubt: the explosive origin of animal life and the case for intelligent design". Harper One, N.Y.,N.Y. 2013, p230-

86. Baker, FR. Kenneth, SJ. "Homiletic and Pastoral Review". "Presuppositions of Darwinism", Editorial Oct 2011

87. Wieschaus, E.F.,taken from tapes at an AAAS lecture, 1982, as quoted by Stephen Meyer in "Darwin's Doubt" page 256-57

88. Meyer, Stephen .p262

89. Ibid p262

90. Behe, Michael. "The Edge of Evolution: the search for the limits of Darwinism". New York Free Press, 2007, p145

91. Durrett & Schmidt. "Waiting for two Mutations". Genetics 180: 1501-9, 2008

92. Hellerstrom, N.P. "the tree as a evolutionary icon: TREE in the natural history museum, London. Archives of Natural History 38:1 ,2011,p-17

93. Rokas, Antonis. "Spotlight: Drawing the Tree of Life". Brod Institute, November 15, 2006. www.broadinstitute. org/news/168.

94. Meyer p122

95. Meyer p133

96. Meyer p143

97. Meyer p143

98. Valentine, J.W. and D.H. Erwin. "Interpreting great developmental experiments: the fossil record. (p92 diagram) in: Development as and Evolutionary Process" . ed. R.A. Raff and E.C. Raff, 71–107. New York: Liss, 1987, [as referenced in Meyer]

99. Meyer p157

100. Huxley, Julian. "The Evolutionary Vision". In: Evolution after Darwin: University of Chicago centennial. Volume three Issues and Education. Chicago, University of Chicago press, p 249-53.

101. Meyer p160

102. Valentine, James W. "On the Origin of Phyla". Chicago university press. 2004,p73]. Note Valentine's work "Why no new Phyla after the Cambrian?" [Valentine J.W. Palaios 10, 1995, pp191-94

103. Meyer p168

104. Sadava, David. et a.l "Life, the Science of Biology", 8th ed. Sinauer Associates and W.H. Freeman,2008.

105. Meyer p367.

106. Meyer pp270-287.

107. McGann, C.J."Mammalian myotube dedifferentiation induced by newt regeneration extract". PNAS 98(24):13699-13704, 2001.

108. Pellitt, Paul and Alistar Pike. "Dating European Palolithic Cave Art:Progress, Prospects,Problems". J. of Archaeological Method and Theory, 14:(1) March 2007

109. Rowe, Marvin W. "Radiocarbon dating of Ancient Rock Paintings". Anal. Chem 81(5):1728-35, March 1, 2009. Also: Ruiz and Rowe. "Dating Methods (Absolute and Relative) in Archaeology of Art" Encyc. Of Global Archaeology:2014, pp2036-42, with 36 references)

110. Rowe p1732, Fig 5

111. Armitage, Ruth A. et al. "Society for American Archeology" 66 (3):476 (July 2001.

112. Watchman . "A Universal Standard for Reporting the Ages of Petroglyphs and Rock Painting". In: Strecker, M.P. eds. "Dating the Earliest Known Rock Art. Oxbow Press, Oxford, pp1-3, (1999)

113. Rowe . :"Dating by ^{14}C Analysis", Handbook of Rock Art Research,Atiamara, N.Y., pp139-166, 2001

114. Pettitt, Paul and Alistair Pike. *Journal of Archaeological Method and Theory, Vol. 14, No. 1, March 2007 (C_ 2007)* "Dating European Palaeolithic Cave Art:Progress, Prospects, Problems". Paul Pettitt1,3 and Alistair Pike2.*Published online: 10 February 2007 [note: paper in book background ch 1]*

115. Vardiman, Larry. Andrew Snelling, and Eugene F. Chaffin. Eds. "Radioisotopes and the Age of the Earth" El Cajon, CA: Institute for Creation Research and Creation Research Society, 2000, Ch 5

116. Humphreys, Russell, Steven Austin, John Baumgardner,and Andrew Snelling. "Precambrian Zircons Yield a Helium Diffusion Age of 6,000 Years". American Geophysical Union Fall Conference, San Francisco, Dec. 2003, Abs #V32C-1047, http://www.icr/research/misc/aguconference.html.

117. Humphreys, D. Russell, "The Earth's Magnetic Field is Young". http://www.icr.org/article/earths-magnetic-field-young/]

118. Lisle, Jason, "Discerning Truth" Master Books, p20-

119. Ibid., p63

120. Ibid., p54.

121. Ibid., p50

122. Ibid., p45.

123. Ibid., p16

124. Ibid., p30

125. Ibid., p35

126. Ibid., p40

127. Ibid., p76

128. Ibid., p76

129. Ibid., p109,124

130. Ibid., p108,124

131. Ibid., p110,127

132. Ibid., p78

133. Ibid., p107,123

134. Ibid., p102,115

135. Ibid., p102,116

136. Ibid..,p110,126

137. Christopher R. Browning, *The Origins of the Final Solution* (University of Nebraska Press 2004, p411.

138. Lee Smolin, Lee. "Trouble with Physics" p63

139. See:Cal Physics Institute," Zero Point Energy and Zero Point Field". paper on line.

140. Boyer

141. Puthoff

142. D'Souza, Dinesh. "What's So Great About Christianity?" Tyndale House. 2007.. pp94-101

143. Lisle, Jason. "Discerning Truth" Master Books, 2010, p7

144. Carlson, N.R. & Heth, C.D.(2009).Psychology the Science of Behavior. Toronto: Pearson Education Canada

145. Vickers, John. "THE PROBLEM OF INDUCTION". The Stanford Encyclopedia of Philosophy.21June, 2010.

146. Vickers, John. "THE PROBLEM OF INDUCTION" (Section 2). *Stanford Encyclopedia of Philosophy.* 21 June 2010.

147. Gray, Peter. Psychology. New York: Worth, 2011.

148. Popper, Karl R. and, David W. Miller. "A proof of the impossibility of inductive probability." *Nature* 302 (1983), 687–688

Chapter 7: Implications of a Godless Campus

1. Vitale, Vince PhD, Oxford Center for Christian Apologetics, see: "Just Thinking" 22(4):18]

2. ibid p21

3. Davis, Bob. Pastor , 9/28/14 on 1Peter

4. Lutzer, Dr Irwin W."When A Nation Forgets God: 7 lessons we must learn from Nazi Germany ".Moody Publishers, Chicago. 2010.

5. Terrell, Richard."Resurrecting the Third Reich", Shreveport, Huntington House,1994, p176.

6. Maxwell, James Clerk, "Discourse on Molecules", Clerk-Maxwell, J. (25 September 1873). "Molecules". *Nature* **8** (204): 437–41. Bibcode 1873Natur...8..437.. doi:10.1038/008437a0. http://www.nature.com/nature/journal/v8/n204/pdf/008437a0.pdf. Retrieved 2012-02-20. Also digitised at *The Victorian Web.* Archived 2012-02-23.]

7. Tayler,G.W.H. quoted in: L. Campbell and W. Garnett, "The Life of James Clerk Maxwell, Macmillan, London, 1882 p.174]

8. Hutchinson, Ian. see http://silas.psfc.mit.edu/maxwell/ "James Clerk Maxwell and the Christian Proposition"

9. [This text was popularized as part of a longer piece commenting on the 2000 U.S. presidential election, which began circulating on the Internet during or shortly after. It may be from Alexander Fraser Tytler, Lord Woodhouselee (15 October 1747 – 5 January 1813) or from the Great Historian Alexis de Tocqueville, there is some uncertainty here]

10. Baskerville, Stephen. WND.com . "Whistleblower", Oct 2013, p22-25

11. Churchill, Winston. "The Gathering Storm", Houghton Mifflin, Boston, 1948, p71

12. Zimmerman, Carle C., James Kurth, Allan C. Carlson. "Family and Civilization", Intercollegiate Studies Inst. Wilmington,ISBN-10 1933859377, 2008. P. 238

13. Graham, Billy. http://billygraham.org/story/billy-graham-my-heart-aches-for-america/, July 19, 2012

14. Kilgore, Randy. "Our Daily Bread", RBC Ministries 59:9. Dec. 11,2013

15. Hunt, Dave. "Great is the Mystery", May 2003, "The Berean Call" xxix (9):3

16. Hunt, Dave. "Great is the Mystery", May 2003, "The Berean Call" xxix (9):4

17. Hunt, Dave. "Great is the Mystery", May 2003, "The Berean Call" xxix (9):3

18. Hunt, Dave. "Great is the Mystery", May 2003, "The Berean Call" xxix (9):3,4

19. ibid, page 4

20. ibid page 26

21. Vitale, Vince PhD, Oxford Center for Christian Apologetics. See:"Just Thinking" 22(4):28

22. Gerlich, G. and Tscheuschner,R.D. (2009) "Falsification of The Atmospheric CO2 Greenhouse Effects Within the Frame of Physics", arXiv:0707.1161v4 [physics.ao-pg] 4 Mar 2009.

23. Zichichi, A. "Meterorology and Climate: Problems and Expectations" in Climate Change and Development. International Conference, Pontifical Council for Justice and Peace, The Vatican 26-27 April 2007, http://www.justpax.it/eng/home eng.html

24. Gerlich, G. and Tscheuschner,R.D. (2009) "Falsification of The Atmospheric CO2 Greenhouse Effects Within the Frame of Physics", arXiv:0707.1161v4 [physics.ao-pg] 4 Mar 2009., p92

25. Houghton et al., Climate Change 1992: The Supplementary Report to the IPPC Scientific Assessment- Report Prepared for IPCC by Working Group I (University Press, Cambridge, 1992)

26. Gerlich, G. and Tscheuschner,R.D. "Reply to "comment on 'falsification of the atmospheric co2 greenhouse effects within the frame of physics' by Joshua B. Halpern, Christopher M. Colose, Chris

Ho-Stuart, Joel D. Shore, Arthur P. Smith, Jörg Zimmermann," International Journal of Modern Physics B, April 2010, Vol. 24, No. 10 : pp. 1333-1359.

27. <u>S@R</u> "Strategies @ Risk, The fallacies of Scenario analysis 4/05/2009 Corporate Risk and other topics. http://www.strategy-at-risk. com/2009/.../the-fallacies-of-scenario-analysis/_

28. Rittel, H. and M. Webber." Dilemmas in a General Theory of Planning". Policy Sciences, 4:155-169. Elsevier Scientific Co Amssterdam,1973.

29. Easterbrook, Don PhD, "Hoax of Global Warming" https://www. YouTube.com/watch?v=ofXQdl1FDGk]

30. Hudson, Matthew. Washington Post review or Nov. 13, 2015. Of a book by Jamie Holms "The Power of Not Thinking" (Crown Books)

31. Monckton, Christopher Walter. twelfth "Climate Conference. Hartland.com. https://www.youtube.com/watch?v=Ebokc6z82cg

32. Moncton, Christopher Lord. "Global Warming is a Hoax by Lord Christopher Moncton", Ideacity.(Toronto Canada) June 18, 2014.

33. Churchill, Winston. *August 24, 1941.*British Library of Information. Churchill's speech on the newest British battleship Prince of Wales

34. Chisholm, G. Brock. Psychiatrist and co-founder of the World Federation of Mental Health. www.psychquotes.com

35. Fitch,Robert E. "The Obsolescence of Ethics", in Christianity and Crisis: A Journal of Opinion, 19(19)(November 16, 1959),pp163-65.cited by Ravi Zacharis in "The Real Face of Atheism", Baker Books, 2013. pp65-66.

36. Vitale, Vince "The Trajectory of Truth" in RZIM "Just Thinking" volume 25(2)pp28-29,2017.

37. ibid

38. Morey, Robert A.. "The New Atheism and the Erosion of Freedom: How to recognize and combat the hidden influence of secular humanism and unbelief in today's society". P & R Publishing, 1994

Bibliography

Adamenko, S. Selleri F. and van der Merwe A. Editors, "Nucleosynthesis-Breakthroughs in Experiment andTheory", *Fundamental Theories of Physics*,

vol 156, The Netherlands: Springer-Verlog, 2007

Adler,Margo. "Drawing down the Moon: witches, druids, goddess – worshippers, and other pagans". Penguin Books, 2006.

Aiken, Henry David, *The Journal of Philosophy* 49:25)789-791, Dec 4, 1952

Anderson, Sir Robert. "The Bible or the Church" . Pickering & Inglis, 1924.

Anonymous M.D., "Unprotected",, N.Y.N.Y: Sentinal, 2006, p68-69.

Baker, FR. Kenneth, SJ. "Homiletic and Pastoral Review". "Presuppositions of Darwinism", Editorial Oct 2011

Barker, William Burckhardt "Lares and Penates", ch 8, "Magi and Monks"

Barnhouse, Donald Grey, "The invisible War", Grand Rapids: Zondervan, 1965.

Barton, Carlin A. "The sorrows of the Ancient Romans: The gladiators and the Monster" Princeton Univ. Press, 1993

Baskerville, Stephen. WND.com . "Whistleblower", Oct 2013, p22-25.

Baumgardner, John R. "In Six Days" John F Ashton ed. Master Books. Green Forrest Arkansas. 2001.

_____. Catastrophic Plate Tectonics: The Physics Behind the Genesis Flood. Proceedings of the Fifth Internatinal Conference on Creationism. R.L. Ivey Jr. (Ed.) pp113-126, 2003.

_____Mendel's Accountant Software. See: http:www.sourceforge. net/progects/mendels account)

_____(see: Sanford, J.)

Bastiat, Federic. "The Law".p 56. BN Publishing 2008.

Behe, Michael. "The Edge of Evolution: the search for the limits of Darwinism". New York Free Press, 2007, p145

Benvenuti, Richard. "The Ninth of Thermidor: the fall of Robespierre", ed. Richard Benvenuti. Oxford University Press, 1970, PP. 32 to – 49.

Bloesch, Doald. "The Battle for the Trinity: The debate over Inclusive God – Language", Ann Arbor, Mi: Servent Books, 1985.

Bork, Robert H.,"Slouching Towards Gomorrah", Harper Perennial, 2003

Bosch, F. et al "Observation of bound-date Beta-decay of fully ionize-d1[87]Re." *Physical Review Letters* 77(26):5190- 5193, 1966.

Boudreaux Edward A. and Eric C. Baxter. "God Created The Earth".2nd Ed. Rocky Mountain Creation Fellowship. PO box 3451, Littleton, CO 80161-3451

Breese, Dave. "7 Men Who Rule the World from the Grave.", Chicago : Moody Publications, 1990.

Bunyan,John."The Works of John Bunyan: A Treatise of The Fear of God", Banner of Truth, 1991.

Bushman (1970). *From Puritan to Yankee: Character and the Social Order in Connecticut, 1690-1765*.

Cal Physics Institute," Zero Point Energy and Zero Point Field". [paper on line.]

Carlson, N.R. & Heth, C.D.(2009).Psychology the Science of Behavior. Toronto: Pearson Education Canada chaos dominates the world...".

Chaplin, Martin. "Water Structures and Science". [http://ww1.isbu.ac.uk/water]

Chisholm, G. Brock. Psychiatrist and co-founder of the World Federation of Mental Health. www.psychquotes.com

Christopher R. Browning, *The Origins of the Final Solution* (University of Nebraska Press 2004, p411.

Churchill, Winston. "The Gathering Storm", Houghton Mifflin, Boston, 1948, p71

_____, *August 24, 1941*.British Library of Information. Churchill's speech on the newest British battleship.

Cicero, De Oratore, 1.2. c. 15. 3:243,254

_____,. "De Natura Deorum". 2.51; Nature of the Gods. pp43-44

Clauss, M."The Roman cult of Mithras" ,Edinburg University Press, 2000.

Coban, Ramazan. Balikesir Univ., 2012. "Ida's research in comparable mythology"

Cohen, Felix S., "Transcendental Nonsense and the Functional Approach" 35 COLUM. L. Rev. 809,821 (1935)

Collins, Steven. "Tall el-Hammam is Sodom: Billington's Hesbon Identification Suffers from Numerous Fatal Flaws with 64 references". *Artifax Magazine*, summer 2012.

Comfort, Ray, "Hitler God and the Bible".p114. WND Books, 2012.

Comte, August. . [1851, VOL 1, 127; E., VOL, 100]

Coursen, Jon. *Application Commentary* Vol. 2:Psalms-Malachi; Nelson Ref. and electronics, 2006

Craig, William Lane. (Oral argument by William Lane Craig ,Talbot school of Theology on John Ankerberg show on 3/13/2016)

Custance, Arthur C. "Primitive Monotheism and the Origin of Polytheism", see: (www.custance.org/Library/Volume4/Part_ll/Introduction.htm)

Custance, Arthur C. *Doorway Papers,* Pat 1, Part V, part VI. A Christian Worldview: a framework of History www.custance.org/

D'Souza, Dinesh. "What's So Great About Christianity?" Tyndale House. 2007.

Dager, A.J. "Vengenance is Ours:The Church in Dominion",Sword Publishers, 1990.

Daly, "Beyond God the Father",Beacon Press, 1993.

Darwin, Charles. "Autobiography" 1887 and Parkyn, Ernest A. "Darwin, His work and influence"

_____. "On the *Origin of Species*",, Chapter Ten: "On the Imperfection of the Geologic Record: On the absence of intermediate varieties at the present day"

_____, The Darwin Papers volume 1. Number XIV "Darwin at Nuremberg Part III Thomas Malthus

Davis, Bob. Pastor , 9/28/14 on 1Peter [http://www.northcountrychapel.com/category/bible_studies]

Dembski, William A. "Mere Creation". Downers Grove: Intervarsity Press,1998.

Derrida "Interviews. 1st ed. Stanford Univ. Press. ISBN 0810103974.

Durant, Will. "Caesar and Christ: A History of Roman Civilization and of Christianity from their Beginning to A.D. 325.N.Y.: Simon and Schuster, 1972.

Durrett & Schmidt. "Waiting for two Mutations". *Genetics* 180: 1501-9, 2008

Dyson, L., M. Kleban, and L. Susskind, "Disturbing Implications of a Cosmological Constant", MIT-CTP-, and *JHEP* 0210:011, 2012.

Edzard et al 1987-1990:s.v. Marduk; Kammenhuber 1990.

Einstein, A. From *The Journal of the Franklin Institute* Vol221 no. 3, March 1936.

_____,. As quoted in *Time*, December 1940, p38, and documented in a youtube video:

_____,"The Expanded Quotable Einstein", Princeton University Press, 2000.

Faludi, Susan, "Backlash: the undeclared war against American Women"(N.Y. Crown, 1981

Fisher, J.T. and L.S. Hawley," A few Buttons Missing". Philadelphia; Lippincott, 1951.

Fodor, J. and M. Piattelli-Palmarini. " *What Darwin Got Wrong*". New York: Farrar, Straus and Giroux, 2010.

Foard, James M."The Nebulous <u>Hypothesis</u>: A Study of the Philosophical and Historical Implications of Darwinian Theory..Editor and Publisher James M. Foard.

Francis, Covers. "The Value of Enlightened Views of Religion" *The Harvard Archives*.

Freeman, Kenneth J. "Schools of Hellas", London: Macmillan, 1922.

G-2. In a War College report May 2011. 163. as cited in Guliuzza Gallagher, Maggie. "Enemies of Arrow's: Hollow the sexual revolution is killing family, and sex and what we can do about it" Chicago: Bonus Books, 1989.

Garber, E., et al (Eds.) <u>Maxwell on Molecules and Gases</u> (1986) MIT press, Cambridge Massachusetts.

Geochronology Encyclopedia vol 19,p783,1985

Gerlich, G. and Tscheuschner,R.D. (2009) "Falsification of The Atmospheric CO2 Greenhouse Effects Within the Frame of Physics", arXiv:0707.1161v4 [physics.ao-pg] 4 Mar 2009, 115pages.

Gianelli,Diane M. "Shock-tactic ads target late term abortion procedure," American Medical News, pub H2920GtT2fK[27MR]

Gitt, Warner, Dr. Professor. "In the beginning was information". Master Books, 2006

Godlman, Gardner, 1878 "Catalogue of the Greek Coins". London (reprinted 1963 Bologna): Houghton 1983,"Coins of the Selecuid Empire in:The Selecuid Kings, 1940.

Good, Harry and James Teller. "A History of Western Education". London: Macmillan, 1969.

Graham, Billy. [http://billygraham.org/story/billy-graham-my-heart-aches-for-america/], July 19, 2012

Gray, Peter. Psychology. New York: Worth, 2011.

Green, John C. "The Death of Adam", The Iowa State University Press, 1959.

Grusin, Richard A. "Transcendentalist Hermeneutics". Durham: Duke University Press, 1991.

Guliuzza, R. "Darwin's Sacred Imposter: Recognizing Missed Warning Signs." *Acts & Facts.* 40 (5): 12-15;2012.

Gurnett D.A., and A. Bhattacharjee. "Introduction to Plasma Physics". Cambridge: Cambridge University Press, 2005.

Haeckel, Ernst, reported in *Fortnightly Review*, London, vol.39, 1886,

Hagenbach, K.R. "German Rationalism, it's rise, progress, and decline" written by his translators Wm. Leonhakd Gage. J. H. W. Stuckenberg. New York: Charles Soribner. MDCCCLXV. (1865)

Haisch, B., Rueda, A., H.E.Puthoff ," Inertia as a Zero-point-field Lorentz Force", *Physical Review A,* Vol 49(2):678-694, 1994.

Harvey, RP and N. Rosenthal. "Heart Development" London: Academic Press. 1999.

Hawking, Steven. And Leonard Mlodinow. "The Grand Design". N.Y Bantam Books..2012.

_____, "God Created the Integers: the mathematical breakthroughs that changed history", Philadelphia: Running Press, 2005.

Heinish, Paul. "Theology of the Old Testament" St. Paul Liturgical, 1955.

Hellerstrom, N.P. "The Tree as a Evolutionary Icon: TREE in the natural history museum, London. *Archives of Natural History* 38:1 ,2011,p-17

Heroditus,1,101

Hess, Moses, "Religion und Sittlichkeit" .

_____, (Holy History of Mankind) "Die Heilige Geschichte der Menschheit" ed. by Shlomo Avineri. Cambridge Univ. Press, 2005.

_____, 12th letter: Rome and Jerusalem the last National Question Hettche, Matt, "Christian Wolff", *The Stanford Encyclopedia of Philosophy* (Spring

2014 Edition), Edward N. Zalta (ed.), forthcoming URL = http://plato.
stanford.edu/archives/spr2014/entries/wolff-christian/>

Hitler,Adolf. "Mein Kampf". From the first section of Vol. 1, Chapter 11:
Nation and Race House PK, Vyas A, Sapolsky R (2011) "Predator Cat
Odors Activate Sexual Arousal Pathways in Brains of Toxoplasma gondii Infected Rats." [see: PLoS ONE 6(8): e23277. doi:10.1371/journal.
pone.0023277.

Hoyle, Sir Frederick. [from an interview by AP pundit George W. Cornel,
quoted from "Times – Advocate", Escondido, California, December 10,
1982, pp. A10-11.See:

http://www.youtube.com/watch?feature=player_detailpage&v=Sk_-
0UiiauU]

Hugh Ross . "The Fingerprint of God. 2nd ed. Promise. 1991 p141.

Humphreys, D. Russell, "The Earth's Magnetic Field is Young". http://
www.icr.org/article/earths-magnetic-field-young/]

Humphreys, Russell, Steven Austin, John Baumgardner,and Andrew
Snelling. "Precambrian Zircons Yield a Helium Diffusion Age of 6,000
Years". American Geophysical Union Fall Conference, San Francisco,
Dec. 2003, Abs #V32C-1047, http://www.icr/research/misc/aguconfer-
ence.html.

Humphries , Russell, "Starlight and Time" Master Books, Green Forest,
1994

Hunt, Dave. "Great is the Mystery", May 2003, "The Berean Call" xxix
(9):3

Hutchinson, Ian. see http://silas.psfc.mit.edu/maxwell/ "James Clerk Maxwell and the Christian Proposition"

Huxley, Julian. "The Evolutionary Vision". In: Evolution after Darwin: University of Chicago centennial. Volume three Issues and Education. Chicago: University of Chicago press.

Ignatius. "The epistle of Ignatius to the Philadelphians, and ante-Nicene fathers, ed. Alexander Roberts and James Donaldson. Grand Rapids, Wm. Erdmans, 1981 1:81

Ironsides, H.A. "Revelation" p31, Kregel reprint 2004. Grand Rapids.IVP NT Commentary on Romans 8

_____," Babylonian Religion"

Jastrow, Robert. Los Angeles Times, June 25, 1978, Part IV, PP. 1,6., As quoted in Hunt, Dave. "in defense of Jeremiah, David. on Daniel 11"

Johnson, Phillip A, "Evolution and Christian Faith" p1. www.ldolphin.org/ntcreation.

Jung M. et al "First observation of bound-state Beta⁻ decay", Physical Reviews Letters 69(15) 2164-2167,1987

Kagan, Don. Yale College final address. "The New Criterion" June 2013.

Kapperler F. and H. Beer. "S-Process nucleosynthesis Nuclear Physics and the Classical Model", Report on.

Progress in Physics 52:1006-1008, 1989.

Kassian, Mary. "The Feminist Mistake: The Radical Impact of Feminism on Church and Culture". Crossway, 2005.

Kegan Paul C. (London:George Bell and Sons, 1901,p89. (PDF Free online) at http://oll.liberty.fund.org.

Kellen, Richard. "Lexington's Rev. John Hancock" . in www.Lexington history.org accesses 3/8/14.

Keller, Timothy. "Counterfit Gods", Riverhead Trade, 2011.

Kennedy, D.J. And J. Newcomb. "What if Jesus Had Never Been Born?"Nashville: Thomas Nelson, 1994.

KEPLER, JOHNNES. "*Harmonies of the World,* by Johannes Kepler", tr. Charles Glenn Wallis.

Kilgore, Randy. "Our Daily Bread", RBC Ministries 59:9. Dec. 11,2013.

Kimball, Roger. "The New Criterion". 32: (9) p3, May 2014. See:"The left's exalted are the left's hierarchy"

Klay. N. et al "Nuclear structure of ^{176}Lu and its astrophysical consequences", *Physical Review* C44(6):2847-2848, 1991.

Koestler, Arthur. "Darkness at Noon, trans. Daphne Hardy ,N.Y. :Bantum, 1941.

Korzybski, Alfred "Science and Sanity", International Non-Aristotelian Library Pub. Co.

Kupelian, David .David quotes Peck, M. Scott ."People of the Lie:The hope for healing human evil". P78,NewYork: Touchstone Simon and Schuster, 1983.

Lane, Pastor Daniel [http://www.armstronginternational.com/node/56765

lecture delivered in the Hall of Christ College Cambridge.Methen and Co., London 1894. P12

Leslie, John. "Modern Cosmology and Philosophy". Amherst: Prometheus Books, 1998.

Lewis, C.S. "Miracles" .N.Y. Macmillan, 1978, 27-28

Lewis, C.S., "Modern Theology and Biblical Criticism" (originally titled "Fern-seed and Elephants"), The Seeing Eye ,New York: Ballantine Books, 1992.

Lewontin, Richard. "Billions and Billions of Demons," *The New York Review*, January 9, 1997.

Lindley, David. "The End of Physics: the myth of a unified theory", Basic Books. N.Y. 2012.

Lintott, Andrew. *The Constitution of the Roman Republic* ,Oxford University Press, 1999.

Lisle, Jason Ph.D "Taking Back Astronomy", Green Forest :Master Books.2001.

_____, "Discerning Truth". Master Books, 2010.

Luther, Martin. "A sermon on keeping children in school", and "Luther's Works," 46:256, Charles M. Jacobs,

ed.Robert Schultz (Phil. Fortress press, 1967

Lutzer, Dr Irwin W."When A Nation Forgets God: 7 lessons we must learn from Nazi Germany ".Chicago:Moody Publishers, 2010.

Lyell, Principles of Geology, London:John Murry, 1932.

MacDonald, William.(ed. Wm Farstad). "Believers Bible Commentary: A complete Commentary in one Volume".Thomas Nelson, Nashville. 1995.

Machen, J. Gresham. "Christanity and Liberalism" 1929. text is free from http://www.christuslibrary.com/

Martyr, Justin volume II (2nd Apology of Justin Martyr)

Marx, Karl and Moses Hess, Sidney Hook Dec 1934, see New International, vol 1.No 55 December 1934, July 5, 1993.

Maxwell, James Clerk, "Discourse on Molecules", Clerk-Maxwell, J. (25 September 1873). "Molecules". *Nature* 8 (204): 437–41. Bibcode 1873Natur...8..437.. doi:10.1038/008437a0. http://www.nature.com/ nature/journal/v8/n204/pdf/008437a0.pdf. Retrieved 2012-02-20. Also digitized at *The Victorian Web*. Archived 2012-02-23.]

_____, Letter to Rev. C. B. Tayler (8 July 1853) in Ch. 6 : Undergraduate Life At Cambridge

_____, Nature, 8:437-442, 1873

McGarry, D.D., "Mediaeval Education ", New Catholic Encyclopedia, San Francisco; Mcgraw – Hill, 1967, five: 113

Mendez, Arnold C. Sr. "Accelerated Radioactive Decay-see www.amendez. com

Meyer, Stephen C. "Darwin's Doubt: the explosive origin of animal life and the case for intelligent design". New York:Harper One, 2013.

Mollenkott, Virginia. "The Divine Feminine: The Biblical Imagery of God as Female". Wipf and Stock Pub., 2014.

Monroe, Kelly,ed, "Finding God at Harvard. Grand Rapids, Zondervan, 1991.

Morey, Robert A.. "The New Atheism and the Erosion of Freedom: How to recognize and combat the hidden influence of secular humanism and unbelief in today's society". P & R Publishing, 1994

Morris, Henry M. . *The Long War Against God*: the History and Impact of the Creation/Evolution Conflict. Grand Rapids: Baker, 1989.

_____,. " The Genesis Record", Grand Rapids: Baker Book House, 1976.

Muggeridge, Malcom. In: *"The Magazine of Ravi Zacharias International Ministries"* 21:4,p6,www.rzim.org , 2014.

NET Bible, note on Genesis 6:11 Biblical Studies Press, L.L.C. version 5.830. 1996 p21. Free electronic access at www.netbible.org

Netterfield, C.B. et al, "A Measurement by Boomerang of Microwave Peaks of the Angular Power Spectrum of the Cosmic Microwave Background ". *The Astrophysical Journal*, 571:604-614, 2003,Jume 1.

Noebel, David A. "Clergy in the Classroom: The Religion of Secular Humanism" 2nd Ed. Summit Press,

Noll, Mark. "The Scandal of the Evangelical Mind". Grand Rapids::Wm. B. Erdman's, 1994.

Nourse, Ruth. "Hijacking of American Education: flip jack turning at Harvard, Part 4-5:Ralph Waldo Emerson._October 1850 to January 1854.

[See::://www.forerunner.com/forerunner/x0285_Hijacking_American_L.html]

Olmstead, Clifton E. (1960), History of Religion in the United States, Englewood Cliffs, N.J..:Prentice-Hall, One, N.Y.,N.Y. 2013

Owen, John." The Works of John Owen 1669", edited by William H Goold, first published by Johnstone and Hunter 1850–1853. Edinburgh: Reprinted by The Banner of Truth Trust, 1965.

Owen,Robert L.,"Uptake and transport of Intestinal macromolecules and microorganisms by "M" cells in Peyer's Patches".*Seminars in Immunology 11*:154-163,1999.

Parker, Theodore. Journal F. (1835-36 reconstituted, pp 190–191, May 1836) quoted in Weiss, John.

"The Life and Correspondence of Theodore Parker". 2 vol. ,N.Y.: Appleton, 1864 1:82.

_____, "letter from Theodore Parker to Greene", 2 April 1834. Mass. Historical Society.

Pascal, Blaise."The Thoughts of Blaise Pascal". Translated from the text of M. Auguste Molinier by C. Kegan Paul,

London: George Bell and Sons, 1901.

_____,"Pensees", No. 72.

Peck, M. Scott ."People of the Lie:The hope for healing human evil",NewYork: Touchstone Simon and Schuster, 1983.

Peirce, C. S. (1893), "Evolutionary Love", *The Monist*, v. III, n. 1. *Arisbe* Eprint. Reprinted in *Collected Papers* v. 6, Reprinted also in *Chance,*

Love, and Logic . *Philosophical Writings of Peirce,* and *The Essential Peirce* v.1

Pellitt, Paul and Alistar Pike. "Dating European Palolithic Cave Art:Progress, Prospects,Problems". *J. of Archaeological Method and Theory,* 14:(1) March 2007.

_____, *Journal of Archaeological Method and Theory, Vol. 14, No. 1, March 2007 (C_ 2007)* "Dating European Palaeolithic Cave Art:Progress, Prospects, Problems".   Paul Pettitt1,3 and Alistair Pike2.*Published online: 10 February 2007*

Plank, Max. "Where is Science Going?". Woodbridge, Conn: Ox Bow Press. 1981. PLL v6.0 (generated September, 2011)

Popper, Karl R. and, David W. Miller. "A Proof of the Impossibility of Inductive Probability." *Nature* 302:687-688, 1983.

Potter, Charles Francis, (a Unitarian Minister), "Humanism :A New Religion", Simon and Schuster, NY, 1930.

Prantzos N, Harissopals S. Proc. Nuclei in the Cosmos pp181-186, 1999. Prince of Wales. *Progress in Physics* 52:1006-1008, 1989.

Rasdall, H. "Universities of Europe in the Middle Ages",vol. i,part 3.

Puthoff see: Haisch et al

Rawlinson, George, ed., Herodotus, appendix to Book 11, p. 250.

Raychaudhuri, S. "Microwave-generated low frequency plasma wave excited in the periphery of the evanescent layer". *Physics of Plasma* Vol 11 number10:4634-4640, October.

Robbins, John W., *The Trinity Review*, Feb.March 1996.

Rokas, Antonis. "Spotlight: Drawing the Tree of Life". Brod Institute, November 15, 2006. www.broadinstitute. org/news/.

Rousas, John Rushdoony, in *"Gold is Money"* by Hans F. Steinholdz. See: www.buchausgabe.de ISBN 9-87991-085-7 204. Bestell-Nr..0297 Seiten, Erschienen,1975.

Rowe, Marvin W. "Radiocarbon dating of Ancient Rock Paintings". *Anal. Chem* 81(5):1728-35, March 1, 2009. Also: Ruiz and Rowe. "Dating Methods (Absolute and Relative) in Archaeology of Art" *Encyc. Of Global Archaeology*:2014, pp2036-42, with 36 references)

Rubin V, and F.W. Kent. *Astrophysical Journal* 159:379, Feb.1970

Rubin, Jerry. "Do it!" New York: Simon and Schuster, 1970).

Russel, Letty. "Human Liberation in a Feminist Perspective: A Theology",Philadelphia, Westminster Press, 1974.

Sadava, David. et a.l "Life, the Science of Biology", 8th ed. Sinauer Associates and W.H. Freeman,2008.

Saflund, G. in "Cretan and Theran Questions" in "Cretan Sanctuaries and Cults: Continunity and change from the late Minoan IIIC to the Archaic Period".by Micke Prent, Brill Academic, 2005.

Sanford, J. and John Baumgartner, Mendel's Accountant. http://www.men-delsaccountant.info/ Also see:*SCPE* 2007. 8:147-165. (supports parallel cluster computers. Software available free online.

Sax, 1992,"A system of nomenclature for quaretz" ,*Archaeometry* 34:11-20.

Schaler, Max." Ressentiment" ed. Louis A. Coser Tran. William W. Holdhime, Glencoe, Illinois .Free Press.

Schlossberg, Herbert. "Idols for Destruction", Crossway Books, 1993.

Schmidt, Alvin J. "How Christianity Changed the World", Grand Rapids: Zondervan pub. 2001.

Schmidt, Wilhelm. "The Origin and Growth of Religion:Facts and theories". London: H.J. Rose, Methuen , 1931.

Schoeck, Helmut." Envy" cf. Ellul, "Betrayal of the West When the gospel of the poor is preached". Liberty Fund, 1987.

Schweitzer, Mary H. et al. "Tyrannosaurus Rex fossil yields flexible tissue" *Science*, (March 25, 2005)

Vol. 307(5717) p.1852 DOI:10.1126/science.307.5717.1852b.

Shoemaker, Stephen P, "The Theological Roots of Charles W. Eliot's Educational Reforms," *Journal of Unitarian Universalist History* 2006-2007 31:30-45.

Silander et al. 2007 Plos Biol 5:922-931.

Sinclair, David, "An Overview on the Bible". 2006

Schlossberg, Herbert. "Idols for Destruction". Crossway Books, 1993.

Smolin, Lee. "The Trouble with Physics: The Rise of String Theory, the Fall of a Science, and What comes next" ,

Boston: Houghton Mifflin, 2006.

Sommers, Christian Hoff," Who stole Feminism: How women have betrayed women", N.Y. :Simon and Schuster, 1994.

Sproul, R.C. "Not a Chance", Baker Books,1999.

Sproul, R.C. from :"No More the Grave" (in Glory to the Holy One) Ligonier Ministries. 2015

_____, "The Holiness of God" . Scripture Press Foundation, 1986.

Sproul, RC Jr.

Steadman, Ray C. "Adventuring Through the Bible". Discovery House Publishers. Grand Rapids,1997.

Steinhardt, Paul J. *Sci Am* 304:36-43 (2011)

Stewart, Don. "The Case For Christianity", Ch.4 (Calvary Chapel Costa Mesa) not (Don Lee Stewart)

_____, "class notes on the veracity of the New Testament"

Stenger, Victor J. "Has Science Found God: the latest results in the search for purpose in the universe".

Stokes, Mitch. "Isaac Newton", Thomas Nelson, Nashville, 2010.

Strabo 14.5.13-15].

Strong, James."The New Strong's Exhaustive Concordance of the Bible" (every word of the Bible). Thomas Nelson. Nashville. 1984

Sullivan, Wilson (1972). New England Men of Letters. New York: The Macmillan Company. ISBN 0-02-788680-8

Teotonio H. et al, *J. Evol. Biol.*, 15:608-617.

Terrell, Richard."Resurrecting the Third Reich", Shreveport, Huntington House,1994,

The New Criterion ,June 2013, "The Struggle for Survival or *W.W.D.D.* -In His Tracks What Would Darwin Do?"

Thomas Pappas, director of Analysis and Production/Threat for the U.S. Arming Training and Doctrine Command Today, Boston: Beacon Press, 1986.

Toynbee, Arnold. "Reconsiderations VOL 12 of the study of history". New York: Oxford University Press. 1961.

Ulansey, David. "The Origins of the Mithraic Mysteries, Oxford University Press, 1989.

_____. " Mithraic mysteries". Scientific American 261(6):130-135 Dec 1989.

Valentine, J.W. and D.H. Erwin. "Interpreting great developmental experiments: the fossil record. (p92 diagram) in: Development as and Evolutionary Process" . ed. R.A. Raff and E.C. Raff, 71–107. New York: Liss, 1987, [as referenced in Meyer]

Van Valen, L. 1989. Three Paradigms of Evolution. *Evolutionary Theory*. 9: 2.

Vardiman, Larry. Andrew Snelling, and Eugene F. Chaffin. Eds. "Radioisotopes and the Age of the Earth" El Cajon, CA: Institute for Creation Research and Creation Research Society, 2000, Ch 5.

Vermaseren, *M.J. Corpus Inscroptionum et Monumentorum Religionis Mithriace,* vol I, and II Vickers, John. "THE PROBLEM OF INDUCTION" (Section 2). *Stanford Encyclopedia of Philosophy.* 21.June 2010.

Vitale, Vince PhD, Oxford Center for Christian Apologetics, see: *Just Thinking* 22(4):18.

Walvoord, John F. "Every Prophecy of the Bible" , Chariot Victor Publishing, Colorado Springs, 1990.

Ware, Henry. "Inquiry" to: 166, 197, 202 as cited in Grodzins, "American Heretic".

Watchman, A. "A Universal Standard for Reporting the Ages of Petroglyphs and Rock Painting". In: Strecker, M.P. eds. "Dating the Earliest Known Rock Art. Oxbow Press, Oxford, pp1-3, (1999)

Weinrich, Max. "Hitler's Professors". Yale University Press, 1946. 2nd ed.

Wellhausen, Juius. "Prolegomena to the History of Israel", Kissinger Pub. LLC, 2010.

Westfall, R.S. "Never At Rest: a biography of Isaac Newton" Cambridge. Cambridge U. Press, 1980.

Wieschaus, E.F.,taken from tapes at an AAAS lecture, 1982, as quoted by Stephen Meyer in"Darwin's Doubt" .

William, Alex and John Harnett. "Dismantling the Big Bang", Green Forest: Master Books, 2005.

Wilson, Edward O., "On Human Nature", Cambridge Mass. Harvard U. Press (1978)

Wiseman, P.J.,Third Preliminary Report on Excavations at Tell Asmar (Eshhunna): quoted by P.J. Wiseman in "New Discoveries in Bablylonia about Genesis", Marshall, Morgan and Scott, London, 1936.

Wolin, Richard. "Preface to MIT press edition: Note on missing text. "The Heidegger controversy. Critical reader MIT press, 1993.

Wurmbrand, Richard, "Marx and Satan", Crossway Books, 1986.

Yeh, C. *J. Applied. Phys.* 5066,1969. And Raychaudhuri S. "Microwave-generated low frequency plasma wave.excited in the periphery of the evanescent layer". *Physics of Plasma* Vol 11number10:4634-4640, October.

Zacharias, Ravi. vol 21.4 R. Zacharias Ministeries. "Morality".

_____, "The end of Reason" , p16, Zondervan 2008 Grand Rapids.

_____, "The Real Face of Atheism", Baker Books, 2013

Zimmerman, Carle C., James Kurth, Allan C. Carlson. "Family and Civilization", Intercollegiate Studies Inst. ISBN-10 1933859377, 2008.

Zuck, Roy B. "The Speakers Quotebook" (1997) ed. By Roy B. Zuck,

Thanks Many Thanks Ron Dickman, Andreas Burger, and Vern Westgate for Critiquing the manuscript. And Alan Golub of www.YourStoryArt.com with cover design help.

Permissions
Scripture Quotations marked:

[NKJV] are taken from the New King James Version. Copyright © 1982 by Thomas Nelson, Inc.

All rights reserved. Used by permission.

[NLT] are taken from the Holy Bible, New Living Translation, Copyright 1966. Used by permission of Tyndall House Publishers, Inc. Wheaton, Ill. 60189. All rights reserved.

[ESV] are from the Holy Bible English Standard Version. Copyright © 2001 by Crossway Bibles, a division of Good News Publishers. All rights reserved.

[NET] are from the NET Bible. Copyright © 2003 by Biblical Studies Press, L.L.C. http://www.netbible.com All rights reserved.

[KJV] are from The Defenders Study Bible. Copyright © 1955 by World Publishers, Inc. Grand

Rapids Michigan 49418.All rights reserved. Notes copyright © by Dr Henry M. Morris, 1995. All rights reserved.

[NIV] are taken from the HOLY BIBLE, New International Version 2011, Copyright © 1973,

Made in the USA
Lexington, KY
27 September 2017